Ideology

transitions

General Editor: Julian Wolfreys

Published titles
BATAILLE Fred Botting and Scott Wilson
NEW HISTORICISM AND CULTURAL MATERIALISM John Brannigan
POSTMODERN NARRATIVE THEORY Mark Currie
FORMALIST CRITICISM AND READER-RESPONSE THEORY Todd F. Davis and
 Kenneth Womack
IDEOLOGY James M. Decker
QUEER THEORIES Donald E. Hall
MARXIST LITERARY AND CULTURAL THEORIES Moyra Haslett
LOUIS ALTHUSSER Warren Montag
RACE Brian Niro
JACQUES LACAN Jean-Michel Rabaté
LITERARY FEMINISMS Ruth Robbins
DECONSTRUCTION•DERRIDA Julian Wolfreys

ORWELL TO THE PRESENT: LITERATURE IN ENGLAND, 1945–2000 John Brannigan
FROM CHAUCER TO SHAKESPEARE, 1337–1580 SunHee Kim Gertz
POPE TO BURNEY, 1714–1779 Moyra Haslett
PATER TO FORSTER, 1873–1924 Ruth Robbins
BURKE TO BYRON, BARBAULD TO BAILLIE, 1790–1830 Jane Stabler
FROM MILTON TO POPE, 1650–1720 Kay Gilliland Stevenson
SIDNEY TO MILTON, 1580–1660 Marion Wynne-Davies

Forthcoming titles
TERRY EAGLETON David Alderson
JULIA KRISTEVA AND LITERARY THEORY Megan Becker-Leckrone
NATIONAL IDENTITY John Brannigan
HÉLÈNE CIXOUS: WRITING AND SEXUAL DIFFERENCE Abigail Bray
HOMI BHABHA Eleanor Byrne
GENDER Claire Colebrook
POSTMODERNISM•POSTMODERNITY Martin McQuillan
ROLAND BARTHES Martin McQuillan
MODERNITY David Punter
PSYCHOANALYSIS AND LITERATURE Nicholas Rand
SUBJECTIVITY Ruth Robbins
POSTCOLONIAL THEORY Malini Johan Schueller
TRANSGRESSION Julian Wolfreys

IMAGE TO APOCALYPSE, 1910–1945 Jane Goldman
DICKENS TO HARDY, 1837–1884 Julian Wolfreys

transitions Series
Series Standing Order
ISBN 0–333–73684–6
(*outside North America only*)

You can receive future titles in this series as they are published by placing a standing order.
Please contact your bookseller or, in case of difficulty, write to us at the address below with your
name and address, the title of the series and the ISBN quoted above.

Customer Services Department, Macmillan Distribution Ltd
Houndmills, Basingstoke, Hampshire RG21 6XS, England

transitions

Ideology

James M. Decker

First published 2004 by
PALGRAVE MACMILLAN
Houndmills, Basingstoke, Hampshire RG21 6XS and
175 Fifth Avenue, New York, N.Y. 10010
Companies and representatives throughout the world

PALGRAVE MACMILLAN is the global academic imprint of the Palgrave Macmillan division of St. Martin's Press, LLC and of Palgrave Macmillan Ltd. Macmillan® is a registered trademark in the United States, United Kingdom and other countries. Palgrave is a registered trademark in the European Union and other countries.

ISBN 0–333–77537–6 hardback
ISBN 0–333–77538–4 paperback

This book is printed on paper suitable for recycling and made from fully managed and sustained forest sources.

A catalogue record for this book is available from the British Library.

Library of Congress Cataloging-in-Publication Data
Decker, James M., 1967–
    Ideology/James M. Decker.
        p.   cm. — (Transitions)
    Includes bibliographical references (p.) and index.
    ISBN 0–333–77537–6 — ISBN 0–333–77538–4 (pbk.)
    1. American fiction—20th century—History and criticism—Theory, etc.   2. Ideology in literature.   3. Literature—History and criticism—Theory, etc.   4. Orwell, George, 1903–1950. Nineteen eighty-four.   5. Faulkner, William, 1897–1962. Barn burning.   6. Subjectivity in literature.   7. Morrison, Toni. Sula.   8. Politics and literature.   9. Literature and society.   I. Title.   II. Transitions (Palgrave Macmillan (Firm))

PS379.D33 2003
813'.50938—dc21

                                                                    2003053649

10   9   8   7   6   5   4   3   2   1
13   12   11   10   09   08   07   06   05   04

Transferred to digital printing in 2006.

Contents

Part II   'Reading' Ideology

Part III   Conclusion

General Editor's Preface

Transitions: *transition* –, n. of action. 1. A passing or passage from one condition, action (or) rarely place, to another. 2. Passage in thought, speech, or writing, from one subject to another. 3. **a.** The passing from one note to another. **b.** The passing from one key to another, modulation. 4. The passage from an earlier to a later stage of development or formation ... change from an earlier style to a later; a style of intermediate or mixed character ... the historical passage of language from one well-defined stage to another.

The aim of *Transitions* is to explore passages, movements and the development of significant voices in critical thought, as these voices determine and are mediated by acts of literary and cultural interpretation. This series also seeks to examine the possibilities for reading, analysis and other critical engagements which the very idea of transition – such as the transition effected by the reception of a thinker's *oeuvre* and the heritage entailed – makes possible. The writers in this series unfold the movements and modulations of critical thinking over the last generation, from the first emergences of what is now recognised as literary theory. They examine as well how the transitional nature of theoretical and critical thinking is still very much in operation, guaranteed by the hybridity and heterogeneity of the field of literary studies. The authors in the series share the common understanding that, now more than ever, critical thought is both in a state of transition and can best be defined by developing for the student reader an understanding of this protean quality. As this *tranche* of the series, dealing with particular critical voices, addresses, it is of great significance, if not urgency, that the texts of particular figures be reconsidered anew.

This series desires, then, to enable the reader to transform her/his own reading and writing transactions by comprehending past developments as well as the internal transitions worked through by particular literary and cultural critics, analysts, and philosophers. Each book in the series offers a guide to the poetics and politics of such thinkers, as well as interpretative paradigms, schools, bodies of thought, historical and cultural periods, and the genealogy of particular concepts, while transforming these, if not into tools or methodologies, then into conduits for directing and channelling thought. As well as transforming the critical past by interpreting it from the perspective of the present day, each study enacts transitional readings of critical voices and well-known literary texts, which are themselves conceivable as having been transitional and influential at the moments of their first appearance. The readings offered in these books seek, through close critical reading and theoretical engagement, to demonstrate certain possibilities in critical thinking to the student reader.

It is hoped that the student will find this series liberating because rigid methodologies are not being put into place. As all the dictionary definitions of the idea of transition above suggest, what is important is the action, the passage: of thought, of analysis, of critical response, such as are to be found, for example, in the texts of critics whose work has irrevocably transformed the critical landscape. Rather than seeking to help you locate yourself in relation to any particular school or discipline, this series aims to put you into action, as readers and writers, travellers between positions, where the movement between poles comes to be seen as of more importance than the locations themselves.

Julian Wolfreys

Acknowledgements

I would like to extend my appreciation to Sonya Barker, Felicity Noble and Anna Sandeman of Palgrave Macmillan for their kind assistance with this manuscript. Thanks are also due to Judy Marshall for her exemplary copy-editing and helpful suggestions. I also wish to acknowledge Mary Edwards, Debra Duhr, and Flora Lowe for their help in locating many obscure materials. Love and thanks also to Suzanne Decker, Siobhan Decker, Anastazia Decker, Evan Decker, and Kenneth Womack for their moral support and friendship.

Julian Wolfreys, however, deserves special mention not only for being a thoughtful editor but for revealing incredible patience when he would have preferred to reach for his revolver. Thank you for sticking with me.

Part I

Theory and Terminology

1   Introduction to 'Ideology'

ideology ... a system of ideas and ideals, especially one which forms the basis of economic or political theory and policy: *the ideology of republicanism.*
■ the ideas and manner of thinking characteristic of a group, social class, or individual: *a critique of bourgeois ideology.* ■ [mass noun] archaic **visionary** speculation, especially of an unrealistic or idealistic nature.   (*The New Oxford Dictionary of English*)

What do Adolf Hitler, Bill Gates, and the Spice Girls have in common? Reasonably expecting the answer to this ostensibly irreverent question to contain a sexually oriented punch line, many people might overlook a less obvious – though intriguing – possibility: ideology. Although media pundits of the latter half of the twentieth century tended to pursue a fairly uniform – and pejorative – definition of ideology, the term possesses a rich, contentious history that covers far more terrain than the contemporary sound-bite version suggests. According to this dominant representation of the concept, ideology primarily manifests itself as an unthinking – whether brutal and oppressive or merely selfish – other, whose rigid, irrational adherence to an overdetermined system or policy defies common sense. As characterized by various western media outlets, then, the ideologue sacrifices open debate for a hermetically closed set of values, and, thus, will refuse to listen to – and may attempt to destroy – anyone with an opposing viewpoint. Ideologues prey on weak and hungry nations. Ideologues reject human rights. As CNN and the BBC would have it, ideologues behave quite like Hitler and not a bit like the Spice Girls. Even the most cursory review of dominant media coverage of, for example, Leonid Brezhnev, Saddam Hussein and Slobodan Milosevic reveals them as unquestionable ideologues.

3

As for Bill Gates, he might qualify as an ideologue under a looser, secondary mainstream definition of ideology that refers to an uncompromising position, but not one that would necessarily hurt anyone in the physical sense or one that would deny the right of others to present a counterargument. Margaret Thatcher might cut a job or two, and Newt Gingrich might not really like females in combat, but they would not personally harm anybody, and neither would Louis Farrakhan or Rupert Murdoch. For the commentators on the Sunday morning news shows, common sense dictates that cartoonish 'butchers' and 'madmen' purvey their ideology with crude, broad brush strokes that contrast negatively with the ultrafine artistry of western capitalism and freedom.

Such a dichotomy between common sense and irrational behavior, however, lies at the heart of most modern discussions of ideology. While it may seem easy – if one employs the above 'obvious' defin-ition of the concept – to declare with Daniel Bell that ideology has outlived its usefulness and that the twentieth century witnessed the 'end of ideology,' to do so would ignore the term's more subtle gradations (Bell 2000). Once perceived as a pervasive process rather than as provincial dogma, ideology's impact becomes clearer. While often characterized as the unchallenged rationalizations of suspect political regimes, ideologies rarely – if ever – function in a monolithic way, and they apply to far more than 'traditional' politics. As the dialogic models of M. M. Bakhtin suggest, divergent ideologies often clash at the level of both discourse ('literal' or symbolic) and material action. Conscious subjects thus gain access to both official and unofficial ideologies, which, in turn, help both to reinscribe and undermine a given social reality. Individuals may thus, for example, interpret the Spice Girls' mantra 'girl power' from both the intended ('official') locus – i.e., women's independ-ence is not contingent on male approval – and from a host of competing perspectives – e.g., despite their claims to the contrary, the Spice Girls' collective voice relied on continued certification by male managers and record executives. In the case of the Spice Girls, observers may or may not consciously reconcile the para-dox ensuing from the different positionings: the 'inferior' class status of the Spice Girls potentially mitigates the subversive intent of the message 'girl power.' Scary, Sporty, Baby, Posh, and Ginger directly or indirectly produced hundreds of millions of dollars, but they received relatively little, while the CEOs of numerous international conglomerates reaped huge profits from the sale of concert tickets, compact discs, clothes, dolls, watches, bicycles, decals, and the like (the full list boggles the mind). The 'girl power,' moreover, also failed to extend to the Taiwanese, Mexican and Honduran (again, among others) factory workers who produced the Spice Girls' product line and who received subsistence wages.

While Terry Eagleton reminds readers that an overapplication of ideology critiques to trivial matters, such as a preference for roses rather than irises, may dilute their effectiveness, the concept of ideology clearly covers more than *Time* or *The Economist* generally suggest. The process of ideology, therefore, refers to the inherent relationships between ideas and material reality, but to avoid the practical limitations of endlessly deferred meanings, Eagleton proposes that 'in any particular situation you must be able to point to what counts as non-ideological for the term to have meaning' (Eagleton 1991, 9). In essence, Eagleton prompts readers to set ideological boundaries, a phenomenon that postmodern theorists would find quite ideological in itself. Nevertheless, although popular usage reduces the word to function, roughly, as a synonym for non-democratic political systems such as totalitarianism, fascism, or communism, one should begin to see that the notion of ideology as process (rather than product) muddles such pat dichotomies. Once one traces the history of ideology from its origins to its current academic incarnations, one will, hopefully, glean a sense of the concept's continuing evolution, and recognize that even reason, that bastion of common sense, may function in an ideological way. Certainly, Hitler fashioned an ideology, but so, too, did Bill Gates.

Although most of the frenetic revelers present at the 1989 dismantling of the Berlin Wall cheered at the imminent passing of Soviet communism, few would have viewed the event as the 'end' of ideology. Indeed, in light of the 29 years of tumultuous history separating Bell's 1960 proclamation regarding the end of ideology from the 1989 demise of the wall, most – if familiar with Bell – would have considered the end of ideology thesis rather naïve and its definition of ideology rather narrow. In Bell's understanding of the term, ideology represents the crude, irrational interests of non-liberal, non-capitalist regimes and the 'conversion of ideas into social levers' (2000, 400). Employing recent memories (and failures) of Nazism and Stalinism as evidence, Bell asserts that ideology lacks political viability and now exists as an unpleasant reminder of 'apocalyptic fervor' (405). Bell, of course, bases much of his argument on the unexamined assumption that western capitalist nations do not rely on ideology to reinforce their claims to Truth. For Bell, as for many historians weaned on the Cold War, ideology is unequivocally 'other,' a pejorative concept signifying a resistance to the 'Truth' embodied in industrial capitalism and its liberal satellites. Ignoring such internal contradictions as racial segregation, educational elitism, homelessness, and gender bias, Bell depicts Anglo-American culture as the non-ideological realm of freedom, democracy, and justice.[1] With their knowledge of Anglo-American involvement in such indubitably ideological struggles as the Vietnam War, the civil rights movement, the feminist movement, the gay and lesbian movement, the youth movement, the culture wars, and Thatcher's privatization movement, most spectators at the destruction of the Berlin Wall would have rejected Bell's optimistic conception of ideology as too dependent on extreme characterizations and binary rhetoric. Faced with so much material evidence, few such participants would have accepted the notion of an ideology-free West.

If, however, ideology fails to conform to the definition set forth by Bell – a rigid set of beliefs foisted on a vulnerable population by a malicious, self-serving elite – how then shall one define it? The answer to this rather ambitious question is fraught with problems and contradictions.

Most modern theorists of ideology would agree that definitions of ideology typically – perhaps inevitably – risk manifesting the very phenomenon they seek to describe objectively. Ideology, such thinkers argue, penetrates our thought processes so deeply that even the language and actions of would-be social critics betray affinities with the network of ideas that dominates their culture. Writers who would hazard a tentative definition of ideology, then, must self-consciously acknowledge the limitations of their approach. In the present case, readers will encounter many counter-definitions in the pages to come and, hopefully, engage the following definition in fruitful debate. For the purposes of this volume, one might define ideology as a reciprocal process wherein subjective, institutional, and political ideas operate within a power web of both the intended and the unanticipated. Under this definition, no ideology can be entirely conscious, for the concept is in constant flux as individuals, institutions, and politics influence one another. Ideology is thus – paradoxically – unstable even as it functions to produce power.

Another possible response to the problem of defining ideology – and quite a popular one – involves some version of the concept of 'false consciousness.' Because of its prevalence in Marxist and Neo-Marxist theory, casual readers might assume that the phrase 'false consciousness' originated with Marx; however, according to extant evidence, Marx himself never used the term (McLellan 1995, 16). Rather, Marx's collaborator, Friedrich Engels, outlined the notion of false consciousness in an oft-cited 14 July 1893 letter to Franz Mehrings: 'Ideology is a process accomplished by the so-called thinker consciously, it is true, but with a false consciousness. The real motive forces impelling him remain unknown to him. ... Hence, he imagines false or seeming motive forces. Because it is a process of thought he derives its form as well as its content from pure thought...' (Marx and Engels 1965, 459). According to Engels' pejorative conception – which draws on notions that Marx and he develop in *The German Ideology* but ignores some of Marx's later formulations of ideology – false consciousness represents a situation wherein subjects mistakenly believe that they act autonomously and independently of material constraint when, in fact, the very basis of their mental activity lies in their relation to socially established modes of production. Divorced from an understanding of materialism, ideas reflect not reality but illusion. While subjects may argue that their thoughts are 'common sense' or 'logical,' a false consciousness view of ideology would suggest that their idealism finds its source in the untenable premise that ideas precede things. Although Engels limited his use of the phrase 'false consciousness' to his intriguing letter, later theorists, as we shall see in chapter 2, seized upon the concept and expanded its significance.

Marx's relationship to the concept – if not the phrase – of false consciousness provides the catalyst for an esoteric, but nonetheless heated, debate among his acolytes. Because Marx wrote at such a prolific rate over an extended period and, perhaps, because many of his texts were published posthumously, many explicators of his work note what they perceive as inconsistencies between Marx's 'early' and 'mature' phases. One such apparent inconsistency involves Marx's conceptualization of ideology. In *The German Ideology,* co-written with Engels in 1845 but not published until the 1920s, Marx refers to 'illusions of consciousness' and discusses the Young Hegelians' desire to 'put to men the moral postulate of exchanging their present consciousness for human, critical, or egoistic consciousness, and thus of removing their limitations' (Marx 1998, 36). Marx further anticipates Engels' later notion of false consciousness when he argues that 'this demand to change consciousness amounts to a demand to interpret the existing world in a different way' (36). A few pages later, Marx explains ideology via the simile of a camera obscura:

> If in all ideology men and their relations appear upside-down as in a camera obscura, this phenomenon arises just as much from their historical life-process as the inversion of objects on the retina does from their physical life-process. ... The phantoms formed in the brains of men are also, necessarily, sublimates of their material life-process, which is empirically verifiable and bound to material premises. (1998, 42)

In the above passages, Marx seems to define ideology quite similarly to Engels. Just as Engels does, Marx attributes ideology to a lack of understanding on the part of a 'subject.' The notion of mental 'phantoms,' moreover, seems to dovetail with the suspicion of idealism evident in Engels' letter to Mehrings. In the camera obscura figure, Marx locates ideology in a privileging of the ideal over the material; for Marx, as for Engels, concrete historical necessity precedes abstract thought. Those who argue otherwise or who only partially grasp historical materialism – for example, Bruno Bauer and Max Stirner, whom Marx severely critiques in *The German Ideology* – practice mystification or rationalization, which blurs the relation between history and conceptualization and, thus, reinforces class divisions.

Nevertheless, despite Marx's apparent early alignment with Engels, many commentators – Theodor Adorno, Antonio Gramsci, and Louis Althusser among them – think that in *Capital* Marx abandoned, or at least radically altered, what they perceive as a limited notion of ideology. In the first volume of *Capital* (1867), Marx develops his theory of commodity fetishism, which many critics argue establishes the definitive Marxian paradigm for ideology. In contrast to Marx's focus on the illusory in the camera obscura trope, commodity fetishism locates ideology in the tangible relations of the marketplace. The transition from product of labor to commodity, Marx writes, yields an 'enigmatic' (1977, 164) situation wherein the 'physical relation between physical things' (i.e., the workers and the products of their labor [165]) dissolves:

> The mysterious character of the commodity form consists therefore simply in the fact that the commodity reflects the social characteristics of men's labour as objective characteristics of the products of labour themselves, as the socio-natural properties of these things. (164–5)

As a commodity, Marx continues, a product has an assigned exchange-value based not on utility (use-value) but on labor-time: 'the determination of the magnitude of value by labour-time is therefore a secret hidden under the apparent movements in the relative values of commodities' (168). The suppression of this 'secret,' Marx argues, 'conceals the social character of private labour and the social relations between the individual workers, by making those relations appear as relations between material objects, instead of revealing them plainly' (168–9).

Rather than characterizing ideology as an inverted relationship between consciousness and reality, therefore, Marx in *Capital* grounds ideology in material reality. The ideology inherent in commodity fetishism drives a wedge between workers and their products and obscures the actual energy and time involved in producing those products. Commodity fetishism, moreover, substitutes the figurative (money) for the concrete, and, thus, further erodes the connections among people. Followers of Marx's logic would claim, therefore, that the 'customer' who exchanges a piece of paper for a cut of beef generally sees only a cellophane-wrapped piece of flesh divorced not only from an animal, but from the ranchers, farmers, drivers, butchers, clerks, machine manufacturers, petroleum suppliers, and others who produced the steak. Workers, thus, become alienated from those who will *use* their products.

As will become evident in later chapters, the two main strands in Marx's conception of ideology largely serve as the flash point for academic debate. Although Marx develops other theories of ideology – notably in his *The Eighteenth Brumaire of Louis Bonaparte* (1852) and in *A Contribution to the Critique of Political Capital* (1859) – the theories he establishes in *The German Ideology* and *Capital* carry the most influence with later thinkers. The camera obscura/false consciousness and commodity fetishism approaches serve as starting points for most post-Marxian discussions of ideology. Because Marx never provides a definitive statement of ideology – one that explicitly rejects the camera obscura simile or else integrates it into his later conception of commodity fetishism – later commentators found his ambiguity fertile ground for amplification and academic discussion and irrevocably linked his name with ideology. One may easily forget, then, that Marx himself did not originate the concept of ideology.

Coined by the *philosophe* Antoine Destutt de Tracy in 1796, ideology originally referred to an ostensibly 'neutral' science of ideas that sought to trace how 'sensation' became thought. Nevertheless, ideology's conceptual pedigree begins much earlier than the Institut de France and, indeed, informs the classical split between idealism and materialism. In discussing his notion of Forms, Plato claims that material reality reflects a flawed version of the ideal. He suggests in his *Republic* (375?BC) that, for example, a craftsperson could never create a table – or even a drawing of a table – which fully captures the concept of the perfect (ideal) table. For Plato, ideas such as Truth, Beauty, and Justice preexist their representations, and these representations serve to distract humanity from transcending the material world. As Plato illustrates in his renowned simile of the cave, only the philosopher attempts to escape from the shadows and 'empty nonsense' of the material world and experience the glaring light of the ideal (1987, 318). Because of the powerful attraction of physical evidence – ideas lack matter – most people reject philosophers and deem them insane (one thinks here of Aristophanes' *The Clouds* [423 BC], for example wherein Socrates is described as gravely contemplating the 'intestinal passage of the gnat' [1973, 118]), but Plato ascribes them the highest place in his ideal society. For Plato, philosophers may more freely distinguish between the material illusions that motivate most subjects and the underlying ideal upon which those distortions rest. While Plato, of course, never uses the word ideology, he does critique contemporary Grecian society by highlighting the process whereby rulers and their subjects derive their beliefs. By chasing after shadows, Plato contends, people ignore the ideal and act irrationally.

Plato's representation of a society in which individuals mistake fabulation for 'reality' underscores one of the major philosophical contributions stemming from the study of ideology: the formulation of the subject. Chapter 2, 'Ideology and the Paradox of Subjectivity,' will explore how a variety of theorists from Plato and Francis Bacon to Sigmund Freud and Louis Althusser employ ideology in constructing their models of subjectivity. Although they reach diverse conclusions, such writers share in common a belief that subjectivity often finds its basis in the mythopoeic. Jean-François Lyotard's 'grand narratives,' Northrop Frye's 'tropes,' Carl Jung's 'collective unconscious': these and other attempts to codify the stories – verbalized or institutionalized – that people tell about themselves and their enemies all focus on the inescapability of cultural myth. Even if individuals fancy themselves 'nonconformists' or even 'revolutionaries,' they nonetheless function within (and react against) the ideological parameters created by the society in which they live. Starting with Plato, several theorists offer ways to avoid such a bleak determinism, but such options (e.g., proletarian revolution or extended psychoanalysis) generally prove difficult at best. Nevertheless, as readers will discover in chapter 2, one value of such formulations of ideology lies in their ability to problematize notions of 'common sense.' It may seem 'natural' for Bill Gates to want to accumulate millions of dollars an hour, but such a phenomenon finds its basis in ideology.

Closely aligned with ideological notions of subjectivity is the concept of culture. In chapter 3, 'Ideology and Institutional Authority,' readers will continue to glean the interconnectedness of subjective and cultural desire. If one subscribes to theorists such as Marx, Georg Lukács, Althusser, and Karl Mannheim, subjective desire mirrors cultural desire. In other words, the 'needs' of an institution (e.g., a religion, government, or family) manifest themselves via ideology and establish a milieu wherein a subject will 'naturally' desire what will benefit the larger institution. Ideas follow the requirements of history. According to this view, therefore, Gates' drive to improve the technological situation of the average citizen finds its root in capitalism's need to find new product outlets. As writers such as John B. Thompson, Marshall McLuhan, and Rosemary Hennessy argue, institutions – beyond their ostensible purpose – exist to perpetuate themselves and their inherent ideologies. Media outlets such as the Internet and television function not only as catalysts for subjective thought, but also as *shapers* of thought. Media 'culture' helps create subjects who – in general – reinforce dominant ideas. The range of ideas, thus, falls within certain parameters. The rise of violence in American schools, for example, might precipitate debate over the proper interpretation of the Second Amendment to the Constitution, but rarely do citizens challenge the validity of their version of democracy itself. Ideology, such thinkers would claim, embeds itself in various institutions so as to become – paradoxically – at once omnipresent and invisible.

Once outside of one's *own* culture, however, ideology often makes itself almost comically obvious, and the external observer cannot but help to notice the ideological scaffolding supporting institutions such as schools, families, religions, and governments. Analyzed in such a naked way – and implicitly compared to competing ideologies – most ideologies will appear crude, overt, dogmatic. In many cases, onlookers will accuse the leaders of alien institutions of propagandizing, social engineering, or worse. Chapter 4, 'Political Ideology,' then, will examine those theorists who consider ideology as a form of direct social manipulation. This perspective gained currency almost from the beginning of ideology's formal history, and most histories of ideology generally credit Napoleon with initiating this pejorative – and by now almost universal – meaning of the term when, upon the occasion of his retreat from Moscow, he chided de Tracy for his 'diffuse metaphysics' (qtd. in Eagleton 1991, 67). Later, thinkers as different as Marx, Bell, Herbert Marcuse, and Jürgen Habermas appropriated Napoleon's usage and ascribed the term 'ideology' to specific socio-political modes of thought. Despite such a philosophical pedigree, however, the mass perception of ideology generally lacks even a modicum of self-reflection and fails to ground its understanding of the concept in the rigorous historical paradigms of the aforementioned writers. Cut loose from the academy and its ideologies, the idea – reinforced by what Althusser refers to as ideological state apparatuses – loses much of its nuance and assumes a more slogan-like character. In this nearly ubiquitous redaction, ideology manifests itself in the extremist sound-bite. Any non-centrist position, whether it regards taxation or grammar school curricula, will likely find itself severely critiqued, if not lampooned, as 'ideology' by the moderate media. Such media will commonly saddle non-capitalist cultures, in particular, with descriptors meant to convey tacit disapproval of an ideology that forsakes their own agendas: 'Muslim extremist,' 'Nicaraguan strongman,' 'cult leader.' Rarely, if ever, though, do such outlets refer to Enron, Nike, Exxon, Texaco, and other ethically dubious corporations as 'capitalist extremists.' In practice, then, ideology effectively doubles back on itself, reinforcing its principles by reifying socio-political alternatives with an ideological label. By calling attention to the ideology undergirding non-moderate, non-capitalist social practices, the media avoid contemplating the ideologies that drive themselves. One may, in fact, apply with profit Jonathan Swift's definition of satire to ideology and declare that the concept 'is a sort of glass, wherein beholders do generally discover everybody's face but their own' (1973, 375).

For students of literature, ideology offers some intriguing interpretive possibilities. As Eagleton observes in his *Introduction to Literary Theory* (1983), the very idea of 'literature' is ideological, but, as he earlier asserts in *Criticism and Ideology* (1978), 'the literary text is not the 'expression' of ideology, nor is ideology the 'expression' of social class. The text, rather, is a certain *production* of ideology' (64). According to Eagleton's theory, students of literature should not consider the text as a transparent rendering of an author's – or an institution's – viewpoint, but should instead avoid simple dichotomies by examining a host of variables and exploring the ways in which text, author, history, and audience converge and contradict one another. Literary representations of history produce ideology as much in their lacunae as in their palpable selections, and the same text can produce quite different ideological effects in different audiences. Chapters 5 through 7 will engage a variety of texts in a series of ideology critiques that will attempt to heed Eagleton's advice and steer clear of mistaking the reflection for the flesh. Hopefully, students will discover how ideology critiques allow readers to navigate between intention and contradiction.

By now it should be fairly clear that ideology contains its own paradox: any attempt to describe ideology necessarily finds itself rooted in ideology. An individual's own historical moment and position will blind her or him to ideology both within a given text and within a particular interpretation of a text. Such a phenomenon may potentially lead either to an endlessly refracting series of interpretive disclaimers or else to a faux (and dangerous) relativism that blithely asserts that Hitler and Tony Blair possess ideologies – or 'grand narratives' – that are no better, or no worse, than one another. Of course, finding an unmitigated relativist would prove quite difficult, and even Lyotard might balk at being the target of cannibalism. The question of positionality, then, becomes paramount here. How can one critique ideology from inside ideology? Can one ever 'escape' from ideology and pursue a purely 'scientific' or 'historical' mode of analysis? In the face of the Holocaust, is it possible to claim that all ideologies are neutral? The final chapter, 'The "Post-Ideological" Era?' will focus on this hermeneutic bind and discuss how a variety of writers, including Raymond Williams, deal with it.

2 Ideology and the Paradox of Subjectivity

Defiant in their subjectivity, two citizens – one from Kosovo, one from Serbia – expressed to an American reporter strikingly similar sentiments regarding their own respective futures and recently completed peace negotiations. The two declarations, edited so as to appear back-to-back in the broadcast, both revealed a stalwart sense of independence. The first speaker, a Kosovar refugee whose tone exhibited ebullient resolve, declared that although Serbian troops forced her to abandon her land, they could 'never take away [her] hope and heart.' The second interviewee, a resident of Belgrade, echoed this assertion with his own avowal that NATO could bomb the city, but it could 'never take away [his] pride.' The interviews, granted, perhaps, 30 seconds of air time, offer an excellent example of an almost Cartesian optimism in the subject, for both seemed to aver that their enemies may persecute them but never *objectify* them: their minds will remain independent despite bodily harm. The political and cultural ideology of the other, in short, will never permeate their subjectivities, for the other may dominate the material realm by annihilating cities or burning identification papers, but it may never penetrate the ideal province of the self. *I think, therefore I am.*

For many theorists of ideology, however, such formulations become problematic, metaphysical. Viewed from the perspective of ideology, **Descartes'** *cogito, ergo sum*, described in his *Discourse on Method* (1637), represents the naïve belief that ideas precede things, that subjectivity rises independently of material conditions. According to those who credit ideology with a major – even central – role in creating subjectivity, the proper statement should read, 'I am, therefore I think.' One's agency is contingent on the convergence of a variety of material factors, from the biochemically random to the economically determined. Subjectivity does not arise merely from the physical ability to think; it grounds itself in the material. The subject, thus, functions not as a truly free agent, but as a phenomenon bound by specific – though flexible – parameters. Because subjects, such as the above interviewees, cannot normally perceive these boundaries, they mistakenly (falsely) assume that their ideal perception of reality is coterminous with Reality.

In coining the term 'ideology,' Antoine Destutt de Tracy hoped to establish a science of ideas and analyze the boundaries of thought. De Tracy's work synthesized the theories of a number of his fellow *philosophes*, such as P. H. D. Holbach, Étienne Bonnot de Condillac, Claude-Adrien Helvétius, and Jean-Jacques Rousseau, and sought to verify abstraction with science. De Tracy postulated that a 'neutral' science of ideas based on reason and empirical evidence could locate – and thus correct – the source of fallacious, metaphysical speculation. Clearly, de Tracy owes much to John Locke, David Hume, David Hartley, and other theorists who perceived a direct correlation between materialism ('sensation') and ideas. Perhaps the major influence on all of these thinkers, however, is **Francis Bacon**, whose concept of mental 'idols' seems a clear antecedent for the belief that ideology affects subjectivity.

Novum Organum (1620), the second volume of Bacon's proposed six-volume *Great Instauration*, critiques contemporary scientific method, which, Bacon argues, erroneously and harmfully proceeds from 'primary notions of things' (1994, 3). In other words, Bacon believes that hitherto, scientists have deferred to established principles, and, thus, manipulated or rationalized specific evidence to conform with such tenets. Instead of altering first principles in the face of aberrations, scientists – because of 'sloth and inertia' (9) – either fail to ask questions or else shoehorn the data into the theory, or 'axiom': 'if they chance to come up against an instance not previously noticed or known, the axiom is rescued by some frivolous distinction, when the more correct course would be for the axiom itself to be corrected' (50). In locating a reason for this, in his opinion, stagnant science, Bacon offers his concept of idols of the mind, which in hindsight certainly qualify at least as a proto-ideology. Dividing the idols of the mind into four categories – Idols of the Tribe, Idols of the Cave, Idols of the Market-Place, and

Idols of the Theater – Bacon attempts to 'forewarn' scientists so that they may avoid false consciousness and seek the 'truth' inductively rather than deductively. Bacon proposes to correct this inversion (Marx's camera obscura trope comes to mind here) by scientific investigations that establish only tentative theories based on the observation of data.

The first rubric, Idols of the Tribe, concerns humanity's predisposition to order the universe, a 'sort of vanity...rife not only in dogmas but also in simple notions' (1994, 57). For Bacon, the idea of a perfectly ordered universe reflects an aggrandized belief in human importance that places unfounded emphasis on subjective perception and cognition. By focusing on principles deduced from limited instances, human understanding falsely assumes itself capable of explaining *every* instance. In a simile striking in its similarity to the camera obscura, Bacon observes that

> all our perceptions, both of our sense and of our minds, are reflections of man, not of the universe, and the human understanding is like an uneven mirror that cannot reflect truly the rays from the objects, but distorts and corrupts the nature of things by mingling its own nature with it.   (1994, 54)

As with the camera obscura trope, Bacon's figure of the uneven mirror centers on the ability of consciousness to depict a warped vision of 'reality.' The commingling of the ideal and the material suggests that subjects project their own biases on to the latter, thereby appropriating the physical realm to forward a variety of self-serving explanations. Rather than striving to observe material phenomena on their own terms, humans 'prefer to believe what [they] want to be true' (59). Subjects generally create, therefore, an ideology that foregrounds received experience and somewhat solipsistically characterizes the natural realm. Such an ideology – built upon a foundation of distortion – prevents subjects from a scientific understanding of the universe.

The second category, Idols of the Cave, refers to the specific prejudices resulting from individual psychology and experience. If in his discussion of the Idols of the Tribe Bacon asserts that human predisposition prompts subjects to project their desires on to the material universe, then in his analysis of the Idols of the Cave he suggests from whence those appetites arise. Using a trope

similar to that Plato employs in his simile of the cave, Bacon argues
that temperament, education, and habit all converge to establish
a subject's 'own private cave or den, which breaks up and falsifies
the light of Nature' (1994, 54). *How* subjects perceive or explain
natural phenomena depends on their specific individual interests,
which, in turn, find themselves shaped by acculturation. As Louis
Althusser later observes, institutions such as families, schools, and
governments tend to perpetuate the ideas that ensure their own
survival, and Bacon appears to subscribe to the view that subjects
take their cues from such institutions, although he does reserve
a place for chance. How, then, may individuals assure themselves
that their scientific theories truly lack ulterior motives? In Bacon's
view, individual subjects who fail to achieve a 'disinterested' balance
between extremes of thought will necessarily blunder when they
attempt to understand the material world. Nonetheless, although
Bacon cautions his readers about the distorting powers of such bias,
he remains rather vague about how individual subjects may solve
the conundrum.

In his critique of the third type of idols, those of the market-place,
Bacon combines his observations of consciousness with speculations
about linguistics. Bacon proposes in his *Novum Organum* that
'words plainly do violence to the understanding and throw everything into confusion, and lead men into innumerable empty
controversies and fictions' (1994, 55). Inevitably, people must ground
their ideas in words, which leads to a situation wherein imprecise
language helps to perpetuate a vicious cycle of ambiguous rationalization, miscommunication, and outright error. Inverting the
accepted relation between ideas and words, which suggested that
subjects regulate language, Bacon argues that language shapes
subjective thought: 'while men believe their reason governs words,
in fact, words turn back and reflect their power on the understanding, and so render philosophy and science sophistical and inactive'
(64). Bacon effectively undercuts the autonomy of the subject by
implying that language – a communal legacy – functions in a
reactionary, self-preserving way. True (non-ideological) thought,
Bacon intimates, stagnates because the language of received, generally false, ideas compels the subject to explain new or aberrant
concepts with words that cling to outmoded imagery. Imagine, for
instance, the problems inherent in explaining post-Einsteinian
physics with a pre-Newtonian vocabulary. However, one cannot

jettison one's entire vocabulary, and although it anticipates the linguistic theories of Ferdinand de Saussure and others, Bacon's explanation of the Idols of the Market-Place generates a paradox, for it, too, consists of words, and Bacon offers little advice on how to avoid false notions borne of language, apart from an admonition to steer clear of 'names of things that do not exist' and careless abstractions (64–5).

Closely related to the Idols of the Market-Place, the Idols of the Theater, those stemming from philosophy, constitute Bacon's final category. Bacon rejects philosophical argument *en toto*, contending that the entire method – rooted as it is in 'fictitious tales' (1994, 66) – fails to explain natural phenomena in an adequate way because of an over-reliance on sophistry, insufficient physical data, and superstition (68). Chiding such luminaries as Aristotle and Plato, Bacon asserts that philosophy eschews experience in favor of preconceived systems into which philosophers manipulate their data. Bacon characterizes such systems as elaborate plays that dazzle their audiences but that nonetheless fail to codify reality. Delivery and rhetoric establish precedence over knowledge and truth, and sweeping abstractions negate 'intermediate causes' (71). Ultimately, Bacon implies, words – rather than thorough experimentation – dictate the results of philosophy.

Obviously, Bacon's Idols of the Mind establish many precedents for future theorists of ideology. Bacon problematizes the notion of a truly autonomous subject, for he depicts consciousness as contingent on received knowledge. Institutions, language, and even biology serve to draw distinct parameters around a subject's mental geography and delimit the products (ideas) of a given psyche. Like Plato, Bacon posits a theory of ideology steeped in the pejorative long before Napoleon chastises de Tracy. Idols, ideologies, produce consciousnesses that misapprehend reality and vainly advertise their own distortions as empirical fact. That Bacon can discover the social roots of false consciousness, however, creates a paradox that will challenge many subsequent thinkers: if misconception plagues humanity, how may Bacon's own mind escape the charge of distortion? For Bacon, the answer lies in rigorous empirical method that reaches only the most tentative of conclusions, but others will view such a position as begging the question. Despite his lack of self-referential criticism, Bacon effectively employs a secular strategy to decenter the subject and challenge established mores, and many later theories of will consist primarily of modifications of this paradigm.

Return for a moment, however, to the Cartesian formulation, *cogito, ergo sum*. For many western readers, the subject, the *I*, lies in conflict with society, with the we. Bacon's belief that our own consciousness may somehow not function independently of an overarching culture runs counter to the apparently ingrained notion of western freedom. Bacon, however, stops short of cultural determinism, for he suggests – and even provides himself as a modest example – that a regimen of disciplined, honest speculation may allow occasional individuals to cast off their thralldom and produce original knowledge. As with Plato, though, Bacon indicates that such mental breakthroughs are most rare, and that the average citizen – while free to a certain extent – will never transcend certain intellectual boundaries. The raw material of ideas may appear limitless to the subject, but Bacon explains that this phenomenon occurs less because of free will than because of ideology's tendency to recycle itself. Humans may possess the ability to create infinite variations on a theme, but the themes themselves (as James Frazer, Carl Jung, Northrop Frye, and others observe in detail) lack the same expanse. In comparison to others, one's cerebral furrows may be relatively deep or shallow, straight or crooked, but they still cut the same ground.

In his *An Essay Concerning Human Understanding* (1690), **John Locke** – who would later have a profound influence on de Tracy (Kennedy 1978, 87) – probes even deeper into the notion of subjectivity. Rejecting the notion of innate ideas much as Bacon does (he even alludes to Bacon's idols), Locke locates the source of moral principles firmly within the subject, as shaped by the environment: 'external, material things, as the objects of *sensation*; and the operation of our own minds within, as the objects of *reflection*, are, to me, the only originals, from whence all our ideas take their beginning' (Locke 1997, 110). Accordingly, a scientist could conceivably discover the locus of a particular thought. This radical notion broke with much of the received knowledge of the day – e.g., the *ideology* of the Church, as represented, for example, by Edward Stillingfleet (Bishop of Worcester) – and heralded the rise of the Enlightenment and political liberalism. Locke's famous *tabula rasa* formulation, which he omitted from the final draft of the *Essay*, holds that the subject arises from an accumulation of impressions, which the subject may then rearrange. For Locke, 'it may come to pass that *doctrines*, that have been derived from no better original than, the superstition of a nurse, or the authority of an old woman; may, by length of time, and consent of neighbours, *grow up to the dignity of principles* in religion or morality... for white paper receives any characters' (1997, 88; emphasis in original). Thought, then, locates its source in a distinctly material realm.

One may readily see that, despite his liberalism, Locke anticipates the Althusserian subject, who, while convinced of his/her 'free will,' inescapably derives thought from the ideology proliferate within the state apparatuses: '*his ideas are his material actions inserted into material practices governed by material rituals which are themselves defined by the material ideological apparatus from which derive the ideas of that subject*' (Althusser 1971, 169; emphasis in original). Via Marx, Althusser simply extends Locke's formulation to a logical conclusion, even if that conclusion reveals a chicken-and-egg-like aporia. If, to Locke, the (pre)subject constitutes a passive 'white paper' waiting to receive impressions, then clearly material reality – from genetic code to state-mandated pedagogy to television sit-coms – shapes 'independent' thoughts like so much malleable clay. Marx and Engels would later codify this concept in *The German Ideology*: 'The production of ideas, of conceptions, of consciousness, is at first directly interwoven with the material activity and the material intercourse of men – the language of real life' (Marx 1998, 42). Although Locke fails to pursue this systematically, in terms of ideology, his empiricist approach suggests that those modes of thinking that most pervade a subject's environment will thus play the greatest role in developing consciousness. By 'reflecting' on the ubiquitous 'sensations' that s/he receives, the subject may produce a 'complex' idea, but such knowledge would necessarily find itself contingent on the ideas of other institutions or people.

The subject must also rely on an imperfect – to Locke – method of expressing his/her ideas: language. Pursuing much the same line of thought that Bacon examines in his idols of the market-place, Locke devotes an entire book of the *Essay* to language and its effects on ideas. Locke notes that words '*signify* only men's peculiar ideas, and that *by a perfectly arbitrary imposition*, is evident, in that they often fail to excite in others... the same ideas' (1997, 366).

In communicating, therefore, the subject must select from a pool of randomly assigned language. For Locke, this phenomenon often leads to confusion or 'abuse.' Speaking in particular of philosophy, Locke argues that 'this gibberish, which in the weakness of human understanding, serves so well to palliate men's ignorance, and cover their errors, comes by familiar use amongst those of the same tribe, to seem the most important part of language, and of all other the terms the most significant' (443). From an ideological perspective, Locke's point underscores the dubious nature of specialized language, be it philosophical, political, or otherwise.

While Locke optimistically calls for subjects to employ words as 'the signs of our ideas only, and not for things themselves' (1997, 444), it seems relatively clear that language serves as a flashpoint for ideology. 'Compassionate conservatism,' 'postmodernism,' 'global economy': according to Locke, such terms tend to replace the ideas that underlie them and muddy the intellectual waters. Locke asserts that many ostensible problems arise from 'this abuse of taking words upon trust' (448), a phenomenon he attributes especially to 'men of letters,' but which certainly applies to politicians ('pacification' of insurgents), educators ('mainstreaming'), industry leaders ('downsizing'), and a host of others. In fetishizing certain words, each institution masks the material significance behind the language. The signifier takes precedence over the 'simple' or 'complex' idea that, for Locke, should be the goal of communication. Theodor Adorno, speaking of the 'jargon of authenticity' claims that this privileging of opaque language proffers 'sub-language as superior language' (Adorno 1973a, 6). Proceeding in the empirical vein that marks the *Essay*, Locke argues that more precise usage would strengthen the bond between idea and word. Clearly, Locke believes that a *science* of ideas should function as the linchpin of any rigorous empirical method.

While Bacon anticipates much of what Locke rehearses in the *Essay*, his influence on ideology and subjectivity was not as pervasive as that of Locke, whose writings helped to spawn the Enlightenment. Even so, Locke's vision of a 'science' of ideas would not take hold – despite the efforts of Hume, Helvétius, Condillac and others – until **de Tracy's** 1796 neologism, 'ideology.' Capitalizing on Locke's notion of 'sensation,' de Tracy asked, 'what is existing if not sensing?' (Kennedy 1978, 45). Emmet Kennedy astutely maintains that de Tracy's question reformulates Descartes' *cogito, ergo sum* (45), and de Tracy – ironically imprisoned during the Reign of Terror for being a reactionary (36) – quite consciously deigned to revolutionize the study of subjectivity. Rejecting the 'transcendental metaphysics' offered by Immanuel Kant[1] in his *Critique of Pure Reason* (1781) and fusing Locke and Condillac's emphasis on perception with Pierre Cabanis' materialist psychology (Lichtheim 1967, 7), de Tracy sought to map the origins of human thought and, by implication, the source of humanity. As de Tracy viewed it, ideology would function as the basis for all future scientific study, for no field could transcend its reliance on ideas and sensation. Religion and other moral speculation, according to de Tracy, find their 'authority' not in a priori, absolute truth, but within the individual mind.

Empirical analysis, de Tracy thought, could strip away millennia of socio-political policy clouded by superstition, prejudice, and metaphysical duplicity. As David McLellan observes, de Tracy and his *philosophe* brethren held that 'the natural and social worlds were pellucid to the rational mind' (McLellan 1995, 6). De Tracy thus ascribed the ultimate source of theology, philosophy, political theory, and other systematic (and oppressive) modes of thought to conditioning, habit. Subjects respond to basic sensations, but they may distort the meaning of those impressions. Because the subject that Tracy contemplated exists as 'the totality of sensitive parts which form a whole...its extension in space is composed of all the sensing parts together, obeying the same will' (cited in Kennedy 1978, 56), it relies heavily on movement and resistance (58). Consequently, the subject's will must consider multiple stimuli and grant more or less attention to them. In this activity, the subject may unduly emphasize one sensation to the exclusion of others – the foundation of metaphysical prejudice. Power, furthermore, results from the imposition of one subject's will upon another.

Once the scientist of ideas could expose them as fabricated myths – rather than as eternal truths – he or she could uproot these harmful concepts altogether and replace them with more benign ideas that meshed with basic human needs. Despite their insistence on the 'neutrality' of ideology, the French *idéologues* believed that discovering the source of human ideas would bring about social change and they merged a humanist, republican political agenda with 'scientific' progress. In essence, then, de Tracy desired to rid the world of false consciousness and supplant it with a rational, unbiased program of social and moral justice. Eagleton remarks that the *idéologues* 'inveighed fearlessly against a social order which fed the people on religious superstition in order to buttress its own brutally absolutist power, and dreamt of a future in which the dignity of men and women ... would be cherished' (1991, 64–5).

As Eagleton points out, however, de Tracy skirts the issue of how the *idéologue* may avoid the errors of the past (1991, 65). If all ideas arise from movement and resistance, then how can the concept of reason itself be immune to scrutiny? As subjects, the *idéologues* themselves would operate from the same limitations as those they were trying to enlighten. Pursuing de Tracy's logic, any idea – freedom, equality, justice – finds its authority not in universal principle but in human distortion. To elevate one's own ideas to the level of absolute truth, then, would be tantamount to megalomania. Clearly, de Tracy's ideology suffers from what Marx – speaking of Ludwig Feuerbach – labels 'inconsistent materialism' (1998, 44). For Marx, the charge of inconsistent materialism applies to those systems that fail to transcend 'the realm of theory' and consider the 'existing conditions of life' (46). In short, de Tracy, by ignoring the paradox that his line of reasoning creates, synchronously mystifies his own ideas and critiques those of others.

Ironically, de Tracy's positive conception of ideology, as outlined in his *Elémens d'Idéologie* (1804–15) failed to outlive its author. As seen in chapter 1, through the sheer force of his will, Napoleon transformed ideology – already ripe for parody among some French intellectuals – into a pejorative, metaphysical concept. According to Napoleon, de Tracy, whose meticulous avoidance of idealism formed the core of his 'science of ideas,' and his fellow *idéologues* were ludicrous dreamers along the lines of those found in Jonathan Swift's parody of the Royal Academy in *Gulliver's Travels*. The French press, sensing Napoleon's mood, followed suit, and the negative definition of ideology took root (Kennedy 1978, 82). Later cemented by Marx's camera obscura analogy in *The German Ideology* and Engels' false consciousness formulation, the perception of ideology as dogmatic adherence to a chimera persists to this day. The popular media tag extremists on both the left and the right as 'ideologues,' and critics of unpopular social programs frequently paint their opponents as attempting to impose their 'ideology' on the unsuspecting masses. Nevertheless, the term invented by de Tracy, and the notions surrounding it, continue to be a focal point for intellectuals of all stripes.

In calling for a metascience that would chart the course of human ideas, de Tracy derided Kant for opaque reasoning and metaphysical reverie. In his *Phenomenology of the Spirit* (1807), however, **G. W. F. Hegel** attempted to combine de Tracy's science of ideas with Kant's belief in a priori knowledge. In so doing, Hegel traced the origin of human ideas to a universal 'spirit' or mind [*Geist*] that fused both subject and object (substance): 'everything turns on grasping and expressing the True, not only as *Substance*, but equally as *Subject*' (1977, 10; Hegel's emphasis). George Lichtheim characterizes Hegel's hybrid as 'a concrete universal which differentiates itself into particular thinking minds' (1967, 13). This observation underscores Hegel's emphasis on the dialectical relationship between human ideas and truth, for it illustrates that an individual must derive a particular thought from the larger pattern of the *Geist*. The trace material of the *Geist* – the history of philosophy – reveals to the discerning reader how a particular thinker could, in fact, arrive at a given concept by displacing its opposite. In other words, the historical (material) record of thought sheds light on the Absolute (ideal) by exposing how new ideas take root in the soil of the old.

For Hegel, Truth, 'the living substance,' stems from 'the movement of positing itself, or... the mediation of its self-othering with itself. This Substance is, as Subject, pure, *simple negativity*' (1977, 10; Hegel's emphasis). A belief in first causes must necessarily lead to a denial of those concepts, for 'the refutation would... properly consist in the further development of the principle, and in thus remedying the defectiveness' (13). The process involved in dialectical movement, therefore, leads to the Absolute. All individual 'subjects,' then, must find themselves co-determined with the *Geist*, or Subject. Effectively, Hegel associates the subject with the other, an interpenetration of opposites. Because of subjectivity's contingence on history, it proves for Hegel a rather problematic issue from the standpoint of ideology, as no one may physically perceive the 'whole' of the Absolute (i.e., all of the past and, thus, all of the burgeoning present). Synthesis, achieved by a systematic examination of the historical and philosophical narratives, can never capture the flux of the current era. As Lichtheim remarks, 'the individual's fate was swallowed up in the dialectic of the process' (1967, 15). The dialectic, then, comprises the history of the Absolute rather than that of a given subject.

The Subject thus displaces the subject, and it is the *Geist*, not the thinking 'I,' that develops through consciousness. Hegel posits that 'the disparity which exists in consciousness between the 'I' and the substance which is its object is the distinction between them, the *negative* in general' (1977, 2; Hegel's emphasis). Consciousness functions as the movement toward the Absolute and as such exists in a limited relation to the whole. By Hegel's definition, then, all particular consciousness is false. Eagleton expatiates:

> One might say, then, that on this view our routine consciousness is itself inherently 'ideological,' simply by virtue of its partiality. It is not that the statements we make in this situation are false; it is rather that they are true only in some superficial, empirical way, for they are judgments about isolated objects which have not yet been fully incorporated into their full context.   (Eagleton 1991, 98)

As Eagleton suggests, Hegel explodes Locke's notion of the *tabula rasa* by denying the autonomy of the individual consciousness. Each subject comprises only a minute component of the Subject wherein the Absolute paradoxically negates itself and moves forward through synthesis. Consequently, Hegel chides those who hold that 'the True consists in a proposition which is a fixed result, or which is immediately known' for their dogmatism (1977, 23). Blind to the scope of the Absolute, those who purport to grasp the Truth simply cleave to but one of its myriad facets. The Absolute of Reason exists in reaction to the Subject and its various redactions, the minute splinters of every thinking 'I' throughout history. The perception of Truth, therefore, tends toward the relative, for new material conditions constantly alter how the thinking 'I' comprehends itself in relation to the world. In *Lectures on the Philosophy of World History; Introduction: Reason in History* (1830), moreover, Hegel describes how the 'cunning of reason' compels individual subjects to distort the material of history to serve the conditions of the present (1981, 89). Unconscious of their role within the *Geist*, yet sincere in their illusory (and, for Hegel, dogmatic) beliefs, such subjects act out of historical necessity without realizing the true catalyst for their behavior. One may readily observe that Hegel's 'cunning of reason' prefigures Engels' notion of false consciousness, for it suggests that individuals fail to recognize the limits of their experience and the existence of an alternative 'truth.'

In challenging the traditional dichotomy between materialism and idealism, Hegel reinvigorated western philosophy. His writings spawned a series of imitators, disciples, and antagonists, most notably the 'Young [or 'Left'] Hegelians' and Karl Marx, although his influence continues today. While they ultimately proved easy targets for Marx and Engels in *The German Ideology*, the Young Hegelians – including Ludwig Feuerbach, Bruno Bauer, Edgar Bauer, F. T. Vischer, David Strauss, and Max Stirner – felt, much like de Tracy and Locke, that by scrutinizing the source of ideas they could enact a more equitable social plan. Hegel's notion that all subjective knowledge exists in a provisional relationship with the Absolute prompted the Young Hegelians to question received political ideas and replace them with a more radical formula. If one could only expose contemporary social policy as a product of inferior thinking, they opined, then one might convince society to implement a political structure based on reason.

Once the radical implications of Hegel's theories permeated German philosophy, institutions of all types faced volleys of historicized treatises. **Feuerbach**, representative of this turn toward materialism and a major influence on Marx, seeks in works such as *The Essence of Christianity* (1841) and *Principles of the Philosophy of the Future* (1843) to release the human subject from the illusions propagated by the abstractions of religion and speculative philosophy. While Hegel holds to a rudimentary belief in religion as a figurative example of his fusion of the ideal and the material, Feuerbach, building on the earlier theories of Strauss, excoriates Christianity – and, by extension, all religious systems – as 'primitive self-consciousness' (1989, 270). Anticipating Marx, Feuerbach also derides philosophy for its grounding in the status quo: 'In that its entire system rests upon these acts of abstraction, Hegelian philosophy has estranged the human being from its very self' (1983, 159). For Feuerbach, Hegel correctly identifies the problem of modern philosophy, but fails to alter the paradigm in any significant way, a charge that Marx and Engels, of course, would later levy against Feuerbach himself. While Feuerbach could not ultimately agree with Hegel's views, he considered them crucial because they offered an escape from the traditional dichotomy between idealists and empiricists and thus admitted the possibility of a new system of thought.

In rejecting the Hegelian Absolute, Feuerbach announced his own project as an attempt to correct the inverted relationship between humanity and ideas: 'The absolute to man is his own nature. The power of the object over him is therefore the power of his own nature' (Feuerbach 1989, 5). Rather than advance a metaphysical Absolute in the Hegelian sense, the dialectical pattern of history charts Humanity's own 'sublime' nature (1989, 7). Through speculative philosophy, individual subjects commit the crucial error of applying their own fathomable capabilities to the entire species, which Feuerbach sees as unlimited and 'perfect' in its essence: 'he can become conscious of his limits, his finiteness, only because the perfection, the infinitude of his species, is perceived by him, whether as an object of feeling, of conscience, or of the thinking conscious' (1989, 7). Like Hegel, Feuerbach ascribes human thought with an absolute quality, but he diverges from his predecessor by imbuing human *potential*, rather than reason itself, with this infinite characteristic. The subject, therefore, circumscribes itself by juxtaposing individual ideas with the unlimited promise of the collective. Hegel and his intellectual brethren, Feuerbach maintains, invert the subject–object relationship between the conscious 'I' and the idea and superimpose human qualities on to abstractions such as 'God.' Feuerbach thus argues that 'the object to which a being is necessarily related is nothing other than its own revealed being' (1986, 9).

In *The Essence of Christianity*, Feuerbach, employing a 'materialist' paradigm, traces the idea of God to its roots in human potential. For Feuerbach, the origins of religion reveal a process of mystification whereby Human subjectivity transforms into a 'divine' object: 'Religion is the disuniting of man from himself' (1989, 33). Drawing from Hegel's Absolute, Feuerbach imbues Humanity with a collective subjectivity that allows him to apply the notion of eternity to the species rather than the individual. The traits of divinity, therefore, refer not to God, but to the human race: 'Man was already in God, was already God himself, before God became man' (50). God and religion, then, represent a manifestation of the unquenched human desire for perfection. By fetishizing the moral qualities represented by Love, religious consciousness embodies God with a human form, Christ, and alienates the human subject from

Humanity itself. For Feuerbach, the Trinity functions as a moral placebo, 'the substitute for the consciousness of the species, the image under which it was made present to the people, and became the law of the popular life' (269). Through the recognition of the human basis of God, individuals may reconnect with Humanity and enact what Feuerbach cites as the 'necessary turning point of history... the open confession that the consciousness of God is nothing else than the consciousness of the species' (270). By 'confessing,' the subject may transcend perceived limitations and actively apply the moral tenets hitherto attributed only to religious fetishes.

While now largely forgotten, Feuerbach's theories helped ignite the modern debate over ideology, for they spurred Marx and Engels, among others, to action. From the standpoint of ideology, Feuerbach represents an important transitional figure. A bridge between de Tracy's 'neutral' notion of an ideological science and Marx's conception of ideology as 'the phantoms formed in the brains of men' (Marx 1998, 42), Feuerbach's inversion of Hegel's Absolute Spirit recognizes the limits of idealism and seeks to empower the subject. By exposing the falsity of religious consciousness, Feuerbach prefigures Marx and Engel's camera obscura simile and suggests how institutions may perpetuate their power by blurring the material nature of their origins. He also suggests that ideology, rather than arising out of pure fantasy, possesses concrete (i.e., material) origins. Nevertheless, as Marx convincingly argues in *The German Ideology*, the materialism that Feuerbach attempts lacks a systematic historical basis and, therefore, shares many of the same problems as 'pure' idealism.

Feuerbach's emphasis on the rather abstract, reductive notion of 'species' undercut his efforts to establish the 'philosophy of the future.' Unlike Thomas Paine in *The Age of Reason* (1794–5), Feuerbach locates his critique of religious mystification in the very strategies that he hopes to subvert. While Paine – languishing in prison and without the aid of a library – problematizes the divine origins of the Bible by rehearsing the historical debate over which texts would fall under the scope of the 'Holy' and which would find themselves labeled 'apocryphal' ('they picked up some loose anonymous essays, and put them together under the names of such authors as best suited their purpose'), Feuerbach relies on a decontextualized notion of 'species' and thus replaces one illusion with another

(Paine 1974, 139). In ignoring the historical fermentation of ideology, Feuerbach forgets Locke's admonition that 'there is no knowledge of things conveyed by men's words, when their ideas agree not to the reality of things' (Locke 1997, 449). Like Ralph Waldo Emerson, who called for a new aesthetic in his essay 'The Poet'[2] yet who in his own work could not resist the calypso song of the English poetic tradition, Feuerbach identified the basic philosophic problem of his time but could not solve it. For Emerson, Walt Whitman would prove the dynamic force who would embody the new poetic vision. As for the 'philosophy of the future,' it would be Marx, not Feuerbach, who would truly revolutionize – and historicize – the materialist paradigm.

While only a few decades old, by the 1840s the term 'ideology' had fallen into relative disuse. Although de Tracy's 'ideology' permeated the general culture of philosophy, the term itself would not enjoy a 'renaissance' until the young Marx seized upon it as the antithesis of the historical materialism that he sought to develop. Ironically, Marx held with Napoleon that ideology represented not an empirical method but a metaphysical illusion harmful to social progress. Consequently, in his *Theses on Feuerbach* (1845 [1888]), Marx heralds the end of ahistorical materialism: 'The chief defect of all previous materialism – that of Feuerbach included – is that things, reality, sensuousness are conceived only in the form of the *object*, or of *contemplation*, but not as *human sensuous activity*, *practice*, not subjectively' (1998, 572; Marx's emphasis). Although Marx appreciates the significance of Feuerbach's efforts, he nonetheless fails to concur with a materialism that lacks a practical base. The fetishizing of ideas, according to Marx, derives from the alienation of the subject from human activity: 'All mysteries which lead theory to mysticism find their rational solution in human practice and in the comprehension of this practice' (1998, 571). The *Theses on Feuerbach* effectively functioned as working points for Marx's more expansive critique of Feuerbach and his acolytes – *The German Ideology* – wherein he would resurrect de Tracy's term for good.

In terms of its tone, *The German Ideology* reveals a rather immature **Karl Marx,** yet the book's ideas represent the kernel that would grow into his magisterial *Capital.* Clearly designed as a polemic, *The German Ideology* snidely derides the ahistorical materialism represented by 'staunch conservatives' such as 'Saint

Max' Stirner and 'Saint Bruno' Bauer (Marx 1998, 36). Feuerbach, while dismissed by Marx, escapes much of the vitriolic rhetoric that marks the sections on the other 'Young Hegelians.' Still, the book's tone undoubtedly played a role in preventing the manuscript from being published until well into the twentieth century. Marx later declared that he and **Engels** nevertheless 'achieved [their] main purpose – self-clarification' (1978, 6). By rejecting the theories of his contemporaries, Marx thus enables himself to announce his own ambitious project: 'what individuals are depends on the material conditions of their production' (1998, 37).

The principal mistake of the Young Hegelians, Marx observes, concerns a 'dependence on Hegel' that precludes a true critique of the Hegelian system (1998, 34). According to Marx, hubris prevents the Young Hegelians from recognizing that they locate their 'materialism' not in the solid realm of historical conditions but in secular abstractions meant to explain religious ones. For Marx, such a phenomenon suggests jousting with windmills, for 'the Young Hegelians have to fight only against these illusions of consciousness' (36). With this statement, Marx, inverting most previous notions of subjectivity, challenges the pseudo-materialism of the Young Hegelians and the notion that changing ideas would lead to social revolution. In a telling passage deleted from the manuscript, Marx proposes a radical revision in the interpretation of subjectivity: 'their ideas are the conscious expression – real or illusory – of their real relations and activities, of their production, of their intercourse, of their social and political conduct' (41). Far from *producing* historical circumstances, ideas *stem from* those conditions. For Marx, ideology represents the culmination of this confused outlook.

The reality of subsistence precedes the formation of ideas. Subjectivity, therefore, depends on social determination: 'Men are the producers of their conceptions ... as they are conditioned by a definite development of their productive forces and of the intercourse corresponding to these, up to its furthest form' (1998, 42). In treating consciousness as autonomous, the Young Hegelians create a fetish of subjectivity and wrest ideas from the very history that produced them. Such an a priori belief in the power of ideas inverts the relationship between social action and theory, a process that, as noted in chapter 1, Marx and Engels liken to a camera obscura. Analyzing the camera obscura simile, Sarah Kofman argues that in it, '[ideology] functions, not as a transparent copy obeying the laws of perspective, but, rather, as a simulacrum: it disguises, burlesques, blurs real relationships' (Kofman 1999, 14). Following Kofman's logic, it becomes apparent that the camera obscura emits not simply a distorted copy of reality, but rather a copy of a copy. For Marx, the Young Hegelians, with their devotion to ideas, naïvely herald their iconoclastic rhetoric without pausing to reflect on how their methods reinforce an ahistorical status quo.

Rejecting such a position, Marx steadily develops a notion of subjectivity that inextricably links historical conditions to the products of consciousness (ideas). Ideology thus stems from an estrangement between the fulfillment of basic human needs and the theories about how those needs would best be met. This alienation inevitably pits the interests of the few versus those of the many and involves a transformation of goods into capital. Once the 'herd-consciousness' – concerned only with procuring enough food, shelter, and clothing for all – fragments because of increases in population and productivity, a division of mental and physical labor ensues:

> From this moment onwards, the consciousness *can* really flatter itself that it is something other than consciousness of existing practice, that it *really* represents something without representing something real. (Marx 1998, 50)

Interestingly, Marx locates the source of mystification at the precise moment when Locke and his fellow empiricists would argue that humans rise above the level of instinct. Seemingly, for the young Marx and Engels, only the pragmatic, materially oriented consciousness functions outside the realm of ideology; the subject trades in illusions, fantasies. Idealists thus arise from a need to quell potential dissatisfaction among those in the population who fail to benefit from the current mode(s) of production. They must, declare Marx and Engels, 'represent [their class] interest in turn as the general interest' in order to solidify social and economic power (52). Once the division of labor places a premium on abstraction, the concept of private property – modeled on the 'latent slavery' of the family (52) – reinforces the schism between individual and collective interests. Commenting on these notions, Eagleton suggests that for Marx and Engels 'ideological consciousness would seem to involve a double movement of *inversion* and *dislocation*' (1991, 78; Eagleton's emphasis). Consequently, ideology both masks the material origins of ideas and establishes those distortions as essential to the ruling hegemony. In this way, ideology represents an *ex post facto* rationalization for economic conditions.

As Marx suggests, the distinction between 'mental' and 'physical' labor results in the self-reification of the former and the devaluation of the latter. Those disposed to mental labor ultimately codify their experience and the resultant epistemology reduces the worth of individual workers by juxtaposing their products with the 'idea' of production, with what Marx deems the 'social product' (Marx 1977, 643). The mechanic, the farmer, the clerk – such workers now merge into a nebulous vapor, indistinguishable from their tools, livestock, and computer terminals. In short, they become 'human resources.' For Marx, this process of alienation – the loss of subjectivity – occurs not through the immediately malicious intent of a powerful hegemony, but via a rather slow shift in the historical conditions that ultimately favored the division of labor (and the concomitant class system). The 'natural' instruments of production gave way to those methods created in response to specific needs. Once successful, the individuals responsible for these new paradigms sought to entrench their power by separating their ideas from the historical conditions that spurred them on. Marx notes that 'all epoch-making systems have as their real content the needs of the time in which they arose' (1998, 488), and the transformation of the subsistence worker into a Taylorized component is no exception.

Glossing Marx's concept of subjectivity, McLellan stresses that 'society was in fact riven by conflicts of interest, but in order for it not to fall apart these oppositions were covered up by ideas which represented attempts to portray society as cohesive rather than conflictual by justifying the asymmetrical distribution of social and economic power' (McLellan 1995, 12). McLellan's observations underscore Marx's point that through ideology even the most ardent critics of society help to sustain the goals of the dominant class. The differences between Labor and Tory, Republican and Democrat, appear significant at first glance, but as Marx would have it, such distinctions are quite superficial, for 'as in general with ideologists ... they inevitably put the thing upside-down and regard their ideology both as the creative force and as the aim of all social relations, whereas it is only an expression and symptom of these relations' (Marx 1998, 444). The various factions fail to recognize that they all take certain concepts for granted (e.g., the right to own property or the value of the Constitution) and, therefore, subscribe to the same underlying ideology no matter what their particular *interpretation* of that ideology might be.

Marx's famous distinction between base and superstructure is of interest here, for it reinforces the notion of ideology as false-consciousness and extends it:

> In the social production of their life, men enter into definite relations that are indispensable and independent of their will, relations of production which correspond to a definite stage of development of their material productive forces. The sum total of these relations of production constitutes the economic structure of society, the real foundation, on which rises a legal and political superstructure and to which correspond definite forms of social consciousness . . . it is not the consciousness of men that determines their being, but, on the contrary, their social being that determines their consciousness.   (Marx 1978, 4)

The institutions of power and their corollary agents, therefore, form an extension to, and a justification of, the material conditions that prompt society to develop particular methods of economic production. Consequently, 'subjectivity' functions not as an autonomous sphere, but rather as an inevitable manifestation of economics: I produce, therefore I am. Subjective 'free will,' therefore, serves as a *totem* of sorts, for its development shadows that of capitalism, which for Marx represents alienation or fetishization. In an inverse relationship, the *idea* of personal sovereignty takes root while productive autonomy dissipates in favor of 'collaborative' (social) production. Of course, in the above passage Marx argues not for a rigid determinism in which an individual's particular course falls along an already plotted graph, but for a set of ranges. By establishing the parameters of society in accordance with economic conditions, Marx underscores the effect that key institutions – education, religion, and law, for instance – have in shaping individual thought. Because of the collective impact of such institutions – which employ varying degrees of systemic 'pressure' – individuals tend to 'take for granted' far more than they realize, and even the most virulent critics absorb a wide range of operating 'truths' from their economically based culture. Such institutional philosophies become ideology not because they accent a particular economic mode but because they *deny* their self-interest and posit themselves as universal truth or common sense.

As one will discover in the following chapter, Marx's notion of ideology transcends the notion of the subject. As he refines his theories in *Capital* and elsewhere, Marx never completely abandons his concept of the camera obscura, but he creates an intricate fusion of institutional superstructure and subjective manifestation. For Marx, the dichotomy between institution and subjectivity proves false, as they both derive from the same historical conditions. Marx, moreover, refrains from assigning a mechanistic correspondence to the relationship between history and ideology, for he recognizes the reciprocity of the two concepts. While ideology may derive from the 'false' value tendered to ideas, few would argue that those ideas themselves have not produced tangible history. In developing his theory of ideology, Marx sought not to deny this relationship, but to balance it and employ a more honest assessment of why certain ideas take precedence.

In *The Genealogy of Morals* (1887), **Friedrich Nietzsche** offers his own contribution to the critique of ideology. Unlike Marx, who privileges scientific method in his treatment of ideology, Nietzsche proffers a highly idiosyncratic conceptualization of subjectivity. Nevertheless, despite his poetic digressions and stylistic tics, the latter thinker acknowledges the socially constructed nature of the self much as his more exacting predecessor does. While Marx locates his discovery in a rational analysis of historical conditions, however, Nietzsche plumbs the depths of the irrational (or, perhaps, the *arational*). Employing Arthur Schopenhauer as his starting point, Nietzsche rejects the findings – and the goals – of the rationalists in favor of an emphasis on *will*, the overwhelming force that seeks self-preservation above all else. Distinct from reason or intellect, will proceeds instinctively to fulfill the requirements of physical life. Abstract endeavors, then, arise from basic biological motives. Altruism, justice, truth: these illusions mask their pragmatic and elemental origins. Even consciousness – the essential building block of subjectivity – finds its roots in the need to maintain basic (or 'animal') functioning. For Nietzsche, the subject constitutes merely one extension of a grand network of delusions.

In *The Genealogy of Morals,* Nietzsche establishes his skepticism of the rational from the outset: 'we knowers are unknown to ourselves' (1956, 149). According to Nietzsche, the pursuit of knowledge yields little of value, for the essential questions remain unasked, too close to recognize. The notion of truth proves, upon inspection, fabricated, for the better part of our existence rests on a foundation of lies. Chief among these is morality, which 'represents not merely a retrogression but even a danger, a temptation, a narcotic drug enabling the present to live at the expense of the future' (155). As with Marx's camera obscura analogy wherein the viewer witnesses an inverted image, Nietzsche's concept of morality (which we may consider as a major element of ideology) presents an image that perverts the relationship between signifier and signified. Far from representing the height of human achievement, morality emblematizes the base preservation of life. Consequently, Hans Barth writes of Nietzsche's theory that 'every class subscribes to a morality appropriate to its interests and its particular will to power' (Barth 1976, 160). Morality is thus contingent on self-preservation and self-justification. Faced with the naked brutality of existence, the majority of humanity requires pacification in order to refrain from madness or paralyzing despair. For Nietzsche, such ultilitarianism undergirds all human ethical codes: 'here are the key ideas of utility, forgetfulness, habit, and, finally, error, seen as lying at the root of that value system which civilized men had hitherto regarded with pride as the prerogative of all men' (Nietzsche 1956, 159). The final variable in Nietzsche's equation – error – proves pivotal to his critique of ideology and the subject.

Nietzsche asserts that contemporary morality – as symbolized in law, theology, and family custom, for example – rests precariously on the logical errors of history, and he offers the dual evolution of good/bad – good/evil as a prime instance of how individual prejudice became codified into ethics. Developing an ethics of power, Nietzsche argues that the etymology of the notion of 'good' points not to the deed itself but to the purveyors of that act, the aristocrats or affluent individuals. Good functions not as a selfless practice but as a self-defining one: 'it was the 'good' themselves, that is to say the noble, mighty, highly placed, and high minded who decreed themselves and their actions to be good, i.e., belonging to the highest rank, in contradistinction to all that was base, low-minded, and plebian' (1956, 160). The quality of 'goodness,' therefore reinforces the disparity of power and, in effect, bolsters the authority of the strong and devalues the weak.

Turning from this branch of the evolution, Nietzsche observes that the subservient classes developed their own etymology for good/evil. Expatiating on many of the principles he outlines in *Thus Spake Zarathustra*, Nietzsche argues that the weak tend to rationalize their impotence: 'the slave revolt in morals begins by rancor turning creative and giving birth to values' (1956, 170). For Nietzsche, the powerful exercise their dominance unconsciously and naturally, and the weak must develop an illusion that justifies their lack of strength. By glorifying actions which they had no alternative but to adopt in the face of dominance, the 'slaves' establish the notions of 'free' will and 'autonomy.' Nietzsche recognizes such concepts as futile attempts to stave off the inevitable, and he suggests that the equation of meekness, resolve, and humility (among others) with 'goodness' is a specious philosophy of the first order. The self-proclaimed 'good' authority now, via the 'sublime sleight of hand' performed by the weak, transforms into an 'evil' oppressor who fails to exercise the newly 'good' virtues of restraint, mercy, frugality, and the like (180). Barth comments, moreover, that in Nietzsche's paradigm, 'equality is a chimera in whose belief only the underprivileged have an interest' (Barth 1976, 161). Determinism cloaked in subjective choice, such moral codes seem, for Nietzsche, calculated less to promote proper action and more to soothe human frailty.

The ideology of power, then, finds itself entrenched in a double falsehood. On the one hand, selfish motives recast themselves as selfless acts, while on the other hand, submission reinvents itself as piety. Both definitions prove dubious, for they involve a misrepresentation of tangible action. In both instances, Nietzsche recognizes a lack of subjective choice, for he assigns both strength and weakness to the realm of the will. Neither the 'bird of prey' nor the 'lamb' may intellectualize their roles; each unconsciously plays a part in a dramatic struggle. Emptied of its metaphysical (ideological) content, existence is synonymous with this conflict.

Subjectivity, then, finds no place in Nietzsche's explanation, for it represents merely the vestiges of 'animal' function. Because no 'truth' – as formulated by philosophers – exists, the mind's 'products' represent no more than an effort to quench particular biological desires. Even conscience, the ideal of personal morality, finds its origins in the prosaic wish to avoid pain (Nietzsche 1956, 193). The subject functions as no more than a conduit for the will to power, and notions of personal identity and autonomy neglect the contrived origins of such concepts. As Lichtheim glosses Nietzsche, 'all thought is ideological; its unconscious function is to serve the life process' (Lichtheim 1967, 29). Within a rational scheme, of course, as Eagleton points out, when *everything* falls under the rubric of ideology the value of the term dissipates: it seems too plastic to possess a practical use. Such metaphysical elasticity, however, serves Nietzsche's irrational paradigm well and unsettles the entire notion of logic and empiricism.

Like Nietzsche, **Sigmund Freud** problematizes the concept of rationalism, but unlike his predecessor, the Austrian recognizes that empirical methods may allow individuals to dissect the unconscious. In later works such as *Civilization and Its Discontents* (1929) and *Moses and Monotheism* (1939), Freud departs from his clinical orientation and examines larger questions of culture and ideology. *The Future of an Illusion* (1927) outlines many of Freud's contributions to the study of ideology and, in particular, religion. As with Feuerbach, Freud seeks the origins of religion in terms of loss. Unlike Feuerbach, however, Freud explains this absence not with humanity's potential, but – more in line with Nietzsche – with its desire to evade pain. Working from his famous tripartite subject,[3] Freud considers how humanity's religious impulses emanate from a subjective position, the pleasure principle, and suggests that 'every individual is virtually an enemy of culture' (Freud 1964, 4).

While Freud (ostensibly) legitimizes 'culture' more than, say, Nietzsche or Marx, he immediately recognizes its sway over the subject: 'every culture must be built up on coercion and instinctual renunciation' (5). Society's most basic institutional enterprises – its churches, schools, governments – suppress individual desire in favor of the communal good. Freud notes that most people prefer leisure to work, regardless of the reasons for that labor (8). Consequently, at the root of all society lies the threat of force. For Freud, the motivation provided by physical force gradually enters the realm of the subject (super-ego) and strengthens the security of the community (14). Here, in the metamorphosis from enforced edict to unwritten idea, lies the source of ideology.

Freud refers to this concept as 'narcissistic satisfaction,' the propensity of a society to tout its successes in order to prevent outcroppings of cultural hostility (Freud 1964, 18). By emphasizing positives – especially in juxtaposition with other societies – a culture may employ less palpable force and rely on citizens to recognize the worth of the community. Individual subjects, therefore, willingly renounce their desires so long as they receive some form of compensation. The strength of this renunciation depends on the distribution of the benefits, of course, and society must campaign indefatigably on its own behalf. Indeed, an effective ideological strategy of this sort may shape society so thoroughly that even its most dissenting members form their subjectivities in relation to such narcissistic satisfaction: 'in spite of their animosity they can find their ideals in their masters' (19). Freud recognizes religion as the essential tool in this ideological struggle for subjective loyalty.

Marking the ideological nature of Freud's thesis, Eagleton characterizes the conceptualization of religion in *The Future of an Illusion* as one that critiques the 'imaginary resolution of real contradictions' (Eagleton 1991, 177–8). In framing this hypothesis, Freud asserts that domesticating nature serves as society's principal task, and he observes that early cultures ascribe the traits of nature to gods (1964, 26–7). The reasons for this assignation are three-fold:

> They must exorcise the terrors of nature, they must reconcile one to the cruelty of fate, particularly as shown in death, and they must make amends for the sufferings and privations that the communal life of culture has imposed on man.   (Freud 1964, 27)

The first two explanations revolve around the unknown, while the third involves morality. As the former two reasons withdraw – because of technological advances – the third takes precedence and forms the cornerstone of organized religion. As one will readily observe, the morality-based notion has a profound effect on the subject, for it both serves as the officially sanctioned explanation for why individuals should delay their gratification and expresses a type of wish-fulfillment: 'illusions, fulfillments of the oldest, strongest, and most insistent wishes of mankind' (51). Phenomena such as faith, eternal reward, and mercy stem from this 'ideology' and attempt to persuade the subject to reject its more tangible (and immediately satisfied) longing in favor of socially constructive activities that will *ultimately* quench desire. Through this process of internalization, 'the laws of culture themselves are claimed to be of divine origin' (28).

Functioning from this perspective, the subject views the requirements of the state not as demands but as moral obligations.[4] Because 'the preservation of human society rests on the assumption that the majority of mankind believe in the truth of these doctrines' (1964, 60), Freud postulates that the prohibition against questioning the authenticity of religious origins and their concomitant moral restrictions functions to defend the 'illusion' from rational (i.e., scientific) thought. Nevertheless, the subject may still exhibit an unconscious need to fulfill primal urges and wage an internal struggle to reconcile the wishes of the culture (ideology) with its own instinctive drives. This conflict manifests itself as neurosis and sublimation, and Freud clearly classifies religion as a type of collective neurosis reminiscent of Marx's camera obscura. Torn between autonomy and the duty to please God [the Father], the subject develops a potentially unhealthy mindset. The subject thus both serves the state and seeks to destroy it – or, at least, to express an autonomy that may contradict the requirements of society. Consequently, Freud observes that the decay of religious influence stems 'not because its promises have become smaller, but because they appear less credible to people' (68). Freud attributes this change to scientific inquiry on the lines proposed by Bacon and Locke. As individuals begin to think empirically, they lose the need for the psychological crutch of religious ideology. Freud, of course, advocates psychoanalysis as a method for destroying misperception and viewing the world in a more transparent way: 'by withdrawing his expectations from the other world and concentrating all his liberated energies on this earthly life he will probably attain to a state of things in which life will be tolerable for all and no one will be oppressed by culture any more' (89). Scientific inquiry, for Freud, represents not an ideology but a liberating paradigm, and through it the subject finds its means of emancipation.

Many theorists, from Jung and Otto Rank to Jacques Lacan and Julia Kristeva, took it upon themselves to modify Freud's concept of religion and to explore its ramifications for ideology. None, however, have been as systematically interested in subjective questions of ideology as **Slavoj Žižek**. In his seminal work *The Sublime Object of Ideology* (1989), Žižek reinterprets Marx (via Althusser) and Freud (via Lacan) in order to problematize the characterization of ideology as false consciousness. For Žižek, the distinction between ideology and reality serves little purpose, for the pervasiveness of the former concept invariably affects – negatively – the quotidian and '[is] more real than reality itself' (Žižek 1994, 30). The 'illusion' sets the tone for physical interaction and impinges on the subject's ability to act spontaneously or autonomously. Žižek conceives of his project as an attempt to liberate the subject from the grips of an ideology that replicates itself within the mind and, thus, leads to an 'externalization of the result of an inner necessity,' as he observes in his introduction to *Mapping Ideology* (1994, 4). Quite apart from Freud's dichotomy of self and culture, Žižek's theory posits that the subject, not the state, now serves as the locus of ideology. Similarly, in contrast to Marx's camera obscura analogy, Žižek argues that ideology consists not of faulty perception, but of a deluded ontological frame of reference.

In *The Sublime Object of Ideology*, Žižek outlines both how this transformation occurred and why it continues to proliferate. For Žižek, the central question of ideology lies not in the content, but in the '*"secret" of this form itself*' (1989, 11; Žižek's emphasis) because the structure, not the substance, offers a clue as to the subjective conditioning that reinforces inequitable material reality. Žižek, therefore, wrests the responsibility for ideology from the culture itself and squarely places it within the subject, who unre-flectively reproduces the 'social symptom' that results in a quite tangible reality: '*"ideological" is a social reality whose very existence implies the non-knowledge of its participants as to its essence*' (21; Žižek's emphasis). The ideology lies so deeply encoded within the basic form of, for instance, capitalism, that the subject cannot even detect its ontological misapprehension. Even those subjects who cynically deride the schism between ideology and social reality reinforce – rather than subvert – the hegemony: 'one is well aware of a particular interest hidden behind an ideological universality, but still one does not renounce it' in any substantive way (29).[5] One may, for example, rhetorically denounce Bill Gates as a corrupt monopolist, but in doing so, one fails to question the motives underlying 'legal' capitalism and thus perpetuates the social symptom.

Within this framework, the subject acts less as an independent, spontaneous entity and more as an unwitting dupe, an object who '*annuls himself as subject*' (1989, 231; Žižek's emphasis). Overt ideological 'propaganda' becomes subordinate to the material: people 'are fetishists in practice, not in theory' (31). Subjects may attempt to distance themselves from justifications of the 'free market,' for example, but their actions betray an almost naïve confidence in the power of money as money, that is to say capital. In fact, Žižek speculates that an ironic distrust of the rhetoric of capitalism (or any other dominant ideology) strengthens such 'ideological fantasies' (33). 'Belief,' he claims, 'supports the fantasy which regulates social reality' (36). In exchange for the (chimerical) pursuit of fantasy objects, the subject allows the illusion to structure reality and interpenetrate the very fiber of existence. By acting in accordance with this fantasy, the subject transforms the raw material of ideology into the concrete transactions of everyday life. Subjectivity thus commodifies itself.

Žižek characterizes this self-commodification as a forced choice: 'the subject must freely choose the community to which he already belongs, independent of his choice' (1989, 165). The subject, of course, fails to recognize the paradox and remains blind to the ideological underpinnings of its actions. The ontological crisis that arises from this paradox inscribes itself into a culture's institutions and posits objectivity for subjectivity, absence for presence. Drawing on Lacanian concepts, Žižek concludes that this paradox damages the symbolic order by creating a 'hystericization' wherein the process of self-objectification traumatizes the subject (181). Objectification instinctively repulses the subject, but the self consists of that very process or 'Thing.' Only by 'evading the dimension of the Thing' (181) may the subject assert itself, but this entails an acceptance of 'brute, senseless reality' as a 'meaningful totality' (230). The subject *is* ideology.

Žižek thus brings us full circle. Whereas Descartes posits that the idea precedes the thing, Žižek argues that the idea is the thing, that the very form of the subject holds the kernels of ideology. From our examination of Bacon onward, however, we witness a generally negative view of the subject in terms of its ability to resist ideology, and, in fact, most – if not all – of the theorists covered in this chapter suggest a certain complicity on the part of the subject with respect to ideological distortion. While Bacon, Locke, de Tracy, Hegel, Feurbach, and even Freud evince a certain optimism that an empirical awareness may free the subject from the chains of its thralldom, even they struggle over the methods whereby individuals can achieve this sense. Marx looks to ground the subject's understanding in historical materialism, but he holds no illusions as to the power that ideology possesses over people. Nietzsche, of course, rejects the subject as a pathetic delusion. In short, most seminal theories characterize the subject's role in the creation of ideology as an enabling one. The subject not only operates from a false position, but it actively shapes that distorted reality and thus reinforces institutional hegemony. In the next chapter, we will see how this reciprocal relationship cements the ideological foundation of society.

3   Ideology and Institutional Authority

Few non-academics would question the assertion that childbirth represents one of the most natural human enterprises, a bridge linking women of all political ideologies and epochs. From the eighteenth through the twentieth centuries, however, many western women experienced childbirth much differently than how most females engaged in it for millennia.[1] Until the mid-seventeenth century, most women did not assume a supine position for the delivery of their children.[2] Instead, as evidenced by birthing chairs and other apparatuses, most employed the squatting posture favored by midwives, who felt that lying on the back prolonged labor. What prompted the sudden shift to the conditions most frequently encountered – and deemed the 'natural' way – by latter-day western women? Clearly, the metamorphosis resulted from the effects of institutional ideology, and birth historians credit Louis XIV of France – whose credo, 'I am the state,' crystallized his autocratic propensities – with popularizing the supine position (Cohen and Estner 1983, 158). In effect, the king's desire to observe the births in his court – the supine posture allowed him to see more – paved the way for the procedural ritual that followed and became so institutionalized as to appear natural. As doctors compelled midwives to yield responsibility for labor and delivery, the practice born of absolute power received technical rationalization: the doctor 'needed' to see in order to complete the 'procedure.'[3] In this way, labor transformed from an event in which midwives assisted women in discovering the position most suited for their own unique birthing processes into an intellectualized operation effectively divorced from biological imperatives.

Advocates of the institutional approach to ideology would argue that one should readily glean from the above example the sense that if ideology can interpolate even the most basic elements of human life, then it certainly can affect human institutions. From this perspective, communal organizations and traditions achieve a self-perpetuating power by detaching themselves from their original – usually self-serving – goals. Because it functions in such a pervasive, systemic fashion, ideology, in effect, protects itself against full-scale intellectual assault and manages to recreate itself even as material conditions change. The very pragmatic source of Louis XIV's predilection for an unobstructed gaze, for example, fades into the recesses of history, but the tangible result of this preference continues to affect millions of women. The fundamental thread that ties theorists of institutional ideology together is a skepticism of societal norms. Such philosophers acknowledge that the very foundations of human commerce rest on ideas. Where theorists as different as Thomas Hobbes, Karl Marx, Louis Althusser, and Marshall McLuhan part ways, however, concerns both the effects of these precepts and society's ability to alter or mitigate those consequences.

At the heart of the various discussions of institutional ideology lies the notion of cultural production, how ideas become reified and, in turn, how these constructs allow for the creation of new concepts. **Jorge Larrain** explains the process of cultural production as a cycle wherein institutions create 'public versions of identity which select only some features that are considered to be representative' and then 'influence the way in which people see themselves and the way that they act through a process of reading or reception which is not necessarily passive and uncritical' (Larrain 1994, 163). The flexibility of Larrain's model underscores its usefulness as a tool for explaining the ideological impact of institutions. Because Larrain highlights the contingent nature of the process, he avoids a prescriptive or deterministic paradigm that attributes a high degree of self-reflexivity or consciousness to the institutions themselves. Instead, he posits a type of feedback loop wherein both institution and subject influence one another and thus he accounts for change not directly dictated by war, revolution, famine or other dramatic events. Clearly, the apparatus – to employ Althusser's term – holds sway over the individual, but the subject exercises some influence on the institution as well. Such a definition of cultural production emphasizes the interpenetration of human behavior and social hegemony and underscores the futility of viewing either in isolation. In order for readers to comprehend

Larrain's synthesis more completely, however, they must examine its theoretical precursors.

Grappling with the problem of institutional authority, **Thomas Hobbes** starts from a position far removed from Larrain's notion of reciprocity. In *Leviathan* (1651), Hobbes announces a paradigm in which an autonomous, centralized state constitutes the only check against the unmitigated anarchy ensuing from individual desire. In order to circumvent the decadent self-interest that would threaten the preservation of the human species, people must obey the dictates of government, which, for Hobbes, represents reason. Placing the state above the ignominious influence of appetite, Hobbes holds that the institutions of government 'restrain' the 'naturall Passions of men' and are in a sense immune to the type of reciprocity suggested by Larrain (Hobbes 1997, 93). Employing an empirical method, Hobbes observes that humans locate their motivation in one of two ways, the quest for pleasure or the avoidance of pain. Leo Strauss notes that Hobbes owes a debt to Epicurus, but asserts that the Englishman modified his predecessor in two important ways. While Epicurus shunned theories concerning the natural human condition, Hobbes grounded his notions of commonwealth on the presupposition that individuals formed societies in order to prevent their inherent rights from eroding (Strauss 1997, 326). Hobbes, moreover, rejected Epicurus' claim that pleasure derived not from unrestrained lusts, but from a more sober existence (326). In both instances, Hobbes' revisions bolster his hypothesis that society functions as a rational constraint on the moral expediency that would result from the innate hedonism of individual humans. Thus, for Hobbes, the commonwealth would by definition exist as a material, rather than ideological, entity.

Intrigued by the pragmatic implications of Galilean astronomy – with its emphasis on bodies in motion – on human knowledge, Hobbes sought to chart the impact of movement on the intellect and society. Serving as Francis Bacon's amanuensis, Hobbes absorbed the former's skepticism of received ideas and admiration of the empirical, and, ensconced in the burgeoning science of his day, theorized that a truly systemic analysis of society could unseat the 'Vain Philosophy and Fabulous Traditions' of the metaphysical schools (1997, 232). Merging cutting edge science with traditional mathematics and Occam's Razor[4] (the belief that the simplest theory that conforms to the facts lies closest to Reality), Hobbes displaces metaphysics with a mechanistic view of society that argued for the material basis of ideas. Despite clear parallels with Bacon's concept of idolatry, Hobbes' theories announce a far bleaker understanding of humanity.

Like Bacon (and Plato), Hobbes holds that the greater part of humanity mistakenly worshipped fancy as Truth: a 'meer Figment of the brain' (1997, 90). For Hobbes, however, no collection of individuals could be trusted to move beyond self-interest in the 'warre of every man against every man' (71). In such an arena, 'the notions of Right and Wrong, Justice and Injustice have . . . no place' (71). Motivated by the desire to avoid pain and pursue pleasure, the typical person displays allegiance to nothing save that which will aid self-gratification. Left to their own devices, Hobbes asserts, human beings would live in a condition of constant turmoil and 'endeavor to destroy, or subdue one another' (69). Existence would, thus, be 'solitary, poore, nasty, brutish, and short' (70). In mechanistic terms, such a phenomenon – left unchecked – would ultimately lead to inertia. Consequently, Hobbes feels that, as with any natural body, humanity needed order placed on it from an outside force: the State.

Rejecting the force of faith as irrational, Hobbes presents the commonwealth, a secular union subject to rational analysis, as the institution that brought order to the closed system of humanity. Because human reason cannot transcend its material basis, it necessarily must fail to comprehend any first causes. Trapped by material effects, humans will never grasp what sets them in motion. Religious faith, therefore, finds its origins in the 'perpetuall feare . . . accompanying mankind in the ignorance of causes' (1997, 61). The State, however, functions as a reasonable counterbalance to the unknown. In enforcing the good of the many over the interests of the few, the commonwealth draws its power by investing one individual (or a small group of individuals) with the will of the multitude. Hobbes claims that such a covenant ensures that humanity will avoid a perpetual state of war. While humans cannot save themselves, the great Leviathan of the State can protect their interests.

Such a pact involves sacrifice, however. All individual actions are now subject to the scrutiny of the various Sovereigns and their agents. Behavior that threatens the commonwealth merits punishment: external forces will check the aberrant motions of individuals.

For Hobbes, 'the source of every Crime, is some defect of the Understanding; or some errour in Reasoning; or some sudden force of the Passions' (1997, 147). The State, in its quest to preserve peace and equilibrium, subdues those desires. Sovereigns are exempt from such restrictions, though, because the transference of power requires absolute faith, the 'dissolute condition of masterlesse men' being far worse than the abuses of a single being (102). Sovereigns who abuse their power inevitably fail, however, because the conditions they create mirror the very lawlessness that their authority bids them to quell.

Hobbes' theories hold several implications for the study of ideology. With his emphasis on the positive aspects of the social contract, Hobbes arrives at a conception of the State that is both 'natural' and absolute. By grounding his philosophy in empiricism, Hobbes decenters the position of religion: all institutions are subordinate to the commonwealth, and all subjects are subordinate to the Sovereign. Anticipating the likes of Marx and Ludwig Feuerbach, Hobbes attributes the institutional manifestations of religion to specific material self-interest on the part of clerics. Religious laws, therefore, do not necessarily adhere to the will of God – although they might – but rather spring from the minds of humans. According to Hobbes, civil law also arises from human interests, but, whereas religion gains its impetus from supernatural forces, the commonwealth receives its authority from the tangible desire to thwart constant pain. The power of the commonwealth is not transcendent, however. The Sovereign must recognize changing circumstances and act accordingly. In this way, Hobbes legitimizes the curtailment of so-called natural rights, for if everyone selfishly pursued unmitigated liberty, no one would succeed. In Hobbes' view, one may not challenge the system itself because to do so would mean the end of all systems. Institutional hegemony may not please everyone, but anarchy would please nobody.

Jean-Jacques Rousseau reaches quite a different conclusion in his *Social Contract* (1762). Starting from a principle very similar to that of Hobbes, Rousseau argues not for despotism, but for a popular sovereignty based on 'natural rights.' Whereas Hobbes posits that the original human condition was one of thralldom, Rousseau claims that 'Man was born free,' a state all the more envied because now 'he is everywhere in chains' (Rousseau 1968, 49). Like Hobbes, Rousseau asserts that political entities stem from an archetypal agreement, but, unlike his English predecessor, he denies the inviolability of that contract. Governments that deny the general will of the people effectively render the original agreement null and void. Immutable human rights exist, and it falls to the governing body to uphold them: 'the social order is a sacred right which serves as a basis for all other rights' (50). Clearly, Rousseau distinguishes between Natural and Institutional laws – much as Martin Luther King, Jr differentiates 'just and unjust' laws in his 'Letter from Birmingham Jail' (King 1964, 82) – with the latter frequently embedding self-interested, self-perpetuating mechanisms that appear normal or 'natural' because of their ubiquity. Such institutional ideology drives a wedge between the people and the societies that they formed to overcome 'obstacles' to self-preservation (59).

Denying Hobbes' chief warrant – that humanity would destroy itself without imposed order – Rousseau likens the concept establishing sovereign inviolability for the common good to 'the human race divided into herds of cattle, each with a master who preserves it only to devour its members' (1968, 51). Rousseau chastises those thinkers – Aristotle among them – who would trace the origins of the State to superior force, be it physical or mental. Such a position, Rousseau observes, would cripple the argument that 'morality' flows from the Sovereign, for 'as soon as a man can disobey with impunity, his disobedience becomes legitimate' (53). One may see here Rousseau's impact on de Tracy and the *philosophes*, and clearly he anticipates Marx's camera obscura characterization of ideology. While Hobbes and Hugo Grotius effectively invest the State with the responsibility of setting the moral tone for society, Rousseau claims that 'goodness' precedes the foundation of civilization: Hobbes had it backwards. In assessing Rousseau's view of the social contract, Hans Barth observes that 'the civil state puts an end to natural equality, and the inequality it initiates is such as to make men dependent on one another. They now no longer provide for their own physical needs with their own hands, but divide their labor so as to produce things collaboratively' (Barth 1976, 69).

Echoing Hobbes' conceptualization of the Sovereign as deriving from the collective desire, Rousseau nevertheless allows the people to retain some modicum of freedom via his notion of the 'general will.' One will recall that Hobbes' citizens sacrificed their autonomy for order. In Rousseau's paradigm, the general will reflects the innate goodness of humanity; the general will cannot help but recognize – and act on – the 'moral' course: 'it is impossible for a body to wish to hurt all of its members' (Rousseau 1968, 63). Disruption of social harmony, he contends, stems from a rift between the general will and the private wills of particular individuals, people who pursue their self-interests and consider 'what [they] owe to the common cause as a gratuitous contribution' (64). Because their narrow designs often conflict with the general will, such people must face the wrath of society at large. The private will is limited, and while it may occasionally attune itself to the general will, 'it is impossible for such a coincidence to be regular and enduring' (69). Thus, the social contract demands that the State serve the general will or else the government loses any legitimate claim to power, a phenomenon that quite obviously threatens institutions based on despotism. By this bargain, humans lose true autonomy but gain 'civil liberty and the legal right of property' (65). In addition, humans obtain the 'moral freedom' to choose between appetite and the aggregate good (65). Theoretically, then, mere individual strength succumbs to collective might.

In practice, however, the general will frequently seems to bend before the superior political strength of an individual. Numerous twentieth-century examples come to mind: Hitler, Stalin, Amin, Gaddhafi. In such cases, the general will and its supposed emphasis on goodness recedes and the private will of the ruler proceeds unchecked. Rousseau recognizes such occurrences, but he explains them by acknowledging that the general will may be 'misled' by unscrupulous private interests (1968, 72). Rousseau claims that the Sovereign 'may not impose on the subjects any burden which is not necessary to the community,' and, thus, the 'commitments which bind us to the social body are obligatory only because they are mutual' (75). Genocide, purges, liquidation: such acts dissolve the reciprocal duties between the general and private wills and, in theory, empower the populace to terminate its relationship with the Sovereign. Without such a safeguard, Rousseau argues, the social contract would paradoxically make life worse.

The ideological implications of Rousseau's arguments in *The Social Contract*, along with those in the *Discourse on the Origins of Inequality* (1755),[5] are immense. Far from viewing the State as a benign institution concerned with shaping the ethical outlook of its citizens, Rousseau characterizes governments as deriving their initial power solely from the people. Subsequent power, moreover, should stem from the general will rather than from the particularized desires of any one sovereign. When one extends Rousseau's arguments – much as Thomas Paine does in *Common Sense* (1776) – one recognizes the rather precarious foundation on which States rest their power. Contra Hobbesian theory, Rousseau's claims divest the State of its moral primacy and expose despotism as the uncontrolled private will of the Sovereign. Reason, too, falls under suspicion, for it frequently masks the hidden agendas of the private will rather than the aggregate desires of the general will. The institutions of government hold no natural or divine position; Rousseau reserves such a state only for the origins of humanity. States, moral codes, laws – these suddenly appear the product of human construction and interpretation. Rousseau thus opens up the possibility that the general will can – and ought – to abolish any harmful government. Popular revolution gains legitimacy – at least in theory – and institutions may no longer claim a priori authority. Rousseau's theories – along with those of John Locke, Charles de Secondat, Baron de la Brède et de Montesquieu, and others – would set the stage for the American and French revolutions.

While one may see certain parallels between some of Rousseau's theories and those of **Karl Marx**, one would be seriously mistaken to assume that Marx left Rousseau and other *philosophe* liberals unchallenged. As Terry Eagleton points out, Marx discards the 'combination of rationalism and idealism' evident in Rousseau because 'social illusions are anchored in real contradictions' (Eagleton 1991, 72). For Marx and his collaborator Friedrich Engels, institutional ideology stems not from an individual sovereign, but because of the 'contract' itself. As discussed in the previous chapter, the Marx of *The German Ideology* inextricably links both ideas and institutions with specific historical conditions. This materialist outlook, refined in *Capital* and elsewhere, denies the primacy of both metaphysics and empiricism and attempts a synthesis. One may not isolate ideas from social activities, for the two categories are reciprocal, dependent. Institutions spring from the same source as abstractions. For example, the same historical conditions that allow for formalized labor unions breed concepts such as minimum wage and overtime. Merely changing the focus of one's ideas, then, cannot radically alter the material conditions that gave rise to an institution.

As noted in the previous chapter, the notion of base and superstructure provides Marx a tool with which to represent the interdependent relationship between subjective and institutional ideology. One will remember that Marx assigns to the 'base' those relationships strictly dealing with economic production, while he claims that the superstructure consists of institutions charged with creating and monitoring social consciousness (and, thus, contributing to the economic structure). A fairly mechanistic metaphor, the base/superstructure model holds forth that – as with the foundation on a house – a society's modes of production precede the development of its other institutions, which one might crudely liken to walls, a roof, and the like. Economic organization, then, limits the options for social design to those paradigms that accept the warrants implicit in a privileged mode of production. The parameters of the debate, in other words, cannot extend beyond the base. Families, schools, churches, militaries, scientific experiments, literary texts – all such phenomena help the dominant mode of production to protect and replicate itself. For example, the extended family preferred by many agrarian societies is cumbersome in a mobile, urban industrialized economy and thus advertising (part of the superstructure) begins to privilege representations of nuclear families.

No matter what the economic system, the base/superstructure model explains how society reinforces the dominant mode of production (and, indeed, how society itself is a reflection of that mode of production). The crucial interpenetration of subjective and institutional ideology occurs because as the superstructure works to justify the economic base, it helps to shape the range of individual responses, which, in turn, assist in erecting or revising other institutions. For example, Marx glosses the liberalism espoused by such philosophers as Rousseau in the following way:

> The sphere of circulation or commodity exchange, within whose boundaries the sale and purchase of labour-power goes on, is in fact a very Eden of the innate rights of man. It is the exclusive realm of Freedom, Equality, Property, and Bentham. Freedom, because both buyer and seller of a commodity, let us say of labour-power, are determined only by their own free will. They contract as free persons, who are equal before the law. Their contract is the final result in which their joint will finds a common legal expression. Equality because each enters into relation with the other, as with a simple owner of commodities, and they

exchange equivalent for equivalent. Property, because each disposes only of what is his own. And Bentham, because each looks only to his own advantage.   (Marx 1977, 280)

According to Marx, the genesis of Enlightenment thought, with its emphasis on personal autonomy, flows not from a 'natural' social contract, but from a need to create consumers for a market economy.[6] Ideals that to liberals such as Mary Wollstonecraft and George Mason seem 'self-evident' arise neither because of an advance in thought nor because of revolutionary zeal, but because of a shift in the modes of production. Warrants such as private property and commodity exchange are left unexamined by liberal humanism, and, indeed, serve as its very base. Thus, institutions that promote liberal values and appear to 'fight the power' – Amnesty International and Berkeley, for example – secretly (and quite unconsciously) help disguise the mores and economic requirements of the power elite.

Advocates of the 'common worker,' therefore, might decry Michael Eisner's Disney salary and stock options not because of the inherent flaws in capitalism but because of the lack of 'equality' evident in the salaries of a corporate CEO and a Splash Mountain line worker. Complaints roar the loudest not when all profits are down, but when a profitable company decides to lay off workers. As Marx writes, 'capital is by nature a leveller, since it insists upon equality in the conditions of exploitation of labour in every sphere of production' (1977, 520). Consequently, institutions designed to promote 'fairness' and 'equality' – such as the legal system or university education – dispense ideology that seemingly offers solutions to far-reaching social injustice but really buttresses the dominant mode of production. Subjects who pass through such institutions cannot avoid a thorough indoctrination in the values of the economic base, even as they seem to desire its destruction. Moreover, as Eagleton remarks, individuals who work within superstructures 'cannot be the ultimate catalysts of revolutionary social change' (Eagleton 1991, 82).

Nevertheless, Eagleton interprets Marx's metaphor as depending heavily on context: 'an institution may behave "superstructurally" at one point in time, but not in others' (83), and Marx himself draws a distinction in volume IV of *Capital*. In this view, certain institutional traits are merely innocuous byproducts rather than

economic supports. A university's decision to eliminate a human-
ities program might reflect a superstructural condition, while its
choice of school colors might simply reflect a dean's preference for
red and black. Cumulatively, however, superstructures make the
economic base and its concomitant relationships seem transparent,
obvious, common sense. In this way, the interests of the State and
the elite become legitimized, become the interests of the people.
The contingent nature of institutional ideology allows for the
appearance of socio-political autonomy, but the ultimate nature
of both discourse and action remains tethered to the economic
base.

While the impact of Marx's metaphor is undeniable (particularly
on Lenin), its meaning continues to be the locus of fierce debate.
Numerous Marxist and Marx-influenced intellectuals argue that
the base/superstructure model of ideology (along with those of the
camera obscura and false consciousness) has been too crudely
interpreted by previous thinkers. Lacking qualifiers such as the one
that Eagleton outlines above, the base/superstructure paradigm
could – according to revisionists – lead to a gross misunderstanding
of Marx and his notions of ideology and could also present a simplistic vision of the subtle interweaving of economic, institutional,
and psychological relationships inherent in a society. One such
revisionist, **Antonio Gramsci**,[7] modifies Marx's model by redirect-
ing the flow from superstructure to base. In his *Prison Notebooks*
(1929–34), Gramsci challenges Marx's contention that altering
ideas at the level of the superstructure will have little effect on the
economic base and the modes of production. While Gramsci con-
cedes that altering the base will reorient the superstructure, he also
believes that revolutionary social transformation *can* occur at the
level of institutional ideology.

Writing of ideology, Gramsci argues that it refers both to 'the
necessary superstructure of a particular structure [i.e., base] and to
the arbitrary elucubrations of particular individuals' (Gramsci
1971, 376). Because of this double signification, Gramsci claims,
many previous studies of ideology commit a series of crucial
mistakes:

> 1. ideology is identified as distinct from the structure, and it is
> asserted that it is not ideology that changes the structures but vice
> versa;

2. it is asserted that a given political solution is 'ideological' – i.e. that it is not sufficient to change the structure, although it thinks that it can do so; it is asserted that it is useless, stupid, etc.;
3. one then passes to the assertion that every ideology is 'pure' appearance, useless, stupid, etc. (Gramsci 1971, 376)

Clearly, Gramsci challenges the 'false consciousness' paradigm of ideology tentatively put forth by Engels and maintains that a significant relationship between institutional ideology and economic change exists. In this way, ideology can claim a positive role in shaping social conditions, a phenomenon denied by previous thinkers. 'Historically organic' ideologies – as distinct from arbitrary ones – help mold group consciousness and support the economic base (376–7). Gramsci further recognizes the split between ideology and material conditions as a theoretical one, for the two concepts are 'inconceivable historically' without one another (377).

From a pragmatic standpoint, the above comments seem closer to Rousseau than to the Marx of *The German Ideology*, for they indicate that social change may occur at the level of ideology. Elsewhere in the *Prison Notebooks*, Gramsci makes his notion of ideological struggle more explicit: 'only the social group that poses the end of the State and its own end as the target to be achieved can create an ethical State – i.e. one which tends to put an end to the internal divisions of the ruled' (259). Through its 'functionaries,' the intellectuals, the State creates a superstructure, 'civil society' that parallels its political and juridical functions (12). This matrix – which Gramsci labels hegemony – ensures the tacit acceptance of governmental control on the part of the subjects, although the 'coercive power' of the dominant group comes into play when the 'negotiation' of the hegemonic level fails (12). In glossing his concept of hegemony, Gramsci extends his definition of intellectuals to comprise not only the architects of diverse arts and sciences, but also a host of other individuals who disseminate ideas, including bureaucrats, teachers, journalists, and the like (13). Gramsci further divides intellectuals into the rubrics of 'traditional' and 'organic,' in which the former represent outmoded functionaries who claim autonomy and the latter exemplify the development of the State's mode of production (6–7). Organic intellectuals allow the State to subordinate the ordinary workers, those whose labor is primarily physical, to the power of the ruling elite.

In this way, Gramsci explicates the failure of his own communist political activities, despite material conditions in Italy that he felt should have made a proletarian revolution historically inevitable. For Gramsci, the proliferation of bourgeois ideology represents a major threat to the burgeoning proletarian consciousness because it posits self-interest for universal interest. Manual laborers might, for instance, cheer for Tony Blair, even as his policies ensure that they will never receive the slightest modicum of power. Without such overt or tacit consent, the State would collapse, despite its more repressive ancillaries (military, police, court systems, etc.). Gramsci labels this phenomenon the 'will to conform' and observes that its strength rests in its ability to convince people in the viability of a fluid class system (1971, 260). The resultant 'work ethic' then masks proletarian alienation with the (ever-receding) hope that eventually the grueling days stooped over a grill or assembling motorcycles will 'pay off' with an entry into the middle class. Schools, advertisers, television programs, books – the organic intellectual class employs these and other products to distort its own interests as those of the proletariat and to suggest the unlimited growth potential of the bourgeoisie. 'Rags to Riches' stories, such as those promoted by Horatio Alger and George W. Bush, reinforce the message, despite the overwhelming evidence that for every John Lennon who rises above his proletarian roots there exist tens of thousands who fail to 'escape.'

By maintaining that ideology acted in a more diffuse way, Gramsci exposed a serious flaw in the dominant ideology thesis preferred by many of Marx's early adherents. According to Gramsci, the State predicates its very existence not on coercive power but on consensus, education, common sense. Such a notion appears to conflict directly with previous interpretations of the base/superstructure model, and while resistance to Gramsci's notion of hegemony remains in some quarters, in many ways Gramsci reestablished the terms of the ideological debate. Clearly, Gramsci's rejection of the false consciousness model opened new horizons in both Marxist and non-Marxist analyses of ideology. After Gramsci, traditional false consciousness interpretations of ideology – particularly at the institutional level – seemed patently reductive, artificial. Instead of focusing solely on economics or coercive institutions, intellectuals began to reflect more seriously on their own role and on how seemingly benign organizations contribute to maintaining the State or, indeed, *are* the State. Those interested in institutional ideology now examined disciplines such as linguistics, literature, history, and science with a much different – and more self-referential – eye.

Before turning to such thinkers, however, one must consider the theories of **Georg Lukács**, particularly those outlined in his *History and Class Consciousness* (1922).[8] Lukács starts from the following premise: 'materialist dialectic is revolutionary dialectic' (1971, 2). He proceeds to claim that before revolution can succeed, it must fuse theory with action: 'the emergence of consciousness must become the *decisive step* which the historical process must take towards its proper end' (2; Lukács' emphasis). In order to accomplish this awareness, 'we need the dialectical method to puncture the social illusion so produced and help us to glimpse the reality underlying it' (5–6). From the above statements, one can imagine that Lukács advances a position similar to Engels' false consciousness. Lukács, however, bases his theory of ideology not on the Marx of *The German Ideology*, but on the Marx of *Capital*, specifically with regard to commodity fetishism. It is here that Lukács locates the force of institutional ideology and develops his concept of reification, the process whereby human activity becomes estranged from human subjectivity.

Because the commodity exchange valorizes things rather than the producers of those things, human activity is reduced to a subordinate position, an 'abstraction of the human labour incorporated into commodities' (Lukács 1971, 87). Reification thus functions as a 'natural' byproduct of the division of labor. As work becomes increasingly compartmentalized, workers lose touch with the consumers of that work and become subject to a psychological fragmentation that mirrors the fragmentation of the commodity's production. One no longer crafts a table and then sells it to another. Rather, one must, say, sand as many legs in 8 or 12 hours as one's supervisor deems fit. Lukács argues that the specialization required for assembly-line production 'transform[s] the basic categories of man's immediate attitude toward the world' (89). Personality or individual circumstance that 'disrupt' the empirically divided tasks have no place in the mechanized workplace and will be 'corrected' by reprimand or termination. In this way, the demands of the commodity exchange seep into the consciousness of workers who – if they are to survive – must adjust their habits to conform with the predetermined pace. For Lukács, 'the atomisation of the individual is, then, only the reflex in consciousness of the fact that the "natural laws" of capitalist production have been extended to cover every manifestation of life in society' (91–2).

Lukács, therefore, claims that institutional ideology strengthens itself by sublimating idiosyncrasy – at least as long as a particular worker's shift lasts – and underscoring the abstract value of labor. Reified individuals assume the universality of the commodity exchange and generally fail to notice the divorce between thing and human use-value: 'the reified mind has come to regard them [commodities] as the true representatives of his societal existence' (93). Immediate experience transmutes into universal experience, and the true nature of the commodity exchange masks itself. Because of the insidious way in which reification alters the spirit of the workforce, it manages to reinforce itself constantly, ultimately appearing in legal codes, educational curricula, and the like. Even labor unions, which purport to protect the worker, emphasize the capitalist economic base by insisting on a strict division of labor.

Differing from Gramsci, Lukács believes that intellectual efforts to battle ideology are futile, for they 'make no effort to advance beyond [capitalism's] objectively most derivative forms' (1971, 94). The totality of the system remains invisible, for the thinkers themselves possess a reified consciousness. Even 'pure' materialist thinkers lack an understanding of the systemic qualities of reification, for they, too, are victims of the very concept they hope to analyze: Lukács observes that the very dichotomy between objective and subjective realities stems from the requirements of the commodity exchange. Only the wage-earning proletariat – by virtue of their own status as commodities – may eventually understand, ironically aided by intellectuals such as Lukács, the overall framework of capitalist society. The bourgeois intellectuals function primarily in a consumptive role, whereas the proletariat comes to recognize the nature of the process itself. *How* the working class moves toward this recognition of the total picture is less clear, as commentators such as David McLellan and Eagleton have noted.

Together, Lukács and Gramsci established the parameters for the twentieth-century debate on institutional ideology. Most current discussions of the subject represent confirmations, expansions, or rebuttals of the opposing principles set forth by the above theorists. Extremely influential in his own right, Althusser, for example, seems inconceivable without Gramsci, while Fredric Jameson clearly owes a debt to Lukács. Crudely put, in his work Gramsci challenges the Marxist orthodoxy by suggesting that ideology *can* be confronted on its own terms, while Lukács – equally affronting to the 'vulgar' Marxists – holds that the superstructure will only change once the proletariat has exposed the economic base. Subsequent theorists, however, refined these positions considerably, applying them in ways that Gramsci and Lukács would probably not have anticipated. Language itself becomes the site of ideology for many latter-day analysts, while the construction of gender, race, national identity, and sexuality attracts special attention from legions of critics concerned with ideological questions. The pages to follow necessarily represent merely a sampling of ideological perspectives, for what was a fairly esoteric subject in previous decades proliferated dramatically in the mid- to late-twentieth century.

Although some pre-twentieth-century thinkers – for example, Bacon and Locke – had noted how language affects thought processes, systematic examinations of the ideology of language exploded in the twentieth century. As Bacon first noted, symbolic discourse holds tremendous – perhaps decisive – influence over how an individual may both generate ideas and act on those ideas. Bacon, Locke, and their followers, however, could not anticipate the seminal work of such linguists as **Ferdinand de Saussure** and **V. N. Voloshinov**, which challenges many basic assumptions regarding language and exposes the ideological components of what one must regard as the most basic of human institutions. Saussure's refiguring of the linguistic sign into signified and signifier, for instance, links concept to sound-image and suggests that the arbitrary nature of this connection reveals that 'every means of expression used in society is based, in principle, on collective behavior or . . . convention' (Saussure 1966, 68). Saussure continues that 'a particular language-state is always the product of historical forces,' a phenomenon that clearly suggests the ideological nature of language (72). Critiquing Saussure, Voloshinov makes this explicit with his assertion that 'without signs there is no ideology' (1973, 9). For Voloshinov, language and ideology form an endless loop from which the subject can not escape: consciousness arises from signs that, in turn, stem from social relationships such as those represented by the division of labor. While later poststructuralists such as Jean-François Lyotard and Jean Baudrillard claim that discourse of 'master narratives' regulates every aspect of life, Voloshinov argues that the 'social material of signs' represents a confluence of thought and practice (12). Within the field of discourse, subjects struggle for linguistic control that has profound effects on material practice. One thinks, for instance, of the Bush–Gore presidential election[9] or of the on-going struggle to define whether a 'patient's bill of rights' should include the right to sue Health Management Organizations.

Many ideological analyses from the mid-twentieth century onward have grappled with language's role in the creation of ideology, even if they ultimately focused on different goals. Many members of the Institute for Social Change's so-called **Frankfurt School**,[10] for instance, examine the impact of language on institutional ideology, even though the movement's primary target involves the naïve and dangerous application of scientific method to social structures. Somewhat paralleling Herbert Marcuse in *One-Dimensional Man: Studies in the Ideology of Advanced Industrial Society* (1964 [1992]), Theodor Adorno's *The Jargon of Authenticity* (1964), for example, explores the 'professional illness' of modern academics and social critics: specialized language (Adorno 1973a, 18). Adorno professes that jargon – and existentialism in particular – conceals the relationship between object and subject, resulting in a pseudo-reality that 'negates the whole man' (14). Hollow abstractions take on a totem-like quality, or, as he puts it in another context in *Negative Dialectics*, 'equip a fallible language with the attributes of a revealed one' (1973b, 111). As with Lukács, Adorno ultimately ascribes this reifying facet of language to economics, but concludes that 'the jargon of authenticity is ideology as language, without any consideration of specific content' (160) and manifests itself as 'a waste product of the modern that it attacks' (45). In other words, language is so alienated from its social characteristics that it fails to recognize its lack of referentiality.

In addition to their exploration of the vacuous relativism inherent in language, the Frankfurt School achieved notoriety for its sustained critique on the hitherto sacred arena of science. From Bacon onward, the West had elevated the scientific method to an exalted status. Citing the neutrality of scientific discourse, advocates of 'enlightened' thought sought to inject empiricism into every facet of society, from economics and psychology to music and sexuality. One need only think of I. A. Richard's zealous efforts to turn the study of poetry into a science or the intelligence tests of Alfred Binet to recognize the overarching dominance of the paradigm. Or think of the push for mandatory teacher testing, resistance to the Kyoto Protocol's 'junk science', and 'focus groups' to see how the paradigm continues to infiltrate modern life. De Tracy himself, one will recall, developed ideology as a *science* of ideas. Marcuse and his colleagues, however, questioned the uncritical acceptance of science as a neutral field. Science, or 'instrumental' reason – even as appropriated by traditional Marxism – represented a means whereby seemingly 'objective' individuals manipulated facts to reflect existing social conditions. In contrast, the Frankfurt group's 'critical theory' sought to expose such apparent harmony as false institutional ideology and an implicit attempt to bring natural forces into abeyance: 'the whole is false' (Adorno 1974, 50). The schism between scientific explanation and fact becomes the realm of the social critic and the conduit for true social change that escapes ideology. By emphasizing the lacunae rather than a comprehensive worldview, critical theorists may gain access to a positive social alternative, although this alternative remains relatively indeterminate.

The objectivity of science is also problematized in the works of such practicing scientists as **Thomas Kuhn, Paul Feyerabend**, and **Stephen Jay Gould**. Kuhn's extremely influential thesis – one which has been appropriated by fields as seemingly diverse as literary criticism and advertising – involves the socially determined nature of paradigm shifts. For Kuhn, science's claim to objectivity is tempered by social mores, ideology. He argues that because 'no paradigm ever solves all the problems it defines' social forces compete to answer the question 'which problem is it more significant to have solved?' (Kuhn 1996, 110). As Kuhn makes explicit, such debate requires scientists to seek guidance using 'criteria that lie outside normal science altogether' (110). Social revolution compels scientists to observe familiar data in new ways, which, in turn, reveal fundamental 'truths' that set the tone for a fresh scientific paradigm. One thinks, for example, of the increased attention to women's health issues concomitant with the social conditions that resulted in an increase in female physicians or of the turmoil of World War II, which resulted in the Atomic Age. While Kuhn finds such institutional ideology inevitable, he regards it as the key to a scientific advancement that is exponential rather than cumulative. Kuhn's text sparked an interest in the ideological underpinnings of science. Feyerabend, for example, attacks the notion of scientific objectivity with a vengeance in *Against Method* (1975 [1993]), a book that equates science with religion. Gould's popular works, such as *The Panda's Thumb* (1980), recount example after example of how ideological false consciousness blinds supposedly objective scientists and dupes them into manipulating facts into preconceived patterns. His essay on 'Women's Brains,' for instance, reveals how the misogyny of scientists such as Paul Broca and Gustave Le Bon clouded their interpretive skills and prompted them to reach conclusions that met a priori assumptions about relative female intelligence. For Gould, personality – as couched in the cultural values of a given era – is always injected into science, although he ultimately believes, along with Kuhn, that paradigm shifts allow scientists to retain a core of basic principles while they simultaneously develop new methods. Other studies, such as Alexander Vucinich's *Einstein and Soviet Ideology* (2001), a study of Soviet science, and Hilary Rose's *Love, Power, and Knowledge: Towards a Feminist Transformation of the Sciences* (1994), offer contemporary examples of how ideology impinges on the scientific.

Another major theorist who questions the supposed objectivity of science is **Michel Foucault**. Commenting on science's relationship to ideology, Foucault observes that 'the role of ideology does not diminish as rigour increases and error is dissipated' (1969 [1972], 186). While Foucault certainly did not confine himself to the study of science, his early critique of psychology in *Madness and Civilization: A History of Madness in the Age of Reason* (1961 [1988]) documents how the silences within the field reveal a keen interest in subordination rather than a benign interest in rehabilitation. Further, Foucault argues that the ideologies that gave rise to the Enlightenment could not support an underclass of the insane without developing a systematic way to exclude them from public discourse: the madhouse. Like the Frankfurt School's principal members, Foucault attempts to resist employing a reductive or totalizing paradigm, and his works are *sui generis* and derisive of 'theory.' As he writes in *The Archeology of Knowledge* (1969), Foucault asserts that his 'aim is most decidedly not to use the categories of cultural totalities...in order to impose on history, despite itself, the forms of structural analysis' (Foucault 1972, 15).

Considerations of power mark a recurrent theme throughout his *oeuvre*, however, and, when aligned with his various structuralist and poststructuralist methods of analyzing discourse, form a fairly consistent critique of institutional ideology.[11] For Foucault, structures – be they literary, juridical, or otherwise – reflect a claim to power. Drawing on the work of Claude Lévi-Strauss – whose own anthropological methods owe a debt to Saussure – Foucault attempts to illuminate the ideological parameters of discourse and the effects of narrative on practice. Speaking of the intertextual network that bolsters institutional power, Foucault writes that 'as soon as one questions that unity, it loses its self-evidence; it indicates itself, constructs itself, only on the basis of a complex field of discourse' (1972, 23). For Foucault, the most telling place to question the 'unity' of discourse appears during 'transitional' periods wherein fledgling paradigms begin to solidify into dominant modes. In Foucault's work, power functions less as a hierarchical phenomenon than as a web that implicates everyone. In *The History of Sexuality: An Introduction*, volume I (1976 [1990]), Foucault rejects mechanistic conceptions of power and ideology, noting that 'by power I do not mean "Power" as a group of institutions and mechanisms that ensure the subservience of the citizens of a given state,' for such manifestations exhibit only the 'terminal forms' of the concept (1990, 92). Rather, he defines power as 'the moving substrate of force relations' that 'comes from everywhere' and 'depends on a multiplicity of points of resistance' for its existence (93, 95). From such a position, Foucault critiques the basic notions of consciousness, representation, and even humanity. Such fixed ideal conceptions are for Foucault fictions that imperfectly capture protean relationships of power and resistance. Although ineffable and lacking in origin, power's effects are felt everywhere, a facet of Foucault's work that prompts Eagleton to muse whether Foucault's definition of power robs it of pragmatic value (Eagleton 1991, 8). Nevertheless, Foucault's influence is beyond question, and he presents a compelling alternative to the more explicitly ideological theories of such luminaries as Althusser and Pierre Macherey.

Foucault's propensity to avoid specific use of ideological theory is somewhat remarkable considering that he studied with **Louis Althusser**, for the latter is the primary figure responsible for the renaissance in the study of ideology. Distinguishing between 'humanistic' and 'scientific' Marxism, Althusser finds the locus of his own work within Marx's notion of production. Here, Althusser finds the rationale of ideology: 'the reproduction of the conditions of production' (1971, 127). For Althusser, a structuralist with affinities to Saussure, this reproduction takes place with the aid of 'ideological state apparatuses,' which he differentiates from 'repressive state apparatuses' such as prisons or military forces (142). While the latter rely on repressive measures, the former employ ideology, although they retain a certain degree of punitive capability. Althusser explicitly states that repressive state apparatuses cannot maintain power for long without the aid of their ideological counterparts (146). Because the ideological state apparatuses fail to use force as effectively as the repressive state apparatuses, moreover, they often act as flashpoints for class struggles.

The multiplicity of ideological state apparatuses evident in capitalist societies leads to a diffuse expression of ideology, but Althusser targets the 'educational ideological apparatus' as the dominant mode (1971, 152). In this way, most – if not all – citizens directly and indirectly absorb the culture that best supports the ruling class. At the same time, schools represent themselves as above ideological suspicion, as teaching the 'basics.' Nevertheless, through their cultivation of social mores, schools help to create or 'interpellate' subjects who readily accept their various roles as workers. Interpellation involves a material practice which formally recognizes the category of the subject. Denying the possibility of a dialectical consciousness, Althusser claims that 'individuals are always-already subjects' by virtue of their relationship to family, church, government, and other institutions (176). The recognition of one's own subjectivity, therefore, is anticipated by ideology. Furthermore, modifying the theories of Jacques Lacan, Althusser suggests that the subject must define and recognize itself through otherness. In this way, the 'vast majority' of subjects function with little guidance, and those who fail to be 'self-motivated' fall under the auspices of the repressive state apparatus (181).

Identity, then, finds itself generally conforming to the needs of the state, with socially constructed subjects carrying out socially constructed roles. Concomitantly, ideas – the pillars of Descartes' *cogito* – exist less as extensions of a particular subject than as the material requirements of the state. The illusory subject might think that an idea is original, but Althusser holds that such concepts are simply self-delusory representations of material practice. 'False consciousness,' therefore, becomes for Althusser an untenable category, as *all* consciousness is necessarily illusory. Indeed, Althusser spends considerable effort in displacing *The German Ideology* from prominence and establishing his singular interpretation of *Capital* in its stead. Althusser explains that, contra Marx and Engels, ideology does have a history, and that it 'is eternal' (1971, 152). To escape from this bind – Althusser reminds his readers that he, too, falls under the grip of ideology – one must turn to science (Marxism).

Althusser's impact on the study of ideology was – and is – enormous. In particular, his impact on literary studies helped change the field. The work of such luminaries as Macherey, Eagleton, Michael Sprinker, and Jameson reflects Althusser's structural approach to ideology, and a quick scan of *Books in Print* or Amazon.com yields countless books with titles beginning with 'Ideology and...'. In distinct ways, the aforementioned theorists apply and modify Althusser's central thesis to examine literature. **Macherey**, for example, argues in such works as *A Theory of Literary Production* (1966 [1978]) and *The Object of Literature* (1990 [1995]) that literature provides the perceptive reader with the means to catalogue ideological contradictions. Rejecting hollow formalism, Macherey concentrates on a definition of structure that includes the writer's negotiation of his or her own culture and received forms. Although he later rejects the Althusserian perspective, **Eagleton** also explores literature's relationship to ideology in such books as *Criticism and Ideology* (1976) and *Literary Theory: An Introduction* (1983). Examining works as ostensibly diverse as *Heart of Darkness* and *Felix Holt*, Eagleton explores the relationships among the general and literary modes of production, the general, authorial, and aesthetic ideologies, and the text (1978, 44). Eagleton eschews readings of texts as simplistic 'expressions' of ideology or class in favor of a more holistic analysis of the ways in which narratives produce ideology (64). In this way, Eagleton 'refuses the spontaneous presence of the work – to deny that "naturalness" in order to make its real determinants appear' (101). In contrast, Sprinker owes at least as much debt to the New Historicists[12] as to Marx in his historically rich examination of Proust, while **Jameson**, on the other hand, fuses the competing strategies of Lukács and Althusser to devise a methodology that exposes how literature interweaves specific historical contradictions to reveal a pattern of dialectic transformation.

In marked contrast to the political activism of the aforementioned critics, the theories collectively (and loosely) known as **poststructuralism** and **postmodernism** reject the possibility of a unified subject or institution. Reacting rather belatedly to the theories of Saussure, the poststructuralists denied the existence of what Lyotard refers to in *The Postmodern Condition: A Report on Knowledge* (1979 [1984]) as 'metanarratives' (xxiii). For Lyotard, social relationships are reducible to heterogeneous, constantly mobile, 'nodal points' of local communication known as 'language games' (15). Jameson, among others, attacked Lyotard's radical modification of Ludwig Wittgenstein as dangerously amoral, a charge often levied against other key poststructuralists such as **Jacques Derrida**, Roland Barthes, Baudrillard, Rodolphe Gasché, J. Hillis Miller, and Paul de Man. In works such as *Of Grammatology* (1967 [1976]) and *Limited Inc.* (1977 [1988]), Derrida explores the possibility of deconstruction, which examines the gaps, paradoxes, and inconsistencies in textual forms and in the play between signified and signifier.[13] One of Derrida's primary discoveries concerns the undecidable nature of the text, a phenomenon he calls 'différance' (Derrida 1973, 129). Provisional meanings melt when juxtaposed with contradictory interpretations and, thus, lead to a series of unresolvable aporia. In this way, texts 'communicate' precisely because determinate meaning has destabilized. In its diverse incarnations, postmodernism poses a number of concerns for those interested in ideology. Broadly influenced by Nietzsche, the postmodernists have been denounced by critics such as Allan Bloom for lacking a moral center and advocating a creeping 'relativism [that] has extinguished the real motive of education, the search for a good life,' and that finds the 'truths' of Gandhi no better or worse than those of Hitler, a claim bolstered by the charge that de Man may have sympathized with the Nazis during World War II (Bloom 1987, 34). Moreover, some postmodern theorists, influenced by sources other than Derrida, characterize social interaction as 'simulacra' or language games, a maneuver that strikes many writers as specious or even callous. Nevertheless, the postmodernists' interest in rhetorical lacunae marks less a desire to rationalize *Mein Kampf* as an effort to underscore the very material production of language and its arbitrary byproduct, sense.

Indeed, one might view deconstruction as a radical exposure of 'false consciousness,' one that unmasks the logocentric quality of 'truth' itself. The postmodernists' insistence that meaning is contingent on the performative and the game, moreover, corresponds strikingly to those materialist theories that emphasize language's shifting social dimensions (Michel Pêcheux comes to mind, for example). Indeed, later proponents of deconstruction such as Barbara Johnson and Marjorie Levinson used the theory as a viable political tool with which to expose institutional ideology.

Another important approach, inaugurated by **Raymond Williams** in his *Culture and Society, 1780 – 1950* (1958 [1983]), cultural studies, challenges the privileging of 'high' culture such as canonical literature and opera to the detriment of 'low' culture such as comic books and hip hop. Williams posits that a thorough comprehension of society cannot occur without an understanding of *all* of its components. The academy's emphasis on high culture, Williams holds, evolved from specific economic and political contexts, specifically the rise of industrialism and democracy. Democracy, with its emphasis on majority rule, posed a hazard to the privileged liberal classes, who constructed their various notions of culture in an effort to erect barriers to power. Thus, within the realm of culture, Williams discovers the ideological residue of advanced capitalism and observes that the very notion of high culture finds its roots in a fear of the mob: 'mass-thinking, mass-suggestion, mass-prejudice would threaten to swamp considered individual thinking and feeling,' hallmarks of the 'cultured' individual (Williams 1983, 298). Williams disputes such claims and announces that in order to evaluate society, one must take into account the 'familiar factual elements' that represent more than a fraction of the population (301). Williams' work was both extended and challenged by such writers as E. P. Thompson, Richard Hoggart, and Stuart Hall. In *The Making of the English Working Class* (1963), for instance, Thompson rejects Williams' model of an organic culture in favor of a dynamic, self-determined cultural formulation, while in *The Uses of Literacy* (1958 [1992]) Hoggart examines the tensions between working-class culture and the superimposition of mass-produced texts. For his part, Hall turns toward Gramsci's concept of hegemony to help explain the 'British' symbolic system, a strategy that complicates Williams' emphasis on the working class by implying that the mass media dissolves class dichotomies.

Apart from Williams, another popularizer of the neoteric field was **Marshall McLuhan**, whose *Understanding Media: The Extensions of Man* (1964) announces that 'the medium is the message' (McLuhan 1964, 23). A social determinist, McLuhan posits that the institutions of communication establish the parameters of human activity and reflect an extension of the human senses. Content, therefore, stems from form. Echoing the findings of Walter J. Ong and others, McLuhan traces the shift from oral to electronic culture and suggests that the widespread alienation and anxiety of the current age reflects a clash of mechanistic fragmentation and electronic integration: 'we are as numb in our new electric world as the native involved in our literate and mechanical culture' (31). In an earlier work, *The Gutenberg Galaxy* (1962), McLuhan, reminiscent of Kuhn, observes several fundamental shifts in human organization, each brought about by a revolution in communication (e.g., the phonetic alphabet, the printing press, the telegraph). The current electronic age, he argues, marks somewhat of a return to the mores of the most primitive cultures, as evidenced by what he calls the 'global village.' McLuhan's relevance for students of ideology lies in his insistence that consciousness and ideas stem from specific technological contexts. Unlike Marx and his followers, however, McLuhan generally drains these contexts of their economic import. For this reason, Williams, among others, reproached McLuhan for being overly reductive and for advocating cultural relativism.

Ironically, **cultural studies** exploded in the academy, and degrees in television studies and popular music proliferate. Lampooned in Don DeLillo's *White Noise* (1985) – which includes references to 'Hitler Studies' – cultural studies now occupies a mainstream position in western educational institutions. Critics such as Antony Easthope, John Berger, the early Roland Barthes, Omar Calabrese, and John B. Thompson, among many others, now routinely examine hitherto pariah subjects such as professional wrestling, western movies, and fast food. For such commentators, every aspect of culture, be it high or low, offers significant ideological substance. In *Literary into Cultural Studies* (1991), Easthope, for instance, asserts that 'history is real but only accessible to us discursively,' a phenomenon that prompts him to avoid compiling totalizing epochal world views (157). Instead, Easthope tries to 'escape mastery' by proffering readings of a multitude of texts – ranging from Benson and Hedges cigarettes to obscure Victorian autobiographies – in order to examine how these might reposition the subject and 'challenge if not circumvent entirely the privileged self-enclosure of the aesthetic' (1991, 138, 166). Positionality also marks the work of Berger, who contends that the ways in which people view images 'are affected by a whole series of learnt assumptions' and that these assumptions lead to 'cultural mystification' (Berger 1977, 11). In *Mythologies* (1957 [1972]), Barthes finds 'myths' that reveal historical forces in such ostensibly ephemeral objects as soap and milk, while Calabrese remarks in *Neo-Baroque: A Sign of the Times* (1992) that 'it is precisely by not producing hierarchies and ghettos among texts that we can discover recurring trends that distinguish "our" mentality...from that of other periods' (xii). Thompson, on the other hand, concentrates on what he calls the 'mediazation of modern culture' (1990, 3). For Thompson, the media's central role in transmitting common images constitutes an 'institutionalized production and diffusion of symbolic goods' that helps to restructure social behavior (219). While cultural studies inevitably employs a wide variety of strategies, one may state that the sum impact on the study of ideology involves the expansion of subject matter, the dissolution of binary oppositions, suspicion of aesthetic-based theory, and the understanding that texts of all sorts are historically constructed and received. Consequently, cultural studies generally reacts quite sensitively to issues of ideology.

Studies of institutional ideology have also played a key role in several key twentieth-century social movements, notably **feminism** and civil rights. From Simone de Beauvoir's magisterial *The Second Sex* (1949 [1989]) and Betty Friedan's highly influential *The Feminine Mystique* (1963 [2001]) onward, most twentieth-century feminists have been concerned with the ways in which androcentric ideologies construct gender roles.[14] Institutions such as the Church, education, marriage, and the legal system all manifest a marked bias towards not only the poor, but the female as well. The ideology perpetuated by these institutions functioned to mystify biological relationships and devalue private (domestic) labor in favor of public work. Even traditionally sympathetic institutions on the political left found themselves accused of perpetuating an ideology little different in substance from that of misogynist medieval clerics. Theorists such as Juliet Mitchell, whose *Woman's Estate* (1971 [1972]) problematizes traditional Marxism's relationship to gender, and Kate Millett, whose *Sexual Politics* (1970) scrutinizes the power code evident in patriarchal literature, observed that reactionary and radical males alike tended to ignore or trivialize the feminine. In addition, French feminists such as Luce Irigaray, Julia Kristeva, and Hélène Cixous were in the forefront of fusing poststructuralism and psychoanalysis to the study of gender. While most feminisms critique ideology at least implicitly, materialist feminism offers a particularly rich vein.

Considering Marx's alleged mistreatment of his own wife, it is easy to recognize why feminists in the mid-1960s and 1970s desired to transform traditional materialist analyses with the burgeoning ideological emphasis of feminist theory. For early practitioners such as Mitchell, the task involved exposing the deficiencies of purely economic critiques and advocating the need for a thorough understanding of the ways in which gender constructions stem from – and contribute to – the economic base. Others, such as Rosalind Coward, sought to undercut the very notion of gender differences, indicating that political and economic struggles are paramount. Toril Moi continues this line of reasoning in *Sexual/ Textual Politics: Feminist Literary Theory* (1985 [2002]), which contends that, despite good intentions, in books such as *The Madwoman in the Attic: The Woman Writer and the Nineteenth-Century Literary Imagination* (1979) feminists such as Susan Gilbert and Susan Gubar indirectly reaffirm androcentric ideology by deferring to Cartesian ontology. Michèle Barrett, on the other hand, emphasizes the relationship between production and consumption, specifically as it intersects with gender. In her groundbreaking work *Materialist Feminism and the Politics of Discourse* (1993), Rosemary Hennessy provides yet another version of materialist feminism, one that 'conceptualiz[es] discourse as ideology,' which helps one 'to consider the discursive construction of the subject, "woman," across multiple modalities of difference, but without forfeiting feminism's recognition that the continued success of patriarchy depends on its systematic operation' (xv). Materialist feminism has its critics, of course, Elaine Showalter among them, who argues for a specifically feminine criticism that rejects masculine ideology altogether: 'gynocritics begins at the point when we free ourselves from the linear absolutes of the male tradition, and focus instead on the newly visible world of female culture' (Showalter 1985, 131).

In *Talking Back: Thinking Feminist, Thinking Black* (1989), bell hooks, on the other hand, excoriates previous feminists – materialist or otherwise – for ignoring issues of race, and in *Other Worlds: Essays in Cultural Politics* (1987) Gayatri Spivak attempts to recognize feminism's relationship with subalternity and postcolonial issues. In particular, hooks offers compelling evidence that the feminist project of the latter half of the twentieth century was singularly concerned with white, middle-class mores, while Spivak notes that western feminists routinely ignore the contributions of women working in locations other than the United Kingdom, France, and the United States: critics such as Nawal El Saadawi and Chandra Talpade Mohanty face far different impediments than do Rachel Blau DuPlessis or Nina Baym. As self-proclaimed 'outsiders', both hooks and Spivak underscore the ideology at work in 'centrist' feminism, just as many materialist feminisms point out Marxism's own blind spots. Such critiques tend to affirm 'false consciousness' models, for they argue that subjects bathed in a particular ideology fail to see their own reliance on preconceived forms. Issues of sexual orientation, national identity, race, critics such as Adrienne Rich, Edward Said, Ngũgĩ wa Thiong'o, and Henry Louis Gates, Jr claim, are inevitably bound up with ideology. Positionality is paramount: one's complex relationships with a host of competing forces shape how one reasons about, reacts to, and represents difference. As Said writes in *The World, the Text, and the Critic* (1983), ideology compels one 'to be too cloistered and too attracted to easy systematizing' (28), a phenomenon that Said contrasts to 'oppositionality,' a strategy that holds a 'suspicion of totalizing concepts' yet 'opposes every form of tyranny, domination, and abuse' (29).

Before turning to questions of political ideology, one further theory requires scrutiny: the **dominant ideology thesis** of **Nicolas Abercrombie, Stephen Hill**, and **Bryan S. Turner**. Whereas most of the thinkers thus far considered agree that ideology holds a central role in the shaping of society, Abercrombie and his colleagues dispute the concept's primacy and even its usefulness. In *The Dominant Ideology Thesis* (1980), Abercrombie, Hill, and Turner reject academic concern with ideological superstructures and assert that 'late capitalism operates largely without ideology' (165). Although they recognize the existence of competing ideologies, the writers problematize the notion that societies possess a monolithic value system, arguing instead for a fragmented set of ideas that hardly qualify as a 'superstructure.' These diffuse, mutually exclusive outcroppings, they posit, lack the coherence and force to champion an overarching model of capitalism. Indeed, they tend to miss their presumed targets – the proletariat – altogether. For this group, satisfying basic necessities such as food and shelter provide the only required impetus to yield to the so-called dominant ideology. Interestingly, Abercrombie, Hill, and Turner's thesis contains a trace of the first theorist under consideration in this chapter: Thomas Hobbes. One will recall that Hobbes' theory of institutional ideology involves the pursuit of pleasure and the avoidance of pain, and Abercrombie and his peers suggest as much with their notion that most citizens simply play along with capitalism so long as they can get three squares and a cot. While Göran Therborn, among others, chides the trio for their overly broad definition of dominant ideology, Abercrombie, Hill, and Turner pose a serious challenge to the work of structuralist Marxists in particular and resurrect the economic determinism of Marx's earliest acolytes. In their treatment of capitalism, however, Abercrombie, Hill, and Turner represent a strain of the end-of-ideology debate considered in the next chapter, which deals with the most widespread definition of ideology: the political.

4   Political Ideology

Ostensibly far removed from academic debates over such niceties as false consciousness and superstructures, questions of political ideology frequently center on realpolitik issues of power. While academics might shudder at such a loose – even simplistic – application of the term, they could hardly dispute the overwhelming evidence that the majority of the population accepts the definitions of ideology propagated by media outlets and politicians. Such definitions, while in no way precise or systematic, broadly fall into two categories of practical usage. The first, and probably most common, characterization of political ideology involves extremism. In this usage, political models that deviate – whether sharply or not – from those of the speaker represent dangerous ideas that will lead, or have led, to serious repercussions for the audience. Furthermore, this pejorative definition of ideology necessitates either an individual or group that would zealously adhere to, and enact, such hazardous dogmas. This definition is inextricably linked to the concept of threatening *action*. One thinks, for example, of Ronald Reagan's reference to the Soviet Union as an 'evil empire,' or of Hillary Clinton's allusion to a 'conservative conspiracy.' The second widely employed definition of political ideology owes somewhat to the 'neutral' usage of the concept offered by political scientists such as Andrew Vincent. Such a depiction of ideology refers to general belief systems, whether they are perceived as menacing or not. Emptied of negative connotation, ideology in this sense applies to beliefs as diverse as anarchism and fascism. In fact, speakers often substitute the slang term 'ism' for ideology.

The preceding descriptive definitions of ideology did not arise fully formed, however. Although the preponderance of media outlets makes it relatively easy to see how such usages are replicated, the underpinnings of these popular definitions find their basis in both the academy and the political arena. Theorists of political ideology maintain that the concept impinges on nearly every aspect of human activity. Unlike the institutional ideologies outlined by such thinkers as Louis Althusser and Antonio Gramsci, however, political ideology tends to exist on a more overt plane and to leave a more noticeable – even predictable – impact on society. Contrary to models such as those offered by the camera obscura or base/superstructure, political ideology – as defined in the popular consciousness – does not rely on inversion or 'deep structure' to make its presence felt. Rather, political ideologies construct a set of core beliefs that directly influences how societies react to variable conditions such as economic flux, militarism, technological progress, religious mandates, and the like. Ruling bodies and their agents, thus, have measurable power over their subjects. George W. Bush, for example, might persuade Congress to pass along a tax rebate to its constituents or Mullah Omar might decide that all Afghani women must wear a *burqa*. In one sense, then, political ideology functions as the locus of power, for such practical decisions should at least ostensibly mesh with the abstract goals underlying, say, Republican conservatism or Taliban fundamentalism.

History, of course, belies such a transparent correlation between political thought and political action. Robespierre's Terror, Stalin's purges, and Roosevelt's 'internment camps,' for instance, all patently contradicted the *ideas* that their practitioners espoused. Despite establishing broad parameters for action, then, political ideology is invariably intertwined with the personalities of those charged with carrying ideas to their fruition. Personal power, while frequently aided by the tenets of such philosophies as 'fascism' or 'liberalism,' tends to be far more free-floating and often adjusts its doctrines on an *ad hoc* basis. Lenin's New Economic Policy, for example, blatantly contradicted his earlier theories, yet it preserved his power in an unstable political environment. Political ideologies are also modified or ignored by a given government's subjects as well. Flouting laws prohibiting the practice, for example, many African-American slaves clandestinely learned to read, while 'Green' movements resist the natural-resource-as-raw-material ethic of capitalism. As Marx points out, systems themselves contain contradictions, such as the free market's 'inevitable' movement toward monopoly. In essence, one must be careful not to exaggerate the uniform nature of a given political ideology, even if one might attempt to delineate its general characteristics.

Abstract qualifiers aside, a linear notion of political ideology continues to thrive in the public consciousness. Typically, such conceptions start from the broad characterization of left-leaning ideologies (e.g., communism, socialism) as sacrificing individual opportunity for equality of result and right-leaning ideologies (e.g., fascism, fundamentalism) as sacrificing individuality for the state. Of course, such ideologies are put forth as extremes when juxtaposed with the 'moderate' position of free-market capitalism in all its various incarnations. The further one 'leans from the center,' the more likely one's political opponent will make use of an unflattering epithet regarding one's affiliation with ideologies of the left or the right. For many, the supremacy and desirability of, for example, a parliamentary government is beyond dispute, is 'common sense.'

Our contemporary (and popular) understanding of political ideology often starts from a relatively monolithic spatial metaphor that the George Orwell of 'Politics and the English Language' might say has lost its 'evocative power' to draw up a visual image (Orwell 1978, 130). This familiar metaphor, of course, describes political ideology in terms of left, center, and right. As is typical of the pejorative usage of the metaphor, a further distinction of 'far' left or right may be applied to those ideologies deemed particularly extreme or dogmatic. Such labels are frequently reserved for one's political enemies, even if those individuals do not happen to hold to an especially extreme branch – or 'faction' to extend the negative connotation – of a given ideology. Students of French political history will recognize this trope as stemming from the Estates-General, where in 1789 'radicals' sat to the left of Louis XVI, while 'reactionaries' sat to his right. The limits of the metaphor quickly become apparent. Neo-nazis, for example, might apply the term 'leftist' to a member of their organization who suspects that lynching might be wrong, while Al Sharpton might find Jesse Jackson too right-wing for his taste. Quite simply, the lack of a set of standards coupled with the *ad hominem* nature of much of the usage, dilutes any accuracy the terms might possess. Nevertheless, politicians and media members alike find the connotative shorthand of such terms irresistible and their propensity to employ the words has filtered down to the talk radio crowd or the unemployed steelworker grumbling to his wife. Attempting to bring a scientific outlook to the debate, many political scientists have attempted to modify the ambiguities that stem from the static model of left–center–right and have developed a variety of competing – and far less popular – paradigms, including what Andrew Heywood calls the horseshoe model (1998, 18) and Hans Eysenck's two-dimensional spectrum (1999). Problematizing the issue further are theories that claim the dichotomy between left and right to be utterly false. A. James Gregor, for instance, argues that 'it has become increasingly difficult to explain the persistence of the right- and left-wing distinctions that were so long labored in the academic literature devoted to accounts of revolution in our time' (Gregor 2000, 6). He ultimately maintains that the relationship among ideologies is often 'curvilinear rather than rectilinear' (128). Gregor and his cohorts, raised in a post-modern academy setting that eschews the dichotomies of earlier generations, certainly have a point. When adolescents lob charges of 'fascism' at parents who despised Thatcher, and Rush Limbaugh paints moderate members of his own party as 'bleeding heart liberals,' the inefficiency of the conservative-liberal model seems beyond dispute. Clearly, people are hurling around terms of which they have little *historical* understanding. Nevertheless, modern political scientists such as Gregor face a perhaps insurmountable challenge in their efforts to denude the language of political ideologies of imprecision. Indeed, theorists positing subjective or institutional models of ideology could assert that it is precisely this semantic ambiguity that allows ideology to be so potent, that being oblivious to one's own position fosters the belief in a 'common sense' worldview sympathetic to the ruling system. Another complicating factor in discussing political ideology is simply the overwhelming number of competing 'isms' and subcategories. In addition to examining familiar ideologies such as liberalism, socialism, and communism, one might also identify and study local-ized movements such as the Luddites, al-Qaeda, the Know Nothings, or Legalism. Most political theorists, however, contain themselves to generalized ideological rubrics. Using such a system, Luddites might exemplify a 'conservative' ideology, while al-Qaeda would represent a 'fundamentalist' worldview. The following discussion will attempt to examine ideology from such a broad-based position.

Perhaps the best place to start a discussion of specific modern political ideologies is with an ideology against which many contemporary western political systems reacted: **feudalism**. Generally, contemporary political theorists regard feudalism as an overdetermined academic abstraction into which medieval societies as diverse as France and Japan were shoehorned in response to a trend toward comprehensive historiography such as that offered by Marc Bloch. Indeed, modern commentators such as Susan Reynolds are fond of observing that the term 'feudal' is an academic construct of Renaissance coinage and that medieval societies did not rely solely on its 'picture' of the state. Nevertheless, in terms of broad ideological strokes, feudalism is a useful concept, especially when viewed in contrast with the ideologies that attempted to discredit it later. As defined by Adam Smith, feudalism represented an economic system predicated on domination. Its chief distinction from prior ideologies was its fusion of the legalistic and the personal. In theory, feudalism decentralized monarchical power and established it in pyramid fashion to a series of overlords, vassals, and peasants. Militarily strong, the overlords offered protection, land (fief), and equipment to their subordinates in exchange for monetary and personal tribute. Legal jurisdiction over the fief would transfer to the vassal so long as he met his obligations to the lord. The governing structure relied heavily on well-defined roles that entailed mutual responsibility. Except in time of war, however, the village was the locus of social activity. Personal liberties were limited, and one's place in the social hierarchy was linked to a divine plan that could not be altered. Land tenure, rather than private property, formed the basis of feudalism's economic structure. Dependent on a weak central government, feudalism atrophied when faced with the more powerful lords of the late middle ages and early Renaissance, although the rigid class system remained in place long after (Russia's serfs, for instance, did not acquire autonomy until the mid-nineteenth century). Indeed, while the organization of the state altered with the demise of feudalism, the lower classes remained with minimal rights.

In sharp contrast to the primacy of social duty inherent in feudalism and its lingering after effects, **liberalism** ostensibly underscores the autonomy of the individual. Although the political use of 'liberalism' finds its origins in the early nineteenth century, its philosophical antecedents – as with those of 'ideology' – appear much earlier and roughly correspond with the Renaissance. Anticipating the skepticism and emphasis on 'human rights' characteristic of liberal thought, the Baconian push for empiricism and the Cartesian emphasis on the individual laid the foundation for modern liberalism, although John Locke and the French *philosophes* provide more immediate influences. Often synonymous with Enlightenment thought, liberalism takes the social contract as an a priori foundation for individual freedom. According to liberalism, such liberty is predicated on humanity's status as '[*animal*] *rationis capax*,' as Jonathan Swift had earlier described it to Alexander Pope (Swift 1970, 265). In this way, Enlightenment thinkers could both acknowledge that 'unnatural' social conditions could lead to individual barbarity and anticipate that humanity's 'innate' potential for reason could not only provide a corrective for such depravity but also establish a society based on principles of Justice, Beauty, and Truth. For much of the western world, classic liberalism is so intertwined with institutional theory and practice as to be virtually unchallenged. At the dawn of the nineteenth century, however, liberalism was by no means secure in its political dominance. Europe looked with amazement, and often horror, at the American and, especially, the French revolutions, where populist ideas were merging with the esoteric theories of Locke and the *philosophes*. Locke's *Two Treatises of Civil Government* (1690 [1988]), for example, propose that individual rights stem from natural law, and, thus, any governmental contrivance to impede those rights should be considered null and void. The quasi-utopian rhetoric of many early liberal thinkers stressed humanity's essential goodness, pointing to the 'noble savage' of the Americas as proof. For such liberals, centralized power unsanctioned by the group inevitably – and somewhat paradoxically – leads to corruption. Tolerance of minority views on governance, religion, culture, and personal behavior is emphasized, and *laissez-faire* economics and personal property form the basis of the liberal market-place. While thinkers such as David Ricardo, Jeremy Bentham, and Germaine de Staël are now generally classified together as 'classic' liberals, liberal viewpoints on many – perhaps most – issues varied widely, and they virulently attacked one another in print, a phenomenon owing, no doubt, to liberalism's stress on the individual. Nevertheless, one may glean a general sense of the ideology and the later 'modern' liberalisms that evolved from it.

The individual stands at the center of classic liberalism. Whereas feudalism had stressed the importance of social duty, liberalism argues for the primacy of self-duty. For the classic liberal, choice must not be hindered by unjustified state restriction or coercion.

Action must be autonomous, so long as it does not impede the liberty of others. Opinions and discourse, however, should be unfettered. John Stuart Mill – while he does argue that opinions that foment a 'mischievous act' could be subject to restrictions (Mill 1984, 119) – discusses the need to limit action but not opinion in *On Liberty* (1859): 'the liberty of the individual must be thus far limited; he must not make himself a nuisance to other people. But if he refrains from molesting others in what concerns them...he should be allowed, without molestation, to carry his opinions into practice at his own cost' (1984, 119–20). To foster such tolerant conditions, liberalism required the destruction or extreme modification of the centralized power characterizing the *ancien régime*. In this way, classic liberalism resembles some forms of anarchy, libertarianism in particular, for it is anti-foundational (and utopian) at its core. For individuals to thrive, the State – and the Church – must return much of its power back to its free citizens and function merely as what Wilhelm von Humboldt describes as a night watchman who protects individuals from the interference of those who would trample their rights (1993, 340). The American anti-federalists offered one expression of this tendency with their opposition to the United States constitution, which they felt centralized power to a dangerous degree. The federalists, who eventually succeeded, felt that rights needed to be ensured more formally, and in this way they anticipated modern liberalism, which agrees with many classic liberal positions but argues for an active government to create the conditions that foster individual liberty.

For the classic liberal, private property is co-extensive with personal liberty. According to this ideological premise, one cannot be truly autonomous if one is beholden to another for one's existence. Contrary to the feudal system, liberalism insists that individuals must have the ability to control the means of production. For Smith, writing in his *The Wealth of Nations* (1776 [1982]), such a phenomenon would lead to a division of labor resulting in free competition. While initially motivated by self-interest, such competition would be guided by an 'invisible hand' that serves the best interests of society as a whole. State intervention, such as taxation or import restrictions, hampers this benevolent self-interest. According to Smith, who was influenced by French Physiocrats such as François Quesnay, mercantilism, an economic theory that favored tariffs and reserves of precious metals, harmed international trade and ignored the natural advantage that nations could exploit by producing goods at the lowest possible cost and trading for those that were more expensive to manufacture. A nation's wealth, Smith observes, lies not in its supply of gold, but in the value of its production. While Smith argues that this form of capitalism will benefit all sectors of society, and, thus, increase personal liberty, Marx and others point out that so-called bourgeois liberalism co-opted these principles in order to exploit the working classes, who owned nothing but their labor, which they ultimately 'rented' to the monied classes.

The obvious discrepancies in the distribution of wealth created (or maintained) by the free-market system led to a fracture within liberalism. Despite empowering individuals to own property, nations still had substantial numbers who did not. Despite professing their citizens to be 'free,' most states also still had varying degrees of oppression. Such ostensible paradoxes led liberalism to consider whether its egalitarian theories suggested an equality of *opportunity* or one of *result*. In the former instance, the removal of governmental barriers was thought to prove enough. Talent, luck, desire, and hard work are naturally distributed unevenly, so it stands to reason that some will succeed where others will fail. The important factor is that everyone has the chance to try his or her hand in the free market-place, all the while having the ability to express his or her opinions and religious beliefs. For the 'modern' liberal, such a state of affairs is intolerable. While the earliest modern liberals did not employ the term 'level playing field,' their belief in legislative remedies anticipates it. The theory of the level playing field posits that preexisting advantages must be minimized, largely through laws – such as the English Reform Bill of 1832 or the United States Civil Rights Act of 1964 – that ensure the civil and fiscal liberties of the downtrodden. Initially (in practice, at least) applying mostly to white males, liberalism eventually extended its purview to women, the poor, racial minorities, gays, and other marginalized groups. Concomitantly, the initial suspicion of federal governments was later replaced by the image of a benign, 'democratic' government designed to assist the weak, particularly in matters of economics and education.

Contemporary liberalism strays far indeed from its classic roots. Whereas classic liberalism downplayed the need for a central government, modern liberalism often seeks to expand it to 'protect' the rights of its citizens. For many modern liberals, the state should not only attempt to guarantee equality of opportunity (generously defined) but should also try to ensure equality of result as well. Public assistance is viewed as a moral duty, a latter-day *noblesse oblige* wherein no individual is left behind. Government ownership of utilities, roads, hospitals, and the like is also seen as serving the public's interest and keeping the avaricious side of self-interest in check. Common liberal issues include abortion, free speech, the environment, labor laws, and educational reform. While laws to protect individual rights existed from the dawn of liberalism – the bill of rights being the most famous example – contemporary liberalism has attempted to regulate virtually all segments of human activity, often employing 'scientific' or 'progressive' tactics. Such 'constructive' (or 'welfare') liberalism designs to prevent the minority from securing its rights at the expense of the majority. William Gladstone's reforms, Franklin Delano Roosevelt's 'New Deal' and Lyndon Baines Johnson's conception of a 'Great Society' perhaps typify this strain of liberalism. Such wide-scale reforms have come under increasing attack, however, and many contemporary liberals, such as Tony Blair, take increasingly centrist positions on many social issues. Regardless, liberalism's broad effects are ensconced throughout much of the western world, a point driven home by the ubiquity of such institutions as jury trials, universal suffrage, and free speech.

While liberalism seeks to storm the bulwarks of a society 'irrationally' bound by the past, **conservatism** attempts to preserve the cherished institutions of social order. As might be gleaned from the above discussion of classic liberalism, however, the face of conservatism changed greatly between the revolutions of 1776/ 1789 and 1848. Indeed, while the conservatives facing Thomas Paine both in the American colonies and in France generally expressed royalist sentiments, classic liberalism – and especially its capitalist economic theories – was so entrenched by the revolutions of 1848 that conservatives now for the most part sought to protect many of the erstwhile radical ideas of the Enlightenment! Opposed to disruptive socio-economic change, conservative ideologies usually attempt to preserve the traditional social order. Consequently, conservative ideologies generally prefer the practical to the ideal and reject metaphysical notions regarding the perfectibility of humanity, as well as the schemes offered to accelerate it. For conservatives, new legislation must be passed only after prudent rumination. Equality of opportunity, not result, is paramount, and attempts to legislate economic equity are misguided and potentially chaotic. Modern conservative ideologies thus tend to be skeptical of governmental bureaucracy and prefer privatization, minimally regulated trade, and local control. In matters of personal liberty, conservatives resist impulsive behavior that could rent the social fabric, but they also recognize the importance of classic civil liberties such as free speech and religious tolerance.

Like liberalism, conservatism did not enter the ideological vocabulary until the early nineteenth century, although its primary tenets have been practiced for millennia. The origins of modern conservatism, however, lie in Edmund Burke's *Reflections on the Revolution in France* (1790 [1999]), which challenged the *philosophes'* a priori belief in natural rights and – prior to the rise of Robespierre – assailed the Revolution's excesses. Ironically, Burke had previously defended the American Revolution, which was premised on many of the same theories he later attacked. Nonetheless, Burke's defense of the American Revolution does reveal some traces of conservative ideology in that it recognizes in the colonial struggle a desire for *established* rights and protections. In contrast, the French Revolution trumpeted a radically new social order that broke with historical precedent and that could prove both corrupt and dangerous. For Burke, as for later conservatives, societal change comes from within traditional institutions rather than from without. According to Burke, who drew some of his ideas from David Hume, a state formed entirely from rational principles ignores the visceral sense of belonging (or 'prejudice') that truly binds a culture together. Tradition transcends individual self-interest, for within it lies a collective knowledge that circumscribes and informs personal reason. As circumstances change, traditional observances evolve, yet they retain the wisdom of previous generations. Thus, ethics – and the concomitant rights designed to protect or enforce those ethics – arise from convention rather than a rational nature: 'as the liberties and restrictions vary with time and circumstances, and admit of infinite modifications, they cannot be settled upon any abstract rule; and nothing is so foolish as to discuss them upon that principle' (Burke 1999, 148). Burke's rejection of natural law portends a skepticism of metaphysics and idealism that continues to mark the conservative ideology.

Burke – who characterized democracy as 'the most shameless thing in the world' – would no doubt have shuddered at the pace of change between the French Revolution and the Paris Commune of 1871 (1999, 150). As mentioned above, the radical ideas of thinkers such as Voltaire and Denis Diderot were perceived as 'universal' or 'common sense' in a relatively short time frame. Despite its first manifestation as what Vincent refers to as the 'negative defensive posture of a declining aristocratic class,' conservatism – ever pragmatic – soon put on the coat of classic liberalism in order to defend the social order against the more extreme views of modern liberalism (Vincent 1992, 56). In matters of economics especially, many conservatives, with the industrial revolution in full bloom, now sought to block potentially costly and tempestuous plans to expand suffrage rights, levy high tariffs, and protect workers. *Laissez-faire* economics coupled with a Hobbesian notion of society-as-moral-guardian formed the basis of such conservative resistance. An example of such theories may be found in the work of Frédéric Bastiat, a conservative economist who strongly objected to the 'legal plunder' of socialism and misguided liberal legislation (Bastiat 2002). Bastiat feels with Smith that the 'invisible hand' will take care of society's needs if government would simply stand aside. A natural harmony would develop in which 'we would not see poor families seeking literary instruction before they have bread' and 'social progress would be ceaseless' (Bastiat 2002). For Bastiat, as for many adhering to the conservative ideology, society would ultimately provide its own correctives for injustice if it would stop trying to legislate behavior. Universal [male] suffrage, represented by such legislation as the British Reform Acts of 1832, 1867, and 1884 and the United States' 15th amendment, was seen by many as dangerous, for a largely illiterate populace could not be trusted to preserve national interests and resist inflammatory liberal rhetoric designed to destroy the traditional social order. Protectionist legislation such as the British Corn Laws was sought to be overturned by many conservatives, such as Robert Peel, although others, like Benjamin Disraeli, objected to pure *laissez-faire* policies. Disraeli's view of 'one nation' conservatism attempted to recognize common national interests among all of Britain's classes, which were manifested in a strong church, a responsible aristocracy, and prudent reform. The rise of trade unions in the late nineteenth century galvanized conservatives, who fiercely opposed bills to regulate child labor, factory conditions, pay, and the like.

Modern conservatism fuses elements of both Peel and Disraeli. Still viewing society as an organic whole, conservatives prize social relationships over extreme individualism, although most conservative ideologies hold that traditional institutions allow for a broad range of personal choice. In this way, personal morality is equated with the sanctity of the community: one's actions should reflect one's responsibility to society. Consequently, many conservative ideologies have strong links to the Church, which is viewed as a repository of historical mores. The family, moreover, is viewed as an extension of this moral authority, and the protection of children from harmful cultural manifestations such as pornography, drugs, and relativism receives much attention from conservatism. European conservatism tends to be more paternalistic than that of the United States, whose conservatives often espouse a 'boot straps' philosophy of economic and educational self-help. The 'new right' conservatism of Margaret Thatcher and the 'supply-side' economics of Ronald Reagan ushered in a phase of conservatism that minimized government interference – including taxation and costly environmental regulations – in economic matters. Marked by concerns for strong defense, Anglo-American conservatisms strongly resisted communism both abroad and within their own nations. Today, conservatism is enjoying an electoral renaissance, dominating the political agendas of many European nations and the United States, and even when liberalism prevails, it often has succeeded by appropriating conservative issues. Ultimately, conservative ideologies seek to preserve the existing order – Russell Kirk writes that 'hasty innovation may be a devouring conflagration, rather than a torch of progress' – and one may see 'conservative' elements within all of the ideologies under consideration in this chapter (Kirk 2001, 8).

To its practitioners, **socialism** offers a corrective both to the individualism of the liberal and the tradition of the conservative. Convinced that the group shapes the individual, socialists argue that the liberal faith in individual good ignores the underlying pathology of social injustice. Pointing to widening gaps between the rich and poor, despite the promises of liberalism and the free market, early socialists believed that the destruction of the *ancien régime* had not gone far enough and had merely substituted one oppressor for another, particularly as the peasant left the field and joined the industrial revolution as 'cheap' labor. Socialism refines the rational principles of the *philosophes* and applies them to every segment of society, not just the middle classes. For the socialist, a society built on Justice must lack the divisiveness of class. Public, rather than private, ownership of the means of production will, according to socialism, lead to a community based on equality and mutual need. Universal access to goods replaces the free market, and the circumstances of work are voluntary: reasonable people will see the necessity of serving the collective to satisfy personal need. Incentives are non-monetary, with many socialisms abolishing money altogether. In some systems, worker cooperatives would barter with one another for needed goods and services. With all of one's needs met, one could experience life as more than economic struggle, and 'self-interest' would wither away, to be replaced with altruism and love. As can be expected with any system based in abstract principles, there are wide variances within the ideology of socialism. Despite – or perhaps because of – its multitude of redactions, socialism proved to be a widely influential ideology, particularly in Europe and Latin America. In the public conscious-ness, however, socialism is often indistinguishable from communism, and it is viewed as an attempt to 'steal' the products of one's labor.

Early instances of the ideology, such as those advocated by Charles Fourier and Robert Owen, are often referred to as utopian (Marx preferred 'uncritical') socialisms. These socialist ideologies revealed a pronounced belief in human perfectibility, a concept broached by the Enlightenment philosophers, and, more distantly, by Thomas More. While many of the theorists of the French and American revolutions reserved the applicability of 'natural rights' to the bourgeoisie, some held with François Babeuf that exclusion-ary practices undermined the very notion of liberty. Babeuf, who was executed by the French Directory for his socialist instigation, produced a 'Manifesto of Equals' (1796), which called for a com-munal state and an end to private property. Babeuf's 'conspiracy of equals' was roundly crushed, but its ideas anticipated many later socialist movements, including that of Fourier. While Babeuf's work generally remained in the realm of the metaphysical, the theories of Fourier provide a methodology for achieving a socialist 'utopia.' Essentially agrarian in nature, Fourier's socialism calls for self-sufficient farming communities or '*phalanges.*' In these communities, such as the one founded by American transcendentalists at Brook Farm, human energies would be channeled in a new, invigorating way that would provide an outlet for the 'passions' as well as allow time for leisurely pursuits. Unlike Babeuf, Fourier retained some measure of private property, and he saw the necessity of rotating pleasant and unpleasant tasks among commune members. Another French socialist, Henri de Saint-Simon, also made use of a modified capitalism. Contra to most socialists, Saint-Simon proposed a hierarchy of classes designed to increase production and improve the lot of the lowest class. Saint-Simon's socialism thus shares many traits with the paternalism of liberals such as Roosevelt and conservatives like Disraeli. A final utopian socialist of importance is Owen, whose experiments in New Lanark and New Harmony (Indiana) proved mixed. Unlike Fourier, Owen applied his theories to industrial as well as agrarian conditions, and he was quite active in the promotion of trade unions, a hallmark of later socialism.

As the utopian socialist experiments failed to produce harmonious communities – a point parodied by Nathaniel Hawthorne in *The Blithedale Romance* (1852 [1985]) – more 'scientific' socialisms began to assess their errors and provide new solutions to the increasingly hostile relations between the working classes and their more affluent employers. Karl Marx – whose communist theories will be discussed below – Louis Blanc, Edith Nesbit, and others developed more pragmatic socialisms that rejected what Marx calls the 'fantasies' of earlier projects (Marx 1978, 497). Blanc eschewed the ornate rhetoric of utopians such as Fourier, grounding his arguments in the practical realm of employment rights, bourgeois avarice, and reform. Blanc, a member of the provisional French government following the 1848 Revolution, recognized that the middle class would not advocate sweeping reforms such as the absolute right to work, and he thus planned a multi-staged socialism predicated first on the enlargement of popular franchise and then, once representatives sympathetic to socialist causes were in place, on the establishment of cooperative means of production. As with Marx, Blanc realized that socialism depended not on the innate goodness of humanity but on specific historical circumstances. Such conditions prevailed in the latter half of the nineteenth century, when schisms between the 'proletariat' and the manufacturers, combined with depressed economic markets, prompted workers to mobilize.

Socialism increasingly identified itself with trade unionism, and socialists such as Eugene V. Debs and Victor L. Berger found a willing audience among the marginalized workers that they addressed. Checks against *laissez-faire* economics such as the eight-hour work day, minimum wage, the right to strike, and collective bargaining all find roots in socialist ideology. The middle classes, however, grew to despise socialism, and sought to suppress the ideology. As suffrage expanded, though, socialist ideology did begin to 'infiltrate' mainstream liberalism and paternal conservatism, ultimately transforming into 'social democracy.' Employing gradualist methods, social democracy attempts to establish a worker's party that will bring proletarian concerns to the political forefront and win victories via education and legislation. Examples of such socialism include Nesbit and Hubert Bland's Fabian Society and the US Socialist Party. Currently, socialism has a strong influence in countries such as Italy, Canada, France, Germany, and Great Britain, and state-run industry is common.

Frequently conflated with socialism, **communism** establishes as public not only the means of production, but the results of that production as well. A 'scientific socialism,' communism views history as a series of 'inevitable' stages culminating in a proletarian revolution that will result in true equality. Free-market phenomena such as competition, private property, and profit are eliminated. While many classic liberals assert that such concepts will lead to personal liberty, communists denounce 'bourgeois freedom' as crude self-interest that necessarily estranges individuals from one another. Only by casting off the chains of self-interest can one be truly liberated. Most communist ideologies also call for the elimination of the Church. Prior to the establishment of a communist state, class antagonism will arise naturally from the imbalances inherent in capitalism. By sharing both the means and ends of production, such divisiveness will abate. Following an economic plan, production will employ principles of social utility rather than profitability. Consequently, the need for political rulers would be eliminated and everyone would live in harmony.

Without question the most influential communist thinker, Marx based his version of communism on the scientific principles of historical materialism, which analyze how human – rather than 'natural' or 'divine' – forces have created the material conditions of society. Human labor shapes societal relations and its concomitant institutions. Dialectical in nature, societal organization results from the struggle between groups with conflicting economic interests, such as capitalists and the proletariat. For Marx, the shift from late capitalism to socialism and then to communism is a precise evolutionary process, for capitalism holds within itself the seeds of its own destruction. The paradox of liberal capitalism is that it eventually moves toward monopoly, placing more wealth ('surplus value') in fewer hands, an intolerable situation that will lead to violent revolt. Marx was extremely prolific, arguing for his theories in such works as the *Communist Manifesto* (1848), *Capital* (1867), and the *Grundrisse* (1857). He did not limit himself to polemics, however, and he took a major role in the International Workingmen's Association, where he successfully battled with Mikhail Bakunin. Many critics have asserted that Marx misjudges the interests of the proletariat, denying them motivation beyond economic need. Marx is also fairly ambiguous in describing when or how the proletarian revolution would occur, specifically since a majority of the proletariat had not yet achieved 'class consciousness.'

Such questions did not sway Marx's followers, however. The sheer bulk of Marx's output, combined with the ambiguities and contradictions arising from his evolution as a thinker, produced a multitude of interpretations and modifications of 'classic' Marxism and, unlike many of the ideologies discussed below, several successful revolutions attempted to implement communist principles. According to Marx, the proletarian revolution should start in the most advanced capitalist nations, such as Germany and Great Britain. In reality, however, communism first arose in Tsarist Russia. Vladimir Lenin, the most politically able of a band of Russian Marxists, rejected the premise that revolution needed to arise from historical conditions (Leon Trotsky would later create the theory of combined development, which is 'an amalgam of archaic with more contemporary forms,' to rationalize this major departure from orthodox Marxism [Trotsky 1973, 4]). Rather than rely on themselves to stage the revolution, the proletariat required – according to Lenin – a revolutionary elite, or vanguard, whose task it would be to develop the communist political, cultural, and economic agenda. Seizing the opportunity of World War I, Lenin succeeded in overthrowing the Tsar and the intermediate government established following his execution. Lenin then proceeded to entrench the vanguard party, which increasingly controlled every aspect of Russian life, a phenomenon that Hannah Arendt studies in *The Origins of Totalitarianism* (1968). Lenin later backed off from his economic plans, instituting the 'new economic policy,' which restored a limited capitalist market. Following Lenin's death, a power struggle between Joseph Stalin, Nikolai Bukharin, and Trotsky resulted in Stalin's victory. The autocratic Stalin solidified the principle of an elite party, killing all who opposed his agenda. Under Stalin and the leaders who followed him, communism lost all pretense of being a worker's revolution. Territorial expansionism – resulting in a 'cold war' pitting Soviet-controlled Eastern bloc nations against NATO – and tight control of Soviet citizens failed to improve, and often dramatically weakened, the standard of living for the proletariat.

As efforts at communism in such nations as The People's Republic of China and Cuba yielded similar results, many contemporary communist and socialist theorists argue that true communism has never truly been implemented, even though dozens of nations claimed to be communist in the twentieth century. Of course, similar objections might be made by partisans of any ideology, for 'pure' ideology is probably impossible, as too many factors and 'vestigial' remnants of competing ideologies drive toward hybridization. With the fall of the Soviet Union, advocates of communism are quick to point out that the human rights violations, aggressive expansionism, and economic and political elitism in that nation were the result not of the ideology, but of corrupt leadership. Distancing themselves from such leaders as Fidel Castro and Jiang Zemin, many contemporary communists seem to look back to utopian communism, although they ground their beliefs in various Marxist texts. As with fascism, however, communism has been perhaps permanently marked by the deplorable historical record of its most visible practitioners, a fact noted with relish by its legion of detractors. Interestingly, Stalin's principal internecine enemy, Trotsky – whom he had assassinated in 1940 – continues to attract followers to his idea of 'permanent revolution' and international socialism. Some of these latter-day Trotskyites encourage the Fabian-like policy of 'entryism,' which believes that communists should penetrate dominant political parties while continuing to work toward communist goals. With the advent of the Internet, communism continues to attract new followers among young idealists.

Nationalism, often associated with conservatism and populism, replaces the personal loyalty evident in feudalism with an allegiance to common identity. A relatively new ideology, nationalism first sought to replace *ancien régime* loyalties to individual leaders with an allegiance to an overarching idea of the State and its concomitant culture. In this way, leaders and political systems may be corrupt, but nations themselves are transcendent. Nationalist ideologies stress the benefits of autonomy and suggest that only a truly unified people may break free from external forces. The source of such unification finds its origin in a number of attributes, including language, religion, natural boundaries, 'culture,' commerce, race, and ethnicity. Predictably, the characteristics defining a nation are subjective and highly contentious, as individuals within the same geographic region may select different traits around which to rally. Redrawing existing political boundaries to conform with a particular vision of national features, then, is often the principal goal of nationalist ideologies. For Benedict Anderson, nations per se are necessarily 'imagined' because a true social contract à la Rousseau is impossible once a population expands beyond the point where 'face-to-face contact' may be maintained (Anderson 1983, 5). Anderson further argues that nationalism is marked by an illusion of 'deep, horizontal comradeship' that creates an impression of community (7). Such communal links are generally strengthened through emotional appeals to 'patriotism.' Toward this end, leaders often romanticize the nation's past achievements and portray citizens' ties to their nations as filial and eternal. Chameleon-like, nationalism usually merges with other ideologies – communism, for example, in 1950s Vietnam, or militarism in nineteenth-century Prussia – and spans the political spectrum from right to left. John Breuilly usefully subcategorizes nationalist ideologies into those involving separation, reform, and unification, wherein the first rubric describes nationalisms, such as Bloc Québecois, that seek to sever their relationship with an existing political entity, the second class (contemporary French nationalists, for example) desires to reenvision an extant state, and the third group (1860s Italy, for instance) attempts to fuse disparate entities into one nation (Breuilly 1985, 12). In nearly all instances of nationalism, psychological, rather than intellectual, motivation drives the movement.

Historically, nationalism finds its roots in the American and French revolutions. As seen in chapter 3, Enlightenment thought rejected the 'divine right' of kings to rule a populace and developed various conceptions of the 'social contract,' wherein individuals agreed to form a government. Consequently, nations and people were viewed as, theoretically, one and the same. Based on this principle, as Heywood observes, nationalism begins as 'a revolutionary and democratic creed, reflecting that "subjects of the crown" should become "citizens of France"' (Heywood 1998, 152). It was not until 1848 and after, however, that nationalism began to show its wide appeal. Otto von Bismarck, for example, capitalized on nationalist sentiments – backed by vigorous force – to create a unified German nation out of hitherto disparate independent states. Bismarck's success illustrates two major aspects of nationalism: myth and compulsion. To gain support for his plans, Bismarck exploited Prussia's historical importance in the region, as well as its past military glory. At the same time, he embarked on a series of wars that both solidified Prussia's power and gave other German states little choice as to their part in the new 'nation.' Eric J. Hobsbawm argues that 'nationalism requires too much belief in what is patently not so,' and Bismarck's 'blood and iron' nationalism seems to confirm him (Hobsbawm 1990). Anticipating many later nationalist movements, Bismarck's pan-German nation forced multitudes to believe in a mythic Germany greater than the sum of its parts.

In the twentieth and twenty-first centuries, nationalism manifested itself in a wide variety of fashions, many of which had little to do with geographical boundaries or political states. Because of the powerful emotions it unleashes, nationalism often prompts fierce resistance and uncritical, dogmatic rhetoric. Nationalisms in Nazi Germany, Japan, Vietnam, Serbia, and elsewhere have questioned the national boundaries of competing states and sparked bloody conflicts. Following Breuilly's paradigm, one may readily see 'separatist' nationalism in the contemporary United States (e.g., the Nation of Islam), Canada (Bloc Québecois), the Middle East (the Palestinians, Zionism), Western Europe (IRA, Basques), and the former Yugoslavia (Serbs, Croats et al.). The rise of the European Union, moreover, has galvanized nationalist sentiments against a global 'new world order' that erases 'traditional' nations such as France and Switzerland. A similar fear of **globalism** (contra nationalism) may be seen in populist American rhetoric casting suspicion on such entities as the United Nations and the World

Court. Interestingly, such opponents of globalism generally also oppose the nationalist claims of minority groups within their boundaries, frequently citing 'history' to support their resistance. Ironically, as this section has attempted to illustrate, nationalism as such is a recent conception, and the geographical boundaries that seem permanent now were typically contingent on conquest, inheritance, purchase, and the like. Nevertheless, nationalist narratives – with their reliance on selective history, sacred talismans, and identity politics – continue to strike an emotional chord with the populace.

Sharing some nationalist characteristics, **fascism**, as opposed to anarchism, grounds itself in the belief that the State – far from being an instrument of oppression – strengthens freedom. As with most ideological terms, the word fascism is frequently, and rather loosely, applied to a wide variety of political philosophies. In common usage, the label 'fascist' most often refers to 'far right' or 'ultra conservative' positions, but lately it is being employed as an invective against dogmatic or 'politically correct' left-wing politics as well. Underlying both applications is a suspicion of the extreme, the rigid, and what Gregor deems '"pathological" political phenomena' (Gregor 2000, 2). The popular usage might best be summed up by the teenager lamenting the curfew imposed by her 'fascist' parents. While such connotations do anchor themselves in a grain of truth, they dramatically oversimplify a complex twentieth-century political phenomenon. Pejorative definitions of fascism emphasize the ideology's interest in control and political chauvinism, but the roots of fascism stem from populist – and often socialist – revolution.[1] Indeed, collectively, rather than individually, oriented, fascism marked a radical departure from the Enlightenment principles of the *philosophes* and a return toward a more Hobbesian view of the state. Paradoxically, strict obedience to one's leader would yield freedom and national superiority. One must willingly accept one's place in the hierarchy to achieve success. Although the individual must not bristle against his or her position in the State, the State itself must exercise its will – often violently – or face extinction or, worse, subordination. Constant movement, then, is integral to fascist ideology, and such motion typically manifests itself via military expansion. For the fascist, passive states, such as Poland in 1939, inevitably yield to the 'natural' order, and in this way fascism combines elements of both Herbert Spencer and

Friedrich Nietszche. Avowedly anti-intellectual, fascism replaces consistent, thoroughly examined doctrine with what has been disparagingly labelled the 'cult of personality': the driving force of a powerful leader. Emotions and will supersede the 'weak' realm of ideas.

The history of fascism, then, is a history of its leaders, some of whom committed atrocities of incredible magnitude in the name of national glory. While fascism and its allied ideology, national socialism, arose (independently) during the post-World War I era, Benito Mussolini, one of its principal founders, argues that it was 'a general reaction of modern times against the flabby materialistic positivism of the nineteenth century' (Mussolini 1959, 411). The fledgling democracies of the late eighteenth and nineteenth centuries dramatically changed the social landscape of the time, but they were frequently inadequate in facing the economic instability brought about by such significant alterations. Consequently, to the working class, many such governments appeared weak and subject to chaos. Fascists such as Mussolini, therefore, initially sought to bring order to their respective countries. In Italy, Mussolini, a former socialist editor, exploited the fears of an eclectic mixture of conservative and socialist sympathizers who were dissatisfied with both economic hardship and the perceived threat of communism. Breaking with the socialists over Italy's (non) participation in World War I, Mussolini organized his Fascist Party nationally in 1921. With meteoric speed, Mussolini became Italy's premier in 1922, after marching on Rome and demanding an audience with the king. Thereafter, Mussolini pursued a policy of aggressive, often brutal, foreign intervention, including invasions of Ethiopia and Albania and an alliance with Hitler's Germany. Spurring his *Fasci di combattimento* fighting units, whose distinctive attire earned them the name 'black shirts,' to quash all opposition – be it from the right or left – savagely, Mussolini indeed stabilized Italian politics, but he did so at the expense of free debate. The nebulous nature of Mussolini's ultimate goals, moreover, tended to subvert any tentative reforms and established the Italian Fascist Party as being 'against' other ideologies but not as having a positivist function of its own. As Richard Thurlow remarks, 'fascism was and is an action-oriented movement, where the function of ideas is to explain behavior more in term of instinct than rationality' (Thurlow 1987, x). Ultimately, it may have been this lack of vision, as well as his doomed alliance with Hitler, that prompted anti-fascist Italians to execute him in 1945. Roger Griffin observes: 'the regime's comprehensive failure to "Fascistize" (inculcate with Fascist values) all but a minority of Italians...was to seal its fate' (Griffin and Krazanowski 1995, 16). Largely dependent upon the illusion of infallible, vigorous leadership, Italy's fascist party never again proved a major force in the country's political scene.

Another major example of fascist ideology may be found in Adolf Hitler's Germany, although some scholars distinguish between Hitler's brand of National Socialism and 'true' fascism. Nevertheless, the similarities between the two ideologies are strong enough to warrant consideration here, and Mussolini did ultimately adopt an official anti-Semitic stance similar to the one that served as Hitler's ideological base. Reacting independently to the economic turmoil spurred by the Versailles Treaty – one thinks, for example, of the image of a German *hausfraü* hauling a wheelbarrow full of cash to buy a single loaf of bread – Hitler's National Socialist German Workers (Nazi) Party rose to power in 1932 with the same preternatural speed of Mussolini's *fasci*. Like Mussolini, Hitler capitalized on the wounded nationalism of his countrymen, but unlike his unfocused ally, Hitler established a much more defined – and harrowing – ideology based on Aryan supremacy, a claim 'empirically' supported by dubious science. Selectively employing symbols of prior German 'glory,' Hitler and his lieutenants (including Paul Goebbels, Hermann Goering, and Heinrich Himmler, among others) devised a myth in which Germany's formidable national power had been drained slowly but systematically by decadent interlopers such as Jews, gays, the physically debilitated, and Catholics. Once such elements were 'eliminated,' Germany would continue toward its inevitable destiny of global domination. Despite the distorted logic of the message conveyed by Hitler's *Mein Kampf* and the deluge of propaganda produced under Goebbels' control, the ideology took hold among many, and the show of force from the *Gestapo* and other organizations compelled the rest to follow, crushing all outward displays of opposition. No aspect of German culture escaped notice of the Nazis. Art, literature, athletics, commerce: all institutions were to exemplify the German 'ideal' and be purged of the 'enervating' influence of the Jew, who was first 'concentrated' into ghettos and then ultimately – and savagely – executed *en masse*. Similar to Mussolini, Hitler believed that territorial expansion offered a testament to his country's superiority. Unlike Mussolini, however, Hitler possessed a massive infrastructure and was far more adept at invading rival nations. Fortunately, Hitler underestimated the fortitude of the Allied nations, and the German juggernaut was destroyed. Facing certain execution, Hitler committed suicide in 1945.

Mussolini and Hitler were no doubt the primary examples of fascist leaders, but they are by no means the only fascists to achieve power. Among others, Francisco Franco, António de Olivera Salazar, Miklós Horthy de Nagybánya, and Jósef Pilsudski all employed fascist ideologies. The lessons of World War II, of course, dramatically lessened the ideology's appeal, but persistent efforts to renew fascism's influence continue. Neo-Nazis and other international fascist organizations have found a modicum of support among disaffected youth (especially adolescent males) by exploiting their racial and economic fears. Ironically, as Griffin points out, contemporary fascism frequently transcends the nationalism of earlier incarnations, opting for a more global outlook (2000, 6). The current movement tends to use a two-pronged approach, offering academic-sounding arguments on the one hand while relying on grassroots anger and organization on the other. Writers such as Alex Curtis and Louis Beame and periodicals such as *Mankind Quarterly* and *Nouvelle Ecole* purport to revise the status quo and expose media-driven 'myths' such as racial profiling and genetic racial equality.[2] At the local level, charismatic leaders such as Matthew Hale, distill the quasi-intellectual language for mass consumption. Many of the converts, race-based spree killer Benjamin Smith,[3] for example, to contemporary American fascism belie the working-class image of Mussolini's *fasci* and possess affluent suburban backgrounds. Vulnerable for a variety of reasons – divorced parents, suburban segregation, lack of popularity, and even simple boredom, for instance – these youth find solace in the racist theories of the street recruiter (or the anonymous web page) and the prospect of 'finally' acting on their angst. While a wide variety of beliefs differentiates the various international fascist movements, they are united in their suspicion of 'aliens,' the United Nations, racial 'impurity,' and American imperialism. Many fascist organizations would balk at the label – and at other appellations like racist or terrorist – preferring names such as 'World Church of the Creator,' 'Front National,' or the 'National Alliance' and espousing 'separatism,' 'pride,' and 'purity.' The euphemisms of 'mainstream' fascist organizations (the trench-level organizations, such as the 'Hammerskins,' of course, thrive on the blunt language of racial hatred) often make it hard at first to distinguish them from more leftist ideologies. In their book *Ecofascism: Lessons from the German Experience* (1996), for example, Janet Biehl and Peter Staudenmaier claim that contemporary fascists have co-opted the rhetoric of the left-wing 'green' ideology, substituting 'overpopulation' for their less popular ideas about eugenics and racial superiority. In this way, contemporary fascism often turns on a curious paradox: its conservative- or libertarian-sounding rhetoric distances itself from its core beliefs.

Entirely at odds with the vision of the State emerging from nationalist and fascist ideologies, **anarchism** altogether denies sovereignty. Whatever their benign intentions, laws collectively work to oppress the individual and reward hierarchical power relations. At the beginning of the twentieth century, the popular notion of anarchy painted an image of wild-eyed, bomb-throwing zealots intent on destroying social harmony. Today, anarchy is frequently associated with teen angst of the sort parodied in Nirvana's video for 'Smells Like Teen Spirit': disaffected, self-mutilating adolescents staging a temporary rebellion against the authority of parents and teachers before ultimately settling into the suburban lifestyle. Neither portrait is very satisfying in capturing the ideological spirit of anarchy, however, and both miss the concept's grounding in rational principles. Nevertheless, both caricatures echo the pejorative origins of the term in the late eighteenth century. Literally meaning 'without a chief,' anarchy was initially used by critics of the French Revolution, such as Edmund Burke, as a description of societal chaos. The positivist definition – sometimes referred to as libertarian socialism – came much later, when in 1840 Pierre-Joseph Proudhon annexed it to his theory of property and absolute liberty.[4] As Proudhon and later thinkers employed the term, anarchy represents not harmful disorder but a return to unfettered liberty. According to Piotr Kropotkin, anarchism so defined constitutes 'a principle or theory of life and conduct under which society is conceived without government – Harmony in such a society being obtained not by submission to law, or by obedience to any authority, but by free agreements concluded between various groups' (Kropotkin 1910). In economic terms, one

might view the barter system as a type of anarchy wherein participants agree to trade their goods and services according to need.
Anarchy in this form is predicated on Enlightenment principles of
reason and thus views human nature as essentially good (but
subject to corruption via externally imposed 'order'). Anarchists,
therefore, scorn a priori thought, preferring to examine each
situation individually and determine a course of action based
on empirical evidence. Anarchism generally opposes hierarchies –
which ultimately stem from violence and oppression – and prefers
cooperative organization. 'Natural' law, rather than human-made
law, governs the anarchist: the universal need for warmth, shelter,
food, security, love and the like would be satisfied if institutional
interference ceased. For many anarchists (Leo Tolstoi is a notable
exception), atheism is a logical extension of the abolition of institutional hegemony. As with any political ideology, anarchy has its
share of factions, some of which will be discussed below.

By linking anarchy to a rejection of property ownership ('property
is the suicide of society'), Proudhon demands comparison to Marx
(Proudhon 1970, 214). Marx himself, however, referred to Proudhon
as an 'ideologist of the petty bourgeoisie' (Marx 1963, 159) who
'deifies' a *dualism* between life and ideas' (Marx 1978, 142, 141;
Marx's emphasis). For Marx, Proudhon commits the classic liberal
maneuver of accepting ideological constructs as eternal. Proudhon,
building upon the notion of social contract explored by Rousseau,
Paine, and other Enlightenment figures, indeed viewed the notion
of human rights as 'eternal,' but he argues that property is an 'anti-
social' natural right (1970, 43). That is, the concept of property
subverts liberty, equality, and security, the three 'absolute rights'
that he seeks to resurrect (43). Property obstructs the free exchange of
products between free individuals because, according to Proudhon,
it is based on the notion of profit. By abolishing property and the
profit motive, society will move closer to the natural ideal, which
for Proudhon involves the three absolute rights indicated above.
Thus, in its first representation, anarchy was closely allied with both
rationalism and socialism and sought to replace state-imposed
order with the 'natural' order that would appear once institutions
such as property were eradicated.

Another early anarchist, Mikhail Bakunin, briefly – and uneasily –
joined with Proudhon and Marx in the First International, but he
and his followers split into an independent organization soon

thereafter. Far more radical than Proudhon, Bakunin advocated a complete break with the past – nihilism – and supported the notion of an armed working class that would overthrow the ruling elite by any means necessary before ultimately living in an ideal cooperative society: 'the urge to destroy is also a creative urge' (Bakunin 1970). In works such as *God and the State* (1916) and *Revolutionary Catechism* (1866), Bakunin attempts to expose the self-serving and mystical status of bourgeois institutions such as the Church and parliamentary government. Peppered with aphorisms such as 'If God really existed, it would be necessary to abolish him,' Bakunin's texts assert that all permanent bureaucracies finally strive to perpetuate themselves, a condition that denies true freedom and frequently leads to war (Bakunin 1970). For Bakunin, even well-intentioned revolutionaries such as Marx err because of their substitution of one system for another and the creation of a new elite. Bakunin did see the need for central organization – isolated local anarchist movements would be easier to quell – but such an institution should be temporary. In its place, an educated populace, free from pecuniary worry, would decide the direction of society via rational consensus. Power would flow upward from the local to the strictly voluntary provincial and larger levels. As Bakunin represented it, then, anarchy involves a two-step process whereby violence must annihilate the bourgeois order before mass cooperation ensues.

Yet another version of anarchy appears in the writings of Georges Sorel, although, as Emma Goldman points out, its origins were in nineteenth-century European labor unions. Sorel advocates direct – sometimes violent – action intended to wrest control of the means of production from the elite classes. Frequently referred to as anarcho-syndicalism, this branch of anarchist ideology is predicated less on theory than on struggle. Indeed, the fascist Mussolini derived many of his concepts from Sorel's work. Nevertheless, anarcho-syndicalism, like other forms of anarchy, denies hierarchical government, opting instead for syndicates – loosely modeled on more moderate trade unions. As with Bakunin's version of anarchy, anarcho-syndicalism required that capitalist production paradigms be destroyed by general strikes, sabotage, and other means before installing a new order in which the syndicates would share power. For Sorel and other advocates of anarcho-syndicalism, traditional avenues such as trade unions and suffrage ultimately enhanced capitalist positions by pitting one group against another. For example, a college-level teacher's union might 'protect' its members' 12-hour class load by 'conceding' a 15-hour load for all members who join the union after the new contract goes into effect. In this way, anarcho-syndicalists would argue, management encroaches on workers' freedoms with the seeming approval of the union. Anarcho-syndicalists reject such methods, preferring aggressive tactics, such as assembly line slowdowns, that would hurt capitalist profits and display the combined power of the workers. Anarcho-syndicalism at first received substantial worldwide support and attracted such thinkers as Goldman and Alexander Berkman. As Goldman writes, 'the ultimate purpose of Syndicalism is to reconstruct society from its present centralized, authoritative, and brutal state to one based on the free, federated grouping of the workers along lines of economic and social liberty' (Goldman 1998, 90). In anarcho-syndicalism, Goldman sees a way to avoid internal dissension, for divisions such as 'seniority' are abolished. Goldman, of course, fuses her conception of anarcho-syndicalism with a sweeping social-libertarianism that embraces hitherto marginalized classes, including women, minorities, and gays. Furthermore, as Bonnie Haaland observes, Goldman extended anarchism well beyond the male theorists of her day and 'formulated a theory of anarchism in which the schism of public and private is absent' (Haaland 1993, 2). Goldman's anarchism, in other words, affected the family hearth as well as the factory. Anticipating later feminist critiques of hidden ideological structures, Goldman argues that even vestigial capitalist organizing principles could threaten the 'true' freedom that her male counterparts claimed to desire. Goldman's anarchism thus calls for a leveling of all hierarchical impediments. Not surprisingly, many of her theories were derided even within the anarchist community.

With the rise of Franco in Spain – where the anarchists had their primary foothold – anarchism lost much of its ideological cachet. Nevertheless, its appeal once again broadened in the late 1960s (especially following Paris in 1968), and it currently attracts thousands of followers worldwide. The Seattle 'events,' as many groups referred to the 1999 protest that ultimately caused over 3 million dollars worth of damage, provide an excellent point of departure for a brief discussion of contemporary anarchy. As with many less popular ideologies, anarchism employs the Internet extensively.

Joined by other Internet-driven ideologies, including various fascist, socialist, and environmental factions, several anarchist movements helped to disrupt the World Trade Organization's meeting in Seattle. Rather than presenting a unified ideology, anarchy now consists of a wide number of subideologies that often appear in conflict with one another. Groups such as Black Flag, the Green Anarchist Network, and the Solidarity Federation certainly do not agree on all points regarding methodology or goals. Some advocated violence, while others adopted the more peaceful course of the Libertarian party, the most extensively organized 'anarchist' movement. Spokespeople for some groups deplored the violent tactics of other anarchist groups, while other anarchists argued that civil disobedience would not accomplish their tasks in an expedient way. The Libertarian Party participates in elections, advocates free-market trade, and seeks to repeal legislation covering victimless crimes, whereas groups such as Black Flag scoff at concessions to traditional capitalism. While its influence does not begin to approach that of more established (and unified) ideologies, anarchism is attracting a growing number of youths worldwide.

Ignoring the 'artificial' boundaries of the State, **fundamentalism**(s) refute anarchist claims and posit that spiritual law should govern individual behavior. A relatively new term, fundamentalism initially referred to a specific early twentieth-century Protestant movement associated with the World Christian Fundamentals Association (founded in 1919). The first of 12 volumes, a 1909 miscellany titled *The Fundamentals* heralded an attempt to explain the inspired Word of God to a broad audience. The title itself may be an allusion to Blaise Pascal's *Pensées* (1660), for Section VIII, thought 556, is titled 'The Fundamentals of the Christian Religion' and exhorts people to avoid blaspheming the Bible (Pascal 1995). Helped by a distribution in the millions, the volume's title soon took on a broader connotation as a movement to preserve Christian orthodoxy. Ultimately, however, theorists applied the label fundamentalism to religions other than Christianity. Evangelical in nature, fundamentalism believes a priori in the infallibility of the holy text (e.g., the Torah or the Koran). Eschewing metaphoric or partial exegesis, fundamentalists insist on a literal, integrative interpretation of scripture that should direct all aspects of behavior. Often viewed as a corrective to progressive heterodoxy, fundamentalism frequently extends beyond the boundaries of the church, and acquires a political element. From the perspective of fundamentalism, secular humanism represents a threat to the spiritual order, a corruption of traditional mores. Its interest in revivalism, therefore, stems from a desire to resist the perceived moral atrophy of society at large. Denouncing secular governments as the decadent manifestations of non-believers, fundamentalists position themselves as being empowered by their Creator, and, thus, as able to act outside the constraint of temporal (profane) law. The propensity toward martyrdom associated with such ideologies exemplifies the steadfast belief that fundamentalists serve only their Creator. The unifying goal of such movements is the establishment of a society based solely on scriptural principles.

While theories regarding fundamentalism are the progeny of the twentieth century, the concept itself probably extends to the prehistoric era and exists in nearly every religion. Faced with secular 'decadence,' or even challenges from other religious leaders, orthodox clerics have attempted to purge their societies of 'impure' elements for millennia. The pilgrim William Bradford, for example, wrote *Of Plymouth Plantation, 1620–1647* (1650?) as a corrective to what he perceived as the 'backsliding' tendencies of the younger generation, while Oliver Cromwell's Puritans might profitably be viewed as a type of 'fundamentalist' movement. In twentieth-century Iran, the Ayatollah Khomeini ousted the Pahlavi regime and established a government based on his (selective) interpretation of the Koran. Khomeini also symbolized a tendency for Muslim fundamentalists to attempt to purge their societies (and, increasingly, the world) of secular influence via violent means, a pattern visible in incidents such as the assassination of Anwar Sadat and the 9/11 attacks. In latter-day America, fundamentalists such as Ralph Reed and Pat Robertson have attempted – rather successfully – to spur the 'moral majority' to political action. Controlling large voting blocs, various fundamentalist groups have united to exercise considerable influence on the platform of the Republican Party regarding abortion, gays, prayer in school, and the like. On the former issue, some fundamentalists echo Khomeini's violent tactics by destroying abortion clinics. Whatever their religion, fundamentalists tend to view themselves as spiritual warriors and look upon non-believers with extreme suspicion. This binary outlook precludes dialogue, for the fundamentalists will not question their 'revealed' truth (i.e., their sacred scriptures). In this way, fundamentalists perceive modernity as antithetical to their beliefs, for any deviation from their religion's origins is insidious. Interestingly, however, most fundamentalists avail themselves of modern technology. One thinks, for instance, of 'televangelists' such as Jerry Falwell or of Osama bin Laden's videotaped messages.

Obviously, such a broad concept as fundamentalism cannot account for individual differences between, say, Southern Baptists and Elijah Muhammad's Nation of Islam. Nevertheless, Heywood points out that 'as a programme for the comprehensive restructuring of society on religious lines and according to religious principles, fundamentalism deserves to be classified as an ideology in its own right' (1998, 294). In the twenty-first century, global fundamentalism is expanding rapidly, particularly in developing nations where wealth is extremely stratified. In promising a heavenly reward in lieu of the crass materialism of their secular enemies, the various fundamentalist groups find many of their recruits among the impoverished. Demoralized by exclusionary economic, social, and political systems, such individuals find hope in fundamentalist words deploring western excess, imperialism, and decadent, selfish rulers. Prior to 11 September 2001, several States had been established on fundamentalist Islamic principles, and despite anti-terrorist sentiments on the part of the United States, the ethos of martyrdom that such governments instill suggests that efforts to destroy them (in Afghanistan, for instance) may, in fact, strengthen their ability to gain legitimacy among the populace. In the United States and Britain, the paradoxical use of technology continues to spread fundamentalist ideology and encourage personal salvation and political activism. Whatever the manifestation, however, fundamentalism looks forward by looking backward to a return to unadulterated religious values in both the public and private sphere.

Like fundamentalism, **environmentalism** premises its ideology on a fluid definition of national borders. Global in scope, environmentalism professes a concern for the delicate balance between national (and self-) interests and ecological sustainability. Timothy O'Riordan describes this phenomenon in terms of 'technocentrism' (the husbandry of natural resources; human society takes precedence) and 'ecocentrism' (complete protection of natural resources; nature takes precedence) wherein the two terms represent extremes on a spectrum (O'Riordan 1981, 2). According to O'Riordan, who later modified his paradigm, most environmental movements fall somewhere in between the two poles. Broadly, environmental ideologies acknowledge that even ostensibly minor changes in an ecosystem may produce long-term adverse effects and that unchecked industrialism will inevitably lead to the Earth's devastation. Through means ranging from protest and government regulation to sabotage and violence, environmentalists seek to stop such phenomena as pollution, species extinction, deforestation, and (sub)urban sprawl. Nearly all environmental ideologies start from the ethical premise that anthropocentrism, or human-centered, ideologies are tragically flawed.

Its rise as an ideology coinciding roughly with the industrial revolution, environmentalism itself crops up periodically throughout recorded history. Benjamin Franklin, for instance, sought to protect the water supply from pollutants. Nevertheless, most pre-nineteenth-century 'environmentalists' conducted their efforts on an *ad hoc* basis, reacting to existing problems rather than looking toward future concerns. In the nineteenth and early twentieth centuries, however, technology and its byproducts encroached upon raw nature to such an extent that individual activists began to organize and call for sweeping reforms. Initially, environmentalists such as Henry David Thoreau called for conservationism, but as the effects of industrialization became more visible, more assertive approaches – like those advanced by John Muir, for example, began to appear, perhaps culminating in Rachel Carson's extremely influential book, *Silent Spring* (1962), and Greenpeace. Muir questioned the long-term efficacy of the so-called scientific logging advocated by such moderates as Gifford Pinchot and called for permanent preservation measures. As the twentieth century progressed, environmental ideologies increasingly became polarized between 'sustainability' advocates like Pinchot, who felt that resources needed to be husbanded in a more rational way, and biocentric proponents like Muir, who rejected a priori beliefs that nature served humanity.

The fierce dialogue between 'free-market environmentalists' and 'ecologism' exemplifies this contemporary split. The former groups, while recognizing the importance of long-term environmental planning, adhere to the concept that natural resources exist for the benefit of humanity. Such factions concentrate their efforts on industrial reform, recycling, reforestation, alternative energy, environmental education, and the like. Some free-market environmentalists also cite scriptural authority against the more radical 'ecologism,'[5] also known as 'green politics': God made nature for human consumption. Ecologism roundly denies this principle and argues that capitalism's exploitation of nature is morally corrupt. In its critique of consumerism, ecologism rejects anthropocentrism and argues for the supremacy of nature. Human needs are considered secondary, and humans must consider the impact of their actions on the larger ecosystem(s). In achieving this task, advocates of ecologism themselves are divided, with some, like those professing a need for 'deep ecology,' preferring peaceful – even spiritual – methods, while others, such as the Earth Liberation Front, might be seen as 'eco-anarchists' in their use of violence. Another popular version of ecologism is ecofeminism, which seeks to connect environmental problems with patriarchal institutions.

Politically, environmentalism is expanding, particularly in Europe, and especially in Germany, where Green Party candidates regularly achieve victory by appropriating a wide range of liberal and socialist platforms. In the United States, the Green Party's Ralph Nader significantly affected the outcome of the 2000 presidential election, and in the United Kingdom, Green Party members have been elected to Parliament. While such popular success generally remains the exception, it suggests a far broader political base than other nascent ideologies – such as anarchism – may claim. One may also register the ideology's growth by the opposition's willingness to appropriate its message – Labour and Democratic candidates frequently point out that conservative environmental policy is flawed – and by the creation of ostensibly nature-friendly legislation such as the United States' 'Clean Air Act.' Another measure of environmentalism's increasing influence is the virulence of 'mainstream' attacks against it. While few talk-radio conservatives even mention anarchism or fascism, they frequently target environmentalists for their wrath, charging that the ideology is merely clandestine socialism or that reports of ozone depletion are based on 'faulty liberal science.' In any event, green politics continues to attract legions of young people and brings its issues to the forefront of the international stage.

Feminism is another ideology that transcends traditional notions of the state. Discovering the roots of injustice in the hierarchical, competitive relationships built upon gender exploitation, many feminisms attempt to develop new social paradigms that eschew aggression and subordination. Generally, feminist ideologies pre-suppose the social construction of gender, although some subcat-egories do employ biological models. In this way, most versions of feminism seek to dissolve or extensively modify every aspect of society where sex hierarchy exists and substitute institutions grounded in equality. Concomitantly, feminism seeks to revalue millennia of female achievements ignored or scorned by men and allow voiceless subalterns to 'speak.' As these two goals suggest, feminism thus acknowledges an unquestionable link between cultural production and political oppression, with the political realm extending far beyond the so-called public sphere. The very structure of institutions such as family, church, school, language, literature,[6] government, and commerce contains both explicit and implicit patriarchal bias that is self-perpetuating. Even so-called liberal and leftist ideologies that are ostensibly sympathetic to equality often fail to deal effectively with this fundamental binary, for it is so entrenched as to be 'internalized' as 'universal.' Feminists attempt to ferret out this insidious hegemony and end the sub-ordination of women.

Prior to the achievements of the feminist movement, women in most societies were legally the chattel, or property, of their fathers or husbands. Most could not legally own property, vote, divorce, acquire an education, practice birth control, or work at jobs other than menial ones or those in the 'pink-collar' areas (e.g., nursing, teaching). The so-called 'first wave' of western feminism (roughly 1789–1920), then, concentrated on securing the basic human rights defined by classic liberalism. Early theorists such as Mary Wollstonecraft, Olympe de Gourges, and Marie Jean Antoine Nicholas de Caritat, Marquis de Condorcet[7] exposed a basic para-dox in the Enlightenment thought of the *philosophes*: while the French Revolution was predicated on fundamental freedoms, full citizenship was not extended to women. Equality, they argued, was not the sole province of men. In the mid-nineteenth century, numerous feminist groups formed in Britain and the United States. Exemplifying the former groups was the one established by Barbara Leigh Smith, which petitioned for passage of the Married Women's Property Act and later formed the *Englishwoman's Journal*, a periodical dedicated to advancing women's issues. Emmeline Pankhurst, a major British 'suffragette,' organized the Women's Social and Political Union, which held major rallies and protests designed to grant women the vote. Initially non-violent, the WSPU ultimately employed violent methods to achieve its goal. Feminist groups in the United States, viewing all oppression as violating the spirit of the Constitution,[8] frequently allied themselves with abolitionist causes. In 1848, Elizabeth Cady Stanton and Lucretia Mott organized the first Women's Rights Convention and composed a 'Declaration of Sentiments' that outlined the group's political concerns. In 1850, the convention went national, and at the second national convention, Sojourner Truth levied charges – that feminists such as bell hooks would echo over a hundred years later – that the movement was primarily concerned with white, middle-class women, a bias reflected in leaders such as Susan B. Anthony. In both Britain and the United States, feminism developed strong links to the labor movement, resulting in actions such as the Shirtwaist Strikes of 1909–10. With the demands asked of women during World War I fully satisfied, the suffrage movement confidently pushed forward, ultimately securing the vote in the United Kingdom in 1918 and the United States in 1920. As the right to vote became closer to reality, other first-wave feminists, such as Margaret Sanger, sought accessible contraception (reproductive control), better working conditions, and an equal rights amendment, among other improvements.

Some theorists argue that first-wave feminism does not constitute an ideology per se, and claim that it resembled a political movement rather than a system of thought. Nevertheless, the 'political' victories of the first wave proved insufficient, for prescribed gender roles and institutionalized sexism thwarted women from achieving – even from desiring – equality with men and the prospect of self-actualization. By the late 1940s, women had not yet achieved parity in the public sphere, and some feminists, such as Simone de Beauvoir, began to critique society's inherent bias against women. In America, the second wave of feminism found its catalyst in the work of Betty Friedan, whose book *The Feminist Mystique* (1963 [2001]) proved tremendously influential and popular. While first-wave feminism generally did not overtly challenge traditional gender roles, second-wave feminism resoundingly objected to such prescriptions, as well as their institutional counterparts. Friedan accumulated tremendous amounts of data that implicated exclusionary social practices in the emotional and physical oppression of women. Founding the National Organization for Women in 1966, Friedan sought to move beyond issues of suffrage and establish true choice for women. A major goal of Friedan and other feminists such as Gloria Steinem, Kate Millett, and Germaine Greer, was to raise the 'consciousness' of the average woman. Faced with severe backlash, such an ambitious task involved not only exposing the 'natural' state of gender relations as a socially created product but demystifying even the most 'liberal' organizations as having a patriarchal structure. Like its predecessor, second-wave feminism looked toward specific political goals as well, including reproductive rights, marital rape, equal pay for equal work, sexual discrimination (in arenas such as education, the workforce, and the family), childcare, female circumcision, and the Equal Rights Amendment (originally drafted by first-wave activist Alice Paul). Additionally, religious, ethnic, and racial minorities, along with economically disadvantaged women, began to organize feminist groups designed for their particular needs. Because it so radically questioned previous ideologies, second-wave feminism is clearly a 'stand alone' ideology, even though it may combine with socialism, liberalism, and the like. Based on the deceptively simple premise that biology is not destiny, second-wave feminism effected sweeping socio-political changes across the globe. As with Marx and Engels' camera obscura simile, second-wave feminism argued that social relations were based on a corrupt, 'upside down' foundation that must be fixed. Denying the dichotomy between the domestic and public spheres, second-wave feminism declared that the 'personal is political.' In so doing, many feminists argued, contra Marx, that gender, not economics, was the basis of social relationships involving power.

With the death of the Equal Rights Amendment in 1982, second-wave feminism came to an end.[9] While many of its goals materialized – such as reproductive rights, no-fault divorce, career choice, and co-education; and the Civil Rights Act of 1964 theoretically ensured legal equality – many other issues remained unresolved. Roughly, one may categorize third-wave feminism in two groups, the popular and the academic. On the popular front, third-wave feminism, while acknowledging the important work of second wavers, seeks to empower women without 'demonizing' men or creating a culture of victimization. Reacting to the perceived 'backlash' against 'radical' feminists such as Andrea Dworkin or Mary Daly, theorists such as Camille Paglia and Susan Faludi reject

separatist rhetoric in favor of a practical feminism that concentrates
on equity rather than on gender. Such a broad-based agenda is
designed to reclaim feminism from its enemies, who have been
successful in tagging 'feminism' as a monolithic quest to destroy
family, church, and country. Encouraging self-definition, many of
the popular third-wave feminists believe that women can be fulfilled
regardless of whether they choose a career, a family, or both, and
they feel that much second-wave rhetoric was damaging to the
self-esteem of those who chose not to enter the workforce. Issues
such as body consciousness, role models, diversity, sexual harassment, domestic violence, cultural representation, education, and
equal pay are pervasive. Autonomy unhindered by the hegemonies
of right or left is paramount, and popular third wavers cover the
political spectrum. Popular third wavers tend to be in their thirties
or younger, a phenomenon that leads some second wavers to accuse
them of historical myopia, neo-conservatism, and even patriarchal
complicity.

   Increasingly academic in focus, especially in France and the
United States, the other major strand of third-wave feminism finds
its primary outlet in women's studies programs, although political
activism continues globally. The ideological characteristics of third-
wave feminism are, as with all of the ideologies described here,
multifold, and often contradictory. Among many of the numerous
feminisms are transfeminism, cyberfeminism, materialist feminism,
Christian feminism, and postmodern feminism. While western
feminists obviously draw their inspiration from a variety of sources,
they often acknowledge French feminists as the pioneers of third-
wave ideology. Women such as Julia Kristeva, Luce Irigaray, and
Hélène Cixous modified poststructuralist theories of psychoanalysis, linguistics, and philosophy to reflect feminist issues long
before their counterparts in countries such as Great Britain and the
United States. In the work of these prolific writers, one sees a concern less with patriarchal structures as such (although all three
women recognize the inherently oppressive assumptions undergirding most institutions) than with attempts to recover, reinscribe, and reinvigorate the feminine as subject. Cixous's concept
of *écriture féminine*, for example, strives to merge written discourse
and the feminine body by exploding binary ('rational,' 'logical,'
'empirical') oppositions designed to trap women in an inferior
position of 'other.' By repositioning the feminine into the realm of

(speaking) subject, such writers subvert the 'universal' or 'natural' truths that subordinate women. Following this line of thought, feminists such as Jane Gallop, Elaine Showalter, Sandra Gilbert, and Susan Gubar have emphasized feminine subjectivity and tradition much more than did, say, Millett or Steinem. Complicating this agenda – and other theoretically inclined feminisms like it – however, are western minority and non-western feminists like hooks, Gayatri Spivak, and Nawal El Saadawi who frequently claim that such academic preciousness reveals a white, middle-class bias that echoes the patriarchy even as it seeks to eliminate it. Questioning the efficacy of 'one size fits all' feminism, hooks, for instance, argues that because oppression transcends gender feminism must include serious analysis of race, class, sexual orientation, ethnicity, and other factors. So-called 'postcolonial' feminists such as Spivak often focus on issues of alterity and also problematize the assumptions of middle-class academic feminists. Clearly, feminism is among the most fragmented of the ideologies under consideration here, but its dramatic proliferation in the last half century also makes it one of the most influential. Regardless of specific methods, feminist ideologies all strive to reconceptualize the way societies view gender and power.

Obviously, any concise grouping of political ideologies is fraught with oversimplification and omission. The subideologies of anarchism alone, for example, are legion, and efforts to establish sweeping rubrics easily fall prey to charges of reductionism. Such essentialism is precisely the point, however, when analyzing how the concept of ideology functions outside of the academic arena. Difference dissolves into easily digestible platitudes that may be spread by any number of media. In this way, the myriad of feminist approaches collapses into Rush Limbaugh's 'feminazi' bent on destroying the heterosexual family, and the socialist becomes Joseph McCarthy's amoral saboteur poised to squelch individual identity. Academics, of course, may scoff at such simple-minded formulae, but they cannot deny the power of these ideological stereotypes. For some, such as Althusser, popular ideological stereotypes combined with an uncritical acceptance of one's own ideology as 'common sense' or 'natural' serve to perpetuate the status quo and its concomitant power base. In this way, even hotly debated issues – such as those in the disputed American presidential election of 2000 – reflect merely different facets of a single ideology virtually invisible to its practitioners. Viewed from the outside, the differences between George W. Bush and Albert Gore, Jr are minimal, despite their apparent disdain for each other's positions. Nevertheless, within the American system, even minor variances within a single party – for example, those between Bush and John McCain – are conceived of as significant ideological polarities.

The 2000 election represents not an aberration but the popular rule in how ideology is perceived by most non-academics. Despite the refinements and qualifications advanced since the late eighteenth-century introduction of the term 'ideology,' Napoleon's populist dismissal of the word doggedly persists. While ideas themselves are not to be feared, in the popular consciousness 'blind' adherence to an individual concept is extremely dangerous. In practice, of course, ideas alone rarely dictate the behavior of an individual, much less an entire government. One need look no further than Bill Clinton to discover an example of a politician whose rhetoric and behavior betray a hybridization of the political ideologies outlined above. A purported liberal, many of Clinton's most successful platforms were culled from his conservative opponents. Expedience, rather than systematic application, seems to drive the typical broker of power. How, then, explain the overwhelming 'misapplication' of the word ideology? How could a distorted, politically motivated definition depose the original meaning?

One might respond, in part, by referring to the frenetic pace that attends modern human activity. As McLuhan points out, media guide our behavior and shape our responses to external phenomena. In the nineteenth, twentieth, and twenty-first centuries, the mass media have shown an increased preference for speed and immediate consumption. A sensational headline, rather than considered (or consistent) content, is the economic imperative. Accordingly, the political landscape has adapted itself in order to reach larger, geographically remote, audiences. The sound-bite has replaced the speech. Such political shorthand translates into a western electorate that receives a tremendous amount of information – a glut really – yet that rarely, if ever, grasps the full picture, possibly because there is no 'complete' view to be had. This latter possibility – that the proliferation of data and ideas has outpaced the human capacity to glean a sense of the 'whole truth' – perhaps provides a clue as to the popular readiness to accept terms that are

undeniably partial and unsatisfactory. In their eagerness to explain –
and thereby control – their environment, individuals conceivably
find solace in the security of compact, unambiguous definitions of
the socio-political phenomena that impact their daily lives. When
one is frustrated by a paycheck that barely covers the rent, one
might hold with populists such as Limbaugh or Mancow Muller
that it was the 'liberal' tax policy that stole the bread from one's
table. Such a tidy strategy preempts the necessity of peering into
the abyss of interrelated – and seemingly unmanageable – factors
that coincide to form a market economy. One might cling to the
precarious hope that if one can target the 'responsible' party, one's
lot might improve. While the political ideologies discussed above
certainly do not exist in any 'pure' form, they will no doubt continue
to endure as long as people attempt to make some sense of their
world.

Part II

'Reading' Ideology

5 Toni Morrison's *Sula* and Subjective Ideology

Critical interpretations of the title character of Toni Morrison's 1973 volume, *Sula*, vary sharply in their assessment of her subjectivity. Staunchly 'individual,' Sula subverts the communal ideology of the 'Bottom' – Medallion, Ohio's African-American quarter – repeatedly. Through such acts as watching her mother, Hannah, burn to death, accidentally (?) hurling Chicken Little to a watery grave, fornicating with Nel's husband (among many others), and assigning her grandmother to a nursing home, Sula distances herself from the *sensus communis* of her birthplace. Although few commentators will unequivocally endorse Sula's behavior, many laud her disregard of 'normative' social standards as an emblem of a subversive feminist consciousness. Jill Matus, for instance, regards Sula as 'a woman...intent on opening all parts of herself rather than folding them away' (Matus 1998, 60) while Wilfred D. Samuels and Clenora Hudson-Weems posit that the character seeks an 'authentic existence' (Samuels and Hudson-Weems 1990, 32). For such critics, Sula offers a critique of the stultifying ideology of the Bottom, which, despite its ostensible reliance on African-American tradition, shadows the 'dominant' ideological paradigm of Medallion and its attendant race-, class-, and gender-based hierarchies. In denying the validity of this hegemony, Sula functions as an exemplar of subjective autonomy. Conversely, a different set of critics, including Trudier Harris and Linden Peach, problematizes this view, arguing that Sula's actions represent not a positive feminist ideology but rather serve as an extreme version of patriarchal self-interest. In such views, Sula is 'a despicable user' (Harris 1991, 54) and experiences a 'failure of spirit' (Peach 1995, 42). Generally, such analyses point to the Bottom's ultimate assimilation of eccentrics like Shadrack, Eva, and Hannah as an implicit condemnation of Sula's excess. Sula's indifference to community fails to bring her joy, and her selfishness prefigures the destruction of the Bottom. A third pattern of reading attempts to reconcile the two extremes by arguing that Morrison advocates neither Sula's Nietszchean amorality nor Nel's unflagging belief in the collective. Pin-chia Feng, for example, observes that Morrison attempts to create 'a new female being who combines Sula Peace's dissruptive yet liberating power with Nel Wright's rootedness in community' (Feng 1998, 77), a point first noted by Deborah McDowell (1988) and Naana Banyiwa-Horne (1985). Sula and Nel fail to profit by their choices because they each suppress a key psychic element. Repeatedly, Morrison suggests that the women are parts of the same whole, and their rift prevents either from achieving true actualization.

While all of the preceding hermeneutic paradigms illuminate the text, they each premise their interpretations on the warrant that Sula is, in fact, an autonomous subject. Sula's self-creation, Sula's implicit affirmation of the patriarchy, Sula's contingent subjectivity – these phenomena all assume that the character is self-determined, is able to operate within a clear ideological framework. If one denies Sula 'pure' agency, however, the above interpretations become difficult to sustain. With her subjectivity in doubt, Sula would conceivably transform into an 'object' of ideology, her construction the product of a furtive communal necessity. Despite external manifestations that align themselves with conceptions of the liberal subject, Sula is controlled by the narrative's 'true' subject, the Bottom.[1] Although Sula appears to engage in a mode of 'free will,' her movements are in fact circumscribed by the collective 'subjectivity' of her society, which requires an 'other' to verify its own existence and blame for its ideological limitations. Intrinsically symbiotic even as it seems mutually repellant, the association between Sula and the Bottom is misperceived by both parties. Indeed, the Bottom's dominant ideology cannot survive without Sula, a relationship evident in the community's ultimate demise. As for Sula, while she intuits her need for the Bottom, her lack of subjectivity prevents her from sustaining *any* relationship, even with herself.

Slavoj Žižek's theories help to explain the ideological paradox inherent in *Sula*. In *The Sublime Object of Ideology* (1989), Žižek describes ideology as 'a totality set on effacing the traces of its own impossibility' (1989, 21). He later remarks that 'the symbolic structure must include an element which embodies its "stain," its own point of impossibility around which it is articulated: in a way it is the structuring of its own impossibility' (183). Within these two observations, Žižek begins to establish the paradox through which one might perceive Sula as an objectified Other rather than as an autonomous subject, for he suggests that any ideology must predicate itself on its opposite. The 'reality' maintained via ideology requires the liminal presence of the 'nonreal,' which must simultaneously be repudiated as myth, illusion, heresy. In this way, the communal *ethos* allows the subject to defer acknowledgement of the 'traumatic real kernel' (45). Departing from Marx, Žižek views ideology as a holistic psychic space rather than as an obfuscated view. Within this space, unsettled by the inexplicable presence of the 'stain,' the subject arises only from 'the void of the impossibility of answering the question of the Other' (178). Subjectivity, according to this reasoning, is a reflexive defense mechanism – a 'mere' rationalization – rather than the Cartesian icon of liberal thought.

Significantly for readers of *Sula*, Žižek further explores the ideological dimensions of the subject in *Tarrying with the Negative: Kant, Hegel, and the Critique of Ideology* (1993), particularly in the passages dealing with 'intersubjective space':

> This paradoxical existence of an entity which 'is' only insofar as subjects believe (in the other's belief) in its existence is the mode of being proper to ideological causes: the 'normal' order of causality is here inverted, since it is the Cause itself which is produced by its effects (the ideological practices it animates). (202)

The key implication for *Sula* in this passage concerns ideological contingency on the *other's* belief. The 'stain' of the other makes the subject necessary in order to explain it away. For Žižek, this inversion *is* ideology. The purpose of this paradoxical relationship concerns the process of 'retroactively ground[ing] [the subject's] own reasons' into a 'spontaneous ideological narrativization of [the subject's] experience and activity' (125, 126). Žižek extends the realm of subjectivity to the larger 'community,' which he observes is an 'elusive entity' that can only 'enumerate disconnected fragments of how it . . . *organizes its enjoyment*' (201; Žižek's emphasis). In this way, the Other stands apart from enjoyment, threatens to destroy it: 'we always impute to the 'other' an excessive enjoyment: he wants to steal our enjoyment (by ruining our way of life) and/or he has access to some secret, perverse enjoyment' (203). Ultimately, '*the hatred of the Other is the hatred of our own excess of enjoyment,*' for the 'stain' reminds the subject of its escapist relationship to the 'traumatic kernel' beyond ideology (206; Žižek's emphasis). If a scapegoat did not exist, we would be forced to invent one. The notion of community, for Žižek, is a tenuous one that depends more on perceptions of alien threats than on mutual similarities. *Post-hoc* ideological narratives thus serve to 'unite' the diverse fragments of enjoyment into a mythic structure. Without the motivation provided by the 'stain,' subjectivity – and thus community – ceases to function and ideology dissolves. Enjoy your nation! = Enjoy your scapegoat![2]

As many critics have noted, Sula functions as the Bottom's scapegoat or 'stain,' but they have not commented on her status as necessary object, preferring instead to underscore her 'extremist' subjectivity (Bjork 1991, 77). If one employs Žižek's paradigm, however, Sula's subjectivity is not only in doubt but non-existent. Objectified, Sula represents the impossible alternative, the escape from all-encompassing reality. More absence than presence, Sula becomes a creation that 'cannot exist.' Her very otherness galvanizes the matriarchal community and spurs it to resist, to erase the stain. Žižek locates this phenomenon, in which the subject excoriates the 'perceived deficiency of the other,' within the 'objectification of the distortion of [the subject's] own point of view' (Žižek 1989, 64). Sula's ostensible liberalism never truly threatens the Bottom. In fact, it *is* a mutilated version of the Bottom's own ideology. While Cyrus R. K. Patell claims that Sula looks for identity 'within herself,' it is the Bottom that constructs Sula (Patell 2001, 165). Any notion of Sula's subjectivity, therefore, dissolves within the scrutiny of the Bottom's communal subjectivity. Her disappearance, as paradoxical as her appearance, is not fully mourned, but the community's contingency on her spectral residue is nonetheless unveiled.[3] Before it can recognize its 'untenable' dependence on Sula, the Bottom is crushed under the weight of its own fears. An application of Žižek's neo-Lacanian principles, then, seeks to recover the traces of this relationship and expose its operation.

Within the framework of the novel, several clues point to such an alternative explanation of Sula and her 'unforgivable' actions (Morrison 1973, 112). Like Herman Melville in *Moby-Dick* (1851), Morrison frames *Sula* around an implausible symbolic blank. The narrative first deposits Sula within textual limbo, leisurely attending to the stories of Shadrack, Helene, Nel, Eva, and others, only to dismiss its nominal title character 24 years before the end of the action. Numerous critics – such as McDowell (1988, 80–1) and Robert Grant (1988, 95) – have pointed to the 'ironic' deferral of Sula's entrance into the novel's action, but her absence nonetheless impacts the reader's interpretation of the narrative. Undeniably, Sula is 'always-already' object. Reified as *Sula*, the narrative 'core,' the ethical 'focus,' Sula is stripped of subjectivity, yet she paradoxically absorbs attention, lingering in the wings, as it were, ready to wrest the story from the Bottom's less 'important' denizens. 'In that place,' the novel begins, 'where they tore the nightshade and blackberry patches from their roots to make room for the Medallion City Golf Course, there was once a neighborhood' (1973, 3). The implications of Sula's presence are revealed from the outset. Impossible as it is, her implicit destruction of the community – embedded in a Western European liberalism at odds with the Bottom's ontology – announces itself before she even arrives on the scene. The title heralds Sula's part in the novel, yet that role is as pure Other. *Sula*, Sula, will be *interpreted* against the subjective will of the collective.

A 'tangible' emblem of this assessment, Sula's protean birthmark operates as a register of the character's objective status. Describing the national fascination with difference as 'purely ideological,' Žižek remarks that communities seize upon distinguishing elements in order to narrativize their own disintegration and 'lost original experience' (1993, 200). Tellingly, though Sula herself fails to remark on the 'meaning' of her birthmark, members of the Bottom do so freely. A part of her, the birthmark nonetheless remains outside of her, exists in the province of the subject. A biological 'stain' of sorts, Sula's birthmark reflects neither her mood nor her autonomy, but instead registers the emotional reaction of the subjects around her. While the birthmark certainly appears a token of Sula's individuality, a celebration of her Nietszchean immunity from quotidian concern, it masks a subtle process of reification. A rose, a tadpole, a rattle-snake, a copperhead, a 'scary black thing,' Hannah's ashes – the increasingly hostile renderings of the birthmark function to decode

Sula, to comprehend her 'attack' on the Bottom's 'enjoyment.' Impossibly standing outside the ideological circle, Sula must be explained, acknowledged. By labeling Sula's birthmark, the community controls the woman, even as the signifier seems to shift at will. As McDowell observes, the varying interpretations suggest that the birthmark announces that Sula 'never achieves completeness of being' (1988, 81). The birthmark's 'readers' reduce Sula's transgressions against the symbolic order into a manageable pathology so that ultimately she may be eradicated. Žižek avers that a society's leader ('Master') must 'dominate the excess by locating its cause in a clearly delimited social agency' (1993, 210). In the Bottom, a *de facto* matriarchy, leadership is putatively collective, and the drive to push out Sula and the imbalance that she creates is, therefore, not centralized. Centralization is, in fact, Sula's primary offense, a phenomenon echoed in her elusive birthmark: In (falsely) claiming agency, Sula poses a threat to the diffuse power structure of the Bottom. Sula's 'experimental life' represents an unnamed, unwanted alternative to the stable enjoyment of the community (Morrison 1973, 118). By calling attention to her birthmark, the Bottom defines the struggle and establishes its 'national enemy' (Žižek 1993, 211).

Why, however, does Sula exclusively merit this intense resistance when other likely targets populate the town? Indeed, the Bottom seems virtually infested with ideological rebels: Shadrack, Eva, Hannah, Tar Baby, Plum – none of these characters provoke the focused prejudice that Sula elicits, even though they, too, appear to act extremely. The town assimilates them nonetheless, a fact noted by Peach (1995, 42), among others. Clearly, the town is leery of the above figures – Harris asserts that Eva, for instance, 'is a slap in the face to all traditional matriarchs' – but ultimately they accept their idiosyncrasies (Harris 1991, 71). Sula receives no such benefit. One might explain this in a number of ways. Grounding her interpretation in the assumption of Sula's subjectivity, Harris posits that she 'is clearly immoral because she sees herself as the center of the universe around which people can revolve or not' (78), while Peach implies that Sula's pariah status finds its roots in the Bottom's uneasy relationship with white society – and, thus, with Sula's familiarity with that world (Peach 1995, 43). Although the extrinsic differences between, say, Eva and Sula may be slight – neither reveals much fear, and both pursue their desires without regard for social censure, for instance – the intrinsic disparity is palpable. The *motivation*, or subjective catalyst, for the Bottom's cast of eccentrics is generally visible, but for Sula, it is either *sub rosa* or non-existent. Her behavior is inexplicable, a 'secret' enjoyment that, for the Bottom's inhabitants, hides any number of perversions. While Shadrack and Plum lose 'perspective' because of the war and Eva and Hannah must fill the void left by their absent husbands, Sula ostensibly drifts at random, following her arbitrary, joyless whim. Patell, who establishes Sula's Emersonian character, nonetheless claims that 'she lacks a crucial ingredient, which proves, ironically, to be a sense of self' (Patell 2001, 164). According to the Bottom's citizens, however, Sula's apparent lack of enjoyment elides her true 'evil' purpose and excessive delight (indulgence): because she 'relish[ed] nothing,' the town 'believed that she was laughing at their God' (Morrison 1973, 115). Sula 'really' enjoys the Bottom's 'Thing,' but she perversely insists on hiding her ecstasy, be it for the carnal knowledge of the town's men or the amorality stemming from her 'foreign' education. She ignores them, yet she cannot stay away. She voices no pleasure, yet she 'steals' Jude from Nel and 'cavorts' (listlessly, paradoxically) with countless other men. Squirrel-like, Sula hordes experiences to employ (enjoy!) another day. Her otherness lies in her refusal to admit her desire, a desire that from the ideological closed circuit of the community MUST exist, but, impossibly, is 'missing' from Sula, despite the obvious stain of her birthmark. The town must rescue itself from Sula's implicit invalidation of its ideology. Žižek describes this reaction as a 'sacrifice' in which 'the destruction of the Other' allows the community to 'purify' itself of its own 'disavowed, repressed content' (Žižek 1999, 194). In denying Sula's autonomy, the Bottom affirms itself.

Sula's status as Other, marked before the narrative begins, is confirmed from the moment she 'enters' the text. In particular, Sula's relationship with Nel – which Lisa Williams positively describes as a 'fusion' (2000, 109) – firmly establishes the girl's difference from the town and its *ethos*. At first glance, the relationship seems liberating for Nel: her subjectivity now flowers, whereas before Helene had apparently crushed it. When one looks closer, however, one recognizes that Nel's agency is utterly dependent on the Other, a phenomenon that prefigures the Bottom's own relationship to Sula. Despite later mythopoeic redactions by both Sula and

Nel herself, Helene Wright's daughter experiences her subjective epiphany *before* meeting Sula: 'I'm me' (Morrison 1973, 28). Nel's utterance – sparked by her mother's Jim Crow-based humiliation during a trip out of the ideological cloister of the Bottom – is a type of mirror in which she recognizes her separation from her family. Tentative though her gesture may be, it intimates that Nel will develop her subjectivity according to the ideology of her system, that she will cast off the will of her mother. Perhaps because of this scene's proximity to the 'bonding' of Nel and Sula, critics such as Patrick Bryce Bjork view the friendship as a 'radical change' helping with Nel's liberation (Bjork 1991, 62). With Sula's advent, however, Nel's subjectivity paradoxically recedes, for it becomes enmeshed in Sula's otherness. Several times, the narrator remarks that the two girls form halves of the same whole, an aside that prompts several critics, such as Williams, to argue for Morrison's rejection of false dichotomies (especially the repellant nature of individual will and communal desire) and creation of a 'unified female imagination' (Williams 2000, 108). Employing Žižek's paradigm, however, one readily sees that Nel's immature subjectivity prompts the girl to confuse the stain of Sula's impossibility with causality. Nel identifies so closely with the Other because she suspects – falsely – that Sula will heighten her enjoyment and complete the separation from her mother.

Temporarily, this appears so. Nel *enjoys* herself more than ever before, partaking in communal rituals of sexuality and play, such as in the 'pig meat' sequence (Morrison 1973, 50). Sula, too, seems to thrive in this relationship, an association far different than the one she experiences within her own family. Even the critical Helene at first approves of Sula's 'influence' on her daughter. Nevertheless, as the Bottom will come to declare, Sula evinces a marked difference from even the most eccentric member of the community – from Shadrack, for instance – in that she betrays *no* fear, a 'sure' sign of her status as interloper, as evil. Her clash with the white thugs, for example, while often taken as 'exciting and disturbing', reveals her distance from the Bottom's ideology, which includes a suspicion of white motives and actions (Peach 1995, 48). Sula stands apart from the rituals of her supposed community. No trickster, she simply cannot adhere to conventional mores because, as the Bottom later 'discovers,' she lacks the 'self-consciousness' that Žižek claims precedes the subject's perception of the object: she cannot 'see' herself (1993, 68). In her haste to escape her mother's gaze, Nel, too, fails to 'see' Sula as a threat to her subjective ideology.

Two other events underscore Sula's otherness: the deaths of Chicken Little and Hannah. In the former instance, Sula hurls the boy to his death, not out of malice but out of indifference. Although Chicken shows his 'frightened joy' and the girls hear his 'bubbly laughter' even as he flies to his imminent death, Sula does not participate in his elation (Morrison 1973, 60, 61). Rather, she acts as though she moves in slow motion, stands outside of the Bottom's temporal and ideological reference. Nel, dangerously allied with Sula, initiates conversation, but her thoughts are not on the community but on the cessation of enjoyment: 'somebody saw' (61). Sula's power over her – her ability to abscond with the Bottom's 'Thing' – confuses her to the point of repressing her shared values. Quickly, Sula, in 'terror' of being unmasked as an infiltrator, invades Shadrack's home, but, as befits her reified status, she finds herself 'Alone' (61). The 'unthreatening' Shadrack, represented by a litany of his transgressions, is discovered by Sula to be benign, a member of the community, subject (61). Unlike Sula herself, Shadrack fights for 'normalcy,' even though his methods, such as National Suicide Day, strain at the parameters of acceptability. His fear of being ostracized from the Bottom – and thus from himself – spur him onward, whereas Sula is utterly numb and cannot (although she makes half-hearted attempts) pierce the veil of self-consciousness. Shadrack's 'gaze turning, turning within her' confirms her otherness, which the outcast announces with a single word: 'Always' (62). Sula is always-already object, and her tearful collapse signifies her permanent estrangement with the Bottom. Significantly, when Sula repeats his cryptic utterance to Nel she replies, 'What?' and the gulf between the two girls is made explicit (63). At the funeral, the gap widens, for it is precisely during such rituals that Žižek locates ideology: 'Nel and Sula did not touch hands or look at each other during the funeral. There was a space, a separateness, between them' (64). Nel recognizes herself in Sula's 'stain,' and the shock of this recognition of the impossible forces her to deny her own participation in both the death of the boy and the cleansing act of the funeral and its 'rivulets of grief or ecstasy [that] must be rocked' (65). The girls do turn toward one another near the end of the ceremony, but Nel is now firmly a subject, 'by definition nostalgic, a subject of loss,' secure in her knowledge of Sula's evil (Žižek 1993, 41).

Mothers hold an ambiguous but important place in *Sula*. While the novel depicts several questionable acts committed by mothers – Eva's burning of Plum, Helene's bullying of Nel, and Hannah's coolness toward Sula, to name just a few – the Bottom's matriarchs stitch the town's social fabric together. Men are present only through their absence, a paradox signaled by their economic infantilization.[4] Sula, however, patently rejects the Bottom's matriarchy, a rupture symbolized in her passive 'reaction' to Hannah's death. Prior to burning to death, Hannah discloses to some friends – and an eavesdropping Sula – that she loves her daughter but 'just don't like her' (Morrison 1973, 57), a singular reaction from a woman who expresses her love freely, even promiscuously. As Sula's mother, though, Hannah recognizes her daughter's stain more readily than do the rest of the town's inhabitants. She senses that Sula's lack of joy is fundamentally different from Eva's (whom she questions regarding love) and flows not from unfulfilled desire but from ideological separation. Whereas Eva burns Plum from a deeply rooted love that cannot bear to witness him destroy the life she once rescued with self-sacrifice, Sula registers no such emotions. She does not, as Feng remarks, fail to act because of 'unspoken anger and bewilderment'; instead, her paralysis stems from her lack of subjectivity (Feng 1998, 84). Sula is detached from the Bottom's matriarchal values and views Hannah's frantic gesticulations as simply another experience to be collected. In contrast to Eva, who, revealing a strength and love beyond her physical capacities, leaps from her window to save her daughter, Sula, healthy, stood 'on the back porch just looking' (Morrison 1973, 78). Although Eva's friends – demonstrating the community's readiness to assimilate ostensibly bizarre behavior – assure her that Sula's reaction was 'natural,' they cannot convince Eva (78). Neither wicked nor perverse, Sula merely 'was interested,' as Eva speculates (78). Lacking subjectivity, Sula cannot love.

Her reactions to Nel's fortunes, therefore, are quite predictable. Never quite forgiving Sula for keeping her subjectivity in check, Nel completes her separation from her childhood friend when she pledges her love to Jude. While Bjork, among others, views Nel's marriage as stifling and Ibsenesque, such an analysis ignores the Bottom's social structure (Bjork 1991, 74). Despite his nominal role as 'head' of the household, Jude's economic impotence clearly installs Nel as the family's ideological center. Ajax, flippantly commenting on the white's treatment of Tar Baby, cuts to the heart of the symbolic emasculation of Jude and the other men when he observes: 'it ain't right to let a grown man lay around in his own shit' (Morrison 1973, 132–3). The 'patriarchy' in Bottom is hollow, and Nel, and most of the town's women, organize the society's enjoyment, celebrate the communal 'Thing.' It is Sula who rejects Nel's *ethos*, not because of her indomitable feminist subjectivity or her Emersonian quest for self, but because she bristles at Nel's formalization of their implicit separation. Nel has vanquished Sula's otherness and re-established her own 'me.' Unlike Sula, Nel senses that Jude's blustering paternalism masks a deep hurt and constitutes an effort to connect with the Bottom's singular enjoyment: 'he needed some of his appetites filled, some posture of adulthood recognized, but mostly he wanted someone to care about his hurt, to care very deeply' (82). In helping to make Jude whole, Nel reinforces the ideology of her community, regenerates her 'nation,' and blots the stain that Sula represents. Despite her apparent enthusiasm for the wedding (still attempting to thwart Nel's subjectivity, she asks to be the lone bridesmaid), Sula departs from the Bottom immediately thereafter. Sula, whom readers learn made little response to Jude's suffering, leaves because Nel's anxiety has ebbed. Unable to stand Nel's enjoyment, Sula flees the scene.

Significantly, upon Sula's return, the town that once made allowances for the girl holds no quarter for the woman. While as a girl Sula emanated a surreptitious otherness, as an adult she clearly stands in opposition to the town's fundamental ideology. Sula's return marks the height of the Bottom's 'nationalism,' a phenomenon predicated on Sula's status as scapegoat.[5] While Sula always seemed somewhat odd to the Bottom's denizens, she now appears dangerous, the source of social cacophony. The 'plague of robins' that ominously announces Sula's return points to her paradoxical existence. Robins are traditionally peaceful heralds of spring, but these are disruptive to the town, startling the citizens out of their complacency, hindering the possibility of enjoyment and arousing 'nationalist' sentiments culminating in a 'vicious stoning' (89). The robins, like Sula, upset the Bottom's ideological equilibrium and arrest its hitherto invisible network of traditions and relations. Because of their near loss of these institutions, the newly nostalgic inhabitants suddenly acknowledge their value and transform into preservationists. Sula, her mind apparently 'tainted' with the bourgeois liberalism of college, the tawdry morals of Hollywood, and the alienation of the city, comes, in the minds of the townsfolk, to represent evil. While the Bottom's doctrine of assimilation precludes forcing Sula into exile or physically harming her, 'such evil must be avoided . . . and precautions must naturally be taken to protect themselves from it' (89). In the novel, such precautions involve scapegoating and the expression of an ardent nationalism. As Žižek would have it, the tension between subject and object bolsters, rather than diminishes, the collective subjectivity: 'their conviction of Sula's evil changed them in accountable yet mysterious ways. Once the source of their personal misfortune was identified, they had leave to protect and love one another. They began to cherish their husbands and wives, repair their homes and in general band together against the devil in their midst' (Morrison 1973, 117–18). Žižek would characterize this phenomenon as a predictably 'reactionary sentimental *Blut und Boden*': the fight stems from a nostalgic reconfiguration of the society's origins (Žižek 1993, 201).

Among Sula's many perceived ideological infractions – which include her 'abuse' of Teapot, her affiliation with Shadrack, and her Dorian Gray-like beauty – are two that particularly suggest her role as object: her (non)sexuality and her rejection of family. Unlike her mother, whose unquenchable desire expresses itself in unmitigated enjoyment and, thus, affirms the joy of the adulterer's wife, Sula trolls among the Bottom's men with casual indifference, which later gives way to 'deep sorrow' (122). Starting with her 'betrayal' of Nel, Sula reveals neither prurience nor envy. She simply mimics the act of love with a pattern of mechanical – albeit (paradoxically) gymnastic – copulation. Apparently lacking a subjective core, Sula first 'samples' Jude out of curiosity, not lust, and then, with a variety of faceless partners, proceeds to engage in coitus (she does not make love, have sex, or fuck) with the sterility of a clinician or – as Nel remarks – 'like [a] dog' (105).[6] Detached from the emotional significance of the act, Sula observes, records, files. It is precisely this dispassionate demeanor that angers her eminently disposable partners and their affronted wives. Sula's unceremonious rejection insults both masculine pride and feminine dignity. Feelings, 'normal' or otherwise, may be channeled into the Bottom's ideology; utter indifference denies the ideology itself and betokens the impossible. Shattering the ideological framework, Sula is thus accused of the highest crimes, including sleeping with Caucasians, the very source of the Bottom's economic oppression.

Compounding Sula's lack of sexual enjoyment is her assault on the extended family. Sula, newly stamped with the impersonal *ethos* of the urban center, does not aim her ideologically antithetical behavior solely against those outside of her family. Sula commits one of the Bottom's worst offenses when she deposes Eva as head of the household. Although liberalism placed increasing emphasis on extreme individualism (culminating, perhaps, in Emerson's version of self-reliance, which itself looked toward Nietzsche's ultimate break with 'morals'), the Bottom, a product of the African diaspora, prizes community above self-interest. One might 'do one's thing' with minimal disturbance, but the matriarchy demands allegiance to kin. Those, such as Boy-Boy, who violate this principle typically flee, but Sula, with her usual 'ignorance' not only fails to leave the Bottom, but she occupies the house of the very woman she usurps, situating herself in Eva's former room. By committing Eva, Sula once again manifests her difference and strikes at the 'nation's' core. Her stock with the townsfolk plummets irrevocably, and those who formerly made allowances for Sula now see her birthmark as a premonition of Hannah's death (and, thus, Sula's 'active' role in it). While Sula famously declares to Eva, 'I don't want to make somebody else. I want to make myself,' she miscalculates her ability to transcend the Bottom (92). She has returned because she *cannot* discover her subjectivity. As her melancholy yearnings later demonstrate, Sula requires the Bottom's ideology to set herself in relief. Her outrageousness, her latent 'me,' derives precisely from her position as Other, and her petulant responses to Eva's (genuine) concern and her studied indifference to the sexual needs of the Bottom's men – and their wives – serve only to reify her. Her sadness, fundamentally inexpressible to herself, stems from her existence apart from the Bottom's ideology: she cannot enjoy her nation.

When she makes her one effort to enjoy self-consciousness and understand her nemesis, she fails miserably. Ajax, who throughout the narrative seems preternaturally self-reflexive, resists the drive to push away Sula, much as the younger Nel had done. By not imposing on Sula emotionally, Ajax seems to be a reflection of Sula's own impulses, but despite circumstances that would ostensibly foster self-consciousness, Sula cannot experience the 'ontological uncertainty of the subject' (Žižek 1993, 71). Instead, she descends into a parody of Nel's maternal enthusiasm and tries to enjoy Ajax too visibly. He doubts the sincerity of her desire, senses its otherness. She does not even know his name. Although she claims to want to 'make' herself, Sula tries in vain to 'become' Nel. Samuels and Hudson-Weems rightly claim that this represents a 'deferment of self' on Sula's part (1990, 47). As a result, Ajax departs, never to return. Sula's shock at discovering her own objectivity precipitates the 'sickness' that ultimately kills her and dismantles the Bottom.

Once Sula lies dying – her ominous otherness dwindling – Nel attempts to understand her. Because of Sula's 'seduction' of Jude, Nel is extremely suspicious of her former friend and resists her explanations. Although she acknowledges their earlier friendship, Nel does not truly reconcile with Sula. Soon thereafter, Sula's death is 'the best news folks up in the Bottom had had since the promise of work at the tunnel' (Morrison 1973, 150). Like Nel, the townspeople fail to forgive Sula, a phenomenon that speaks to their blindness concerning her important role in the creation of the Bottom's ideology. Ultimately, both Nel and the town's inhabitants suffer the consequences of denying Sula. For Nel, Sula's death forces her to recognize the evil within herself. Žižek observes that such realizations recast 'moral rectitude [as] radical Evil' (1993, 49). Her repressed memories regarding Chicken Little – hitherto projected onto Sula – are released and Nel must confront her own part in the boy's demise, fusing herself and Sula into one: 'girl, girl, girl girlgirlgirl' (Morrison 1973, 174). The town itself also literally and figuratively collapses under the absence of Sula. Their scapegoat gone, the Bottom uncharacteristically turns outward to remove the evil that threatens its enjoyment. Medallion's white hierarchy – endlessly deferring its promise to grant the Bottom its economic autonomy – becomes the target of the town's wrath. Acting against evil rather than assimilating it and drawing from its power, many of the Bottom's residents destroy themselves along with the tunnel on the final National Suicide Day. Ultimately, the Bottom's ideology dissolves without Sula, and the town fragments, finally becoming a white suburban golf course, what Denise Heinze refers to as 'ideological miscegenation of the worst sort' (Heinze 1993, 122).

As Žižek suggests, the subject 'always-already ha[s] chosen evil' (Žižek 1993, 98). Nel and the Bottom both recognize too late that they always-already carry evil within them. While they fiercely attempt to preserve the structures and institutions of their enjoyment, their very efforts establish the conditions of its opposite. Their desire calls up – is dependent on – their fears, and they exist self-consciously only by recognizing the stain in their midst. While they condemn Sula for her 'ignorant' transgressions, they require her otherness and lose themselves when she expires. Žižek would see in this relationship the 'conditions of possibility coincid[ing] with the conditions of impossibility' (1993, 171). Rather than imposing her subjectivity upon the Bottom, Sula is gazed upon, constructed. Within Sula converge elements both of the Bottom's ideology and its destruction. 'Radical Evil,' Žižek writes, 'is conceivable only against the background of the constitutive antagonism' (224). In this manner, ideology both 'produces' and 'threatens' itself. Ideology, furthermore, is a prerequisite to subjectivity rather than a projection from it. The tragedy of *Sula*, then, is neither Sula's 'extreme' actions nor Nel's 'conventionality,' but the women's mutual misrecognition. They not only fail to see themselves within each other, but they never even detect their own roles within the ideological matrix.

6 William Faulkner's 'Barn Burning' and Institutional Ideology

Most critics of William Faulkner's 'Barn Burning,' written in 1938, view the story as a 'coming-of-age' tale which pits blood ties against societal responsibility. Proponents of this interpretation generally argue that Sarty Snopes experiences a crisis in which he must negotiate the murky waters of duty. Sarty, torn between a desire to maintain loyalty to his family and a nascent moral sense that – increasingly – condemns his father's actions, ultimately discovers as a mature man that a code of ethics grounded in binary categories of 'good' and 'evil' is unsatisfactory in comprehending the range of human actions. Sarty's jejune moral confusion, coupled with Faulkner's intricate narrative technique, thus makes 'Barn Burning' a complex background on which critics may consider a series of ideological 'opposites,' including Southern/Northern, agrarianism/ industrialism, aristocracy/sharecropper, violence/nonviolence, and individualism/communalism, to name just a few. Complicating this picture, Faulkner's own views – as well as the perspectives of his contemporaries – frequently come into play as foils to the choices of characters such as Sarty, Ab, Flem, and Major de Spain. For such critics as Edmond L. Volpe, then, the text becomes what Terry Eagleton disparagingly labels the 'expression of ideology' (Eagleton 1978, 64). In this way, the work supposedly reveals a tension between 'competing' ideologies that is or is not resolved in varying degrees. Volpe, for instance, may therefore confidently remark, 'the clue to Sarty's conflict rests in its resolution' (Volpe 1980, 75).

Eagleton, however, denies such a static model of ideology. For him, ideology manifests itself as a 'ceaseless reciprocal *operation* of text on ideology and ideology on text' (1978, 99). As both a 'product and producer' of ideology (89), the text 'is the process whereby ideology produces the forms which produce it' (84). The text, thus, is neither a mere repository of a writer's ideological agenda (conscious or otherwise) nor a simple manufacturer of ideology. Rather, it is both. The text's lacunae are indeed the result of ideology, but the text most definitely helps to create both those absences and other, future gaps as it operates on its audience. Binary oppositions present within a given text, therefore, represent not simply a conflict or ideological residue but ideological production.

Eagleton's paradigm of ideology raises a number of issues relative to 'Barn Burning.' As alluded to above, the story manifests a number of ostensible dichotomies that easily lend themselves to 'readings' of one sort or another. Myra Jehlen, for example, might interpret Faulkner's work as expressing 'ambivalence' concerning two models of southern agrarianism (Jehlen 1978, 22), while James B. Carothers might emphasize the 'irreconcilable ideals of loyalty to [family] and loyalty to ... justice' (Carothers 1985, 62). If, however, one adheres to Eagleton's model, then one quickly sees the insufficiency of such monologic interpretations. Eagleton's dynamic description of ideology seems preferable to more static paradigms because it not only allows for multiple readings across the historical continuum but it also helps explain how those diverse interpretations reflect the 'logic' of the text and the absences therein. 'Barn Burning' does not only function as a warehouse for the ideology of its characters/author. It also serves as an ideological factory of sorts that 'deformatively' *produces* the real while 'nevertheless [carrying] elements of reality within itself' (Eagleton 1978, 69). One must, therefore, devise a strategy that takes the conflicting elements of 'Barn Burning' into account without reducing them to fixed entities.

While 'Barn Burning' expresses a number of ideological conflicts that seemingly yield a 'schizophrenic' text, the story may more profitably be considered as an example of what Mikhail Bakhtin refers to as polyphony.[1] Although individual commentators may seize upon particular ideological strands, they may not be able to reconcile the whole. Bakhtin views this (failed) quest for synthesis as a necessary function of ideology, which for him constitutes a partial representation of a dynamic experience. Analyses that concentrate on ideological particulars are, for Bakhtin as for Eagleton, reductive and unproductive. To break free of ideology – or at least to recognize its limits – one must resist the temptation to view it in isolation. The concept of polyphony, as Bakhtin describes it in regard to Fyodor Dostoevski, refers to a reimagining of the text as 'a plurality of independent and unmerged voices and consciousnesses' (Bakhtin 1984a, 6). The various moments of cultural production evident in the text – including antebellum southern socio-economics, reconstruction, Depression-era historicism, and androcentrism, among others – thus manifest themselves as an 'opposition, which is never cancelled out directly, of many consciousnesses,' which 'do not merge in the unity of an evolving spirit' (26). Dialogic, polyphony contrasts with the monologic – or ideological – in that it combats the urge to elevate one element (even should that aspect be 'dominant' within a particular sphere) above the rest. In this way, no consciousness 'entirely becomes an object for the other[s]' (18). Ideology, which Bakhtin provisionally defines as 'separate thought' that manifests itself in a 'system,' ignores, downplays, or attempts to erase the multiplicity of voices at play in the world, no one of which is ever 'cancelled out' (92; 26). Thus, privileging one voice, that of Faulkner, say, or that of young Sarty, produces ideology.

Ultimately, any attempt to *apply* Bakhtin's theory to a text – even one as short as 'Barn Burning' – will fall 'victim' to ideology. Clearly, uncovering all of the consciousnesses within a given work is futile, for individual limitations compel readers to be 'deaf' to many of the voices represented. Historical circumstance dictates whether or not one's perception regarding a 'voice' will be acute. Second- and third-wave feminisms, for instance, helped to create conditions in which gender issues – hitherto unexamined – became 'obvious' within 'Barn Burning.' Similarly, voices that the average student of 1950 may have found overwhelming, such as the lingering effects of Reconstruction on the 'modernization' of the South, have become mere whispers to the typical student of the twenty-first century. A project to examine polyphony within 'Barn Burning,' then, is by definition contingent, but such an undertaking may at least raise an awareness of the plurality of voices within the story and suggest some of the effects this dialogism has on interpreting Faulkner's tale.

'Barn Burning' – indeed, Faulkner's entire *oeuvre* – is well suited for a discussion of polyphony and its subversion of ideology. One need not be alert to polyphony, however, to recognize some of its manifestations in 'Barn Burning.' In fact, most considerations of the story concentrate in some way on the debates that Sarty has with himself, both as a young boy and as a man. Faulkner's characteristically complex use of narrative form foregrounds the text's apparent interest in dialogue, if not dialectic. Choices abound in the story. Sarty must decide, for example, whether or not to lie, to reveal his father's plans to de Spain, and to rationalize his father's actions. Later in life, Sarty, who chose to betray his father – an act that he falsely believes led to Ab's death – struggles in his attempt to reconstruct his father's motives and ethical premises. Nevertheless, while such possibilities do reflect reality, they do so in a partial way that Bakhtin calls 'monological-intentional' and that ignores the multi-level 'condition' of society (1984a, 25, 27). For Bakhtin, Sarty's intentions exist alongside those of all other ideologies. As Bakhtin makes clear, polyphony involves more than the actions of a character, the designs of an author, or the social context of a reader. The text represents an 'essence independent of... second-hand ideological refraction' that serves as a forum for competing ideologies without collating or intermingling them (27). In each of the story's four primary movements – which one might label trial, exile, contract, and betrayal – one may witness what Bakhtin elsewhere describes as a carnival of voices shouting its multifold song (1984b, 4–5). Through an examination of these movements, one may glean a sense of how polyphony functions in 'Barn Burning.'

The tale's first movement, trial, starts *in medias res* and immediately announces one of several ideological conflicts within the narrative: 'The store in which the Justice of the Peace's court was sitting smelled of cheese' (Faulkner 1961, 3). From the outset, readers will notice the tension between the privileged, but increasingly outmoded, planter class and the economically deprived poor whites. The court, far from being an institution of the people, is described in proprietary terms, a paternalistic realm wherein disputes between common folk are resolved by a Justice with a 'kindly' face (5). This stately arena contrasts sharply with the olfactory presence lingering in the room. Underscoring Sarty's progress on Maslow's hierarchy of needs, the cheese wafting through the store reminds the boy of his pressing hunger, an urge that prompts him to sense – falsely – the smell of 'hermetic meat' emanating from the store's tin cans, modern commodities that ironically undercut the Justice's property-based authority (3). As the hearing continues, the dichotomy between the Snopses and the Justice is further emphasized by Sarty's thoughts of '*Enemy! Enemy!*' and the Justice's extralegal dictum, 'leave this country and don't come back to it,' a sentiment that Ab responds to with 'something unprintable and vile' (5). Ab's disdain for the law is reinforced by a reference to a horse he stole in the midst of the Civil War: the debate over slavery and states' rights was not Ab's fight, just as the conflict over modernization is not his struggle. Everyone in the room, of course, realizes that Ab indeed set fire to Harris's barn. Their interpretations of his action, however, range from Sarty's grudging familial acceptance to Harris's violent outrage. The poles of this debate seem to suggest that Faulkner wishes his audience to form an *ex officio* jury and cast judgment on this class conflict. Such a phenomenon mirrors the condition of Sarty himself, whose burgeoning conscience has begun to stage a debate between the proto-proletarian instincts of his father and the beleaguered pre-Reconstruction mores of the Justice: '*he aims for me to lie*, he thought, again with that frantic grief and despair. *And I will have to do hit*' (4–5). Initially, then, Sarty decides to confirm his father's perspective, but not without reservations stemming from his budding identification with the remnants of the antebellum social order represented by the Justice. His private thoughts are not evident, however, when he attacks a much larger boy who has impugned his family name with the label 'barn burner,' although Sarty's temper may rise more from having the term applied to himself rather than to Ab (6). Despite these somewhat obvious ideological 'intentions' of the decaying aristocracy (the Justice is 'shabby, collarless, graying') and the sullen, increasingly more brazen lower classes represented by Ab, however, the trial's lacunae announce other voices in the chorus (4).

Bakhtin's representation of polyphony would not deny the dominance of the preceding voice, but it would decry placing exclusive emphasis on it. Such a state would constitute an ideological position: 'only error individualizes' (Bakhtin 1984a, 81). Employing this principle, it is possible to peer beyond the 'form-shaping principles' of ideology and avoid their concomitant grounding in a 'unified [and, for Bakhtin, faux] spirit' (84, 31). Two of the absences within the trial section include the voices of Caucasian women and African Americans. Neither group is visible at Ab's trial, but both contribute to the polyphony of voices within the text. Despite benefiting to a degree from the social organizations of both the paternalistic old South and the liberal push toward economic modernization that seeks to replace it, Caucasian women had little direct influence on either system. At the affluent end of the spectrum, women of the 1890s had long since ceded their most tangible power base of the antebellum years (their control over the bodies of 'house' slaves), yet most were actively discouraged from taking part in the activities of the New Woman as represented, say, by Charlotte Perkins Gilman. Placed in a submissive role, many such women possessed skills that were increasingly devalued in a market economy.[2] Those at the other end of the spectrum hardly fared any better, as the newly instituted, quasi-feudal methods of sharecropping condemned women to brutal labor with little prospect of reward.

The lack of women at the trial, therefore, underscores the one-sidedness of the debate: women are affected by social change, yet they are not granted representation. Even a young boy like Sarty rates at least a whisper in the public discourse. In the trial section itself, the voice of the more affluent women does express itself despite the absence of corporeal women.[3] The canned food that Sarty fantasizes about represents one aspect of the new economy. The 'labor-saving' phenomenon in theory liberates those who can afford the tins of food from preparing meals and provides them with more leisure time. Such escapes may have proven bittersweet, however, for they allowed women more time to contemplate their lot.[4] The cans, moreover, both represent the commodified labor of the workers who prepared the food and tins and transported them to the store and accentuate the plight of the poor women who will rarely be in a position to avail themselves of the product of that labor, in many instances the sweat of either themselves or their husbands. The text thus reveals women, in however muted fashion, chiming in on the debate over modernization expressed in the story. Obviously, as will become even more evident in the next section, the lack of a public voice does not silence the various groups of women, and the text juxtaposes their ideological intentions along with the rest.

African Americans also assert their voices in the trial section. While Reconstruction economics might ostensibly pit liberalism against Jeffersonian paternalism (Jehlen 1978, 21–2; Railey 1999, 7), they might also be viewed as a referendum of sorts on the economic status of the newly freed slaves. The bleak prospects for poor white social mobility were still far better than those open to African Americans. Promises of land went largely unfulfilled, and share-cropping became practically the only way for African Americans to farm. As Reconstruction progressed, the token public representation for African Americans dwindled away, eventually to be replaced by the legal segregation of Jim Crow. Poor whites, resenting the improved state of the former slaves, viewed African Americans as a legitimate economic threat, a division that the gentry enabled. Such conditions, obviously, do not foster wide-scale participation in public discourse. Nevertheless, African Americans add their ideological intentions to the mix of the trial scene. Via the testimony of Harris, who futilely attempts to use a former slave as evidence against Ab, African Americans express their dissent. Harris' 'strange nigger' serves a dual role in the proceedings (Faulkner 1961, 4). Acting as a go-between for Ab and Harris, the man's presence is at once tangible and ethereal. Ab 'employs' the man as a visible insult to Harris, whom Ab views as pretentious. In turn, the freeman exposes the social and racial hierarchy of the planter class by speaking freely with a so-called superior. The subject of the conversation, moreover, is a not-so-subtle threat against Harris' property, a warning issued by Ab but, by virtue of being uttered by an African American, reflecting widespread fears of racial mayhem directed toward the landed class. The man's subsequent 'disappearance' – a circumstance aided by Harris's inability to 'see' the African American as a distinct individual – reflects both the insubstantial nature of such apprehension and its very real conse-quences, lynching being the most explicit. The ability thus to fade into the background becomes, as Ralph Ellison would later explore, both a curse and a blessing. As expressed in this section, African-American concerns voice themselves through a double discourse wherein 'he say' (4) transmogrifies into 'I say' while still remaining 'out of sight.' The planters enjoy, although at a decreasing rate, the products of African American labor, yet they cannot particularize the source of such commodities. The African-American voice adding to the plurality of 'Barn Burning' here describes the occasional benefits of such narrow-mindedness.

In the next movement of the text, the story's narrative flux is paralleled by the peripatetic nature of the Snopes family. A metonym for the 'rootless' life of the sharecropper, the Snopes' nomadic existence at once reflects justice and injustice. For the planter, the Snopeses have betrayed the personal relationships at the heart of the paternalist system. The animalistic Ab represents the very worst in the poor whites, and his refusal to see the 'mutual' benefits of sharecropping condemns him to a hardscrabble life of poverty and violence. According to the fading aristocracy, Ab's lack of vision compels him to miss the reciprocity in the relationship, the economic advantages for both the tenant and landlord. His eviction from the community is thus deserved and just. Ab, on the other hand, expresses no passion in his resistance. The ceaseless caravans to different locales spark no outward bitterness, nor do they lead to reckless outbursts of violence. Ab is deliberate in his actions, but pure hatred seems lacking and only a distilled sense of passive-aggressive behavior signals his latent emotion. Clearly, though, Ab feels that his labor entitles him to more power than it does.

Independent of both of the above voices is the concept of private property. The struggle between the two parties is based in part on the notion that individuals may own land. The planters desire to retain their control, while Ab's actions suggest that he believes that land should belong to those who work it. One might suggest that Ab does not represent widespread resentment, but Kevin Railey's observation that 'planters who rented land to blacks would find their barns or houses burned to the ground' suggests otherwise, particularly with regard to the system's racial component (Railey 1999, 9). Regardless, neither argument proffers the suggestion that land should be held in common or that the products of labor should be shared. Such an option certainly existed in the 1890s, and by the Depression of the 1930s it was widespread in the United States. A socialist or communist solution to the modernization debate is an option unvoiced by the figures in the story – or by Faulkner himself – but the text's polyphony allows it to co-exist with the ideological intentions of the characters.[5] The source of Ab's negative actions, private property 'graphically exemplifies' how its attendant conditions dehumanize the Snopes family and turns them alternately into automatons laboring for others or brutes, scrambling to find what should – by virtue of their work – already be theirs: food, shelter, security, clothing (Byrne 2002). Instead, they must haul the 'sorry residue of the dozen or more movings which even the boy could remember' from site to site, all the while possessing the foreknowledge that the next 'paintless two-room house' would hold prospects no different than the ones before it (Faulkner 1961, 6, 9). Apparently beyond the ken of the warring classes is the possibility that individuals such as Ab Snopes might become less alienated and dangerous should private property and the conditions it creates be abolished. Suggesting an interpretation that contemplates the story's 'complex interplay of diverse perspectives,' Marilyn Claire Ford states that 'glamorizing' Ab as a proletarian warrior neglects the character's similarities to the system he detests: 'he tyrannizes his wretched family mercilessly' (Ford 1998, 536). The 'wolf-like independence' that separates him from his community might dissolve should its foundation – class tension – disappear (Faulkner 1961, 7). While the characters might not recognize it, the narrative's polyphony allows such a prospect to express itself.

Yet another set of voices in this section arise from Sarty's psychological development. Sarty's chronological duality manifests itself for the first time in this movement, and the narrative perspective reveals an outward manifestation of the overall polyphonous nature of the text. R. Rio-Jellife asserts that this strategy allows 'the two strains [to] qualify or subvert one another, and amplify ironic overtones sounded among discrepant voices' (1994, 104). One might add with Bakhtin that such qualification extends to other voices as well. In the 'exile' phase of the text, the voices of the immature and mature Sarty express their positions, but they do not compete with one another. Young Sarty exhibits a naïve critical position regarding the exile, whereas the older Sarty evinces a more complex, self-aware mode. While Ab still controls the boy's physical movements – he prevents Sarty from pursuing the 'moonlike' antagonist with a single flat command: 'go get in the wagon' – his influence on the child's mind, particularly its sense of ethics, is visibly waning (Faulkner 1961, 6). Released from the claustrophobic and unfamiliar realm of the courtroom, Sarty twice attempts to analyze his father's recidivism, only to censor himself. Sarty's naïve position prompts him to view Ab's actions from without, from their effects: '*Forever* he thought. *Maybe he's done satisfied now, now that he has...* stopping himself, not to say it aloud even to himself' (7). Sarty here reveals that he is moving beyond the self-pity ensuing from his desire to establish roots and toward an absolute sense that his father is wrong and amoral. He cuts himself short, however, because the conflict between his mental development and his familial loyalty has not yet reached the crisis point implicit in his full name, Colonel Sartoris Snopes, a appellation that Richard Godden notes '[is] forced historically apart' (1997, 129). Ab's patriarchal eye still follows him within the confines of his consciousness.[6] Interestingly, Ab apparently detects Sarty's wavering dedication – possibly because the boy is too silent, too reflective – and, after delivering a blow that is 'hard but without heat,' lectures him, 'you got to learn to stick to your own blood or you ain't going to have any blood to stick to' (Faulkner 1961, 9). For the callow boy, Ab's binary seems exhaustive; a choice must be made, once and for all. This cognitive paradigm echoes the ideological intentions demonstrated by the older characters and their respective classes.

Viewing the events from a temporal and spatial distance, though, the mature Sarty problematizes such a limited view. Contemplating Ab's practice of economical fires, Sarty – via free indirect discourse – progresses from incredulity over the notion that a man so heedless of the property of others should be careful in starting fires to the thought that Ab's fugitive status during the war may have ingrained the custom within him. Ultimately, though, he rejects this for a metaphoric interpretation that casts fire in the role of the 'deep mainspring of his father's being' (8). The mature Sarty thus recognizes in Ab's actions more than a visceral hatred for the social order that tries to emasculate him. Rather than the black and white justice demanded by Harris, Sarty offers an alternative that makes allowances for the enigmatic forces that drive Ab onward. Such catalysts are beyond the comprehension of everyone, including Ab, and might be characterized as the unconscious. Sarty realizes that this unconscious is ineffable, but he nonetheless believes that understanding irrational behavior is impossible without pondering its existence. Sarty's position is indicative of the *possibility* of forgiveness in a way that the assessment of his younger incarnation is not. The mature Sarty is thus far more ambivalent about Ab than even the confused young boy, for experience has taught him to distrust moral prescriptions and arrogant certitudes. Not quite a moral relativist, Sarty does rebuke Ab for his arson ('if I had said they wanted only truth, justice, he would have hit me again'), but he no longer sees his father, à la Harris, as an unthinking beast or as completely inscrutable (9). Rather, Sarty attempts to contextualize Ab's behavior and dissect it accordingly.

At the periphery of this debate over Ab's character, but nonethe-less impacted enormously by it, are the repressed females of the Snopes family. As in the previous section, women are physically marginalized, but their voices are enlisted in the text's polyphony. Sarty's mother, irrevocably bound to Ab and his vengeful ways, must move from domicile to domicile without protest. Her distress over this lack of physical autonomy manifests itself first in tears and then in concern over Sarty's wounds, a reaction that Ab rebuffs with a brisk 'get back in the wagon' (7). Sarty models his father's behavior when, in response to his mother's concern, he commands her to 'lemme be' (7). In this way, both father and son elevate their own sense of power at the expense of the mother. Still carrying the clock, now broken and 'stopped at some fourteen minutes past two o'clock of a dead and forgotten day and time,' that served as her dowry, Mrs. Snopes futilely attempts to live with some sense of dignity (6). Her daughters, however, bristle at the prospect of yet another move and openly defy Ab: 'likely hit ain't fitten for hawgs' (9). Although Ab bullies them into compliance ('you'll hog it and like it'), the sisters, described pejoratively as 'big, bovine, in a flutter of cheap ribbons,' nonetheless announce an alternative discourse that exists alongside those of Ab and the others (9). Their ridicule of the shack undercuts both the sharecropping paradigm and the patriarchal institutions that bolster it. Seen in this light, their seemingly 'bovine' indolence might comprise a subversive strategy designed – however unconsciously – to expose the moral hollowness of paternalism. Unlike their mother, the sisters make no pretense about their condition. While a monologic reading of the story might concur with the negative assessment of the narrator regarding the sisters, a dialogic interpretation allows them their own voice without judging it in isolation.

The third movement, contract, continues Sarty's tutelage in the ways of blood kin. Bent on emphasizing the content of his lecture with a physical demonstration, Ab tells Sarty that he 'reckon[s to] have a word with the man that aims to begin tomorrow owning me body and soul for the next eight months' (10). Far from showing his landlord the deference demanded by the paternal system, Ab designs to make his presence felt, and he wants Sarty to witness his actions. Sarty's mother recognizes that Ab may subvert yet another contract and weakly attempts to stop him from taking the boy, but to no avail. On the way to the de Spain house, Ab willfully steps in a pile of manure. Ab's action mocks the superior attitude of the landlord by confirming the tenant's status in the relationship as 'inferior' and bringing latent fears about degenerate behavior to the fore. While Ab recognizes that he cannot change his situation without sacrificing his basic needs, he does evince a proto-proletarian consciousness that vaguely senses the need for fundamental structural transformation from a feudal society to one of equals. Clearly, Ab sees that the system itself will never recognize him as a man; therefore, he will behave like a beast. Blatantly ignoring admonitions to leave, Ab tracks dung across Lula de Spain's rug, a possession costing, perhaps, more than Ab earns in a year, and certainly valued more than the labor that made it possible. Ab notes this fact to Sarty when he oberves the de Spain mansion's lustrous white paint: 'that's sweat. Nigger sweat. Maybe it ain't white enough yet to suit him. Maybe he wants to mix some white sweat with it' (13). Ab intuits the commodity fetish pervasive to the Southern economic system and notes its basic injustice: aristocratic luxury stems from lower-class toil.

As Ab probably predicted, the soiled rug yields negative consequences, and de Spain, a 'linen-clad man on a fine sorrel mare' orders him to clean the rug (13). The imbalance in their social class pronounced by the symbolic power of the horse, the two men interpret the dictum in vastly different ways. De Spain assumes that the rug will be returned in its original state, but Ab, literally interpreting the charge, employs crude methods of cleaning the item, which results in 'long, water-cloudy scoriations' (15). The hermeneutic schism is significant, for it both physically recasts Sarty's inner debate and parodies the rug's value as a commodity. In the first instance, Sarty, attracted to the hitherto unknown material wealth represented in the rug (Tony Fabijancic [1994], for instance, remarks that the boy, 'experiences a surge of joy' at seeing the mansion' and its 'aura of power'), must contrast the pull of objects with the labor that produced them (87). The de Spains seem majestic, regal, in large part because of their possessions. Ab appears crude, animalistic, chiefly because he denies the inherent worth of commodities (or, perhaps, because he recognizes that *his* [devalued] work creates the value within the material). The latter construction works by juxtaposing the labor that Ab's daughters put into cleaning the rug with its utter *lack* of value after they have completed the task. Ab's parody continues as he 'hunche[s]' the rug onto the porch with a 'thunderous' sound, an action that clearly denies importance to the possession and satirizes his own role as beast of burden (16). De Spain, of course, is not satisfied, and attempts to increase the terms of Ab's contract in order to 'teach [him] to wipe off [his] feet before entering [Mrs. de Spain's] house again' (17). The class warfare becomes palpable in this scene, with de Spain taking the role of an intellectual and moral superior who must educate his inferior. Ab most certainly is not a gentleman, but de Spain feels that his tenant must learn to respect those who are.

The above conflict plays a major role in shaping young Sarty's ethical sense. Initially, Sarty is both surprised and honored to accompany his father to the de Spain house. Because Sarty notices that Ab had 'paused afterward to explain why' he had hit him, the boy realizes that he has experienced a rite of passage toward man-hood (10). The de Spain estate impresses him as being as 'big as a courthouse,' an observation that unwittingly – but tellingly – merges the economic and judicial systems (11). Immediately, Sarty detects the gulf between the de Spains and the Snopeses, a gap that functions as an ethical boundary. Although he cannot express the thought in words, Sarty assumes, falsely it turns out, that the polarities of the class hierarchy – represented by the 'peace' of the estate – will protect the de Spains from Ab's arson: 'people who are a part of this peace and dignity are beyond his touch' (11). Sarty's feel-ings stem from an identification with the ideology of paternalism, which offers the working class 'security' in exchange for labor. In 'ideal' paternalism, a transference of 'pride' takes place from landlord to tenant. Sarty's mesmerized reactions (he was 'deluged as by a warm wave') strongly suggest that the boy unconsciously validates this ideal (12). His horror regarding Ab's treatment of the rug, moreover, foreshadows his ultimate rejection of Ab's theorem regarding duty to family above all else. Rather than approve of Ab's petty rebellion, Sarty is repelled and begins to conflate aristocratic self-interest with moral value: what is good for the de Spains is good for all. While vestiges of his loyalty to family remain – his admiration for Ab's mule-like march with the rug, for example, or his protest of de Spain's alteration of the contract: 'you done the best you could' – Sarty's allegiances seem to shift markedly to the propertied class (17). As the week progresses, Sarty experiences relief in the fact that Ab has not burned down de Spain's barn, a temporary serenity that belies his vocal objections to de Spain's penalty: 'maybe this is the end of it' (18). Sarty has internalized the de Spain's ideology.

Also apparently subscribing to the de Spain ideology is the African American servant who chastises Ab. At first glance, the old man seems perfectly dedicated to Lula and her rug. The servant protests loudly at Ab's loutish behavior and attempts to get him to leave the premises. When one examines the scene closely, however, one may detect a complicity between Ab and the butler. Historically distinguished from 'field' slaves, African domestics enjoyed some privileges, yet their proximity to the commodities earned by their brethren's labor visibly reinforced their own low status. Employing various covert means, such domestics often tried to control or devalue such commodities, despite harsh retaliation if they were discovered. In this instance, the servant – who has clearly watched Ab's stroll through the excrement – perhaps enables the white man in his destruction of de Spain property. Although the servant possesses a lifestyle far superior to that of Ab, the sharecropping system's dual division of class and race definitely placed Ab higher on the social scale. Thus, the man knew that his outward objection to Ab's entering the house ('wipe your foots, white man, fo you come in here') would be brushed aside: 'get out of my way, nigger' (12). The servant could have prevented Ab from entering simply by locking the door. By letting him in, however, he all but seals the fate of the rug, no doubt one of many symbols of his own inferiority in the eyes of the de Spains. Lula, predictably, neither looks at Ab nor listens to her servant's weak explanation ('I tried ... I tole him to ...') and focuses her attention on her property (13). Without any negative consequences for himself – other than, perhaps, a reprimand for opening the door – the old man exploits the racial bias in the aristocratic system and engages in a seditious act that silently concurs with Ab's assessment of whose sweat built the house.

In the story's final movement, betrayal, Sarty reaches a seemingly irrevocable decision regarding the placement of his loyalty. Not comprehending that his father, not Major de Spain, initiated legal action, the boy at first assumes that Ab is once again on trial for arson and that, this time, the charges are unwarranted: 'he ain't done it! He ain't burnt ...' (19). Sarty desperately believes that Ab has finally given up his resistance to the moral order. Ab meets the boy's outburst with habitual coolness, ordering him out of the court. Sarty ignores this mandate, a defiance that prefigures his ultimate betrayal of his father's ethical code. At the end of the trial, when Ab is ordered to pay a portion of his crop over and above his initial contract, Sarty exclaims that de Spain won't get anything. For his part, Ab makes a final gesture to 'convince' Sarty of the need to support family no matter what the stakes. Trying to initiate the boy, Ab buys some cheese and 'divide[s] it carefully and deliberately into three,' a sort of mock trinity designed to show Sarty that, as a man, he should establish a united front with his family (22). As a condition of his faith in family, Sarty is later commanded to participate with his father and brother in the ritual of barn burning by fetching the accelerant. Because he assumed that no one would dare burn down a house as splendid as that of the de Spains, Sarty is completely taken aback: '"what..." he cried. "What are you..."' (23). Confused at this seeming paradox, Sarty contemplates absconding, but finally complies. However, the boy tries to appeal to his father's ethical center – one which ironically stems from the 'high' moral code of the de Spains – and asks, 'ain't you going to even send a nigger?' a question that reveals Sarty's ultimate detachment from his father's *ethos* (23). Ab, divining Sarty's final defection, prompts his wife to hold her son, but, ready to turn thought into action, he escapes and alerts de Spain. Later, hearing what he believes to be the gunshots that end Ab's life, a remorseful Sarty whispers 'he was brave' (26). Nonetheless, 'he did not look back,' his ideological intentions revealed at last (27).[7]

Bakhtin suggests that an author's ideological intentions necessarily reflect those of his characters but that a polyphonous text transcends such limitations. The plurality of voices in 'Barn Burning' does resist the call to decide the 'legitimacy' of the ideologies manifest in the various characters. Is Ab pure evil, or is he a proletarian hero? Is Sarty justified in his betrayal, or is he complicit with the very forces that keep him in tattered, disintegrating clothes? While Faulkner seemingly invites his readers to judge the boy's decision – Carothers holds that 'explicit judgment is a constant technique' in the story – the writer's own ambivalence undercuts this effort (Carothers 1985, 61). Neither the narrator nor the older Sarty ultimately define the ideological imperative for the story, and it is quite clear that all of the various voices possess strengths and weaknesses that make them insufficient in and of themselves. The Snopses' migration (and, more subtly, the upheaval of the Depression during which Faulkner wrote) tangibly emphasizes this ideological flux: each locale/position begins to look equally barren. 'Barn Burning' resists becoming mere polemic, however, for it simply cannot choose a monologic perspective. The dichotomies dissolve into the chorus of indicative of dialogic consciousness, an 'uneasy and unstable balance of forces and ideologies,' as Railey terms it (1999, 10). As with Faulkner's own conflict over the character of the new South, Sarty's struggle cannot resolve itself.[8] 'Barn Burning' thus conforms to Eagleton's view of the text as both being informed by ideology and producing ideology, for its many voices express distinct ideological positions yet they contribute to an entity that is occasionally quite at odds with those intentions.

7   George Orwell's *1984* and Political Ideology

From its release in 1949, George Orwell's *1984* has been considered a stinging indictment of totalitarian ideology. Unlike many other texts, Orwell's novel seems overtly to suggest its ideological underpinnings and place aesthetic considerations squarely in the background.[1] For critics such as Richard Lowenthal (1983, 209) and Tosco R. Fyvel (1984, 73), Orwell provides a transparent – but nevertheless powerful – condemnation of Stalinism and a prescient warning against the proliferation of totalitarian methods. In this light, Orwell, working from a 'common sense' socialist position that eschews dogmatic rhetoric, exposes the dehumanizing qualities of systemic terror. Both sympathetic and hostile critics usually ground their discussions of *1984* in the assumption that Orwell offers 'substantially little more than an extension into the near future of the present structure and policy of Stalinism' (Rahv 1987, 14). For the inhabitants of Oceania, ideology – irrational and sadistic – crushes not only the feeble resistance of 'rebels' like Winston Smith and Julia, but also disintegrates the human spirit and transmogrifies it into a repository of platitudes. Aided by what Rob Kroes deems a 'dislocation of human understanding by linguistic sabotage,' the Inner Party employs ideology to eliminate the very possibility of thought (Kroes 1985, 85). According to such interpretations, Orwell sets his dystopia in England as a check against factions within British socialism that he feels are open to influence from Stalinism.

Alternately, however, Erich Fromm, in a tantalizingly brief section in his discussion of the novel, points readers of *1984* not only toward the Soviet Union but toward the United States and the West as well. For Fromm, Orwell excoriates the capitalist West for many of the same tendencies evident in totalitarian states, claiming that 'managerial industrialism, in which man [sic] builds machines which act like men and develops men who act like machines, is conducive to an era of dehumanization and complete alienation, in which men are transformed into things and become appendices to the process of production and consumption' (Fromm 1983, 267). Fromm's assessment of Orwell's dual purpose seems apt, for while Big Brother and Emmanuel Goldstein certainly resemble Stalin and Trotsky in both physiognomy and philosophy, using the geographic 'logic' of the novel, the setting is awry, for a disguised Soviet Union would appear to suggest Eurasia rather than Oceania. Airstrip One owes its allegiance, moreover, to a more distantly western entity, which certainly suggests the United States.[2] In a three-superpower world (Eastasia/China represents the third power), totalitarianism has spread far beyond its Stalinist roots. Antony Easthope validates such a perspective, observing that 'liberal democracy is complicit with the totalitarianism it would condemn in that it supports the undemocratic structures of corporate capitalism and state paternalism' (Easthope 1984, 267). Although Lowenthal rejects postulations such as those offered by Fromm and Easthope, arguing that 'Orwell did *not* believe ... that the social conformity of advanced capitalist democracies ... was essentially similar to totalitarian party dictatorship,' he offers little in the way of evidence to support his purported knowledge of Eric Blair's thoughts (Lowenthal 1983, 209). Indeed, one cannot simply dismiss Fromm's intriguing comments out of hand, for they at least offer a potential explanation for the demise of free market capitalism and its leading exponent, the United States, an account that asserts that the 'danger [of totalitarianism is] ... relatively independent of ideology' (Fromm 1983, 267). One might, in fact, posit that Orwell's use of totalitarianism predicates itself on the end of ideology.

In his best-selling *The End of History and the Last Man* (1992), Francis Fukuyama examines the demise of totalitarianism in Eastern Europe and suggests that the victory of liberal democracy, which represents an 'ideology of potential universality,' portends the end of history – and, thus, ideology (42). In its attempt to dominate, the totalitarian state swims meekly against the relentless current of human progress. For Fukuyama, the whole point of empirical methodology is to bolster human security and conquer nature in order to fulfill material wants (76). Because totalitarian governments emphasize collective security rather than individual desire, they fail to mesh with what Fukuyama regards as the inevitable course of human history. While occasional ruptures or discontinuities have appeared, the fundamental historical pattern indicates a consistent prejudice for liberal democracy. Totalitarianism ignores this controlling principle and, thus, with its 'bankruptcy of serious ideas,' cannot sustain its internal logic indefinitely (39). Simply stated, there is 'now no ideology with pretensions to universality that is in a position to challenge liberal democracy' (45). China's ideological threat 'is finished' (36) and Islam 'has virtually no appeal outside those areas that were culturally Islamic to begin with' (46). With astonishing surety, Fukuyama posits that liberal democracy (usually of the capitalist variety) echoes the innermost desires of humanity and, in its purest form, will mark the end of history. Although 'a host of problems like unemployment, pollution, drugs, crime, and the like' will still exist, the absence of any 'deeper sources of discontentment' will preclude a return to history and its ideological posturing (288).

Opposing Orwell's vision of totalitarianism, Fukuyama holds that 'the most fundamental failure of totalitarianism was its failure to control thought' (1992, 29). While doublethink and thoughtcrime might serve for interesting fiction, Fukuyama is clearly skeptical of their practical applications. Despite concerted attempts to exercise state authority within the confines of the human mind, the innate need for *thymos* (self-recognition) undercuts efforts to control individual imagination (162). Confidently employing an essentialist view of 'human nature,' Fukuyama suggests that psychological terror of the sort practiced by O'Brien can never completely efface the quasi-instinctive drive to improve material conditions and seek recognition. Discontent might become liminal, but it will ultimately explode (if the regime's own decaying infrastructure does not collapse beforehand). Totalitarianism, based on a *megalothymian* principle of state superiority, must fail in the face of *isothymia*, 'the desire to be recognized as the equal of other people' (190). Because 'recognition based on groups is ultimately irrational,' the neo-Hegelian Fukuyama inverts Marx's premise and argues that totalitarian communism holds its contradiction within itself (242). Control based on abstractions – even ostensibly positive ones – pales in comparison to control based on collective practice. In denying the agency of its citizens, totalitarianism grounds itself in limited self-interest (consequently, Fukuyama would not accept O'Brien's notion of self-perpetuating power). Because its discipline derives from innate tendencies, liberal democracy stands a much stronger chance of outlasting history. Based on the 'scientific' fulfillment of the human desire for comfort (the economic imperative) and the 'natural' drive for rational autonomy, the final incarnation of capitalist democracy – according to Fukuyama – would result in a 'completely satisfying' state (206).

Fukuyama characterizes his world-without-history as a peaceful place where wars are irrelevant (ideological jealousy being obsolete) and humans are content (1992, 311). Interestingly, he also holds with Alexandre Kojève that art and philosophy will disappear for want of subject matter: the possibility of change would not exist (311). As with well-fed dogs dozing in the sun, humans would have no need to look beyond their own noses (311). If they were inclined, artists could repeat themes and approaches, but they could not innovate. Fukuyama does not lament such a loss, however, for the absence of ontological and epistemological friction would create conditions so blissful that no one would desire to pursue visions of a better life. Creativity would be channeled through other means, such as economic and scientific activity (315). While survival would not depend on entrepreneurs or increased efficiency, the natural desire for *thymos* would find an outlet in such activities.[3] Plenty of opportunity, then, would exist for those who felt some inner compulsion to do more than simply scratch their full bellies or enjoy the latest gadget. The 'homogeneous' world, therefore, would not constitute the ontological equivalent of a coma, but rather would represent the culmination of all human desires and instincts. Unlike Ursula LeGuin's Omelas, however, such a utopia would not be founded – according to Fukuyama – upon an essential injustice but upon ideology-free, 'natural' principles that all humans hold in common. Any inequality that remains at the end of history would not be traced to systemic imbalances but rather to the 'natural inequality of talents' (291). For Orwell, however, the end of history is far from the sunny paradise that Fukuyama envisions.

In *1984*, Orwell depicts not only Stalinist brutality pursued to its vicious extreme. The narrative also presents a horrifying vision of the consequences of absorbing an ideology so completely, so unquestioningly, as to eliminate ideology altogether. In this way, *1984* represents not an *example* of ideology but a world *without* ideology. As Winston's position in the Ministry of Truth reveals, history has ended in Oceania, replaced by a ubiquitous present less convinced of its own righteousness than unaware of any alternate ontological possibilities. Unlike Fukuyama, Orwell conceptualizes the end of history as a grim, vacuous realm where struggle has ceased and canine-like contentment is omnipresent. Paradoxically, Orwell's Oceania, free of political strife and economic dissatisfaction, represents not a utopia but a dystopia. Curiously, Orwell depicts ideology – utterly vanquished and annihilated beyond possibility – in a romantic, even nostalgic, way in *1984*, for its absence leads to a dispassionate, soulless existence that must manufacture a faux ideological opponent to avoid the risk of mass psychological implosion. For Orwell, the prospect of erasing ideological difference elicits not celebration but fear, for a society without debate – even among a tiny elite – is a society that breeds terror. As Winston's tormentor O'Brien points out, Oceania's ideology-free system substitutes self-perpetuating 'collective' power for inefficient individual power, which is based on the possibility of resistance and dies with its owner (Orwell 1983, 218). Oceania contains no endings, no beginnings, no history. It is.

Although the system that Oceania represents is definitely suggestive of totalitarianism, it would be better characterized as post-totalitarian. Irving Howe calls for such an interpretation, remarking that 'the world of 1984 is *not* totalitarianism as we know it, but totalitarianism after its world triumph' (Howe 1982, 332). One finds more support for Howe's observation in Hannah Arendt's magisterial work on totalitarianism. For Arendt, totalitarianism represents an attempt to destroy the need for *consensus iuris*, the process whereby society agrees to a set of laws, and 'make mankind itself the embodiment of law' (Arendt 1968, 462). In this way, 'totalitarian policy claims to transform the human species into an active carrier of a law to which human beings would otherwise only passively and reluctantly be subjected' (462). Arendt's formulation of totalitarianism, furthermore, states that 'ideologies are never interested in the miracle of being,' preferring the realms of 'becoming' and 'perishing' to the victory itself (469). Arendt focuses on process, on the heinous but dynamic act of bending a people to the 'will' of an idea. Totalitarianism gains its momentum from both the rhetoric and act of terror, inscribing the latter within the former: terror is the method by which the idea will be absorbed by – not imposed on – an unwilling and foolish public (for its own good). Much as suspects, under extreme duress, honestly confess to crimes that they did not commit, the inhabitants of a totalitarian society eventually come to believe in the very government that injures them. The pain stops when acceptance is absolute. Arendt, however, clearly suggests that totalitarianism without an enemy or a backslider portends the end of ideology: 'it would mean the end of history itself if rudimentary classes did not form so that they in turn could "wither away" under the hands of totalitarian rulers' (464). Such is the state of affairs in Oceania.

The 'becoming' and 'perishing' of which Arendt speaks do not exist in Oceania, a realm of the infinite present. Orwell indicates that the process of becoming ended years ago for the leaders of Oceania and its enemies: 'the purpose of all of them was to arrest progress and freeze history at a chosen moment' (1983, 167). Isaac Deutscher views such comments as evidence that 'Orwell saw totalitarianism as bringing history to a standstill' (Deutscher 1982, 342). While the state continues to 'fight' its enemies, Goldstein's *The Theory and Practice of Oligarchical Collectivism* (a parody of Trotsky's *The Revolution Betrayed* [1937]) reveals that a geographic and technologic equilibrium prevents the three superpowers from expanding their territories in any but the most tentative way.[4] In effect, the regimes engage in the simulacrum of war in order to prop up an obsolete class structure. While Ruth Ann Lief argues that 'Party unity is assured by adherence to a common ideology,' her proposition assumes a conscious sense of direction lacking (even according to O'Brien) in Oceania, where hollow ritual has replaced burning idealism (Lief 1969, 93). The phenomenon that Fukuyama labels the 'crisis of authoritarianism,' the inability for *megalothymian* self-interest to subsume human desire, fails to materialize in Oceania, and the system continues to lumber on long after its original practitioners are dead (Fukuyama 1992, 13). Although totalitarian measures still exist, they are no longer required to transform the overwhelming majority into zealots for the party. As Fyvel points out, 'there is not even any political ideology left to oppose, so that resistance becomes nonsensical' (Fyvel 1984, 77). So effectively has the system reprogrammed the citizens of London – and by extension all of Oceania – that rebellion has to be either fabricated, as in the case of the innocuous Parsons, or else cultivated, as with Winston. While the former represents the discovery of 'repressed' anti-Big Brother sentiment by children, the latter signifies a more curious situation in which Winston's halting gestures against conformity had been observed and tolerated for at least eleven years (Orwell 1983, 212). A totalitarian state, no doubt, would have crushed such behavior at its first signs, but a post-totalitarian government, in search of any 'enemy' that could regenerate the 'becoming'/'perishing' binary, might attempt to 'grow' Winston's discontent like a hothouse flower, cutting it down only after it had reached full bloom. While Winston assumes that 'purges and vaporizations were a necessary part of government,' such instances seem to stem more from habit than from necessity (41). The citizens have internalized doublethink and need little in the way of real monitoring: even the telescreens, representing a high-tech panopticon, frequently have no guardian on the other side, for everyone lived 'from habit that became instinct' as though 'every sound [they] made was overheard' (6–7).[5]

Oceania thus exists as a paradox, for while it craves enemies, with their concomitant positionality (spatio-temporal starting/ending points), it nonetheless cannot subvert its own ultimate victory as represented in its atemporality. The defamiliarization of time, most famously represented in the novel by the clock striking thirteen, is the culmination of Oceania's decades-long project of obliterating the past and making the future irrelevant (5). O'Brien sums up this tendency as he catechizes Winston during his 'reintegration': 'who controls the past controls the future; who controls the present controls the past' (204). Consequently, the Party places complete stress on the immediate moment, blurring any chance of temporal comparison. Winston, for example, can only crudely determine the year ('it was never possible nowadays to pin down any date within a year or two'), for the continuum itself represents the unthinkable: time before Oceania (10). The speaker at a Hate Week rally, furthermore, finds no problem in informing the crowd mid-sentence in condemnation of Eurasia that their enemy is, and always was, Eastasia (149). Julia has little conception of how many sexual partners she has had, and the old prole whom Winston queries seems not to project any knowledge of life before the Party. Five-year plans never seem to end, and Big Brother (or Goldstein, for that matter) never ages. Winston's own memories seem impossible, and the antique shop he frequents is fraudulent (perhaps everything it contains has been created by members of the Party) and superfluous: there is no call for antiquities in a society of ubiquitous presence. The Party has, in effect, ruptured the very fabric of time and rendered it meaningless outside of the present. Unlike Fukuyma and his contention that the end of history will be characterized by the 'smallness of its actual remaining inequalities,' Orwell views such omnipresence with fear and loathing (Fukuyma 1992, 295). For Orwell, the bureaucratization of society that Fukuyama anticipates in a post-historical society yields not only efficiency but an enervating lack of motivation. Because the past does not exist, no one exhibits a sense of progress (apart from the pseudo-progress depicted in counterfeit reports of 'record' output of consumption goods and the like), and, as the future is an alien concept, no one can set long-term goals and is doomed to a static death-in-life. By implication, Orwell suggests that as long as ideology exists, struggle prevails and hope continues. In Oceania, the Party has vanquished hope forever, the Brotherhood not withstanding.

Oceania's post-ideological status manifests itself most clearly in Winston's job at the Ministry of Truth. Charged with expunging 'errors' from printed material, Winston's department adjusts all texts to conform with the requirements of the present. Since the Party cannot make mistakes, any discrepancies between the printed word and official policy must be eliminated: 'all history was a palimpsest, scraped clean and reinscribed exactly as often as was necessary' (Orwell 1983, 36). Such a step, however, is superfluous, for the Party's doctrine is so pervasive as to constitute reality rather than ideology. Even should references to Party miscalculations escape detection, it is doubtful that anyone would notice because the sheer weight of the present would overwhelm the past. Old newspapers, like Winston's 'ancient' paperweight/talisman, would hold no appeal for the Party faithful, who would subscribe to whatever the current speaker imparted. Just as doublethink could explain away anti-Eurasia war posters as the work of Goldstein-influenced saboteurs, it could ascribe images of non-persons or narrative inconsistencies to the handiwork of Big Brother's enemies. The parameters of thought are such that – except in the increasingly sporadic cases of 'pure' subversion evident in the (literally) dying breed of Winston's generation – Party inaccuracy is utterly impossible. Even had Winston retained the surreptitious photograph of Jones, Aaronson, and Rutherford, he would hardly have been in a position to convince anyone of its origin, despite his belief that 'it was enough to blow the Party to atoms' (67). O'Brien, for example, easily dismisses it as pure 'invention,' even though Winston has seen the picture, prompting Winston to question his own sanity (211). While smuggled copies of Solzhenitsyn or Pasternak may have resonated with furtive Soviet dissidents, their Oceanic counterparts would have been viewed as the products of Oceania's 'enemies' and, thus, discounted accordingly. Counter-ideology is invisible, particularly among children and young adults who, of course, were born after the Party's hegemony was complete. As O'Brien tells Winston, the Party 'cut the links between child and parent' (220). Even the hazy memory of ideology is recast as fantastic. Winston's rebellion, therefore, amuses, rather than infuriates, the Inner Party, and exemplifies the futility of resistance. No one hears him.

Apparently, most people in Oceania unquestioningly accept their system as signifying the terminus of human development. No viable alternative to the Oceanic worldview exists, for Orwell suggests that Eastasia and Eurasia are quite similar in outlook: they 'are not divided by any genuine ideological difference' (153). More important, however, is the absence of even the *sub rosa* desire for such an option. Orwell's largely undifferentiated characters – caricatures, really – truly seem to bask in their existence, reveling in their hate for Goldstein and applauding Big Brother in 'electric thrill' (244). Of those characters that Orwell does delineate in more detail, only Winston and Julia rebel overtly, and for Winston, Julia's resistance is 'from the waist downwards,' a phenomenon indicating instinctive physical hunger, rather than ontological questioning (129).[6] The *thymos* that Fukuyama requires for ontological viability seems for all but a few citizens – such as Winston – to manifest itself in unwavering dedication either to bureaucratic functions or to various social superstructures such as group hikes or the Spies. Art and philosophy are produced – quite efficiently – by machine, and political dissent is rare to the point of suggesting mental aberration. People throw themselves eagerly into state-sponsored activities such as the Junior Anti-Sex League and the two-minutes hate. Apart from Winston, fear, which Philip Rahv claims results in a 'psychology of capitulation,' seems eerily absent from Oceania (Rahv 1987, 16). Contentment, a prerequisite for Fukuyama's post-ideological world, is rampant.

The bounty that Fukuyama anticipates for such a society, however, materializes only in tepid gin, razor blade shortages, and chocolate of dubious quality. The efficiency that Fukuyama claims will outpace traditional social groups and portend the fulfillment of desire, furthermore, aids only disembodied power (Fukuyama 1992, 77). Inequality is institutionalized and revered: 'freedom is slavery' (Orwell 1983, 17). While the average citizens of Oceania have little to do with war per se, they nonetheless endorse it, despite Fukuyama's assertion that post-historical contentment will yield the cessation of war (Fukuyama 1992, 311). In effect, Orwell seems not only to have envisioned the end of history long before Fukuyama, but he turns that vision on its head. For Orwell, Winston may represent the 'last man,' but he certainly does not present a very compelling case for the end of history.[7] As an ideological warrior, Winston appears woefully inadequate. Lacking any sense of ideology apart from a vague and instinctive emptiness, Winston gropes along without purpose. Despite numerous outward signs that would preclude collaboration, Winston attempts to enlist Julia and O'Brien in his 'cause,' a foolish decision given that Winston has little idea as to their goals. Physically and mentally mediocre, Winston represents hope in a world devoid of struggle. His ultimate impotence (underscored by his initial inability to achieve an erection with Julia) manifests itself both in his wildly imprudent actions – particularly his establishing a love nest and failing to destroy Goldstein's book upon detection – and his ultimate 'reintegration' and love for Big Brother. O'Brien, assured that no ideological alternative exists, extirpates Winston's heterodoxy with ease: Winston's 'mind shriveled' (Orwell 1983, 214). Orwell clearly has little faith in the potential for revolution in a post-totalitarian state.

Even Goldstein's book offers little in the way of ideological opposition to the Party, a fact stemming, no doubt, from its being a product of O'Brien's authorship. Winston learns the answer to his question 'why?' but he certainly fails to discover any ontological alternative. Although Orwell's imitation of Trotsky's prose style presents a lucid history of Oceania's post-totalitarian methods – including the use of war to destroy surplus goods (155) and the principles of doublethink (176) – it does not appear to spur Winston on to consider ideological alternatives. Julia, moreover, falls asleep when Winston reads her *The Theory and Practice of Oligarchical Collectivism* not only because of her general contentment but because Goldstein's book fails to generate any revolutionary ideas. Orwell suggests that were Big Brother himself to read the text over the telescreen the impact would not be enough to over-come the desensitization to ideological conflict inherent in a post-totalitarian society. Rob Kroes considers such a phenomenon the result of 'an effort aimed at the total surrender of intellectual and moral sense' (Kroes 1985, 86). Oceania's residents, including Winston ('what most oppressed him was the consciousness of his own intellectual inferiority'), have ceded their ability to think to the system itself (Orwell 1983, 211). The country's political machinery is exposed to Winston, but without a viable counter-ideology he lacks the critical vocabulary to articulate alternatives and work toward its realization. Oceania's citizens are so stripped of independent thought that they cannot reinterpret society and imagine a distinctly different entity. Access to sexual partners, the refinement of Newspeak, the possession of a glass object – these acts hardly qualify as full-scale ideological rebellion. Winston exists at the margins of the Party, but he never leaves the circle itself, for his creative abilities are simply too atrophied to reenvision society. Once he is imprisoned, for example, Winston hardly proves a worthy adversary to O'Brien, who, convinced that history has culmin-ated in the concept of pure, self-perpetuating power, glibly swats away the criminal's confused objections. In Orwell's formulation, once the threshold of totalitarianism has been passed, a return to ideological struggle is impossible. While Fukuyama argues that totalitarianism is a historical aberration that represents a 'pathological condition' that will inevitably be corrected, Orwell's dystopia presents a stark counterpoint that explicitly maintains the 'condition' could become permanent if other ideologies are rendered unthinkable (Fukuyama 1992, 128).

Orwell's fear, therefore, lies less in the propositions of a particular ideology than in the absence of ideology. Nearly all ideologies advance a mythic future wherein its enemies have been vanquished. Concurring with Fukuyama, such self-mythologies present claims to historical finality, postulating that the past merely represents a prelude to the wondrous realm wherein every human desire will be fulfilled. In presenting Oceania as a society divested of possibility, Orwell critiques the principle of ideological inevitability and presents not a heavenly dream but a hellish nightmare. Valorizing the liberal subject, Orwell depicts Oceania as a subhuman society filled with witless citizens who cannot recognize their own subjugation. Even the elite class has been stripped of mental responsibility, for power itself is in control. The compartmentalization of human behavior and emotion has resulted in a bureaucratized, soulless state that cannot even remember its own original idealism. Once intent on destroying its ideological rivals, Oceania now drifts through an endless gray day of empty slogans and pointless tasks. As with unthinking beasts, the denizens of Oceania represent interchangeable parts of a collective unconcerned with individuation; the collective lurches instinctively forward, protecting its power for no other reason than to survive, like so many gnats forgoing sustenance in order to produce the next generation. According to Orwell's conception, all of the human attributes that Fukuyama links to historical struggle – Art, Philosophy, Beauty, Truth, Justice, Love – vanish when a society loses its contrasts, but unlike Fukuyama's paradigm, Orwell's model inscribes total contentment as a pejorative. Such a notion is unquestionably intertwined with what Marx would deem bourgeois liberalism, but it also functions in a rather conservative way, a trait noted by Philip Goldstein (2000, 44) and Carl Freedman, who points out Orwell's ambivalence toward the socialist project (1988, 167).

Written in a post-war era when Britain's status as imperial power had diminished considerably and permanently, *1984* mightily resists the changes promised by either American capitalism or Soviet communism. The novel elides the process whereby the superpowers entrenched their positions, but it emphasizes how their respective ideologies would produce draining, homogenizing effects if extended to their logical conclusions. Orwell, then, clearly rejects the utopian vision for which Fukuyama yearns. Far from yielding self-actualization, a conflict-free society irreparably damages the very essence of humanity and transforms life into a perfunctory trudge toward undifferentiated existence. The dingy milieu of Oceania betokens political stasis, ideological uniformity – which is to say it has no ideology at all. Any political system – be it communist, capitalist, or otherwise – that totally expunges dissent risks a devolution into utter imbecility. While O'Brien prizes Oceania's methods as being superior to the crude tactics of Hitler and Stalin and recognizes in his society's system the apotheosis of power itself, he fails to acknowledge that complete efficiency robs that power of significance. None of the powerless even discern that they lack power, and Inner Party members – being utterly interchangeable – lack true understanding beyond their function.

All sense of irony has been banished, and O'Brien, like Symes before him, is too good at his job and will inevitably be reprogrammed himself. As many critics, such as Lowenthal (1983, 210) and Gordon Beauchamp (1984, 75), have pointed out, Orwell offers not a prophecy in *1984* but a warning. He rails against all ideologies with pretensions toward comprehensive explanation, against any system so hubris-filled as to intimate that human civilization could not transcend its 'truths.' Orwell strongly suggests that the importance of Life lies, far beyond issues of economics and political creeds, within the process of resistance. Even Winston's meek overtures of rebellion constitute a grand Life when contrasted with the jingoist bravura of an Inner Party member, who, like Fukuyama's dog, merely exists. Ultimately, Orwell reveals a vision wherein Fukuyama's complacent, post-historical dog should be euthanized in order to clear the way for the return of ideological chaos and its attendant humanity.

Part III

Conclusion

8 The 'Post-Ideological' Era?

Responding by telegram to an obituary in the *New York Journal*, Mark Twain announced that 'the reports of my death have been greatly exaggerated' (1897). One would certainly not be misguided to follow Twain's advice with regard to the beleaguered concept of ideology, whose death-knell has prematurely tolled for over half a century. As Andrew Heywood wickedly proclaims, 'history [and with it ideology] has ended on a number of occasions in the last few centuries' (1992, 278). Despite the over 2100 books pertaining to ideology that one discovers on an unscientific search of amazon.com, theorists as diverse as Francis Fukuyama, John Horgan, Katie Roiphe, and Slavoj Žižek trumpet that we now live in a 'post-ideological' age. Although none of the above would claim that world turmoil has ceased, many would posit (at least during the 90s) that the struggle over the mechanism for change has been replaced by debate over pragmatic solutions to local problems. For example, echoing – and often citing – the work of earlier 'end-of-ideology' theorists such as Raymond Aron, Daniel Bell and Seymour Martin Lipset, conservatives such as Fukuyama and Milton Friedman confidently announce that Marx's formulation regarding historical inevitability was incorrect: free-market capitalism, not socialism, was the final step in the process of historical evolution. The decline of communism in the former Soviet Union and Eastern Europe marks the culmination of ideological struggle.[1] While conflicts will continue to exist, democratic capitalism contains the 'solutions' for such problems within itself. For such theorists, ideology per se is as outmoded as a whalebone corset.

The pervasiveness of such 'consensus' could be witnessed in such diverse manifestations as the 'lipstick' feminism of Karen Lehrman, the cultural relativism of Stanley Fish, and the general political malaise of the American electorate. 'Agreement' over the death of ideology reached its apogee, however, during the American presidential debates in October 2000. With the perception of unmatched economic prosperity and 'relative' world peace still before the viewing public, the campaigns of both Albert Gore and George W. Bush eschewed the extreme elements of their platforms in favor of centrist rhetoric that took it for granted that capitalism and its corollary institutions, such as individual autonomy, globalization, and free enterprise, represented not ideological distortion but the *absence* of ideology. Implicit in their (non)argument is the belief that modification of the American system should only occur as refinement, adjustment. While they ostensibly attempted to 'distinguish' themselves from one another, Bush and Gore practically tripped over themselves in agreement over the issues. Revealing 'end of history' demeanors, the candidates simply had little to say to one another. Any substantive differences that may have existed between the two men collapsed into quibbles over the practical methods of how to 'get the job done.' With communism 'out of the way,' America could settle down to the hard work of extending the benefits of capitalism to 'everyone.'[2] Clearly, socialized medicine undercuts the spirit of free enterprise, so the United States should focus its attention on a 'bill of rights' for patients: should it include a provision to sue one's HMO? That millions of citizens had no HMO to sue received little mention. The ideology-free system, of course, will eventually get around to solving such minor inconveniences. Not surprisingly, the election was one of the closest in American history, for the economy and the 'lack' of ideological opposition had apparently transformed the presidency from ideological spokesperson (Ronald Reagan, say) into the role of caretaker. As long as 'everyone' possessed an overflowing stock portfolio, even a moral delinquent like Bill Clinton could occupy the White House. While 'conservatives' and 'liberals' might have disagreed over school vouchers or taxes, they fundamentally agreed on the primacy of democratic capitalism.

One year later, however, few would have subscribed to the notion that history – and with it ideology – had ended. The attacks of 11 September 2001 poignantly underscored the narcissism of the post-ideological premise. As George F. Will observes, 'in 2001, a delusional, pre-modern enemy lashed out at American symbols – iconic buildings – and instantly magnified American power by dispelling an American mood – call it end-of-history complacency'

(Will 2002). One might add that such complacency is often the result of hegemonic dominance and that 'empires' from Rome to Turkey have succumbed to similar 'decadence.' That global capitalism – particularly the American version – dominates the international scene is hardly in dispute, but Will's characterization of the 'mood' of the 1990s underscores that ideology can become so pervasive as to be virtually transparent, as to reflect a false consciousness, in fact. In the 1990s, 'mainstream' American politics could not see alternative ideologies through the glare of its own recent victories and confused historically particularized success with universal acceptance (apart from the dissent of a few 'rogue' leaders, such as Saddam Hussein and Moammar Gaddhafi, who were more or less contained). With only one 'superpower' still in existence, the assumption arose that most nations, 'first-world' or not, all desired the increased material comfort that would result from globalizing the principles of the free market and the rational subject. Foreign policy turned away from ideological struggle and toward 'methods of delivery': how can individuals best participate in the economy? How can they best exercise their freedom? Desire for the 'goods' was clearly a priori. As Osama bin Laden dramatically demonstrated, however, such 'post-ideological' warrants were tragically delusional. Vladimir Tismaneanu would recognize bin Laden's brand of political Islamism as a 'fantasy of salvation' that 'articulate[s] collective hopes and anxieties in aggressive ways' in order to 'stimulate fears and ecstasies, illusions and redemptive expectations' (Tismaneanu 1998, 27). For Tismaneanu, such fantasies arise precisely when the hegemony seems most victorious: the physically vanquished retreat to an unquestioned myth that channels fear of disintegration into eschatological action. 'Defeated' ideas thus contain the capacity to perpetuate themselves violently instead of fading away.

Tismaneanu's thesis suggests that as long as humans are capable of thought, ideology will persist. Ideas can definitely outlive their hegemony. The end-of-ideology proponents could have done worse than to consult the theories of Raymond Williams pertaining to ideology's longitudinal properties. In *Marxism and Literature* (1977), Williams proposes that culture functions not as a transparent reflection of hegemony but as a web of 'dynamic interrelationships' (121). While one may easily mark 'changes' in the dominant ideology along a diachronic continuum, one would be overly reductive to do so, for, according to Williams, a synchronous approach to culture yields not only the hegemonic superstructure but elements of dissent as well. Williams identifies these divergent social components respectively as residual and emergent cultures. Residual culture refers to ideological practices of an earlier time. Far from being a petrified entity with no impact on the present, residual ideology 'is still active in the cultural process' (122). In some cases – Williams cites religion as an example – residual culture is assimilated into the dominant paradigm, but in others it remains a viable ideological alternative. In the United States, for instance, industrialization effectively blotted out the notion of subsistence farming as an economic model, yet some erstwhile urbanites, disenchanted with their 'treadmill' existence, have sold their possessions and 'returned' to the land. Such neo-Thoreauvians frequently characterize their relation to the dominant culture in pointedly ideological terms.[3] Unassimilated residual culture always possesses the potential to threaten the dominant culture, for it exposes ideological inconsistencies. Similarly, emergent ideologies arise from lacunae in the dominant ideology. For Williams, such 'new meanings and values, new practices, new relationships and kinds of relationships are continually being created' (123). Williams cites the notion of a new class as an example (124). The degree to which such emergent cultures are oppositional to the dominant culture (and successful in their difference) suggests the vehemence with which the latter will attempt to appropriate the former. Informing both the residual and emergent cultures is the supposition that '*no mode of production and therefore no dominant social order ever in reality includes or exhausts all human practice, human energy, and human intention*' (125; Williams' emphasis). One might profitably add 'human history' to the list.

Williams, writing from his own ideological premise, correctly observes the inexhaustibility of ideology. As the previous chapters illustrate, figurations of ideology long predated Destutt de Tracy's 'invention' of the term. Disagreements over the meaning of ideology – whether it is applied to subjects, institutions, or politics – underscore both its constructed nature and its inescapability. Although Karl Marx and others argue that ideology mystifies historical relationships and, thus, can (inevitably) be overcome, the linguistic basis of the concept – a potential 'unifying' principle of ideology is that it cannot transcend its own signification – points one back toward Williams's more pragmatic approach. Simply put, the suggestion that ideology, and with it 'history,' has ended (or can end) occludes both human practice and human thought, both the empirical and the metaphysical. In effect, such a 'mood' effaces the possibility of free will *and* predestination, for, situated in an endless present, it refuses to confront either the past or the future. For George Orwell, as seen in chapter 7, such a scenario might manifest itself in a historical contigency based not on the interpretation or (de)construction of meaning, but on the physical (re)creation of artifact. The Internet's hypertextuality notwithstanding, such a possibility would require the extirpation not only of all objects, but of all human memories as well. Williams's tripartite conception of culture exposes the ludicrous nature of such a proposal, which would need, in effect, to level both the constructed (and constructing) Cartesian subject *and* its other in the 'objective' world and return to what Sigmund Freud speculated was the 'oceanic' state prior to differentiation (Freud 1961, 11). 'Pure' unity – nothingness? – would function as the prerequisite to an end of ideology. Residue, trace, stain – all such notions implicitly deny such a state, even as they may critique conceptions of the 'pure' binary. The subject-text may hold its contradiction within itself, but it nonetheless *does* exist in the world, *does* pay its taxes, *does* rail against its 'enemies,' *does* dream of utopia, and, one might add, *does* negotiate institutional superstructures, including politics. A 'pure' society (or subject) devoid of ideology could not contemplate, or use, the residual culture of the past, nor would it desire to create emergent counter-cultures. Such a society could not even recognize its own 'ideology-free' superiority, for it would have no basis for comparison, the need for history eradicated, the stain blotted.

The Internet functions nicely as an example of how Williams's paradigm demonstrates the inextinguishable nature of ideology. Most lists of major developments since the 'fall' of communism would include the increased public access to the Internet (particularly the World Wide Web). While the Internet existed long before the nineties, the advent of increased modem capabilities and providers, such as America Online, allowed millions of (mostly middle-class) individuals to experience cyberspace. Despite the concurrent rise of pornographic and 'hate' sites, the technology found itself widely hailed as offering an alternative to the hegemony.

Advertisements for Internet products portrayed the 'new' medium as a utopian locus where all knowledge could be had at the touch of a button, while 'cybertheorists' lauded a new realm where people could dispense with socially dictated pretense and act like 'themselves.' Ideas, not prejudices, would control interpersonal responses. Distinctions such as race, gender, and class would not drown out the significance of one's thoughts. Diffident geniuses could now shine without fear of social stigma, while ideologues could sample new ideas and soften their outlook on those different from themselves. Further, borders (even temporal ones) would collapse when faced with the limitlessness of the Internet. Little children in Iowa could 'interface' with their counterparts in Albania and alter misperceptions of life in both places. In sum, many individuals cast the Internet as a 'classless' virtual society where subject, institution, and politics existed if not in harmony than at least in peace. Ideology would fade away.

While the Internet does indeed develop what Williams would label an emerging culture, it certainly fails to escape the influence of both the residual and dominant cultures. The very 'facelessness' of the Internet aids residual ideologies in their resistance of the dominant culture. To a certain extent, authority for divergent opinions is masked.[4] One might, for instance, build a site dedicated to the discredited views of Franco or (ironically!) advocate a return to a 'simple' agrarian existence. Fundamentalist cultures, rhetorically in opposition to the cult of technology, provide another instance of residual ideology actively engaged in proselytizing via the Internet. While the Internet is seemingly antithetical to residual culture, it cannot escape the realities of human practice. Williams points out that residual culture does not mean obsolete culture. Residual culture has active practitioners because the dominant culture has failed to meet a crucial need. Consequently, any emergent culture that fails to address such needs must also expect resistance. Although the celebrants of the Internet point out its quasi-utopian properties, they ignore its often ancient ideopolitical content, which frequently runs counter to the mythos of progress.

Similarly, they overlook or disregard the many ways in which the dominant culture colonizes the Internet and replicates its authority. Despite suggestions that a new subjectivity is possible on the Internet, the medium subtly reinforces hegemonic models. For instance, the most popular search engine, Googol, employs complex logarithms to impose structure on the sprawling cyber world. An essential component in Googol's method is an individual site's popularity: 'mainstream' voices (even on manifestly 'alternative' subjects such as anarchy) rise to the top, while other views are effectively silenced – rarely do users examine the content of page 109 of a search. Online discussion groups might serve as another example, for they frequently 'monitor' responses for breaches of 'netiquette.' Such practices attempt to impose normative standards of 'order' and intellectual discourse on users, punishing them, in effect, if they deviate from (dominant) societal mores. Similarly, the use of iconic glosses on written discourse (for example, the sign ':)' denotes that a post is meant in a friendly way) attempts to mimic body language, tone, and the like, a phenomenon that subverts the notion of a subjectivity based on 'ideas' alone. Physical characteristics are enlisted to decipher meaning, a technique that echoes the dominant culture's stress on appearance. Dominant institutional ideology expresses itself in a variety of ways as well, including the omnipresent capitalist signifier '.com,' which strikingly contrasts with representations of the Internet as an alternative to the corporatization of thought. Additionally, published content (even 'radical' content) not in the public domain is typically made available only for a fee.[5] A less visible way in which dominant ideologies are reflected within the emergent Internet culture pertains to access. Underprivileged populations are far less likely to log on to the Internet, a fact that mirrors the class divisions of the dominant culture. An apartheid system of sorts has developed in which a significant portion of the population is shut out of a major source of both economic potential and information. In such ways, the dominant culture both seizes on those elements of the Internet that reflect its superstructures and attempts to subvert the potentially transformative power of the emergent culture.

One might explore the Internet's relationship to political, subjective, and institutional ideology in much finer detail, but suffice to say that for the purposes of this volume it functions admirably as a synthesizing example. The medium strongly suggests that ideology's importance as a concept will not 'end' any time soon. All of the theorists under study in the previous chapters would find the Internet a most fascinating development with much to say about the nature of ideas. 'Subjective' theories of ideology, such as those forwarded by Freud or Ludwig Feuerbach, might examine the Internet as a narrativization of human desire, while 'institutional' theories of thinkers like Marx or Thomas Hobbes might view cyberspace as an extension of sovereign power. 'Political' theories of ideology would undoubtedly comment on the proliferation (ghettoization?) of anti-hegemonic voices on the Internet. Contemporary theorists like Judith Butler or Terry Eagleton will continue to identify, codify, and annotate instances of ideology. They will persist in their quarrels about what constitutes ideology and in positing alternate explanations for how it works and how (or whether) it might be overcome. Do we live in a post-ideological age? Hardly, but human thought will nonetheless persevere in its quest to discover such a tempting chimera.

Notes

1 Introduction to 'Ideology'

1. Bell, unlike Francis Fukuyama, carefully avoids equating the end of ideology with utopia or near-utopia.

2 Ideology and the Paradox of Subjectivity

1. In his 'De la Métaphysique de Kant,' de Tracy explicitly excoriates Kant for his lack of scientific method and chides him for developing 'the inverse of reasoning' in the *Critique of Pure Reason* (cited in Kennedy 1978, 118–19).
2. In 'The Poet,' Emerson calls for a radical poetic aesthetic that would eschew the artificial constraints of meter and adopt an 'organic form.' Interestingly, Emerson also developed the concept of the 'oversoul,' which owes much to Hegel's *Geist*.
3. In his *Introductory Lectures on Psycho-Analysis* (1915–17), Freud dissects the subject into three parts: super-ego, ego, and id. These correspond roughly to conscience, consciousness, and desire. The ego attempts to regulate between the super-ego and the id.
4. Freud fails to suggest, however, that religion fulfills its ostensible moral purpose: 'in every age immorality has found no less support in religion than morality has' (1964, 68).
5. Žižek distinguishes between cynicism – the classic ideological response to social reality – and 'kynicism,' the 'popular, plebian rejection of the official culture by means of irony and sarcasm' (1989, 29). In the latter instance, subjects appeal not to reason, but to parody. The subject mocks the gravity of official doctrine by exposing the self-interest of the principals. *Saturday Night Live* and *Mad TV*, for example, lampoon the ultra-earnestness of political candidates through caricature. In one such skit, Bill Clinton's famous empathy ('I feel your pain') is undercut by a portrait in which he cannot restrain his sexual impulses for even a moment.

3 Ideology and Institutional Authority

1. In the late twentieth century, a burgeoning natural birth movement – spawned in large part by midwives and feminist critiques of the male-dominated realm of obstetrics – questioned both the routine use of the

supine position and the over-application of Caesarean sections that resulted from such procedures. Consequently, larger numbers of contemporary women are opting for squatting or other natural labors. Interestingly, however, the trend applies much more to affluent and educated women than to other socio-economic groups.

2. Some women, of course, did lie on their backs for labor and delivery. The current natural child birth philosophy holds that the best position coincides with the *mother's* comfort and not with any uniform medical practice or recommendation. Interestingly, in 2001 The Royal College of Obstetricians documented that only 52% of deliveries were natural – the others being induced, Caesarean, or instrument-aided – (Drudge 2001), and the Royal College's Induction of Labour Guideline Group claimed that many Caesarean sections occurred for 'social' rather than medical reasons (2001).

3. Midwifery, of course, never completely faded in the West, and the absolute institutionalization of the supine position did not occur until hospitalization became the standard in the twentieth century.

4. In his *Quodlibeta Septem* (1320), William of Occam, an English philosopher, postulated that 'entities should not be multiplied unnecessarily.'

5. In this text, Rousseau anticipates Marx's theories about private property establishing the foundations of social inequality.

6. To recognize the saliency of Marx's point, one need only recall the circumstances of the American Revolution, which drew heavily on French rhetoric and ideas, and its roots in populist tax disputes.

7. For further discussion of Gramsci, see Moyra Haslett's *Marxist Literary and Cultural Theories* (2000), chapter 2.

8. That Lukács later retracted his position in *History and Class Consciousness* is irrelevant to the study at hand, for the influence of his theories was immediate and widespread.

9. Both sides, of course, chastised various courts for their decisions to include or exclude ballots, and charges of 'subjective' (read political) legal interpretation abound.

10. Besides Adorno and Marcuse, the Frankfurt School, whose prolific members theorized from the 1930s to the 1970s, included such luminaries as Walter Benjamin, Max Horkheimer, and Friedrich Pollack.

11. See Mark Currie's *Postmodern Narrative Theory* (1998) and John Brannigan's *New Historicism and Cultural Materialism* (1998) for extended discussions of Foucault's changing methodology.

12. See Brannigan for an extensive analysis of New Historicism.

13. Julian Wolfreys extensively covers Derrida's project in *Deconstruction•Derrida* (1998).

14. Obviously, space considerations limit discussion of this complex subject. For further information see Ruth Robbins' *Literary Feminisms* (2000).

4 Political Ideology

1. In *The Faces of Janus: Marxism and Fascism in the Twentieth Century* (2000), Gregor makes the provocative argument that fascism is

remarkably similar to communism in its philosophical underpinnings. Roger Griffin further claims that fascism 'is directly opposed to conservatism' and 'set[s] out to create a new type of total culture' (2002, 1).

2. One strategy that combined both elements involved Holocaust revisionism. In the early to mid-1990s, college newspapers across the United States received full-page advertisements, complete with footnotes, that claimed the Holocaust to be an elaborate hoax. Many campuses refused to run the advertisements, but many did, often with disclaimers that cited first amendment rights as the basis of their decision to display the proclamations.

3. Smith, who killed three people and wounded nine others, claimed that he had been influenced by Hale's arguments. Hale denied advocating violence.

4. William Godwin anticipates Proudhon in his *Enquiry Concerning Political Justice and Its Influence on Modern Morals and Happiness* (1791): 'No man must encroach upon my province, nor I upon his' (1985, 198). In critiquing the social contract, Godwin comes to the conclusion that humans must be guided by their own understanding, as compulsory law approximates 'external slavery' (200). Even positive laws are ultimately injurious, for they substitute self-interest for reason.

5. Ernest Haeckel coined the word 'ecology' in the nineteenth century, during the midst of the industrial revolution. Haeckel's term refers to the relationship of flora and fauna with their organic and inorganic environments.

6. See Ruth Robbins' *Literary Feminisms* for an extended discussion of feminist theory and its implications for literary study.

7. While some feminists deny the ability of men to practice feminism, the majority would include males such as Condorcet, John Stuart Mill, and Charles Fourier as important feminist thinkers.

8. Abigail Adams unsuccessfully petitioned her husband to word the Constitution explicitly to grant full rights of citizenship to women.

9. The proposed constitutional amendment failed to be ratified by the minimum number of states (38) required.

5 Toni Morrison's *Sula* and Subjective Ideology

1. Denise Heinze, for instance, implies that the Bottom functions as a 'character' unto itself (1993, 125).

2. In *Tarrying with the Negative* (1993), Žižek reconfigures his famous phrase 'Enjoy your symptom!' as 'Enjoy your nation as yourself!' (200). While Žižek concerns himself with national identity, he allows room for interpreting 'nation' in a broader sense than that conveyed by terms such as 'state,' 'government,' or 'sovereignty.' Žižek's reference to community as a 'shared relationship toward a Thing' suggests that a nation is not confined to geo-political boundaries (201). The Bottom, then, while maintaining an adjunct status to Medallion, might profitably be viewed as a national entity.

3. Sula's enigmatic presence parallels that of the title character of Morrison's *Beloved*. In both books, the non-recognition of the 'stain' results in a dissolution of community.
4. The Bottom's economic structure is dependent on the caprice of the white community, which dangles the prospect of the tunnel before the men, only to replace the fantasy of self-sufficiency with sporadic menial jobs. With the exception of Shadrack, all of the town's men seem to flee or else are 'superficial, immature, untrustworthy, [or] anonymous' (Samuels and Hudson-Weems 1990, 46).
5. One might make the case that Sula functions not as scapegoat but as scapegrace. Feng posits that Sula represents a 'masculine' ideology and 'assumes the prerogatives of a man' (1998, 92). Sula herself signifies on Sojouner Truth's 'ain't I a woman,' claiming 'I'm a woman and colored. Ain't that the same as being a man?' (Morrison 1973, 142).
6. Notice that Morrison contrasts Sula's torpid sexuality with Nel's impassioned subjectivity, casting off the third-person perspective for a direct look into Nel's consciousness. For Nel, Sula is truly an object.

6   William Faulkner's 'Barn Burning' and Institutional Ideology

1. Some readers may object to the pairing of Eagleton and Bakhtin as a naïve critical maneuver that ignores the differences between the two. I certainly acknowledge that such incongruities exist. However, both Eagleton's definition of ideology and Bakhtin's concept of polyphony seem to make allowances for one another. Eagleton intimates that a text contains – and produces – a multiplicity of ideological 'absences,' a phenomenon suggestive of polyphony. In arguing for polyphony, moreover, Bakhtin scolds critics who 'are enslaved by the content of individual heroes' ideological views,' a perspective that Eagleton echoes (Bakhtin 1984a, 8–9). The analogy ultimately breaks down, of course, but it is undeniably useful for describing 'Barn Burning' and ideology.
2. Bakhtin's application of polyphony as it referred to Dostoevski was predicated on a pantextual reading of the writer's works. Space limitations prohibit such a project here, but Faulkner's fictive universe certainly would allow for similar consideration. Faulkner's 'A Rose for Emily,' for instance, in part portrays the effects of economic obsolescence on the title character, a formerly affluent woman whose well-being now depends on the charity – sans the name – of one of the town's prominent citizens.
3. Women, as with African Americans, may physically be present in the courtroom, but their literal silence betokens at least a symbolic absence.
4. The fugitive slave Frederick Douglass reports a similar phenomenon in his *Narrative* (1845) regarding his new found ability to read (Douglass 1968, 55).
5. Of course, alternatives such as anarchism, fascism, and the like also add their voices to the narrative's plurality. Space considerations do not permit examining them here.

6. For a discussion of the patriarchal eye see Ragan Gita's 'A Feminist Rereading of Poe's "The Tell-Tale Heart."' *Papers on Language and Literature*, 24 (1988): 283–300.
7. Of course, he does look back, as the 'older' Sarty makes clear.
8. Explicitly mentioning 'Barn Burning,' André Bleikasten suggests that Faulkner ultimately 'extend[s] his sympathy to the oppressed' (1995, 13), but Jehlen intimates that when writing the Snopse Trilogy – to which 'Barn Burning' is a prelude – the author may have 'finally settled at the conservative pole of his ideological ambivalence' (1978, 131).

7 George Orwell's *1984* and Political Ideology

1. Numerous critics, including Anthony Burgess and Jeffrey Meyers, have chided Orwell for his rather cumbersome style in *1984*.
2. Orwell writes that Airstrip One is a 'province' of Oceania, which subverts any notion that English Socialism has led to totalitarianism (1983, 7). Clearly, totalitarianism was imported to London from a futuristic America.
3. In this context, any 'art' would be more akin to that described in Donald Trump's *The Art of the Deal* than to the discussions in Walter Pater's *The Renaissance: Studies in Art and Poetry*.
4. Of course, the war has very real consequences for the subaltern populations existing at the margins of the central powers. The constant upheaval reifies these peoples into a slave class and obstructs the avenues of assimilation or subversion possible in a time of peace. Their status as chattel represents a far more dangerous and dehumanizing prospect than the bleak but 'secure' existence experienced by the inhabitants of Oceania. Even criminals such as Winston eventually find their suffering abated – albeit via reeducation and death – but the subalterns must face eternal bondage without even a bottle of Victory Gin to dim their consciousness.
5. Vita Fortunati perceptively remarks that 'Oceania represents the panoptic *society par excellence*' (1987, 145). Michel Foucault, of course, famously describes the theory and practice of the panopticon in *Discipline and Punish: The Birth of the Prison* (1995, 195–228).
6. If one accepts the veracity of Winston's clandestine photograph, then one might count the three disgraced Party leaders as providing dissent above the waist. Given the Thought Police's methods, however, one must be wary about the authenticity of the document. 'Charrington,' Goldstein's book, O'Brien's 'look' – all of these represent counterfeit sedition designed to entrap Winston.
7. Christopher Norris reminds his readers that the working title of *1984* was *The Last Man in Europe* (1984, 256). Such a title clearly indicates Orwell's disgust for end-of-history complacency.

8 The 'Post-Ideological' Era?

1. As seen in chapter 3, postmodern theory offers quite a different approach to the 'end' of ideology, effectively exposing all 'metanarratives' as

linguistically based constructs. Postmodern theorists such as Paul de Man and Jean-François Lyotard view 'reality' as a linguistic construct and, thus, meet 'metanarratives' with suspicion. One may easily expose ideologies purporting to explain the 'truth' as mere historicized self-interest. A major effect of postmodernism's skepticism of overarching narratives was, thus, a growing distrust of hierarchical or binary thought. Since thought may neither be true nor false (consciousness), any attempt to systematize or codify reflects not an external reality but rather the partial – and historically constructed – view of a subject who is also contrived. Many individuals, such as Fredric Jameson, Allan Bloom, and Jane Flax, excoriated postmodernist arguments for their implied (perceived?) cultural relativism and attendant endorsement of patently dangerous 'versions' of reality. Flax provides a typical criticism:

> Postmodernists intend to persuade us that we should be suspicious of any notion of self or subjectivity. Any such notion may be bound up with and support dangerous and oppressive 'humanist' myths. However, I am deeply suspicious of the motives of those who would counsel such a position at the same time as women have just begun to re-member their selves and to claim an agentic subjectivity available always before only to a few privileged white men. It is possible that unconsciously, rather than share such a (revised) subjectivity with the 'others,' the privileged would reassure us that it was 'really' oppressive to them all along.   (Flax 1990, 220)

Defenders of postmodernism's 'political' elements, such as Linda Hutcheon, view such critiques as misinterpreting the concept and failing to see the liberatory impetus behind it: the exposure of all metanarratives as ideological potentially 'frees' one from ideology.
2. The billion-plus Chinese are frequently elided from discussions of communism's ultimate demise.
3. See Anne La Bastille's *Woodswoman II: Beyond Black Bear Lake* (2000), for example. Williams suggests that such a phenomenon may, in fact, also serve as a 'leisure function of the dominant order itself' (1977, 122).
4. Criminal investigation units, such as Scotland Yard or the Federal Bureau of Investigation, immediately began developing techniques to locate 'criminal' users. For all but the technological elite, such methods effectively set up a discrepancy between the façade of anonymous usage and the 'reality' of cyber 'signatures.' Had Michel Foucault witnessed the dramatic rise of the Internet, he would have no doubt noticed a similarity between the technology and Jeremy Bentham's panopticon. Although they may not be aware of the surveillance – may, in fact act in the false belief that it does not exist – users leave traces of their presence that are perhaps even more palpable than DNA residue. Like Orwell's Big Brother, the agents of the dominant ideology are always 'watching,' if only after the fact (crime).
5. One example of a 'radical' journal that charges users to view their content is *Red Orange: A Marxist Journal of Theory, Politics, and the Everyday*.

Annotated Bibliography

Since one might arguably maintain that the history of ideology parallels those of (at least) philosophy and politics, no attempt at a comprehensive bibliography has been made below. Instead, the bibliography concentrates on general discussions of ideology *qua* ideology and tries to provide samples of subjective, institutional, and political approaches to the subject. Central texts, such as Louis Althusser's *Lenin and Philosophy* and Karl Marx's and Friedrich Engels's *The German Ideology*, have been discussed at length above and are thus not included here.

Baker, Houston A., Jr. *Blues, Ideology, and Afro-American Literature.* Chicago: University of Chicago Press, 1984.

Analyzing what he calls the 'economics of slavery,' Baker explores theorists such as Michel Foucault, Roland Barthes, Hayden White, and Marx. Baker suggests that readings of African-American literature would profit by an application of 'archaeological' methods that reveal how uniquely 'unofficial' history – manifested in such phenomena as the blues – is bound up in material practice. Baker, therefore, advocates studying the vernacular not only as a diachronic reaction but as possessing synchronous 'subtexts' as well. Of particular note for the study of ideology in general is chapter 2, which traces the impact of ideology on the study of African-American literature.

Ball, Terence, and Richard Dagger. *Political Ideologies and the Democratic Ideal.* 4th edn. New York: Longman, 2001.

Ball and Dagger provide an accessible introduction to both classical and emergent ideologies, including gay rights and neo-nazism. Although their focus is necessarily broad, the authors do an effective job of connecting philosophical premises to specific movements and actions. Discussion ranges from the influence of Locke on liberalism to the impact of *The Turner Diaries* on the American 'militia' phenomenon.

Baradat, Leon P. *Political Ideologies: Their Origins and Impact.* 7th edn. New York: Prentice-Hall, 1999.

Revealing a vaguely leftist paradigm, Baradat approaches political ideologies chronologically. His concise discussion relies heavily on contemporary application. Baradat pays particular attention to the ideological impact of communism's decline in Eastern Europe.

Barrett, Michèle. *The Politics of Truth: From Marx to Foucault*. Stanford, CA: Stanford University Press, 1992.

Despite the comprehensive outlook implicit in her title, Barrett concentrates primarily on the two thinkers she explicitly mentions. Rejecting Marx's claim to empiricism, Barrett attempts to expose a number of contradictions in Marxist thought. While accepting the notion of ideological mystification, Barrett echoes Abercrombie, Hill, and Turner's critique of the 'dominant ideology thesis' before endorsing Foucault's concept of discourse.

Barth, Hans. *Truth and Ideology*. Trans. Frederic Lilge. Berkeley, CA: University of California Press, 1976.

Barth traces the metamorphosis of ideology from a 'science of ideas' to a pejorative political concept. He faults philosophers such as Marx and Nietzsche for conflating truth with ideology, a 'self-contradiction.' A priori distinctions between truth and falsehood subvert ideology's empirical claims and reinforce its political agendas. Such a phenomenon 'undermines the foundation of... social life.'

Bell, Daniel. *The End of Ideology: On the Exhaustion of Political Ideas in the Fifties*. Cambridge, MA: Harvard University Press, 2000.

In this new edition, Bell revisits his influential theory regarding the demise of the left. With the decline of Communism, Bell suggests that the world is ironically becoming more politically fragmented than before. Bell views this phenomenon as a return to the 'primordial identities of peoples.'

Bracher, Karl Dietrich. *The Age of Ideologies: A History of Political Thought in the Twentieth Century*. Trans. Ewald Osers. New York: St. Martin's, 1984.

Bracher explores connections between scientific progress and totalitarian ideology. In so doing, he observes that pre-twentieth-century ideologies lacked the conspicuous need to justify themselves intellectually. Modern media accelerate such self-rationalizations because they provide a direct and immediate link to the public and allow for unheard of competition among various ideologies.

Eagleton, Terry, ed. *Ideology*. New York: Longman, 1994.

Eagleton's reader collects seminal documents in the study of ideology ranging from its inception as a field of inquiry to the present. Besides choosing crucial passages from such notables as Marx and Engels, Georg Lukács, and Karl Mannheim, Eagleton selects contributions from such thinkers as Clifford Geertz, Alvin Gouldner, and John Frow. Eagleton also adds a thorough introduction that considers ideology historically and analyzes competing usages of the term.

——. *Ideology: An Introduction*. New York: Verso, 1991.

Eagleton offers an indispensable, sophisticated analysis of post-Enlightenment ideology and its diverse historical manifestations. Employing numerous engaging examples, Eagleton problematizes both overly broad and overly narrow definitions of ideology. He argues that ideology is less a set of discourses than a set of effects within those discourses.

Grimes, Alan P., and Robert H. Horwitz, eds. *Modern Political Ideologies*. New York: Oxford University Press, 1959.

Grimes and Horwitz collate a number of key primary documents concerning democracy, capitalism, socialism, communism, elitism, and nationalism. Although dated, the volume samples the thought of thinkers ranging from John Locke and Karl Marx to Jawaharlal Nehru and Mao Tse-tung. The editors also provide a brief, liberally slanted, introduction for each ideology.

Hawkes, David. *Ideology*. New York: Routledge, 1996.

Hawkes studies ideology from its origins to the postmodern era. Locating a common theme of modern considerations of ideology within an 'imbalance' between subject, object, and representation, Hawkes analyzes representative philosophers within such traditions as empiricism and idealism. No index.

Ingersoll, David E., Richard K. Matthews, and Andrew Davison. *The Philosophical Roots of Modern Ideology: Liberalism, Communism, Fascism, Islamism*. 3rd edn. New York: Prentice-Hall, 2000.

Ingersoll, Matthews, and Davison attempt to illuminate the interrelationship of ideological theory and political practice by examining the historical context of four major ideologies. The text summarizes key concepts and illustrates discrepancies between thought and action. The authors critique the end of history thesis and point to the dramatic resurgence of 'theopolitics' as proof of ideology's currency.

Kennedy, Emmet. *A Philosophe in the Age of Revolution: Destutt de Tracy and the Origins of 'Ideology'*. Philadelphia: American Philosophical Society, 1978.

Since de Tracy's work is not readily accessible to speakers of English, Kennedy's book is an extremely valuable resource for learning about the 'superscience' of ideology. Kennedy interweaves de Tracy's biography with the growth of the philosopher's most lasting contribution to the history of ideas. The book examines de Tracy's influences as well as his involvement in the French political scene and suggests that despite its claims to neutrality, the 'science of ideas' was politically charged from the start. The volume concludes with a discussion of de Tracy's impact on later thinkers. A detailed bibliography of works by and about de Tracy is also included.

Kofman, Sarah. *Camera Obscura: Of Ideology.* Trans. Will Straw. Ithaca, NY: Cornell University Press, 1999.

Kofman analyzes the camera obscura simile in the works of Marx, Freud, Nietzsche, and Descartes. She argues convincingly that despite revealing a desire to transcend metaphor (and the falsity of ideology), the thinkers in question nonetheless ground their critiques of ideology in figurative language. Kofman explains, moreover, that Marx in particular lacked scientific understanding of the camera obscura simile, for if one follows the trope to its logical conclusion, 'then ideology should set itself right on its own.'

Larrain, Jorge. *The Concept of Ideology.* Athens, CA: University of Georgia Press, 1979.

Larrain provides a sensitive, erudite examination of ideology from its roots as a psychological system to its apotheosis as a 'social contradiction' and to later post-Marxist accounts that introduce (or reintroduce) positivist, psychological, sociological, and semiological conceptions of the term. Besides presenting the basic ideological premises of Marx, Antonio Gramsci, Roland Barthes, and others, Larrain critiques the various explanations and exposes their various limitations.

——. *Ideology and Cultural Identity: Modernity and the Third World Presence.* Cambridge: Polity, 1994.

Larrain discusses the nexus of ideology, reason, and cultural identity in order to critique the construction of the modern 'other.' He also argues that most conceptions of ideology are too polarized and advance either 'rational' or 'irrational' models that Larrain finds inadequate. In the theories of Jürgen Habermas, however, Larrain discovers a viable alternative that synthesizes the opposing paradigms and allows that identity functions both as a historical construction and as an active 'project.'

Levine, George, ed. *Aesthetics and Ideology.* New Brunswick, NJ: Rutgers University Press, 1994.

Levine's collection includes essays by a number of important thinkers, including Derek Attridge, Peter Brooks, Myra Jehlen, Mary Poovey, and Arnold Rampersad. The volume starts from the premise that focus on ideological matters has resulted in a devaluing of the aesthetic in literary criticism. Levine argues that ideological strategies that ignore the aesthetic fail to account for how texts 'get their work done.' While the essays by no means present a monolithic view of the aesthetic, they do all problematize its relationship to ideology. By historicizing the aesthetic without dismissing it, the collection seeks to integrate ideology with poetics.

Lichtheim, George. *The Concept of Ideology and Other Essays.* New York: Vintage, 1967.

Lichtheim's essays investigate ideology from a diachronic point of view that nevertheless rejects the notion of historical 'logic' or inevitability.

Lichtheim grounds his treatment of the ideological tradition in an awareness of contemporary (circa 1967) trends. In the title essay, he explores conceptions of ideology from Francis Bacon to Mannheim, ultimately critiquing those theories of ideology that stray from false consciousness by substituting a 'limited practical relevance' for intellectual discourse. Other essays consider such subjects as the revolutions of 1848, existentialism, and metahistory.

Mannheim, Karl. *Ideology and Utopia: An Introduction to the Sociology of Knowledge.* Trans. Louis Wirth and Edward Shils. New York: Harvest, 1985.

Mannheim defines ideology as a fictional construct geared toward solidifying social order, a phenomenon he finds antithetical to human needs. In contrast, the fantasies of utopianism, while equally fabricated, resist stasis and encourage transformation (destabilization of the status quo). For Mannheim, ideas are context-based. Because ideologies resist change, a sociological approach to ideology must try to expose the historical 'tendencies' that led to a particular fiction about life and its concomitant control mechanisms.

MacIntyre, Alasdair. *Against the Self-Images of the Age: Essays on Ideology and Philosophy.* South Bend, IN: University of Notre Dame, 1999.

MacIntyre critiques major modern ideological discourses, such as Marxism and psychoanalysis, claiming that they present inadequate pictures of human practice. The discourse of such ideologies is patently solipsistic and fails to understand the principles and philosophies of rigorous social science, which MacIntyre believes may provide social philosophers with the tools to comprehend human behavior.

McLellan, David. *Ideology.* 2nd edn. Minneapolis: University of Minnesota Press, 1995.

McLellan's concise guide covers a wide array of ideological approaches and includes chapters on Marx, the Marxist tradition, the non-Marxist tradition, science and ideology, and the 'end of history,' among others. McLellan does an admirable job of outlining the primary contributions of numerous ideological thinkers. Although McLellan generally – but by no means always – employs a descriptive strategy, he ultimately concludes that ideology penetrates all systems 'in so far as they are implicated in an asymmetrical distribution of power and resources.'

Pines, Christopher L. *Ideology and False Consciousness: Marx and His Historical Progenitors.* Albany, NY: State University Press of New York, 1993.

Pines reconsiders neo-Marxist suppositions that distance Marx from Friedrich Engels's characterization of ideology as false consciousness. Pines argues that false consciousness has been widely misinterpreted by such commentators, and asserts that Marx did, in fact, subscribe to a theory of social illusion. In supporting his thesis, Pines traces Marx's connection to the substantial false consciousness tradition, which originates in Bacon and continues through G. W. F. Hegel and Ludwig Feuerbach. Pine then explains how Marx synthesizes the tradition not simply in his early work but in *Capital* as well.

Plamenatz, John. *Ideology*. London: Praeger, 1970.

In his first chapter, Plamenatz surveys various ways in which ideology has been used, but he concludes that post-Condillac usage (de Tracy is oddly absent from the discussion) is unified in its reference to a system of ideas that is fundamentally limited. Plamenatz discovers the broadest conceptions of ideology in the philosophy of Kant and Hegel rather than in that of the *philosophes*. He then explores notions of ideology as social conditioning and self-rationalization before turning to a study of Marx. He concludes with a treatment of political ideology, which he claims has a reciprocal relationship with ideology in the broader sense and, thus, both informs and is informed by such representations.

Thompson, John B. *Ideology and Modern Culture: Critical Social Theory in the Era of Mass Communication*. Stanford, CA: Stanford University Press, 1990.

Thompson's penetrating study focuses on the ways in which 'mediazation' impacts ideology. He suggests that most prior considerations of ideology lack a developed sense of how modern methods of communication provide ideology with 'a new scope and complexity' by extending the realm of symbolic form. Such symbolic forms are inextricably linked to hierarchical structures so that meanings are 'mobilized in the service of dominant individuals and groups.' To analyze such symbolic forms, Thompson develops a paradigm of 'depth-hermeneutics,' which is a hybrid methodology comprised of social-historical analysis, discursive analysis, and interpretation (re-interpretation).

Vincent, Andrew. *Modern Political Ideologies*. London: Blackwell, 1992.

Vincent analyzes the history and principal traits of political ideologies from the Enlightenment to the present. He offers a concise but sensitive general discussion of ideology that places the concept in historical context and questions the existence of 'pure' ideology: 'all ideologies are internally complex, intermixed, and overlapping.' Vincent's treatments of various ideologies, such as liberalism and anarchism, examine the ideas not as monolithic entities but as competing strains of a similar approach to society.

Watkins, Frederick M. *The Age of Ideology – Political Thought, 1750 to the Present*. Englewood Cliffs, NJ: Prentice-Hall, 1964.

Watkins inquires into the ideological basis for revolution. Surveying the major ideologies of the last two centuries, he starts from the premise that a unifying factor of all modern ideologies is a belief in the perfectibility of human existence. He also postulates that ideologies are inherently binary. After extended historical discussions on such political ideologies as fascism, socialism, and political Catholicism, Watkins concludes that ideology is in 'decline' in the West and that although it has been marked by an 'explosive increase' in non-western societies, ideology will diminish as 'backward areas [sic] ultimately succeed in catching up with the West.'

Williams, Howard, Gwyn Matthews, and David Sullivan. *Francis Fukuyama and the End of History.* Cardiff: University of Wales Press, 1997.

The authors place Fukuyama in a philosophical tradition extending from Immanuel Kant to Karl Popper. Ultimately, they critique Fukuyama's position from a variety of angles, including the postmodern. Of special interest is Fukuyama's 'dual role as political actor and...political philosopher.'

Williams, Raymond. *Marxism and Literature.* London: Oxford University Press, 1977.

While Williams's book discusses a broad array of Marxist principles, several chapters pertain to ideology – including one specifically dealing with the term and another discussing base and superstructure. In a chapter called 'dominant, residual, emergent,' moreover, Williams modifies Marx's concept of base/superstructure to describe material practice not accounted for in superstructural institutions. Williams identifies three basic usages of the term ideology: a set of beliefs typical of a group; illusory beliefs that contrast with empirical reality; and the production of meaning. Williams argues that critics may apply scientific methods to social practices, including art and literature.

Žižek, Slavoj, ed. *Mapping Ideology.* New York: Verso, 1994.

Žižek's collection overlaps minimally with that of Eagleton and concentrates on contemporary theories of ideology, including those of such writers as Pierre Bourdieu, Richard Rorty, Fredric Jameson, Michel Pêcheux, and Seyla Benhabib. In a provocative introduction, Žižek questions why theorists have 'suddenly' resurrected the concept of ideology. Žižek, typically juxtaposing cybersex with the waning of socialism in Eastern Europe, answers that ideology critiques presuppose a 'privileged place' wherein a 'subject-agent' may 'perceive the very hidden mechanism that regulates social visibility and non-visibility.' He suggests that conceptions of ideology that rely on such normative representations simply 'enslave' the critical subject-agent within ideology. Žižek thus identifies a new need for 'postmodern' discussions of ideology that avoid the latent self-congratulatory methodologies of previous critiques.

Bibliography

Abercrombie, Nicolas, Stephen Hill, and Bryan Hill. *The Dominant Ideology Thesis*. London: G. Allen and Unwin, 1980.

Adorno, Theodor W. *The Jargon of Authenticity*. Trans. Knut Tarnowski and Frederic Will. Evanston, IL: Northwestern University Press, 1973a.

——. *Negative Dialectics*. New York: Seabury Press, 1973b.

——. *Minima Moralia: Reflections from a Damaged Life*. Trans. E. F. N. Jephcott. New York: Verso, 1974.

Althusser, Louis. *Lenin and Philosophy and Other Essays*. Trans. Ben Brewster. New York: Monthly Review, 1971.

Anderson, Benedict. *Imagined Communities: Reflections on the Origin and Spread of Nationalism*. New York: Verso, 1983.

Arendt, Hannah. *The Origins of Totalitarianism*. New York: Harcourt, 1968.

Aristophanes. *Lysistrata and Other Plays*. Trans. Alan H. Sommerstein. New York: Penguin, 1973.

Bacon, Francis. *Novum Organum*. Trans. Peter Urbach and John Gibson. Chicago: Open Court, 1994.

Bakhtin, Mikhail. *Problems of Dostoevsky's Poetics*. Trans. Caryl Emerson. Minneapolis: University of Minnesota Press, 1984a.

——. *Rabelais and his World*. Trans. Hélène Iswolsky. Bloomington: Indiana University Press, 1984b.

Bakunin, Mikhail. *God and the State*. New York: Dover, 1970.

Banyiwa-Horne, Naana. 'The Scary Face of the Self: An Analysis of the Character of Sula in Toni Morrison's *Sula*.' *SAGE* 2 (1985): 28–42.

Barth, Hans. *Truth and Ideology*. Trans. Frederic Lilge. Berkeley, CA: University of California Press, 1976.

Barthes, Roland. *Mythologies*. Trans. Annette Lavers. New York: Hill and Wang, 1972.

Bastiat, Frédéric. 'The Law.' *Mondo Politico*. 2002. 14 July 2002. <www.mondopolitico.com/library/thelaw/toc.htm>

Beauchamp, Gorman. 'From Bingo to Big Brother: Orwell on Power and Sadism.' *The Future of Nineteen Eighty-Four*. Ed. Ejner J. Jensen. Ann Arbor, MI: University of Michigan Press, 1984. 65–85.

Beauvoir, Simone de. *The Second Sex*. Trans. H. M. Parshley. New York: Vintage, 1989.

Bell, Daniel. *The End of Ideology: On the Exhaustion of Political Ideas in the Fifties*. Cambridge, MA: Harvard University Press, 2000.

Berger, John. *Ways of Seeing*. New York: Penguin, 1977.

Biehl, Janet, and Peter Staudenmaier. *Ecofascism: Lessons from the German Experience*. San Francisco: A. K. Press, 1996.

Bjork, Patrick Bryce. *The Novels of Toni Morrison: The Search for Self and Place within the Community*. New York: Peter Lang, 1991.

Bleikasten, André. 'Faulkner and the New Ideologies.' *Faulkner and Ideology: Faulkner and Yoknapatawpha, 1992*. Ed. Donald M. Kartiganer and Ann J. Abadie. Jackson, MS: University Press of Mississippi, 1995. 3–21.

Bloom, Allan. *The Closing of the American Mind*. New York: Touchstone, 1987.

Bradford, William. *Of Plymouth Plantation, 1620–1647*. New York: McGraw-Hill, 1981.

Brannigan, John. *New Historicism and Cultural Materialism*. London: Palgrave Macmillan, 1998.

Breuilly, John. *Nationalism and the State*. Chicago: University of Chicago Press, 1985.

Burke, Edmund. *Reflections on the Revolution in France*. New York: Oxford University Press, 1999.

Byrne, Mary Ellen. '"Barn Burning": A Story from the '30s.' *Center for Faulkner Studies*. October 2002. 15 October 2002. <www.2.semo.edu/cfs/barn.html>

Calabrese. *Neo-Baroque: A Sign of the Times*. Princeton, NJ: Princeton University Press, 1992.

Carothers, James B. *William Faulkner's Short Stories*. Ann Arbor, MI: University of Michigan Press, 1985.

Carson, Rachel. *Silent Spring*. London: Penguin, 1962.

Cohen, Nancy Wainer, and Lois J. Estner. *Silent Knife: Cesarean Prevention and Vaginal Birth after Cesarean*. South Hadley, MA: Bergin and Garvey, 1983.

Currie, Mark. *Postmodern Narrative Theory*. London: Palgrave Macmillan, 1998.

DeLillo, Don. *White Noise*. New York: Viking, 1985.

De Man, Paul. *Aesthetic Ideology*. Ed. Andrzej Warminski. Minneapolis: University of Minnesota Press, 1996.

Derrida, Jacques. 'Différance.' *Speech and Phenomena*. Trans. David Allison. Evanston, IL: Northwestern University Press, 1973. 129–60.

——. *Of Grammatology*. Trans. Gayatri Chakravorty Spivak. Baltimore, MD: Johns Hopkins University Press, 1976.

——. *Limited Inc*. Trans. Samuel Weber and Jeffrey Mehlman. Evanston, IL: Northwestern University Press, 1988.

Descartes, René. *A Discourse on Method, Meditations on the First Philosophy, and Principles of Philosophy*. Trans. John Veitch. New York: Everyman's Library, 1995.

Deutscher, Isaac. '*1984* – The Mysticism of Cruelty.' *Orwell's 1984: Text, Sources, Criticism*. 2nd edn. Ed. Irving Howe. New York: Harcourt, Brace, Jovanovich, 1982. 332–43.

Douglass, Frederick. *Narrative of the Life of Frederick Douglass, an American Slave; Written by Himself*. New York: Signet, 1968.

Drudge, Matt. 'The Demise of Natural Childbirth.' *The Drudge Report*. 13 June 2001. <www.drudgereport.com/flashxx.htm>

Eagleton, Terry. *Criticism and Ideology: A Study in Marxist Literary Thought*. New York: Verso, 1978.

——. *Ideology: An Introduction*. New York: Verso, 1991.

——. *Literary Theory: An Introduction.* Minneapolis: University of Minnesota Press, 1983.

Easthope, Antony. 'Fact and Fiction in *Nineteen Eighty-Four.*' *Inside the Myth: Orwell: Views from the Left.* Ed. Christopher Norris. London: Lawrence and Wishart, 1984. 263–85.

——. *Literary into Cultural Studies.* New York: Routledge, 1991.

Emerson, Ralph Waldo. 'The Poet.' *Selected Writings of Emerson.* Ed. Donald McQuade. New York: Modern Library, 1981. 303–25.

Eysenck, Hans J. New Brunswick, NJ: *The Psychology of Politics.* Transaction, 1999.

Fabijancic, Tony. 'Reification, Dereification, Subjectivity: Towards a Marxist Reading of William Faulkner's Poor-White Topography.' *Faulkner Journal* 10 (1994): 75–94.

Faulkner, William. *Selected Short Stories of William Faulkner.* New York: Modern Library, 1961.

Feng, Pin-chia. *The Female Bildungsroman by Toni Morrison and Maxine Hong Kingston.* New York: Lang, 1998.

Feuerbach, Ludwig. *The Essence of Christianity.* Trans. George Eliot. Amherst, MA: Prometheus, 1989.

——. *Principles of the Philosophy of the Future.* Trans. Manfred Vogel. Indianapolis: Hackett, 1986.

——. 'Provisional Theses for the Reformation of Philosophy.' *The Young Hegelians: An Anthology.* Ed. Lawrence S. Stepelevich. Cambridge: Cambridge University Press, 1983. 156–72.

Feyerabend, Paul. *Against Method.* New York: Verso, 1993.

Flax, Jane. *Thinking Fragments: Psychoanalysis, Feminism, and Postmodernism in the Contemporary West.* Berkeley, CA: University of California Press, 1990.

Ford, Marilyn Claire. 'Narrative Legerdemain: Evoking Sarty's Future in "Barn Burning."' *Mississippi Quarterly* 51 (1998): 527–40.

Fortunati, Vita. '"It makes no difference": A Utopia of Simulation and Transparency.' *George Orwell.* Ed. Harold Bloom. New York: Chelsea House, 1987. 139–50.

Foucault, Michel. *The Archaeology of Knowledge and the Discourse on Language.* Trans. A. M. Sheridan Smith. New York: Pantheon, 1972.

——. *Discipline and Punish: The Birth of the Prison.* Trans. Alan Sheridan. New York: Vintage, 1995.

——. *The History of Sexuality: An Introduction.* Vol. I. Trans. Robert Hurley. New York: Vintage, 1990.

——. *Madness and Civilization: A History of Insanity in the Age of Reason.* Trans. Richard Howard. New York: Vintage, 1988.

Freedman, Carl. *George Orwell: A Study in Ideology and Literary Form.* New York: Garland, 1988.

Freud, Sigmund. *Civilization and its Discontents.* Trans. James Strachey. New York: Norton, 1961.

——. *The Future of an Illusion.* Trans. W. D. Robson-Scott. New York: Doubleday Anchor, 1964.

——. *Introductory Lectures on Psychoanalysis.* Trans. James Strachey. New York: Norton, 1977.

——. *Moses and Monotheism.* New York: Random House, 1987.

Friedan, Betty. *The Feminine Mystique*. New York: Norton, 2001.

Fromm, Erich. Afterword. *1984*. By George Orwell. New York: Signet, 1983. 257–67.

Fukuyama, Francis. *The End of History and the Last Man*. New York: Free Press, 1992.

Fyvel, Tosco R. '*1984* as a Satire on the Relations between Rulers and Ruled.' *And He Loved Big Brother: Man, State, and Society in Question*. Ed. Shlomo Giora Shoham and Francis Rosentiel. Strasbourg: Council of Europe, 1984. 85–96.

Gilbert, M. Sandra, and Susan Gubar. *The Madwoman in the Attic: The Woman Writer and the Nineteenth-Century Literary Imagination*. New Haven, CT, Yale University Press, 1979.

Gita, Rajan. 'A Feminist Rereading of Poe's "The Tell-Tale Heart."' *Papers on Language and Literature* 24 (1988): 283–300.

Godden, Richard. *Fictions of Labor: William Faulkner and the South's Long Revolution*. Cambridge: Cambridge University Press, 1997.

Godwin, William. *Enquiry Concerning Political Justice and its Influence on Modern Morals and Happiness*. New York: Penguin, 1985.

Goldman, Emma. 'What Is Syndicalism?' *Red Emma Speaks: An Emma Goldman Reader*. Ed. Alix Kates Shulman. New York: Prometheus, 1998. 87–101.

Goldstein, Philip. 'Orwell as a (Neo)Conservative: The Reception of *1984*.' *MMLA* 33 (2000): 44–57.

Gould, Stephen Jay. *The Panda's Thumb: More Reflections in Natural History*. New York: Norton, 1980.

Gramsci, Antonio. *Selections from the Prison Notebooks*. Trans. Quintin Hoare and Geoffrey Nowell Smith. New York: International, 1971.

Grant, Robert. 'Absence into Presence: The Thematics of Memory and "Missing" Subjects in Toni Morrison's *Sula*.' *Critical Essays on Toni Morrison*. Ed. Nellie Y. McKay. Boston: G. K. Hall, 1988. 90–103.

Gregor, A. James. *The Faces of Janus: Marxism and Fascism in the Twentieth Century*. New Haven, CT: Yale University Press, 2000.

Griffin, Roger. 'Fascism.' 2002. 20 July 2002. <www.brookes.ac.uk/schools/Humanities/staff/FAECRGL.htm>

——. 'Interregnum or Endgame? Radical Right Thought in the "Post-Fascist" Era.' 2000. 20 July 2002. <www.brookes.ac.uk/schools/humanities/Roger/2457/POSTWAR.htm>

——, and W. J. Krazanowski. *Fascism*. London: Oxford University Press, 1995.

Haaland, Bonnie. *Emma Goldman: Sexuality and the Impurity of the State*. New York: Black Rose, 1993.

Harris, Trudier. *Fiction and Folklore: The Novels of Toni Morrison*. Knoxville, TN: University of Tennessee Press, 1991.

Haslett, Moyra. *Marxist Literary and Cultural Theories*. London: Palgrave Macmillan, 2000.

Hawkes, David. *Ideology*. New York: Routledge, 1996.

Hawthorne, Nathaniel. *The Blithedale Romance*. New York: Penguin, 1985.

Hegel, Georg W. F. *Lectures on the Philosophy of World History; Introduction: Reason in History*. Trans. Hugh Barr Nisbet. Cambridge: Cambridge University Press, 1981.

——. *Phenomenology of the Spirit.* Trans. A.V. Miller. New York: Oxford University Press, 1977.

Heinze, Denise. *The Dilemma of 'Double-Consciousness': Toni Morrison's Novels.* Athens, GA: University of Georgia Press, 1993.

Hennessy, Rosemary. *Materialist Feminism and the Politics of Discourse.* London: Routledge, 1993.

Heywood, Andrew. *Political Ideologies: An Introduction.* 2nd edn. London: Palgrave Macmillan, 1998.

Hobbes, Thomas. *Leviathan.* Ed. Richard E. Flathman and David Johnston. New York: Norton, 1997.

Hobsbawm, Eric J. *Nations and Nationalism since 1780.* Cambridge: Cambridge University Press, 1990.

Hoggart, Richard. *The Uses of Literacy.* New Brunswick, NJ: Transaction, 1992.

hooks, bell. *Talking Back: Thinking Feminist, Thinking Black.* Boston: South End Press, 1989.

Howe, Irving. '*1984*: History as Nightmare.' *Orwell's* 1984: *Texts, Sources, Criticism.* 2nd edn. Ed. Howe. New York: Harcourt, Brace, Jovanovich, 1982. 320–32.

Humboldt, Wilhelm von. *The Limits of State Action.* Ed. J. W. Burrow. Indianapolis: Liberty Fund, 1993.

Jameson, Fredric. *Marxism and Form.* Princeton, NJ: Princeton University Press, 1971.

Jehlen, Myra. *Class and Character in Faulkner's South.* Secaucus: Citadel, 1978.

Kant, Immanuel. *Critique of Pure Reason.* Trans. Norman Kemp Smith. New York: Bedford/St. Martin's, 1965.

Kennedy, Emmet. *A Philosophe in the Age of Revolution: Destutt de Tracy and the Origins of 'Ideology'.* Philadelphia: American Philosophical Society, 1978.

King, Martin Luther, Jr. 'Letter from Birmingham Jail.' *Why We Can't Wait.* By King. New York: Mentor, 1964. 76–95.

Kirk, Russell. *The Conservative Mind: From Burke to Eliot.* 7th edn. Washington, DC: Regnery Publishing, 2001.

Kofman, Sarah. *Camera Obscura: Of Ideology.* Trans. Will Straw. Ithaca, NY: Cornell University Press, 1999.

Kroes, Rob. 'A Nineteen Eighty-Foreboding: Orwell and the Entropy of Politics.' *Nineteen Eighty-Four and the Apocalyptic Imagination in America.* Ed. Kroes. Amsterdam, NY: Free University Press, 1985. 85–96.

Kropotkin, Piotr. 'Anarchism.' *Encyclopedia Britannica.* 1910 edn.

Kuhn, Thomas. *The Structure of Scientific Revolutions.* 3rd edn. Chicago: University of Chicago Press, 1996.

La Bastille, Anne. *Woodswoman II: Beyond Black Bear Lake.* New York: Norton, 2000.

Larrain, Jorge. *Ideology and Cultural Identity: Modernity and the Third World Presence.* Cambridge: Polity, 1994.

Levine, George, ed. *Aesthetics and Ideology.* New Brunswick, NJ: Rutgers University Press, 1994.

Lichtheim, George. *The Concept of Ideology and Other Essays.* New York: Vintage, 1967.

Lief, Ruth Ann. *Homage to Oceania: The Prophetic Vision of George Orwell.* Athens, OH: Ohio State University Press, 1969.

Locke, John. *An Essay Concerning Human Understanding.* New York: Penguin, 1997.

——. *Two Treatises of Government.* Cambridge: Cambridge University Press, 1988.

Lowenthal, Richard. 'Beyond Totalitarianism?' *1984 Revisited: Totalitarianism in Our Century.* Ed. Irving Howe. New York: Perrenial, 1983. 209–67.

Lukács, Georg. *History and Class Consciousness: Studies in Marxist Dialectics.* Trans. Rodney Livingstone. Cambridge, MA: MIT Press, 1971.

Lyotard, Jean-François. *The Postmodern Condition: A Report on Knowledge.* Trans. Geoff Bennington and Brian Massumi. Minneapolis: University of Minnesota Press, 1984.

Macherey, Pierre. *The Object of Literature.* Trans. David Macey. Cambridge: Cambridge University Press, 1995.

——. *A Theory of Literary Production.* London: Routledge, 1978.

Marcuse, Herbert. *One-Dimensional Man: Studies in the Ideology of Advanced Industrial Society.* Boston: Beacon Press, 1992.

Marx, Karl. *Capital: A Critique of Political Economy.* Vol. I. Trans. Ben Fowkes. New York: Vintage, 1977.

——. *Contribution to the Critique of Political Economy.* New York: International, 1989.

——. *The Eighteenth Brumaire of Louis Bonaparte.* New York: International, 1984.

——. *The German Ideology Including Theses on Feuerbach and Introduction to the Critique of Political Economy.* With Friedrich Engels. Amherst, MA: Prometheus, 1998.

——. *Grundrisse: Foundations of the Critique of Political Economy.* Trans. Martin Nicolaus. New York: Penguin, 1993.

——. *The Marx-Engels Reader.* 2nd edn. Ed. Robert C. Tucker. New York: Norton, 1978.

——. *The Poverty of Philosophy.* New York: International, 1963.

——, and Friedrich Engels. *Selected Correspondence.* Moscow: Progress, 1965.

Matus, Jill. *Toni Morrison.* New York: Manchester University Press, 1998.

McDowell, Deborah E. '"The Self and the Other": Reading Toni Morrison's *Sula* and the Black Female Text.' *Critical Essays on Toni Morrison.* Ed. Nellie Y. McKay. Boston: G. K. Hall, 1988. 77–90.

McLellan, David. *Ideology.* 2nd edn. Minneapolis: University of Minnesota Press, 1995.

McLuhan, Marshall. *The Gutenberg Galaxy: The Making of Typographic Man.* Toronto: University of Toronto Press, 1962.

——. *Understanding Media: The Extensions of Man.* New York: Signet, 1964.

Melville, Herman. *Moby-Dick.* New York: Bantam, 1981.

Mill, John Stuart. *On Liberty.* New York: Penguin, 1984.

Millett, Kate. *Sexual Politics.* New York: Ballantine, 1970.

Mitchell, Juliet. *Woman's Estate.* New York: Random House, 1972.

Moi, Toril. *Sexual/Textual Politics: Feminist Literary Theory.* 2nd edn. London: Routledge, 2002.

Morrison, Toni. *Beloved.* New York: Plume, 1987.

——. *Sula.* New York: Plume, 1973.

Mussolini, Benito. 'The Doctrine of Facism.' *Modern Political Ideologies.* Ed. Alan P. Grimes and Robert H. Horwitz. New York: Oxford University Press, 1959. 410–24.

Nietzsche, Friedrich. *The Birth of Tragedy and the Genealogy of Morals.* Trans. Francis Golffing. New York: Anchor, 1956.

Norris, Christopher. 'Language, Truth, and Ideology: Orwell and the Post-War Left.' *Inside the Myth: Orwell: Views from the Left.* Ed. Norris. London: Lawrence and Wishart, 1984. 242–62.

O'Riordan, Timothy. *Environmentalism.* 2nd edn. London: Routledge, 1981.

Orwell, George. *1984.* New York: Signet, 1983.

——. 'Politics and the English Language.' *In Front of Your Nose: The Collected Journalism and Letters of George Orwell, Volume 4, 1945–1950.* Ed. Sonia Orwell and Ian Angus. New York: Harvest, 1978. 127–39.

Paine, Thomas. *The Age of Reason.* Secaucus: Citadel, 1974.

——. *Common Sense.* Mineola, NY: Dover, 1997.

Pascal, Blaise. *Pensées.* Trans. A. J. Krailsheimer. New York: Penguin, 1995.

Patell, Cyrus R. K. *Negative Liberties: Morrison, Pynchon, and the Problem of Liberal Ideology.* Durham, NC: Duke University Press, 2001.

Pater, Walter. *The Renaissance: Studies in Art and Poetry.* New York: Mentor, 1959.

Peach, Linden. *Toni Morrison.* London: Macmillan – now Palgrave Macmillan, 1995.

Pines, Christopher L. *Ideology and False Consciousness: Marx and His Historical Progenitors.* Albany, NY: State University Press of New York, 1993.

Plamenatz, John. *Ideology.* London: Praeger, 1970.

Plato. *The Republic.* 2nd rev. edn. Trans. Desmond Lee. New York: Penguin, 1987.

Proudhon, Pierre-Joseph. *What Is Property: An Inquiry into the Principle of Right and Government.* Trans. Benjamin Tucker. New York: Dover, 1970.

Rahv, Philip. 'The Unfuture of Utopia.' *George Orwell.* Ed. Harold Bloom. New York: Chelsea House, 1987. 13–20.

Railey, Kevin. *Natural Aristocracy: History, Ideology, and the Production of William Faulkner.* Tuscaloosa, AL: University of Alabama Press, 1999.

Rio-Jelliffe, R. 'The Language of Time in Fiction: A Model in Faulkner's "Barn Burning."' *The Journal of Narrative Technique* 24.2 (1994): 98–113.

Robbins, Ruth. *Literary Feminisms.* New York: St. Martin's, 2000.

Rose, Hilary. *Love, Power, and Knowledge: Towards a Feminist Transformation of the Sciences.* Bloomington, IN: Indiana University Press, 1994.

Rousseau, Jean-Jacques. *Discourse on the Origins of Inequality (Second Discourse). Polemics and Political Economy, Vol. 3.* Trans. Judith R. Bush, et al. Ed. Roger D. Masters and Christopher Kelly. Hanover, PA: University Press of New England, 1993.

——. *The Social Contract.* Trans. Maurice Cranston. New York: Penguin, 1968.

Said, Edward. *The World, the Text, and the Critic.* Cambridge, MA: Harvard University Press, 1983.

Samuels, Wilfred D., and Clenora Hudson-Weems. *Toni Morrison.* New York: Twayne, 1990.

Saussure, Ferdinand de. *Course in General Linguistics*. Trans. Wade Baskin. New York: McGraw-Hill, 1966.

Showwalter, Elaine. 'Toward a Feminist Poetics.' *The New Feminist Criticism: Essays on Women, Literature, and Theory*. Ed. Showalter. New York: Pantheon, 1985. 125–43.

Smith, Adam. *An Inquiry into the Nature and Causes of the Wealth of Nations*. Ed. R. H. Campbell and A. S. Skinner. Indianapolis: Liberty Fund, 1982.

Spivak, Gayatri Chakravorty. *Other Worlds: Essays in Cultural Politics*. London: Routledge, 1987.

——. *The Post-Colonial Critic: Interviews, Strategies, Dialogues*. Ed. Sarah Harasym. New York: Routledge, 1990.

Strauss, Leo. 'From *Natural Right and History*.' *Leviathan*. By Thomas Hobbes. Ed. Richard E. Flathman and David Johnston. New York: Norton, 1997. 320–33.

Swift, Jonathan. *Gulliver's Travels*. 2nd edn. New York: Norton, 1970.

——. *The Writings of Jonathan Swift*. Ed. Robert Greenberg and William B. Piper. New York: Norton, 1973.

Thompson, E. P. *The Making of the English Working Class*. New York: Vintage, 1963.

Thompson, John B. *Ideology and Modern Culture: Critical Social Theory in the Era of Mass Communication*. Stanford, CA: Stanford University Press, 1990.

Thurlow, Richard. *Fascism in Britain: A History, 1918–1945*. London: Olympic Marketing Corporation, 1987.

Tismaneanu, Vladimir. *Fantasies of Salvation: Democracy, Nationalism, and Myth in Post-Communist Europe*. Princeton, NJ: Princeton University Press, 1998.

Trotsky, Leon. *The Revolution Betrayed*. Trans. Max Eastman. New York: Pathfinder Press, 1973.

——. *The Russian Revolution: The Overthrow of Tzarism and the Triumph of the Soviets*. Trans. Max Eastman. Ed. F. W. Dupree. Garden City, NY: Doubleday, 1959.

Trump, Donald. *Trump: The Art of the Deal*. New York: Random House, 1993.

Vincent, Andrew. *Modern Political Ideologies*. London: Blackwell, 1992.

Voloshinov, V. N. *Marxism and the Philosophy of Language*. Cambridge, MA: Harvard University Press, 1973.

Volpe, Edmond L. '"Barn Burning": A Definition of Evil.' *Faulkner: The Unappeased Imagination: A Collection of Critical Essays*. Ed. Glenn O. Carey. Troy, NY: Whitston, 1980. 75–82.

Vucinich, Alexander. *Einstein and Soviet Ideology*. Stanford, CA: Stanford University Press, 2001.

Watkins, Frederick M. *The Age of Ideology – Political Thought, 1750 to the Present*. Englewood Cliffs, NJ: Prentice-Hall, 1965.

Will, George. 'Danger Remains After Six Decades.' *Sacramento Bee*. 8 September 2002. <www.sacbee.com/content/opinion/will>

Williams, Lisa. *The Artist as Outsider in the Novels of Toni Morrison and Virginia Woolf*. Westport, CT: Greenwood, 2000.

Williams, Raymond. *Culture and Society: 1780–1950*. New York: Columbia University Press, 1983.

——. *Marxism and Literature.* New York: Oxford University Press, 1977.

Wolfreys, Julian. *Deconstruction•Derrida.* New York: St Martin's, 1998.

Žižek Slaovoj, ed. *Mapping Ideology.* New York: Verso, 1994.

——. *The Sublime Object of Ideology.* New York: Verso, 1989.

——. *Tarrying with the Negative.* Durham, NC: Duke University Press, 1993.

——. 'There Is No Sexual Relationship.' *The Žižek Reader.* Ed. Elizabeth Wright and Edmond Wright. Malden, MA: Blackwell, 1999. 174–205.

Index

CPSIA information can be obtained
at www.ICGtesting.com
Printed in the USA
LVOW08s1735180517
535029LV00002B/204/P

in Nasiriyah. What had happened to the CIA plans to facilitate the Iraqi surrender and line up allies among the Iraqi tribes weeks earlier? Why had his phone calls to "Bob" gone unanswered? But there was too much mayhem to pose the question. Berdy made eye contact with "Bob" but never had a chance to exchange words. Fortunately for "Bob" and his passengers, the route beyond Curley was too dangerous for Berdy's Bradley to travel by itself: Koppel would not be making it to downtown Baghdad. Berdy would be able to escort "Bob" and his comrades south toward 2nd BCT's original attack positions near Objective Saints.[26]

Before the push downtown, the U.S. military had expected that the main battle would be with the Special Republican Guard. At Curley, however, most of the fighting had been against foreign Arabs and jihadists. Interrogation reports indicated that the Arab fighters were organized into platoons of thirty to forty and that there were an estimated 200 to 300 at Curley. Many had been brought over from Syria in buses and trucks and had only been in Iraq a few days. Some had military training but none were professional soldiers. Of the thirty enemy prisoners of war captured at Curley, twenty-eight held Syrian passports and neither of the two Iraqis taken prisoner was a soldier.[27]

"Most of what we found was Syrian, Syrian mercenaries, that had been recently conscripted to come over here and fight us," recalled Felix Almaguer, the intelligence officer. "This was based on the interrogations we had during the actual battle. The leaders were generally individuals who had some experience in some kind of Hezbollah or Hamas militia. It was very easy to spot them. We had been told by Special Operations Forces the night prior, look for older gentlemen with beards that look distinguished, look like they could be a religious leader, or a spiritual leader. And in fact when we found the EPWs [enemy prisoners of war] it was very easy to find the leader, because he pretty much matched the description word for word and we selected the individual that we believed to be the leader, and sure enough, he was the leader."

According to the enemy's defensive scheme, there were fewer
Arab fighters proportionately at the intersections closer to the
center of town and more of the Special Republican Guard. At
Larry, Arab fighters made up about half of the resistance. At
Moe, the majority of enemy combatants were from the Special
Republican Guard. "As you moved along it became more and
more of an Iraqi fight," Almaguer recalled.[28]

While Perkins was battling downtown, the CIA received a tip that
Saddam and his two sons were meeting at a house around the
corner from the Al-Saa restaurant in the Al-Mansur district of
Baghdad. The CIA report was received at 12:45 p.m. The restaurant, the CIA also noted, had traditionally been used by the Iraqi
Intelligence Service for meetings. Within an hour a B-1 bomber
dropped four 2,000-pound satellite-guided bombs on two separate buildings, turning them into a mountain of debris. It was an
impressive feat of airmanship and one of the most notable decap-
itation strikes of the war. The Air Force had worked hard to
reduce the "sensor to shooter" time to the bare minimum when
striking what it called TSTs, time-sensitive targets. The B-1 crew
were awarded Distinguished Flying Crosses for their efforts.

In Washington, U.S. officials hoped the fate of the Iraqi leader
and his sons had finally been sealed. After the fall of Baghdad the
U.S. Army would truck away the ruins to the Baghdad airport so
intelligence experts armed with the latest DNA technology could
sift for signs of Saddam and his aides. The staff of the restaurant,
however, said that eighteen innocent Iraqis had been killed in the
blasts.

Interrogations conducted by U.S. intelligence after the war
pinpointed the numerous safe houses Saddam had been shuttling
among during the war. According to the classified study by the
Joint Forces Command, Saddam was not in the area at the time
of the attack. Like the strike at Dora Farms, the bombing had
been based on faulty CIA intelligence. On April 7, Saddam had
in fact met early in the day at a safe house Qusay used as an alternative Republican Guard command post, which was far from the
site of the air strike. Saddam convened a meeting after that at the
former residence of the Spanish ambassador, who had evacuated

the capital. The Iraqi leader stayed that night at the home of Abd Hameed, his personal secretary. The CIA's informant who provided the original tip may have been the victim of a ruse by Saddam's intelligence operatives to expose disloyal Iraqis and may have been executed, the JFCOM study noted.

In all, Moseley's command carried out 156 TST attacks during the war. Of these, fifty were against targets where the Iraqi leadership was thought to be, four were against "terrorist" targets, and 102 were against suspected infrastructure for WMD or the artillery and rockets to deliver them. As it turned it, "most of the leadership strikes were offset from where Saddam stayed during the war, denying him use of government buildings, but not threatening his life," the JFCOM report noted.

Despite repeated attempts to decapitate the regime, none of the top fifty-five officials in the Iraqi government were killed by an air strike. The TST attacks could only be as good as the intelligence they were based on. The postwar interrogations also showed that, by chance, Perkins's two Thunder Runs had come within one and a half miles of two locations where Saddam stayed during the war, including the house where Aziz had read Saddam's eight-page letter. None of this was known to the U.S. ground commanders at the time. All they knew was that the Iraqi resistance had not ceased. Twitty's battalion had done its job. Most of the R2 package made it through. Perkins was able to stay the night. The 2nd BCT had claimed a portion of western Baghdad. But the eastern part of the city was still up for grabs.[29]

At the land war command headquarters in Kuwait, McKiernan sensed that Baghdad was falling and the regime was dissolving. The conditions had radically changed from the prewar planning, but it now looked like the V Corps and Marine forces would be able to gain control of Baghdad far more rapidly than anticipated. McKiernan was thinking about his next steps. When could he get into Baghdad himself with his forward command post to start working with those Iraqis who would be part of the post-Saddam solution? Where was Saddam? How could the 4th ID be quickly projected into northern Iraq? When would the rest of the forces flow into Kuwait and on to Iraq? As a result of Perkins's unexpected fight to the heart of Baghdad, McKiernan and Franks faced some new opportunities and decisions.

CHAPTER 21

The Second Battle for Baghdad

Jim Mattis liked to command from the front and as his division closed on Baghdad he positioned his command post on Highway 2, just east of the Diyala River, the last obstacle between the Marines and the capital. Marine artillery fire reverberated through his field headquarters as he gathered his commanders to go over his plan to attack into the eastern sector of the city. For all the detailed preparation the Marines had done to get to Baghdad, surprisingly little planning had been done for how to take the city when they got there. The general idea was for the 1st Division to attack from the northeast to cordon off the northern part of the city and then conduct raids in and out of Baghdad on critical targets.

Meeting with his commanders on April 6, Mattis sketched out his plan. Joe Dunford's RCT-5 would carry out the main attack, crossing the Diyala River to thrust into the capital from the northeast. Steve Hummer's RCT-7, meanwhile, would cross the Diyala in the south and attack into the Al-Rasheed military complex—a secondary attack to distract the enemy and pin down the Iraqi defenders. The trouble was that after racing toward Baghdad, Mattis's attack was in danger of becoming stalled at a critical moment. As it fought north on Highway 6 the day before, Lieutenant Colonel Bryan McCoy's 3/4 had flown a Dragon Eye drone near two bridges that crossed the southern stretch of the Diyala and was surprised to see that they were still intact. McCoy thought about seizing the spans before the Iraqis destroyed them but the bridges were beyond his limit of advance.

Mattis, who was wary about seizing the bridges while the bulk of his combat power was still battling its way up the highway, decided he needed more time to get ready for the push across the river.[1]

By April 6, however, gaping holes had been blown in the spans. Compounding the Marines' problems, there were no bridges at all on the northern stretch where Mattis wanted to launch his main attack. A fifty-yard-wide channel stood between the Marines and the Iraqi capital. Waving his hand over a map, Mattis gave an urgent set of instructions: "Find me crossing points." The job of spanning the Diyala fell to Lieutenant Colonel Niel Nelson, the commander of the Marines' bridge battalion. Laying bridges had not been one of the Marines' priorities before the war, but Nelson had worked hard to prepare his unit. He had canvassed the military establishment for spare parts and practiced river crossings with Blount's 3rd ID in North Carolina. In the months leading up to the war, Nelson had drawn up plans to lay bridges across the Euphrates, Tigris, and the Gharraf canal, which ran toward Kut. It seemed that he had plans to cross every body of water but the Diyala. Crossing the Diyala was an unexpected assignment.

When Mattis asked him how long it would take to find a crossing point for Dunford's RCT-5, Nelson estimated that the job could be done in six hours. In reality, neither he nor anybody else in Mattis's division knew much about the terrain to the north, but he felt he had to tell the general something. Nelson was improvising now. Reconnaissance units from RCT-5 and RCT-1, as well as engineers from Nelson's battalion, would move north along a twelve-mile stretch of river and somehow find a way across.[2]

The intelligence at the Marines' command post indicated that the northern stretch of the Diyala was defended by Iraq's 42nd Armored Brigade, but as the Marines' 1st Light Armored Reconnaissance Battalion headed north on Highway 2 it was clear that the Iraqi resistance was breaking down. The Iraqi brigade had dispersed to make itself less of a target for U.S. air strikes and, after being hammered by B-52s, Iraqi soldiers had quickly abandoned their armor. The Iraqi tanks were still warm when the

Marines got to them. As with the Medina and Baghdad divisions, the Iraqis' fear of U.S. airpower was as crippling as the air strikes themselves. The 1st LAR got a small taste of that airpower when a Navy F-14 Tomcat suddenly appeared, mistook the Marine reconnaissance unit for the enemy, and without clearance from forward air control unleashed a 500-pound bomb. Fortunately, the F-14's aim was bad and the bomb landed on the far side of a sand berm, shielding the Marines' LAVs from the effect of the blast. One mistake had canceled another; a potential friendly fire disaster became a minor footnote.[3]

While Iraqi resistance was crumbling, so was the terrain. Two obstacles stood in the way of suitable crossing sites. One was the fragile, steep riverbanks, which required a major engineering effort to emplace a bridge across the Diyala. The second was the lack of suitable roads to the river. Some routes were little more than donkey trails and others were crisscrossed with irrigation canals and culverts—some made of wood and tin—capable of withstanding at best five to ten tons, far too little to support a seventy-ton tank. To even get to the crossing site the engineers would have to construct an approach from scratch.

After several hours of searching, an impatient Mattis pressed Nelson for a fresh estimate when the elusive crossing point would be found. Trying to buy some more time, Nelson said he needed another six hours. Still, it was beginning to dawn on Nelson why there were no Iraqi bridges in the vicinity: the river in that area was virtually unbridgeable. "The Babylonians hadn't found crossing points there in 2,000 years," Nelson recalled. "The banks were made of brittle hard-packed clay that had been used and reused over centuries."

While Nelson's search went on, Marine units were stacking up on Highway 6. Instead of thrusting into Baghdad they were caught in the mother of all traffic jams. "The place looked like a parking lot," recalled one Marine officer, who noted that the division had inadvertently created "a potentially lucrative target for the Iraqis." Mattis had touted the value of speed to unhinge the enemy and reduce the vulnerability of his forces, but now his division was stuck at the doorstep of the capital.

After twenty hours of futile searching, Nelson drove south to

Mattis's command post and recommended that the division abandon its effort to bridge the Diyala in the north. Attacking from the east, lower on the river, would still enable Dunford's regiment to enter the capital through Saddam City, the Shiite-dominated area that would hopefully be sympathetic to the Americans. It would also put the regiment in position to move north to Kirkuk should McKiernan call on the Marines to secure the oilfields there, a mission that the Marines had already learned might be handed to them after the battle for Baghdad was won.

There was a way to traverse the lower Diyala. With air and artillery support and the help of mine-clearing gear, Marine combat engineers had been able to reach the damaged bridges on the southern stretch of the river. A quick inspection of tunnels on the near side of the river found no evidence of additional explosives. The southernmost span could be made usable by installing a ribbon bridge over the gaps. A nearby footbridge could be made passable by gathering debris from the near riverbank and stuffing it in the holes. To the north, the Marines planned to bring up an AVLB, a collapsible bridge that is carried folded up in an armored vehicle, and lay it over the large breaks in the span.

As Perkins was preparing to attack downtown on the evening of April 6, Mattis finally discarded the northern attack route. He decreed that the Diyala would be bridged in the south at first light the next day and that Hummer's RCT-7 would lead the attack. After almost a day of delay, the Marines would turn the southern Diyala into a major thoroughfare.[4]

As the Marines planned their next move, McCoy moved stealthily and alone to the Diyala to size up the damaged bridges for himself. While prone on the ground he was startled to see a French news photographer in bright civilian clothes taking his picture. McCoy was worried that the photo shoot would give away his position, but quickly calculated the photographer was between him and any fire from Iraqi defenders on the far bank. The media had its uses on the battlefield. If the photographer was prepared to serve as an unwitting decoy, McCoy was not about to complain. The battered bridges were just part of the problem. The Iraqis had also laid a minefield on the far side, which the Marines would have to make their way through as well. Hummer would have plenty of firepower to draw on when RCT-7 fought across the bridges. Cobra attack helicopters, with Hellfire missiles, would hover, M1 tanks would scan the far bank, and artillery would engage in counterbattery missions.[5]

Colonel John Toolan, who had replaced Joe Dowdy as commander of RCT-1, would also do his best to help. To take some of the pressure off Hummer's regiment, Toolan offered to conduct a supporting attack: his amphibious AAVs would swim across the river and attack into the city on the northern flank. The Marines had traveled hundreds of miles in the aluminum AAVs, but this would be the only amphibious operation of the war. The maneuver would not be without risk. Some of the AAVs had been received so soon before the war that the Marines had not had a chance to check their seals and bilge pumps. Toolan figured he would hedge against that by ordering the crews to ford the river with the top hatches open so they could jump out if the armored vehicles began to sink. Fording the river meant that Toolan's assault force would be separated from fuel, ammo, and other logistical supplies that would have to link up later once the far bank was secured. It was the sort of bold move that Toolan's predecessor would have been unlikely to propose; Mattis quickly approved the plan.

The Iraqis, however, sensed the attack coming. Intelligence reports indicated that the Iraqis were rushing to stiffen their defenses at the anticipated crossing points. That evening, the Marines and the Iraqis engaged in a two-hour firefight as Iraqi forces moved to the far riverbank to prepare for the Marine crossing. Iraqi observers hidden in buildings on the far side were directing artillery and mortar fire at the Americans. One round scored a direct hit on an Amtrack, killing two Marines.

Corporal Jeremiah Day had helped to clear Iraqi mines on the way to the Diyala the day before and knew that his platoon would be needed again. The platoon prepared for the day by wolfing down an MRE. Most of the platoon had only had one meal the day before and they did not know when they would have a chance to eat again. Day's platoon received a welcome order to shed their cumbersome chemical protective gear and fight in their camouflage uniforms. If the Iraqis had not used chemical or germ weapons against the Marines while they were parked on Highway 6, it was doubtful that they would do so now. That was one fewer danger to worry about.

Two M1 tanks were the first to arrive at the damaged bridge. They immediately began scanning for the enemy on the far bank and provided covering fire while the AVLB bridge was installed. Rolling across the span, a platoon of tanks established a 180-degree defense to guard the flanks. The external fuel bladders had been removed from the tanks. An M1 had been hit and burned up on Highway 6 and with the bladders in place enemy fire could turn a tank into a blazing inferno.

The protection provided by the tanks was all to the good, but Day's platoon needed to advance in front of the armor to clear the minefield. The most lightly protected Marines would be at the tip of the spear. Riding in their thinly armored AAVs, the platoon approached the mines and fired a MICLIC line charge. The charges were effective when they worked. This one did not. Though the line shot forward, the charge failed to detonate. The platoon had two additional MICLIC charges, but wanted to save them in case it ran into more mines on the way to downtown Baghdad. There was another way to set off the charges: what Marines called a "Medal of Honor run," a reference to the battlefield medal, which was almost always awarded posthumously.

Lance Corporal Biamchimano grabbed a stick of C4 plastic explosive and a timing device, raced to the butt of the line charge, placed the charges, and then scampered back unscathed to the AAV. There was a huge sympathetic explosion as the MICLIC blew a channel through the mines. As the dust cleared, the platoon could see that some mines remained. The minefield had been dense and even the blast from the line charge had not destroyed all of them. The platoon would need to make a few more Medal of Honor runs. Corporal Cobian and Lance Corporal Eubanks prepped two Bangalore torpedoes in the back of the

AAV. The Bangalore, which was first devised by the British army to blow gaps through barbed wire and used by the U.S. Army for the D-Day invasion in World War II, was essentially an explosive at the end of a long, expandable tube. It was also a simple but effective means of breaching obstacles, but required that the Marines run up to the minefield to employ it. The Bangalore blasts widened and deepened the lane.

With a path blown through the minefield, the Marines left the AAVs again to mark the lanes, sticking flags in empty, upended cans of ammo to designate the entrance, left side, and exit of the route the vehicles were to take. As Day and his comrades were checking the lanes, they were surprised to see that some of the mines had survived the MICLIC and the Bangalores and were sitting on the fringe of the lanes, close enough that they could blow the track off a wide vehicle like an M1 or damage any vehicle that strayed ever so slightly from the path. Sergeant Adam Lauritzen bent down to move a mine and cast a fatalistic glance at Day. It was a look that said "if it happens it happens." Lauritzen would either get the job done or he would be "a pink mist and a memory," Day recalled. Lauritzen moved the mine without any harm to himself, and then moved two more. Day and Lance Corporal Diaz joined in. By noon the lane was clear and the follow-up units were able to cross.

When the Marines reached the far side they began to explore some of the tunnels on the far bank only to discover five charges that had not detonated but were wired to explode. Gunnery Sergeant Smith followed the wires tied to one explosive until it led to an enemy fighter who had been killed by fire from the M1s before he could blow up the final section of the bridge. By the end of the day Hummer's RCT-7 had crossed the Diyala and all but captured the Rasheed airfield complex, which was the regiment's limit of advance in accordance with McKiernan's intent to establish the Baghdad cordon, but not to occupy the city itself. Scouring the Rasheed medical facility, the Marines found five pairs of camouflage trousers, some with traces of blood, which came from U.S. troops. The Marines had stumbled on the trail of the U.S. soldiers from the 507th and aircrew from the ill-fated Apache deep attack, who had been captured early in the war.

The American prisoners were nowhere to be found, but the Marines found three truckloads of decomposing Iraqi bodies near a mortuary.[6]

Toolan's supporting attack was also successful. Marines cheered as each AAV made its way across the river without sinking. The Iraqis were astonished by the "floating tanks." Once across the Diyala and under intermittent sniper and mortar fire, RCT-1 moved quickly north and crossed a canal[7] to cut off Highway 5, a main highway into Baghdad from the north.

By the time Perkins had fought his way downtown, Mattis's division had crossed the river and begun to cordon off the city from the north. The engineers of the 8th Engineer Battalion made bridge repairs and installed additional expeditionary bridges to accommodate the traffic of supporting and logistics units. Mattis's Marines ringed Baghdad from the east and were ready to attack into the city. U.S. signals intelligence was reporting that the Iraqi communications were in a state of panic. In a video conference among the commanders, John Abizaid cautioned that the fighting would become more difficult as the U.S. forces proceeded downtown. The regime was still intact, and the shrinking battlespace increased the possibility of "blue on blue."[8]

As Mattis edged in from the east, Perkins was struggling to hold on to his foothold in the regime area. Perkins had played to the international media. By April 8, the entire world knew that the Americans were in downtown Baghdad. But while Perkins's brigade controlled an important swath of the capital, his unexpected arrival meant he was the only force in a city the land area of Boston but with a population of some six million.

With the Tigris as a boundary for U.S. Army forces and the Marines largely on the eastern fringe of the capital—the eastern bank of the Tigris—the Al-Mansur district and most of the eastern sector of the capital had become a temporary sanctuary for the Fedayeen and Special Republican Guard troops. By coordinating with Division, Perkins could call in air strikes and even artillery on targets on the eastern side of the Tigris and his tanks and soldiers could shoot across. But the U.S. Army had to stay on their side of the river. The battle for Baghdad was messy enough without allowing Army thrusts across the river into the Marine sector, possibly resulting in fratricide.

The Iraqis and their foreign jihadist allies, however, were under no such restrictions. At the Republican Palace, Flip DeCamp was worried about the Iraqi counterattacks. His 4-64 Armored Battalion had easily taken the palace grounds, but there were five bridges just north of the palace complex that facilitated west-to-east traffic across the Tigris, and Perkins's brigade did not control any of them. The Al-Jumhuriya bridge, which fed into a major intersection just north of the Republican Palace, gave cause for worry. The brigade was getting reports that dozens of vehicles were driving across this and other bridges, dropping off fighters who would pick up RPGs and AK-47s from the numerous caches hidden on the west side of the city and then head back to get more reinforcements. DeCamp was also concerned about a park on the other side of the major intersection just north of the palace area, which was dotted with Iraqi bunkers and fighting positions.

As Iraqi fighters streamed across, Perkins tried to shore up his position by requesting an air strike to take out one of the bridges. This time, Blount endorsed the request only to have McKiernan turn it down. Destroying bridges in downtown Baghdad was not a step McKiernan was prepared to take at this point. He did not want to destroy the capital to save it. Perkins had gotten his brigade downtown; now his soldiers would have to stanch the flow of Iraqi fighters across the Al-Jumhuriya. The only way to block the fighters was to get the brigade's tanks and fighting vehicles on the bridges—or at least at the intersections near them. Eric Schwartz's 1-64 Armor Battalion had its hands full clearing the parade field and Crossed Sabers monument area, and was not in a position to help. DeCamp's battalion would have to take on the job itself.

DeCamp delegated the seizing of the intersection adjacent to the Al-Jumhuriya bridge to Captain Phil Wolford, one of his most aggressive company commanders. The intersection was on the other side of a triumphal arch known as Assassins' Gate, where Haifa and Yafa streets crossed. Wolford called on his mortar platoon to fire on the intersection and did not halt the mortar attack until he was 200 yards away. First Lieutenant Maurice Middleton, the commander of an infantry platoon attached to Wolford's company to provide more foot soldiers, had the lead for the company. As Middleton approached the arch, jeeps were dropping off enemy fighters who were toting RPGs and taking up positions in the archway. The platoon shot several TOW anti-tank missiles at their foes near the arch and Wolford's tanks fired its main guns as the company moved into the intersection.

The thrust into the intersection put Wolford's company in the center of a giant kill sack. The Iraqis were firing from bunkers directly ahead in the park. The company was taking fire from recoilless rifles to the left. Enemy fighters were also shooting from the roof and upper floors of the Ministry of Planning and other buildings in the intersection. "We were pretty much receiving fire from all directions," Middleton recalled. The company did not have fire superiority. The Iraqis were giving as much as they were getting.

Within minutes, a tank platoon sergeant was wounded by a sniper. Wolford's tank was hit by enemy fire, which blew out the driver's vision blocks and knocked out the sight for the .50 caliber machine gun. One enemy shot caused a spent shell casing to ricochet off Wolford's neck, which sent him reeling. The company commander slammed his head against the hatch as he fell down and blacked out. The soldiers feared their company commander had been mortally wounded. As Wolford regained consciousness he started to reload his .50 caliber, but saw that his tank loader had been shot. The company now had two wounded soldiers and no way of stopping the enemy fire or controlling the intersection. Wolford needed some serious help from the Air Force. For the first time in the war, Perkins's soldiers pulled back, returning to the palace area to clear it so that close air support could be brought in.

Soon, four A-10s arrived and began to shoot up the park with their Gatling guns. The Ministry of Planning was pulverized by JDAM satellite-guided bombs dropped by an F/A-18. Wolford called on his mortar team again to hit the Iraqis. By the time the company returned, enemy resistance had been sharply reduced. The company shot its way through the park and then turned its attention to the RPG teams prowling the riverbank and small boats of Iraqi fighters trying to get across.[9]

After fighting through the intersection, the next step was to take control of the bridge. As Wolford moved his tank into position he was concerned about fire from a tall building at the far eastern end of the bridge and wanted the brigade to call in an air strike on the structure. Meanwhile, soldiers in Schwartz's battalion found a Motorola radio the Iraqis had been using and turned it over to the battalion's intelligence officer. Major Rick Nussio, the executive officer for the battalion, was told that the radio chatter indicated that the Iraqis had a spotter who appeared to be monitoring the brigade and directing fire. The spotter was reported to be in a building with a Turkish restaurant. The information was passed to DeCamp's battalion.

When Lieutenant Middleton received the word about the Iraqi spotter, he forwarded it to the rest of his platoon on the bridge, including Sergeant Shawn Gibson. Gibson's M1, Red 2, had moved onto the bridge. The air was hazy but Gibson's tank systems gave him a good look. He saw a figure in a building in the distance looking at him with binoculars. He hit the zoom button to bring his scan to 10-power magnification. The figure was standing on a balcony and pointing. Gibson called Middleton, the platoon leader, and reported what he had seen. "Roger, I see it," Middleton replied, who asked how far away the observer was. "1,760 meters," Gibson replied. Middleton told Gibson to stand by. Less than ten seconds later, he told him to take out the target. Red 2 lased and fired his main tank gun. Wolford thought they had taken out the forward observer.[10]

In his command track, Perkins had fielded Wolford's request for an air strike on the tall building at the far end of the Al-Jumhuriya bridge and was trying to coordinate the attack. As he was discussing the strike, Greg Kelly, a correspondent for Fox News and a former Marine, approached Perkins. Perkins needed to be careful so as not to hit the Palestine Hotel. Western journalists were gathered there. That was the first time Perkins had heard of the Palestine Hotel. The hotel was a strange place. The international media had moved there from the Al-Rasheed, after being quietly alerted by the Pentagon it might be a target. The Pentagon knew that the Americans were concentrated at the Palestine. It was on the no-hit list for Moseley's command center. Iraqis had also calculated that the Americans would be unlikely to strike the hotel and had been using it for their press operations. Other unsavory visitors had also moved into the hotel for the same reason.

As Perkins sorted out the situation, Chris Tomlinson, the Associated Press reporter who was embedded with the brigade and a former Army captain, tried to contact the AP reporter at the Palestine by e-mail. The message bounced back, so Tomlinson called an AP colleague in Qatar, who in turn tracked down an AP employee in Amman, Jordan, who had stayed at the Palestine. While Perkins listened on a Thuraya satellite phone, the employee described the Palestine, depicting the tan hotel as pink. Perkins was still struggling to identify the buildings on the far side when Tomlinson called his AP contact in Qatar and suggested that it pass on a message to the reporters at the Palestine. They should mark their position by hanging white bed sheets out the windows. He was told it was too late. The hotel had been struck. Smoke was pouring out of the hotel and journalists were running out the front.

Hearing that the hotel had been hit, Perkins turned to his ALO, the air liaison officer who traveled with the brigade and coordinated the air strikes. Did the Air Force bomb the Palestine? No such air strike had been conducted, the officer insisted. Perkins called DeCamp. Did 4-64 fire on the Palestine? DeCamp had no idea. He too had never heard of the Palestine. With the brigade commander demanding an answer, DeCamp pressed Wolford: "Did you fucking hit the Palestinian hotel?" Like DeCamp, Wolford drew a blank. Apart from the general injunction against destroying mosques and cultural sites, the only building his company was specifically ordered not to damage was the Republican Palace along the river. As Wolford sought to figure things out, scouts reported sheets hanging from a building across the river. Wolford told DeCamp that was the building the tank had struck. "Okay, cease fire on that building. I'm coming over to talk to you," DeCamp said.[11]

A CENTCOM spokesman initially justified the attack on the Palestine, asserting that the soldiers had been fired at by enemy fighters in the hotel. Further investigation later determined that there had been no fire from the hotel. A military inquiry absolved the tank crew, concluding that in attacking a suspected spotter it had been acting within the rules of engagement. Still, the inquiry sidestepped the main reason for the episode: the failure to alert the ground forces attacking into Baghdad about the unique status of the hotel. The brigade had been careful not to attack the Al-Rasheed Hotel until it determined the media was not present and would have been cautious in its approach to the Palestine as well had it known about it. CENTCOM and the Pentagon knew that American and other journalists were based in the Palestine, but neither Blount nor his brigade commanders were made aware of this.

For Perkins, the episode was replete with irony. He had sought to turn the tables on the Iraqi information ministry by showing the media his soldiers had made it to the heart of Baghdad. He wanted the international media to cover the brigade's exploits and the professionalism of his soldiers. That was also Blount's reason for ordering Erik Berdy to try to get Ted Koppel to downtown Baghdad. Now one of the brigade's tanks had inadvertently attacked the media that he was hoping would chronicle his success. Taras Protsyuk, a Reuters cameraman, and José Couso, a cameraman for Spain's Telecinco, were fatally wounded.

As the Marines were battling their way across the Diyala, Dan Allyn was maneuvering to isolate the city from the west. Under Wallace's original plan to ring Baghdad with U.S. military units, Dave Petraeus's 101st Airborne was to seize the Iraqi military base at Taji on the northwest outskirts of the capital. That would have provided Wallace with an additional airfield and enabled U.S. forces to cut off the routes leading to the capital from the west and north. But the problems the Army had encountered with Iraqi air defenses had led Wallace to turn again to the tanks and Bradley Fighting Vehicles in Buff Blount's 3rd ID. With Grimsley at the airport and Perkins attacking into the city, the task had been handed to Allyn.

Allyn had played a supporting role since taking the Highway 1 bridge and the Tallil air base, first fighting to contain the Iraqis at Samawah and then penning in the Fedayeen at Karbala. Throughout the push to Baghdad, his brigade had been used as something of a 3rd ID reserve with battalions loaned to Perkins and Grimsley to reinforce their attacks. Now, for the first time since the Highway 1 bridge, his brigade would be at full strength again. Allyn's command M113 had broken down on his final day of operations in the Karbala Gap, so he headed north in an unarmored Humvee. With the collapse of Baghdad seeming close at hand, Allyn was not to occupy Taji, but to block two bridges and an intersection that led west and north from the city. The hope was that this would not only stop Saddam and his cohorts from fleeing west but would also put Allyn in position to drive into the capital himself. It was a small but important change that would draw Allyn's brigade into the battle for Baghdad.[12]

The first leg of the journey took Allyn to Terry Ferrell's 3-7 Cavalry Squadron, which had been sent west of the capital on April 3 to cut the routes there and protect the division's western flank from the Hammurabi Division, which had been positioned west of the capital as part of Saddam's misguided effort to guard against an attack out of Jordan. In his push west of Baghdad, Ferrell had gotten himself into more of a fight than he had anticipated. U.S. F-16s, A-10s, and British Tornados had targeted Iraqi T-72s on the western outskirts of the city and Ferrell headed to the area soon afterward to confirm the battle damage. As the squadron drove to the supposed site of the destruction it discovered that a battalion of the Iraqi tanks was not only intact but positioned behind a sand berm to the right. The Americans had blundered into a confrontation with Iraqi armor.

With his tanks and artillery, Ferrell made short work of the T-72s, destroying some twenty tanks. It was a small taste of what the Americans had once thought would make up most of the fight: a head-on clash with Iraqi armor and another object lesson in both the U.S. proficiency in mechanized warfare and the gaps in battlefield intelligence. After the episode, Ferrell had continued to screen the division's left flank, going as far as the intersection of Highways 1 and 10 east of Fallujah. But despite the skirmishing in the west and north by Blaber and other Special

Operations Forces, the territory beyond was a veritable no-man's-land. Allyn's route to the northwestern bridges passed right through it.[13]

As Allyn arrived at Ferrell's forward checkpoint, the brigade's scouts pulled their Humvees over to the side of the road so that J. R. Sanderson's armored battalion could take the lead. As Sanderson's battalion moved forward, Captain Clay Lyle, the Apache Troop commander in Ferrell's squadron, came on the radio and cautioned that Allyn's 3rd BCT would be in contact with the enemy within 400 yards. The warning turned out to be uncannily accurate. Sanderson's soldiers came under RPG and machine gun attack from both sides of the road, and later took fire from Iraqi BMPs and tanks. As Sanderson's battalion moved through an S-turn, Private Brian Huxley was hit squarely by an RPG as he was returning fire from an M113. Huxley was part of the engineer unit that dismantled obstacles the Iraqis had erected to slow the American advance. Sanderson had sought to use a series of code words for casualties so as not to unnerve his troops, but the word soon spread on the net: just twenty minutes into its drive north Allyn's brigade had its first KIA of the war.

With artillery and A-10s softening the resistance ahead, the brigade pressed on, bypassing resistance whenever possible to maintain momentum. With little intelligence on the enemy, Sanderson relied on reports from the pilots to gauge his foe. "It was all movement to contact," he recalled. "There was very little intelligence and what we did get was often wrong. The best intel came from talking to the pilots." Six hours after Sanderson forged ahead, Allyn's brigade received an intelligence report identifying the enemy it had already faced. Here was yet another example of how the speed of the attack exceeded the ability of the intelligence systems to support it.

Sanderson's battalion fought its way through a company of Iraqi BMPs and an air defense battery, and then hooked right to block a major highway bridge over the Tigris, as well as a secondary bridge 3 miles to the north, another potential escape route from Baghdad. Baghdad was now isolated from the northwest—if the U.S. troops could solidify their control.[14]

Like Perkins, Allyn sought a secure place to lodge his command post and decided to move it inside an Iraqi building: the Arab Petroleum Institute, a modern one-story structure off a highway. "We had been through direct fire engagements throughout the day," recalled Allyn. "I think everybody had finally taken a breath and said, 'Okay, we own this ground.' " After determining the area was reasonably secure, Sanderson ordered his ammunition and fuel trucks to drive up to the site. The brigade was running low on fuel and ammo and the institute appeared to be away from the main fight.

About forty-five minutes later, an Iraqi advanced toward the Americans motioning as if he wanted to surrender. The Americans ordered the Iraqi to lie prone on the ground, a precaution against suicide bombers, and kept their guns trained on their would-be prisoner. Almost immediately, they came under fire. The Iraqis were trying to blow up the fuel and ammunition used to support the American advance. There were no front lines and rear areas in the battle for Baghdad. Allyn's brigade command post and the supply trucks were in the middle of a firefight.[15]

Private Kelly Prewitt was in the front seat of the ammo truck at the head of a five-vehicle supply column. Just nineteen, Prewitt had joined the Army to find himself and had been trained as a tanker. With the division's tank crews at full strength the new recruit was given the seemingly safer job of driving supply trucks. As the supply trucks came under fire, Prewitt and the other drivers jumped out to take cover in the institute's compound. Prewitt did not get far before a tracer round tore a hole in his right thigh. Wounded, Prewitt began to drag himself along the road using his arms and hands. He was in the middle of a shooting gallery, severely injured and alone. As bullets whizzed across the highway, Sergeant Jimmy Harrison heard somebody yelling for a medic and was alarmed to see a soldier crawling in the street and nobody rushing to help him. Harrison left his M16 behind with a comrade providing covering fire and climbed over the fence outside the institute. Doffing his helmet, Harrison started to crawl forward before sprinting the last 30 yards to the injured private.

Prewitt reported that he felt numb and could not see. His pupils were dilated and he was in shock. With bullets flying around them, Harrison gave Prewitt his 9mm pistol while he tried to administer first aid. Harrison had his hands full dealing with Prewitt. If the Iraqis approached, Harrison would tell him where to aim. "You'll be okay," Harrison said. "If I tell you, just squeeze the trigger." As the drama unfolded in the middle of the highway, other soldiers from the brigade staff ran out to help Harrison carry Prewitt back to the institute and drive away the vulnerable supply trucks. But they could only salvage three of the vehicles. As ammunition in Prewitt's truck began to cook off, it ignited the fuel truck directly behind it. For hours, the area was racked with fiery secondary explosions.

Two of the brigade's Bradleys and J. R. Sanderson's M1 helped to repulse the attack. Now the race was on to save Prewitt, who needed to be urgently evacuated to the division rear. A request was made for a helicopter. The soldiers marked out a landing zone and waited. Eventually, the soldiers got the word. The Medevac helicopters were not flying. The news went down hard with Harrison and the rest of the soldiers. Prewitt's situation was desperate and they would have to drive him sixty miles to the rear. The private died en route. This brief episode in the war spoke volumes about the nature of the conflict. The brigade had suffered two dead in the battle for Baghdad—a truck driver and an engineer. The Iraqis had tried to stifle Perkins's attack by lobbing a missile at his command post and cutting his supply line to the city. Now, Allyn was encountering similar tactics.[16]

"After several weeks of fighting our tanks and Bradleys, the enemy knew he could not do anything significant to our tank and Bradley formations," recalled Allyn. "So he had begun targeting our soft-skin vehicles and our logistics vehicles. I am absolutely convinced that once they infiltrated this location here to the northwest, they surveyed it and figured out where they could do some damage to us. Their intent was not just to kill one or two Americans. It was to attempt to cause a situation that would kill a large number of Americans and also hurt our supply status."

With Perkins downtown and the Marines pushing in from the east, the Tigris River bridge was one of the few spans under Iraqi control. Captain Stu James's Assassins Company had rapidly seized the near side of the bridge, but it would have quite a fight on its hands to stop the Iraqis from coming across. Iraqi armor and vehicles were prowling the far bank along with hundreds of fighters in and out of uniform. The Iraqis had not seemed to appreciate the importance of the bridge until the Americans showed up on the western bank and were now preparing a major counterattack to recapture it.

Sanderson was worried an enemy attack would overburden his overstretched force. Sanderson had just four companies to secure about 2 square miles of battle space. He had encountered fanatical fighters in Kifl and knew it would take a lot to prevent the Iraqis from overrunning his position. At Kifl he had fought to save a bridge; now he wanted to drop it. Dropping the bridge would leave Sanderson with one less problem as he struggled to control his interior lines. Sanderson called Allyn and urged an air strike to take out the Tigris bridge. During the Gulf War, the Air Force had bombed bridges with abandon; in this war the destruction of a bridge was not a decision to be taken lightly. Allyn, however, agreed with Sanderson's assessment. The bridge had to go. Allyn took his request to Blount. The word came down that higher-level commanders had given permission to drop a small bridge to the north. The Iraqis were not massing to counterattack across that span, but bombing it would give the brigade one less objective to defend and allow it to shift forces. In Blount's view, the bridge Sanderson was on was key to the link-up with the Marines and the encirclement of Baghdad.

Even so, holding the Tigris bridge required all the firepower Allyn could muster. Desperate to hold off the Iraqis, Sanderson called for "final protective fires," a last-ditch artillery and mortar barrage to prevent friendly forces from being overrun. It was the only time that the Army used the procedure during the war. The brigade's artillery began an intensive thirty-minute bombardment, supported by some of the division's artillery. A-10s swooped in to bomb the far bank. All told, more than seventy enemy vehicles were destroyed.[17]

The Iraqis, however, were not through. A T-72 started to cross the bridge and was knocked out by an M1. First Lieutenant

McKinley Wood, a platoon leader with Alpha Company, was ordered to cross the bridge and see if the Iraqis were forming yet another counterattack. As Wood led two tanks onto the bridge, there was a large explosion followed by another. Having failed to mount a counterattack and open a route to the west, the Iraqis were trying to destroy and deny the bridge to the Americans. As at Kifl, the demolitions failed in their objective. Wood pulled back and began firing at the Iraqis across the river. Iraqi soldiers began taking off their uniforms so they could blend into the population. Baghdad was isolated from the west and east now.[18]

In the final days, it was impossible to tell from the air which Iraqi tanks were operational and which had been abandoned, so Moseley instructed his aircrews to "keep killing it all." Moseley's warplanes also kept pounding Iraqi airfields. The Iraqi air force had not sent a single plane aloft, but Moseley would not take any chances. He would hit the airfields until Franks told him to stop. Still, the upsurge of fighting on the northwest outskirts of Baghdad led to the loss of an allied plane: an A-10 that had been shot down by a Roland antiaircraft missile while supporting Allyn's brigade. Another barely managed to make it back to base. The aircraft were flying low and had been silhouetted against clouds. It was the first U.S. warplane to be knocked out of the sky by the enemy. The pilot ejected and was in hiding and trying to elude capture until he heard the unmistakable shout of a 3rd ID team that had been sent to rescue him: "Hey, pilot dude."

At CENTCOM, Franks and his top aides were struggling to keep up with the rapidly changing developments on the battlefield. Franks had made his first visit to the U.S. forces in Iraq on April 7. Overcome by emotion, Franks had drawn his generals together at Conway's field headquarters at Numaniyah, instructing them to hold hands and say a prayer thanking God for the looming victory. With Perkins's rush downtown, Iraqi fighters launching counterattacks from the eastern section of the city, and Mattis and Allyn itching to get downtown, the idea of conducting raids in and out of the city had been overtaken by events. In a morning teleconference on April 9, McKiernan, Wallace, and Conway settled on a new plan to assault Baghdad. Mattis would be given a green light to attack from the east and would seize the Directorate for General Security, the air force headquarters, the Ministry of Intelligence, the Ministry of Oil, and the Fedayeen command center. The Army would push from the west and the forces would meet in the middle. By this plan, they would capture the key city locations. All three leaders recognized that they had very little solid intelligence to shape their attacks but also knew the time was at hand to push hard to exploit the crumbling regime's defensive efforts.

RCT-7 headed downtown. Lieutenant Colonel Chris Conlin's 1/7 seized Baghdad University on a peninsula-like spit of land opposite the Republican Palace. In doing so, Conlin also overran the home of Iraq's deputy prime minister, Tariq Aziz. McCoy's 3/4 and tanks from 1st Tank Battalion drove into the city's riverfront complex of embassies and hotels. Continuing the attack, 3/7 captured government buildings, including the high-rise Ministry of Information, which was cleared of snipers floor by floor.

To the north, Toolan's RCT-1 advance in its zone was opposed only by snipers until Lieutenant Colonel Jeffrey Cooper's 2/23 came upon the Directorate for General Security, the walled headquarters of Saddam Hussein's internal security police off the Al-Dawrah Expressway. Cooper's Marines were met by heavy fire from approximately 100 loyalists within the compound as well as attacked outside by gun-mounted technicals. Nine Marines were wounded before the compound was taken. Iraqis not killed in the engagement blended into the neighborhood. The Marines received a friendly reception in Saddam City, but were astonished by the wholesale looting. In the absence of any guidance about looting, Mattis ordered his Marines to do what they could to protect hospitals and critical installations as long as it did not interfere with their combat mission. As for looters in general, Mattis said, "We didn't come to Iraq to shoot some fellow making off with a rug." Focused on digging out the last of the defenders, the Marines did little to restore order.

To the west of the city, Allyn dispatched a battalion toward the airport on April 8. Blount wanted to clear the battle space that existed between 3rd BCT in the northwest, 1st BCT at the airport, and 2nd BCT in the center of Baghdad. The next day, Sanderson's 2-69 Armored Battalion charged downtown from the northwest. The forces were converging on the city from all sides.

It was Corporal Edward Chin, a tanker with 3rd Battalion, 7th Marines, who stole the spotlight by hooking a cable from a tank retriever to a statue of Saddam—draping the head of the monument with an American flag—so that it could be hauled to the ground. As soon as Franks saw the flag on CNN he called McKiernan. McKiernan had already called Conway. Displays of the U.S. flag were officially forbidden. CENTCOM did not want to be perceived as an occupying army. There was a sense that Baghdad had been captured, but the battle for the capital was not over yet.[19]

In the early hours of April 10, Lieutenant Colonel Fred Padilla moved west around Baghdad's outskirts to seize one of Saddam Hussein's opulent palaces on the northern bank of the Tigris River. Earlier, the battalion had been welcomed after they crossed the Diyala. In one instance, Padilla and his sergeant major, Kenneth Jones, were brought to an ominous-looking walled compound by a group of agitated Iraqis who crossed their hands at the wrists as though handcuffed and lowered their hands knee-high. The two Marines interpreted the crossed hands to signify prisoners, but the other signal was unclear. As the Iraqis grew more agitated, Padilla called for some Marines to break through the heavy gate of the compound. About 150 dirty, bruised, and malnourished children, some as young as seven, rushed out and ran screaming to the open arms of the waiting crowd. What the Marines had uncovered was a children's prison, whose inmates were presumably locked up as punishment for their families' disloyalty to the regime. Their warders had fled, but left the children imprisoned. Upon reunion with their families, grateful parents descended on the colonel and his sergeant major with kisses of gratitude. "I don't go for that shit," Jones said to one. "Go kiss the colonel."

The mission to take the palace was different. Padilla was faced with uncertainties. His maps were not detailed and there was very little intelligence about the enemy. He had no idea about the loyalties of the population in that part of Baghdad. He had decided to attack at night when few civilians would be on the streets and to take advantage of the battalion's night vision capability. Anticipating a tough fight, Padilla left most of his soft-skinned vehicles behind. One Humvee per company was loaded with emergency ammunition and other supplies to help sustain the attack.

With Captain Blair Sokol's Alpha Company in the lead, the battalion plunged south into the darkness on Highway 2 beginning what Padilla called "the longest night"—a nine-hour running gun battle. Concealed in the buildings on either side of the four-lane highway, the enemy opened up on the column with small arms, machine guns, and RPGs. Firing right and left the column drove deeper into the city until the entire battalion was engaged and casualties were mounting. According to Padilla's map, there was a three-way intersection four miles down the road. The battalion was to turn right at a mosque and follow Antar Street to the palace. As Sokol approached the mosque, he ran into a blizzard of fire and hooked right. In the confusion of battle, however, Sokol had turned too far. He had led the battalion onto a road heading northwest, away from the palace. Realizing his error, Sokol ordered his company to jump the median to head back to the intersection. With the battalion now moving in both directions on a divided highway, Padilla screamed an order over the radio: "Fire only outboard!" Already taking enemy fire from both sides, there was danger of the Marines firing into each other as they reversed course past one another. Compounding the problem, Alpha Company's command AAV was hit by an RPG, lost a track, and ground to a halt.

Trying to salvage the situation, Captain Jason Smith, the Bravo Company commander who was positioned at the rear of the column and knew where the palace was, offered to take the lead. "I've got the route up to the palace," he radioed his battalion commander. Unlike Sokol, Smith had no tanks but at least he knew where to go—or thought he did. After reaching Al-Maghrib Square, Smith himself took a wrong street under fire at a traffic circle. He, too, quickly realized his error and also reversed direction. More than ever, the attacking column was in disarray. Padilla was worried that things might get out of control and he might not make it to the palace.

Making matters worse, Padilla received a new order from Joe Dunford, his regimental commander, directing him not only to capture the palace but also seize the Iman Abu Hanifa Mosque, a mile and a half beyond the palace around a bend in the Tigris, where Padilla was told Saddam might be taking refuge. Padilla was also told to grab some Baath Party buildings a half-mile northwest of Al-Maghrib Square, where American POWs were thought to be imprisoned.

Padilla ordered Bravo Company to continue to the palace and followed behind. He sent Alpha to attack the mosque. Shawn Blodgett's Charlie Company was ordered to seize the suspected POW site. The battalion commander now had three companies under heavy fire going in three different directions, none in a position to provide support for the others and no reserve. In retrospect, Padilla thought the confusion might have had a silver lining: any Iraqi defenders trying to divine the Marine plan would have been thoroughly mixed up. "I think it may have unhinged their defensive game plan," Padilla said. "There were Marines everywhere. They [the Iraqis] must have thought the entire 1st Marine Division had hit them."[20]

At early dawn the Marines could see the Tigris River and the palace, an elegant complex surrounded by a high wall. Smith's Marines dismounted and attacked the defenders, who were dug in outside the wall. An armored bulldozer was ordered up to smash down the gate, but the Marines found the gate open. Bravo Company rushed into the palace complex and began clearing it building by building, room by room. To the Marines' surprise the palace was empty. All the defenders were fighting from outside the complex and continued to do so. Even with the capital full of invading soldiers and Marines the Iraqis were wary of entering one of Saddam Hussein's residences. Padilla established his command post in the palace and, protected by its walls, called for a helicopter medical evacuation for twelve of his increasing casualties.

Meanwhile, Sokol's company followed the road abutting the river to the mosque, where he ran into intense fire from the mosque and the adjoining buildings. His gunnery sergeant, Jeffrey Bohr, was killed while evacuating a wounded Alpha Company Marine. A tank and two or three AAVs were also knocked out. (Thirty-three RPG hits were later counted on the tracked vehicles.) Padilla was afraid Sokol would be pinned down and exhorted him to keep moving.

The battle seemed to hang in the balance when Dunford radioed that he was sending a company of M1s from the 2nd Tanks. Padilla immediately dispatched it to reinforce Alpha Company. By this time it was daylight. Alpha Company's forward air controller called for air strikes from F-14s, F/A-18s, and A-10s stacked overhead. The A-10s marked the enemy locations and the fixed-wing aircraft made multiple runs at "danger close" range. With the arrival of the tanks and air support, the tension disappeared from the company commander's radio reports. Although mosques were protected sites, this one had been turned into a fortress, abrogating its sacrosanct status. Supported by air and M1 tanks, Sokol launched his assault on the mosque, hoping to kill or capture Saddam. After a four-hour fight and under covering fire from the tanks and AAVs, the dismounted Marines blew a hole in the wall of the mosque, rushed in, and overran it.[21]

Facing furious firefights and cut off from the bulk of their supplies, Padilla's Marines were short of ammo. There was a way to rush ammunition to the Marines but it was risky: a section of vulnerable CH-46 Sea Knight helicopters under the command of Captain Larry Brown had landed at the Iraqi Airborne Training Facility in Baghdad. They were better suited to flying supplies in the rear than dashing without an armed escort into a hot landing zone. Brown's crews began breaking out the pallets of ammo and packing machine gun rounds and smoke grenades on the choppers—some 3,000 pounds of ammunition in all. Then, flying fifty feet over buildings and dodging electrical wires, Brown took the first CH-46 in, landing at a designated spot near a swimming pool.

As the Marines unloaded the helicopter, a second CH-46 anxiously waited to land. As the firing picked up, the pilot decided that he was better off landing in a marshy area away from the main landing zone and taking his chances on the ground than providing the enemy with an easy target in the sky. In all, the helicopters made five runs, only one of which was escorted by

Cobra attack helicopters. The Marines captured twenty-two prisoners at the mosque, all armed, many dressed in black and identified through documents as Syrians. But once again there was no sign of Saddam Hussein. A CH-46, on the final run of the day, picked up most of them, as well as a trove of secret papers and files. All the litters on the chopper had been stripped to make more room for cargo. So the crew chief had the prisoners lie down sideways, stacked them like Lincoln Logs, and strapped them down with cargo straps.[22]

Charlie Company had no luck in locating the American POWs at the Baath headquarters. Under fire, but supported by air strikes, Blodgett's Marines stormed the Baath Party buildings. They found evidence that the captured Americans had been there, but had been moved. The "Battle of the Mosque," as it became known, was over. It had cost seventy-seven casualties and was the last major battle for Baghdad. By April 10, it was clear that Baghdad had fallen to the Army and Marines.

At his air war command post near Riyadh, Buzz Moseley had been keeping up the pressure. He was still concerned that the Iraqis might have some Scud missiles squirreled away in western Iraq and he was determined to keep the Iraqi airfields out of action and deprive the Iraqi air force of any opportunity to take to the skies. He also had an unusual problem. Rumsfeld's aides had pressed CENTCOM to drop a new bomb: the "Massive Ordnance Air Blast Bomb," a 21,700-pound behemoth of a weapon that had been promoted by J. D. Crouch, a senior civilian official. The huge bomb was a successor to the "Daisy Cutter" that had been used to create landing zones in Vietnam by eviscerating swatches of jungle. The weapon was designed to produce a large mushroom cloud and the theory was the massive blast would frighten the enemy into submission and have the psychological effect of a nuclear blast.

John Jumper, the Air Force Chief, thought the weapon was hardly needed in Iraq. "I was not excited about it," he recalled. But Franks had been inclined to placate the civilians at the Pentagon by giving the weapon a try. The CENTCOM commander had told Moseley that the Air Force should bring two of the MOABs to the region "so we can help the designers do their work." Two of the bombs had been transported to Al Udeid while several Daisy Cutter bombs were shipped to Romania on their way to the Gulf.

Finding targets for the weapon was no easy matter. The MOAB was designed to be dropped from a vulnerable and slow-moving C-130, and it seemed singularly inappropriate for an air command that was committed to precision warfare and limiting collateral damage in Iraq. Moseley dutifully discussed a plan to drop the MOAB and Daisy Cutters for three days and to monitor the effects, but he remained unenthusiastic. "Unless we have a different mindset, dropping them in a city with a CEP of about 3,000 feet does not make much sense," Moseley said. CEP was a technical term that signified the radius of a circle in which the weapon could be expected to fall 50 percent of the time. In other words, the MOAB would produce a mammoth bang, but it was hardly an accurate weapon. To the relief of the Air Force, the war ended before the bomb was used. The Iraq War would record a number of air war firsts, including the first time that B-1, B-2, and B-52 bombers were all in a single bombing raid, but the MOAB would not be one of them.[23]

As he watched Iraqis celebrating Saddam's fall on television, Moseley decided to catch one of the first C-17s to the Baghdad airport to get a firsthand look at the victory his aircrews had worked so hard to achieve. Before he left, he mused about the war. The air war commander was conflicted. "I've got mixed emotions about this," he confided to an aide. "We've conquered a country today and for the first time we started it."

The aide quickly corrected the general: Iraq had been "liberated."

"You're right," Moseley added. "That's a better way to describe it." One day, Moseley ventured, Iraq would become the jewel of the region.

On April 12, McKiernan's early entry command post was loaded into C-17s, which made a blacked-out, eerily quiet flight to the

Baghdad airport. The vans of communication gear were moved into an airport hangar that months before had been picked from reconnaissance photos as the site of his initial headquarters. Now that the capital was in U.S. hands McKiernan would direct the final stages of the war in the north and the beginning efforts to rebuild the country from his new headquarters on the outskirts of the Iraqi capital. He would be the senior general on the ground.

Wandering around the pitch-black airfield with Command Sergeant Major John Sparks, a close friend and adviser, McKiernan surveyed the destroyed planes and debris around him. McKiernan had no idea how many Iraqis might come forward to help or who they might be. There was no provisional government in waiting. Jay Garner was still organizing his team in Kuwait and there was very little direction from on high. McKiernan was entering a new and very uncertain phase.

CHAPTER 22

Saddam's Great Escape

On April 9, Saddam made his last appearance before the faithful. Riding in a Mercedes he stopped in the Al-Adhamiya district of northwestern Baghdad, jumped out of the vehicle, and vowed to carry on the struggle. Then he vanished as quickly as he had appeared, returning to one of his numerous safe houses in the sprawling Iraqi capital. It was clear to the Iraqi leader that the noose around his neck was tightening. One member of Saddam's party later told U.S. interrogators that the group decided it was time to get off the street after spying U.S. tanks maneuvering across the river in the Al-Azimiyah district, where the Marines were battling for the mosque. The day that Saddam had thought would never come was at hand: Baghdad was overrun with U.S. troops. It was time to abandon the capital.[1]

The next day, Saddam, his two sons, his personal secretary, Abd Hameed, and his bodyguards set off in a convoy of a dozen or so vehicles. The convoy came under fire and the entourage forced their way into a residence and hid there until the following morning. Saddam's massive palaces and government buildings had long since been abandoned. The Iraqi leader was on the run now and heading west.

Saddam's next destination was Anbar Province, a vast Sunni region west of Baghdad that contained the restive cities of Ramadi and Fallujah and offered the best refuge in Saddam's hour of crisis. The region was friendly to Saddam and had a long, porous border with Syria, Jordan, and Saudi Arabia. It was also largely void of allied forces. The only coalition troops in the

region were the teams of U.S., British, and Australian commandos that were roaming in search of WMD and regime leaders on
the run—what the military called "high value targets" or HVTs.
They were a danger for Saddam but were too few to seal off all
his possible routes for escape.

Saddam proceeded to a safe house in Ramadi, which turned
out to be not nearly as secure as the Iraqi leader would have had
it. After he got to the sanctuary on April 11, the building next
door was bombed at 2:00 a.m. An hour later, Saddam and his
sons hit the road again, spending the night in their vehicles,
parked in an orchard. Allied warplanes were prowling the skies
and hunting for Iraqi convoys. This was one time when there was
no safety in numbers: Saddam and his sons decided to split up.

Qusay and Uday hopscotched their way across western Iraq,
moving from Bija, Mayadin, and Maah until they made their way
to what they thought would be a safe haven in Damascus, Syria.
For all of their difficulties with Washington, however, the Syrian
authorities decided that Saddam's sons were too hot to handle.
They forced Qusay and Uday to return to Iraq, where they made
their way to the northern city of Mosul. Saddam, for his part,
sought refuge initially in the western Iraqi town of Hit.[2]

Now that Baghdad had fallen, McKiernan needed to seize the
northern oilfields near Kirkuk and take Tikrit, Saddam's
regional base of support and a potential rallying point for his
loyalists. He also needed to deploy American troops in the north
to augment the modest Special Forces there so that the region
would not dissolve into bitter ethnic fighting among the Kurds,
Arabs, and Turkomans. Before the invasion, McKiernan's staff
had identified the ethnic fault lines in the north and fretted about
the potential competition for control of Kirkuk and Mosul and
the threat of Turkish intervention. McKiernan was convinced
that he needed a U.S. ground presence north of Baghdad, all the
way to the Turkish border.

McKiernan did not have the 380,000 troops that Zinni had
determined in his 1003 plan would be needed to control all of
Iraq. The allied troops would be distributed in a wide belt that

extended from Mosul and Kirkuk in the north to Basra and the Shiite area in the south. As for western Iraq, the U.S. military would have to cut some corners and Anbar would be one of them. The U.S. military presence there would be an "economy of force." As for sealing the borders, Dell Dailey's Task Force 20 and later the 3rd Armored Cavalry Regiment could try to patrol them, but there were nowhere near enough troops. That was a task that McKiernan hoped would be taken up, in time, by a new Iraqi military and whatever troop contributions could be rustled up from allied nations.

Franks endorsed McKiernan's strategy and passed on his guidance in a video conference. As U.S. forces ventured north, Franks wanted them to cut off the pipeline that was transporting Iraqi crude to Syria. The Syrians had allowed foreign fighters to cross into Iraq and were no friends of the Pentagon. "Find out where the knobs are to shut off the oil to Syria—they've been assholes, they continue to be assholes, so I want to turn off their oil," Franks said.

Franks also had another matter on his mind. With Saddam out of power, the Turkish government was beginning to complain that Turkomans in northern Iraq were being harassed by the new law in the area: the Kurds who were allied with the U.S. Franks had little sympathy for Ankara's position. "Tell the Turks they can kiss my ass," Franks said. The CENTCOM commander was still smarting from Turkey's refusal to let the coalition open a northern front. As for the enemy, Franks made it clear that the remaining pockets of Iraqi forces were to surrender promptly or be destroyed. "I'm interested in exploitation, in killing those who need to be killed and targeting what needs to be targeted. Let the youngsters know that they should be as lethal as they need to be. We need to still be very much offensively inclined. The only negotiating we'll do is either you capitulate or we'll kill you. Don't get jerked around, be tough in negotiations, either you surrender or we kill you period."

On April 10, McKiernan told Jim Conway that the Marines would have the Kirkuk mission. Buff Blount's 3rd ID had its hands full trying to maintain order in western Baghdad. Dave Petraeus's 101st was busy dealing with Karbala and Najaf and had temporarily contributed a brigade to Blount's efforts in the Iraqi capital. Shortly after Conway was given the Kirkuk assignment, however, it was switched. The Peshmerga and the SOF that were working with them had already raced ahead to Kirkuk. The Marines would take Tikrit instead. The next day, John Kelly, the Marine assistant division commander, was told he had twelve hours to organize a task force and set off.

Because of the need for speed and the uncertainty of bridges ahead, Kelly decided not to bring any tanks, AAVs, or other tracked vehicles. They were too heavy, required regular maintenance, and guzzled lots of fuel. Instead, the task force would be a form of light cavalry built around the division's three Light Armored Reconnaissance battalions supported by a company of truck-mounted infantry, an artillery battalion, a service support unit, a detachment of SEALs, and an air control and support team. All told, the force numbered 4,000 troops and 600 vehicles. Kelly named it Task Force Tripoli, alluding to First Lieutenant Presley O'Bannon's Barbary War exploit. Tikrit was on the western side of the Tigris, while the Marines were on its eastern bank. The fastest and most secure route was to use the northern Baghdad bridge to cross the river and zoom up Highway 1. This, however, meant passing through the U.S. Army zone. When Kelly proposed the route he was told it would take twelve hours to coordinate the passage. Clearly, joint operations still had a way to go. "I was in disbelief that it would take that long, so I said screw it. If we have to, we can build a bridge in twelve hours." The task force would find a crossing point farther north.[3]

How much fighting Kelly would have to do along the way was uncertain. Saddam was born in the village of Awja, just south of Tikrit, and the city was a bastion of support for the Iraqi leader and home to many of the leading figures in the regime. The Marines had already made a few shallow probes north and had encountered enemy resistance. While the Marines had been taking control of Baghdad, Lieutenant Colonel Steve Ferrando, the reconnaissance battalion commander who had protected Joe Dowdy's flank on the way to Kut, had been ordered to go twenty-five miles north to Baqubah, where a Republican Guard brigade headquarters was reported. Just ten miles into the journey, Ferrando ran into Iraqi forces in one of the stiffest defenses he had encountered in the war. The Iraqis were in fortified positions, supporting one another. Withdrawing for the night, Ferrando assaulted the positions at daylight with substantial support from Cobra helicopter gunships. To Ferrando's surprise an Iraqi approached him afterward and warned of an ambush site at a crossroads just south of Baqubah, the first time he had received a tip from a local. The tension heightened when the lead squad leader rounded a turn in the road in his Humvee and started screaming into his radio, "Tank! Tank!" Circling the area a Cobra pilot asked dryly if the supposed T-72 was to the "right or left of the irrigation pipe propped up in the road."

The Iraqi had been truthful regarding the ambush at the crossroads. An Air Force F-16 and other air support were used to take out the Iraqi defenders. After Ferrando seized the Republican Guard headquarters he discovered two trailers in a palm grove—trailers that resembled the mobile germ warfare labs Colin Powell had warned of in his February address at the United Nations. Ferrando thought he had hit the jackpot until the Marines broke into the trailers and discovered they were nothing more than Russian-made field kitchens.

Another probe took place on the morning of April 12 when Lieutenant Colonel Dan O'Donohue's 2nd Battalion, 5th Marines, supported by a battery of artillery, drove north to check out a report on American POWs and to investigate an old pontoon bridge that crossed the Tigris at Swash. The POW report turned out to be groundless. The bridge was a different story. Captain Myle Hammond's Golf Company was in the lead and the first to arrive at Swash. Two AAVs from 1st Platoon were sent to secure the far side of the bridge, which was part of another town named Tarmiya.

Hammond did not have an Iraqi interpreter with him, but an artillery forward observer who was mingling with the people in the town found an Iraqi who spoke some English. As the Marines were monitoring the bridge, a car crossed the far bank and the Iraqi driver made a hand motion as if firing a gun. Pressed into service, the English-speaking Iraqi talked to the driver, who explained that there were large caches of weapons on the far side of the river. Assuming the weapons had been abandoned, Hammond asked the driver when he had last seen Iraqi soldiers. The driver said the Iraqi troops were there now. After the driver left, the residents of the town also began to move east. It seemed clear that something was about to happen. Hammond went back to his vehicle, but before he could radio the platoon on the far side, two RPGs struck one of the AAVs. The Marines on the far side were pinned down by small arms and RPG fire.

The Marines on the near side provided supporting fire and Hammond called for artillery and air strikes. As the Marines pounded the enemy, the Marines left Tarmiya and returned to the east bank of the Tigris. The Marines had four wounded, some seriously, but estimated that they had killed some sixty enemy fighters. Clearly, the fall of Baghdad had not signaled the end of enemy resistance.[4]

That afternoon Task Force Tripoli headed north with Lieutenant Colonel Duffy White's 1st LAR in the lead. With no electricity and therefore no operating traffic lights, the traffic on the outskirts of the city was a nightmare. Units snarled in the crush of automobiles were simply told to catch up with the main column as soon as possible. As the task force drove north through narrow village streets, Marines used poles to raise the sloping utility wires so the vehicles, and their radio antennas, could pass. Kelly made no effort to secure a supply line to Baghdad. He cut his lifeline, counting on Marine aircraft for needed support. By the time the task force reached Swash, there was no more resistance. The main danger was the bridge itself. It was so rickety that each of Tripoli's 600 vehicles had to cross one at a time. The drivers were under orders to keep their doors open so they could jump out if the bridge began to collapse, but it never did.

After crossing the river at a snail's pace, Tripoli sped through the night without opposition to Samarra, the only town of consequence before Tikrit. The route was littered with abandoned Iraqi armor and artillery. By dawn on April 13, Kelly had bypassed Samarra to the west and was racing the remaining twenty miles to the southern outskirts of the city. As Kelly moved north, Lieutenant Colonel Stacy Clardy's 3rd LAR was left behind at Samarra to establish a blocking position outside the town and prevent attacks against the task force. That day, a group of sheiks from Samarra approached Clardy's unit to ask the Marines to stay clear of their town. The sheiks insisted there were no Baathists there and Clardy assured them he would not attack the town if the Iraqis did not cause any trouble. Staff Sergeant Randy Meyer, a member of a human intelligence team, made contact with an Iraqi policeman who insisted that there was something of interest to the Americans in the town after all: U.S. prisoners of war.

Ever since the ambush of the 507th Maintenance Company in Nasiriyah and the shoot-down of Dave Williams's Apache helicopter, the rescue of U.S. POWs had been a top-priority mission. But as the Marines put it, POW sightings seemed as frequent as Elvis sightings. For the most part, these leads had been tantalizing but unfruitful. After an hour of questioning, Meyer gave the Iraqi informant his GPS receiver and instructions to go to where the Americans were being held and enter the coordinates into the device. The Iraqi did as instructed and upon returning sketched the location. The Iraqi captors, the informant said, wanted to get rid of the prisoners but were scared that the U.S. would kill them. They also were equally concerned that if they surrendered the prisoners, the Baathists would kill them. Clardy remained skeptical. The task force had passed Samarra and his blocking mission was over. Earlier reports that prisoners were being held in Baqubah had been untrue. But if there was the remotest chance to free American prisoners, Clardy did not want to leave any stone unturned. "I had orders to go to Tikrit and be there in four hours," Clardy recalled. "We sent a platoon from Delta Company with the coordinates, the Iraqi sketch map with a description of the house."[5]

Since his Apache had been shot down and he was taken captive near Karbala, Dave Williams had been through a punishing ordeal. Williams and his fellow crewmate, Ron Young, had been hauled to Baghdad, where they learned a few days into their captivity that there were other American prisoners nearby. Yelling out to them, Williams learned they were soldiers who had been ambushed on Saturday morning, but communication was difficult as Williams was generally kept several cells away from the other prisoners. Subsisting on a bowl of rice a day, Williams lost twenty-five pounds. He was subjected to death threats. His captors had taken his Seiko watch in Karbala and given him nothing more than a thin blanket. He slept on the floor. The walls of one of his cells were splattered with bloodstains, pieces of skin, and hair. Like all pilots, Williams had heard the story of Michael Scott Speicher, the Navy lieutenant commander whose F/A-18 was shot down on the first night of the Gulf War and who had been declared missing in action. There had been no definite proof that he was alive or dead and some in the Pentagon had wondered if he might have been held prisoner for thirteen years. Williams did not see how he could endure a lengthy captivity in such conditions. "I don't know how those guys did it in Vietnam," Williams said. "I really don't. Because I didn't feel like I was going to make it a year, or certainly any longer than that. You're totally helpless . . . dependent on your captors for even the basic necessities. I hardly ever slept, and we were getting bombed all the time. I wouldn't wish my treatment on my worst enemy."

On the twelfth day of his captivity, he suffered a distressingly close call when the Iraqis set up an antiaircraft gun on the roof of his Baghdad prison and began to fire away at the U.S. planes. Williams could hear the empty cartridges clattering on the tin roof overhead. With air raid sirens blaring Williams was back in the war again, but now he would be on the receiving end of U.S. fire. Confident that the U.S. planes would be striking back, Williams ran to each corner of his cell, trying to figure out which might be safest. The first bomb threw him to the floor. The second bomb landed nearby. "Afterward, I lay there for a minute or two," Williams recalled. "Then I stood and brushed off some of the bricks and debris. I started yelling out to the other kids, and Ron answered. The bombs had ripped the welded tin roof off my cell room, and I could see clouds."

Some of the walls of the building had tumbled down from the blast. When the Iraqi captors returned they seemed surprised to find their American prisoners alive. Gathering the prisoners, they moved them to an array of Baghdad facilities until Williams was handcuffed, blindfolded, and driven out of town in an ambulance. Williams was afraid that the American prisoners might be on their way to Syria or perhaps being hauled off to a remote spot of the country for execution. He knew he was moving north because the setting sun was always to his left.

When the POWs arrived at their destination they were put in a single room. Williams was the senior officer present and began to take responsibility for the five young soldiers from the 507th, several of whom had been wounded in their ordeal. Edgar Hernandez had been hit by a bullet in his right arm, Shoshana Johnson, an Army cook, in both legs. Joe Hudson had taken three rounds to the lower back. It had been four days since their bandages had been changed. Williams insisted that the Iraqis provide fresh bandages. After claiming that all the pharmacies were closed, one of the Iraqis secured those and other medical supplies that night. "The Iraqis had a hard time understanding something," Williams recalled. "Shoshana is Panamanian. Edgar is Hispanic. Joe is Philippine, and Patrick [Miller] is from Kansas. The Iraqis could not conceive how we could all have been in the same army and not fight one another. One Iraqi said to me, 'You no fighting each other? Why?' "

The POWs had just received their morning bowl of rice when they heard the roar of diesel engines outside the door. After getting lost a few times in a warren of streets and alleys, a Delta Company platoon, led by Second Lieutenant Brett Eubanks, had found a house matching the informant's description. The Marines pounded on the door. After receiving no answer, they burst in. "The door crashed open and Marines stormed in, yelling, 'Get down! Get down! Get down!' They looked just like the steely-eyed killers you'd imagine them to be," Williams recalled. "The Iraqis got down quicker than we did, and rightfully so." Then the Marines began shouting, "If you're American, get up."

Williams stood up and declared, "I'm Chief Warrant Officer Dave Williams, United States Army." A Marine responded, "You're going home, bud." As the Marines brought the POWs to the waiting LAVs, the soldiers could see where they had been kept: in a house in a walled compound on a Samarra street. The ambulance that had brought Williams there was next to the house, its siren and rooftop light covered by a green blanket. Johnson began crying from sheer relief.[6]

Kelly had led Task Force Tripoli to the outskirts of Tikrit when he got a call from Clardy. "The battalion commander was saying, 'We've got POWs,'" Kelly recalled. "And I was saying to him, 'How the hell could you have POWs? You never reported any contact. How the hell did these guys get captured?' I thought he was telling me that Marines had been captured." Clardy explained that he had freed seven American POWs and asked what he should do with them. Kelly said, "I think we ought to send them home." The POWs were given a quick medical checkup and flown to safety in Marine CH-46 helicopters. After Clardy's Marines rounded up the Iraqi captors, some of the POWs entreated the Marines to let them go. "I guess they treated the prisoners decently and they didn't want anything to happen to them," Clardy said. Clardy acquiesced and freed the Iraqis. His focus was catching up with the rest of the task force and getting to Tikrit.[7]

Like Tarmiya, Tikrit had already been the scene of a violent skirmish. After leaving the Haditha Dam, Blaber's Delta Force had continued to swing north. In early April the Delta Force had been involved in a serious firefight. When half a dozen Iraqi SUVs maneuvered toward C Squadron, the commandos blasted the two lead vehicles with Javelin missiles, triggering a violent brawl. The squadron took casualties: one soldier suffered a broken jaw when he was grazed by a bullet and another was shot just below his body armor. The squadron broke contact while other Delta troops killed and captured some of the enemy. While interrogating the prisoners, Saif Ataya discovered that they were members of a 100-strong force from the town of Seniya, 25 miles to the east.

Back at Ar'ar, Sergeant Major Iggy Balderas coordinated the air attack. Armored MH-60 helicopters attacked the enemy along with F-16s and other aircraft. Franks himself was at the Delta command center at Ar'ar when the clash was taking place and checked on its progress. It was a lopsided battle. More than sixty enemy fighters were killed. Despite the victory, the episode had a sour outcome for Delta.

To Medevac the critically wounded soldier, Balderas called on Black Hawks, which were at Ar'ar and ready to go. But they were on call for another mission: a Dell Dailey operation to film one of Saddam's empty palaces as part of an information operations campaign. It took four and a half hours to Medevac the injured Delta operator, who later bled to death. Later that night the Black Hawks flew Dailey's commandos to the empty palace and a combat camera crew filmed every bit of the staged attack. The tape was flown to a psychological operations team based in Kuwait, but never used.

A week later, Delta set up a desert encampment, which they called Grizzly, 13 miles to the west of Tikrit. Delta was joined by Rangers, Army Special Operations helicopters, Team Tank, and human intelligence teams. Leaving the Ar'ar command post, Blaber flew there to run the operation. He was in control of a small but lethal force he called Wolverines, after the teenagers who took on an invading Soviet army in the B movie *Red Dawn*. The mission was to raid Highways 1 and 12 north of Baghdad, capture senior Iraqi officials who were trying to escape, and generally sow panic and confusion in enemy rear areas.

The move was not without its drama. On April 9, Captain Shane Celeen, along with his fellow tankers, was heading to seize a nearby airfield when his M1 vanished into a forty-foot-deep hole and flipped over. The plunge nearly severed the hand of the tank loader and trapped the crew. Upside down, out of radio contact, and operating by flashlight, the crew administered first aid and tried to figure a way out of its predicament. Finally, Private First Class Christopher Bake wiggled through the driver's hatch and dug a tunnel through the sand beneath until he was clear of the upended tank. The injured loader was passed through the tunnel. Celeen had to doff his bulky chemical protective suit to squeeze through and emerged in nothing more than combat boots and underwear, soaked in blood and spilled diesel fuel. Team Tank later blasted the M1 with two main gun rounds to prevent any sensitive materials from falling into the hands of the Iraqis and then pressed on.

On April 11, after a week of marauding on the outskirts of Bayji and Tikrit, Blaber and Delta officer Bill C. decided it was time to begin encroaching on Tikrit. Before departing, Blaber explained his strategy. His intent was to instill fear and panic in the enemy forces occupying Tikrit. At no time would the Delta Force allow itself to be decisively engaged by larger enemy forces, or get caught in an urban area that would allow the Iraqis to cut them to pieces. Blaber's final words to the assembled force were, keep your backs to the desert at all times.

Led by Bill C., the force departed Grizzly under the cover of darkness and drove to their objective: a highway cloverleaf on the edge of Tikrit. Bill C. positioned one tank on each ramp of the cloverleaf, covering all four cardinal directions. The enemy quickly began swarming to the area. Bill C. noted that all the roads leading into town had been either blocked or barricaded so that only a single vehicle could pass. Trenches dug along the road were stocked with weapons and ammunition.

A complex situation suddenly became worse when one of the M1's tracks became snarled in a strip of utility wire, and two Delta soldiers had to brave enemy fire to cut the cable to free the tank. As Delta fought off the Iraqis, Blaber received a call from Major General Dell Dailey, who was monitoring the melee from his command post at Ar'ar. Dailey had his own idea of how the operation was to proceed: Delta was to fight its way north and do a Thunder Run through Tikrit. Like Dave Perkins's Thunder Run through Baghdad, it would shock the enemy and test their defenses.

Delta was not the 3rd ID and Blaber had no intention of engaging in a slugfest in urban terrain. Blaber told Dailey that he was willing to talk about a future operation in the heart of Tikrit but this would not be it. The Delta team planned to pull back into the desert. "Negative! Negative!" Dailey shot back. He wanted Delta to attack through downtown Tikrit now. Blaber stood his ground and said that Bill C. had already been ordered to return to Grizzly. Dailey was furious. As a member of Dailey's staff described the scene, just as Dailey was about to respond, the radio in his Ar'ar command center blew a fuse. Dailey slammed his radio headset down in disgust.

Over the next several days, Delta continued to conduct raids on the outskirts of the city, with mixed results. It searched in vain for Speicher, the missing Navy pilot from the Gulf War, and hunted for an underground facility that the CIA believed might contain WMD. The suspected prison where Speicher was supposedly being held turned out to be a hospital that had never treated an American. When he got to the suspected underground structure, Bill C. called Blaber with the results of the raid. Bill C. said sarcastically that his soldiers were looking at dead coals. The site was actually a barbecue pit—the most mundane structures had been cast as part of an ominous WMD infrastructure by American intelligence.

Several days later, Delta and Team Tank raided Highway 1 near Bayji, a town north of Tikrit, the first of numerous forays into Bayji. With the help of Saif Ataya and Nazzar, another Iraqi-American attached to Delta, the commandos were able to learn about the Baathists in the area and where to find them. The result was the capture of five of Saddam's bodyguards, the chief of staff of the Iraqi air force, and numerous ministers in Saddam's inner circle.

By and large, Delta's collaboration with Team Tank had been a plus. It gave the commandos more firepower and surprised the Iraqis by deploying M1 tanks in their rear. The combination of SOF and conventional forces was precisely the sort of imaginative thinking that the Pentagon had promoted as part of its program of transformation and reflected the trust that McKiernan had developed with Dailey.

But there was a setback. Team Tank and the SOF were also not always familiar with each other's tactics, all of which led to disaster one night. A Ranger commander made the mistake of sending a Humvee in front of the tanks without informing Team Tank. When the enemy began shooting at the tanks, one of the M1s mistook the Ranger vehicle for the enemy and blasted it with a main tank round, killing one of the Rangers' controllers who was responsible for calling in air and artillery strikes. When the Special Operations Command put out its official history of Team Tank, the deadly episode of friendly fire went unmentioned.[8]

Two days after Delta's raid on Highway 1, Task Force Tripoli arrived on the outskirts of Tikrit with Duffy White's 1st LAR in the lead. White ran into some resistance, killing some and taking prisoners, including foreign fighters. "We got passports from them; they were Syrians, Jordanians, and some others," he recalled. The 2nd LAR under Lieutenant Colonel Eddie Ray, whose battalion had distinguished itself earlier on the march to Kut, swung north and blocked Highway 1. That cut the road north. A city bridge across the Tigris was bombed, restricting access to the east—one of the few occasions when U.S. forces struck a bridge.[9]

Kelly spent part of April 13 investigating a new intelligence tip: Saddam was dead and buried in a village south of Tikrit. Kelly was given the grid coordinates of the suspected burial site. When the Marines arrived at the site the neighborhood was abandoned. There were no residents and no freshly dug grave. After finishing with the detour, Kelly was ready to move north again. The sudden appearance of the Marines caught the local Iraqis by surprise. Many were on their way to work when the LAVs appeared. One gas station owner drove up to find a command group parked at his pumps. "He was astounded and didn't know what to do," Kelly recalled. "So after hesitating, he simply unlocked the door to his office and opened up for business."

By dawn on April 14, the main body of Kelly's task force began to enter the city. Monuments and tributes to Saddam Hussein were seen on every street, leaving no doubt about Tikrit's allegiance. West of the city, tanks and artillery were spotted in revetments. They appeared unmanned, but were hit by Tripoli's covering aircraft as insurance. The Marines had little need for air support in Baghdad and had dozens of warplanes and helicopters scouring Tikrit for targets. But as 1st LAR passed through the city's gates it came under machine gun and RPG fire, which damaged one LAV. What ensued was a running gun battle, but opposition was spotty and was quickly ended by overwhelming

Marine air and the accompanying infantry. The Marines were amazed at the number of weapons and ammunition depots abandoned in and around the city. White stated, "We even found thirty-one helicopters parked in the trees, half of which were probably still flyable. They were American-made, some German, some Russian ones, and a Hind or two."

The anticipated battle for Tikrit had not amounted to much. After the initial firefights, the Baathist forces had either fled or gone underground. Getting Tikrit back on its feet was a priority. Kelly installed his command post in the opulent palace above the Tigris but did not allow Marines to bed down in them for fear of appearing too much like conquerors. Kelly met with the local sheiks and urged them to form an interim council. He wanted them to take responsibility for the restoration of services to the city and manage its day-to-day affairs. Meanwhile his Marines set up checkpoints throughout Tikrit and began to track down regime holdouts. Much of the population had fled the city upon the approach of the Americans, but came back in droves days later. Their fear of the Marines was overridden by fear that Kurdish renegades would swoop down from the north and catch them undefended outside the city. With the Marines there, their anxiety over the Kurds was allayed and some semblance of order was restored. But on the outskirts of Tikrit, there were robberies, looting, and shootings.

Nonetheless, Kelly decided he had entered the postwar phase of operations. He ordered his Marines to take off their flak jackets and helmets and circulate among the locals. An ad hoc Tikriti police force was organized. Vigilante checkpoints were disbanded. The Marines, who had been involved in pacification programs in Central America during the 1920s and 1930s and later in Vietnam, had drawn upon this experience when planning in Iraq. Yet it was clear that loosely organized resistance groups— known as "the Shadow Regime"—still intimidated the population. They were hunted down, but were not eliminated.[10]

Within a few days, Task Force Tripoli received orders to turn over their area of operations to Ray Odierno's 4th ID. Now that he had an additional Army division at his disposal, McKiernan had divided the battle space in accordance with his original campaign plan: the Army would secure northern Iraq and Baghdad while the Marines and British controlled the south. Cooperation between the Army and the Marines had been good from the outset of the campaign to the seizure of Baghdad, though at Tikrit there was disharmony: Kelly believed he had already transitioned to postwar operations; Odierno thought that his late-arriving division was still in the combat phase of the campaign. Odierno had been told his mission was to attack north, seize the Iraqi military complex at Taji airfield at Balad, and then advance to Tikrit as quickly as possible.

Apache helicopters from the 4th ID flew into the Marines' battle space without coordination with Kelly's task force and began to strafe abandoned enemy armor, vehicles that were close to the Marine LAR units. Major Ben Connable of the Marines said that Odierno's staff "felt they were coming to Tikrit not to relieve us, but to rescue us." A draft history prepared by the 1st Marine Division was equally critical. "US 4th ID had missed the combat phase of OIF [Operation Iraqi Freedom] and was determined to have a share in the 'fighting.' . . . Stores that had reopened quickly closed back up as the people once again evacuated the streets, adjusting to the new security tactics. A budding cooperative environment between citizens and American forces was quickly snuffed out." According to the Marines, a senior officer with the 4th ID made it clear that the Army had a different prescription for Tikrit when he remarked, "The only thing these sand niggers understand is force and I'm about to introduce them to it."

Lieutenant Colonel Gian Gentile, the executive officer of the 1st BCT of Odierno's division, confirmed that the 4th ID went into Tikrit "hard" but insisted it was for valid reasons. He said that the Marines, in their zeal to demonstrate that the war was over, had limited the number of checkpoints and did not patrol at night. "The velvet glove applied by the Marines in Tikrit covered up some dangerous problems and conditions," Gentile noted. "The perception among Iraqis was that the American occupation forces would do from little to nothing to stop them from looting ammunition and weapons." On his first night in Tikrit, Gentile said, a combat patrol from his brigade came upon thirty Iraqis looting weapons from an abandoned Iraqi base. A sharp firefight ensued and about fifteen Iraqis were killed.

The differences between the units were evident on April 19 when a traditional tribal feast was arranged between the Marines and Sheik Fahran al-Sudaid and important Kurdish and Arab tribal leaders in northern Tikrit. The goal was to facilitate the transfer of command. Kelly and his staff attended the dinner. Odierno's division was represented only by his sergeant major.[11]

On April 21, the relief in place was completed and Task Force Tripoli made its way south to the 1st Marine Division staging area at Diwaniyah. It left convinced that the good work it had done would soon be undone by 4th ID heavy-handedness. For its part, the 4th ID was convinced that the Marines were naive in thinking they had left matters under control. The question of how best to deal with Iraq after the regime's fall remained a matter of dispute as resistance persisted and grew in subsequent months.

North of Tikrit and Baqubah, U.S. forces had an entirely different issue to deal with. When Baghdad fell, the Iraqi resistance there crumbled, dissolving the Green Line. In Kirkuk, Iraqi soldiers had shed their uniforms and blended into the populace. The police had disappeared from the streets. Along with a delirious celebration, rioting and looting were rampant. The problem the Americans faced was not pushing the Iraqis out, but controlling the Kurds who were rushing in to fill the power vacuum in the north.

In the Kurdish city of Sulaymaniyah, Lieutenant General Pete Osman, heading the largely symbolic Military Coordination and Liaison Command, had worked hard to keep the Kurds in line. But when Jalal Talabani, head of the PUK, called he knew he had trouble. "They're looting! They're rioting in Kirkuk!" Talabani exclaimed. "We need to do something! I've got to send Peshmerga." Kirkuk had been home to thousands of Kurds until Saddam began to push many out and bring in Arabs in a calculated effort to alter the ethnic balance and solidify his hold on the oil-rich region. The Americans were afraid that the Peshmerga would try to expand the Kurdish sphere of control southward, possibly provoking a Turkish military intervention. Osman urged Talabani to stay calm and let the U.S. military deal with the unrest in Kirkuk—to no avail. Talabani's Peshmerga rushed forward.

Unable to restrain the Peshmerga, Osman contacted Colonel Bill Mayville, the commander of the 173rd Airborne Brigade, which was headquartered at Bashur, and warned him that the Kurds had rushed south. Mayville, in turn, contacted Lieutenant Colonel Ken Tovo, the commander of the Special Forces 3rd Battalion, which had been working with the Kurdish forces in that area. The 173rd was under the SOF's command in the north. Mayville wanted to know what he was to do about the Kurds. He did not have enough forces to "capture" the city. Mayville had been preparing to fight Saddam's forces, not restore law in an area that was now officially in friendly hands. Tovo replied that, as Mayville did not have a combat mission, his job was to "just stabilize the situation." "The 173rd was having a very difficult time accepting what they were facing. They were all about fighting Iraqis and force ratios and how they were going to handle the threat. They just couldn't come around to the realization that wasn't their problem."12

Mayville got the 173rd on the road and, by the end of the day on April 10, advance elements entered Kirkuk. The following morning, to the surprise of the Americans, Kirkuk was returning to normal with only pockets of disorder, mostly the doing of Peshmerga. "There had been a good deal of rioting and looting, but there was a sense of calm," said Osman. "The people seemed happy. They had gotten the rioting out of their system and seemed ready to settle down." Some Kurdish police from Sulaymaniyah arrived to help restore order.

But the crisis was not over. A 173rd roadblock on the approaches to the city reported that Talabani and "a huge escort" were heading for the city center. By the time Osman arrived on the scene, Talabani was already giving a speech and taking questions from the media at city hall. Osman was alarmed at how this would play in Ankara. The Kurdish leader was not only in Kirkuk but acting very much as if he was now in charge. An SOF officer managed to whisk Talabani away from the microphones and cameras and into the mayor's office, where Osman confronted him. Osman told him his presence as head of the PUK, the Patriotic Union of Kurdistan, was going to give the Turks the excuse they were looking for to cross the border. "But this is my home," retorted Talabani. "I don't give a damn if this is your home," shouted Osman. "Get your guys and get out of town before you cause a war we don't need." A chastened Talabani left the city. Forty-eight hours later calm had fully returned to Kirkuk. The police slowly reemerged while paratroopers of the 173rd patrolled the streets and chased renegade Peshmerga out of town.

In Washington, Colin Powell made an urgent phone call to Abdullah Gull, Turkey's foreign minister, promising that the Peshmerga would be persuaded to leave. Powell also agreed that a small number of Turkish officers could accompany U.S. forces into the city. By April 9, U.S. forces had taken control of Kirkuk's 300 unscathed oilfields. On April 11, Gull expressed satisfaction with the situation, saying, "There is no need at this time for intervention on our part," while clearly implying that the option remained.[13]

Mosul proved to be a bigger challenge than Kirkuk. Even as the battle for the Tebecka crossroads was taking place, the Peshmerga attacked and captured the town of Ayn Sifni, thirty miles north of Mosul. The Kurds closed in on the beltway around Mosul, which was designated the limit of advance. At a joint meeting with Waltemeyer the two Kurdish groups got into an angry shouting match. Masoud Barzani's KDP people had heard that Talabani's PUK was in Kirkuk in violation of all agreements. Officials from the two groups were at each other's throats and neither side was particularly interested in talking with Waltemeyer. Frustrated, Waltemeyer went to Dohuk, where he met with two dozen representatives of various regional factions. He told them that the Americans were going into Mosul and solicited their assistance. By day's end, however, he had no commitments. That night Waltemeyer received reports that Mosul was on fire and being looted.

The next morning Waltemeyer learned that the commander of the Iraqi V Corps, which had defended Iraqi territory south of the Green Line, wanted to formally capitulate at a designated meeting point south of Dohuk. When Waltemeyer arrived, he recalled, "it looked like Woodstock with guns." Waltemeyer was not the only one who had been informed of the event. The surrounding hills were covered with trucks and thousands of Peshmerga. It was soon apparent that the Iraqi general had nothing to surrender but himself. The Iraqi V Corps had evaporated and was a corps in name only. Sensing this, the Kurds began mounting their trucks for a drive into Mosul. It was clear the door to the south was wide open.

Waltemeyer grabbed a rifle and ran to the front of the column and aimed at the lead Kurdish vehicle—a dramatic confrontation between two allies. To his relief the column came to a halt and three hours of parlaying ensued. It was clear to Waltemeyer that somebody would have to go to Mosul and that he should be the one. Trying to stop the Kurds from claiming the city, Waltemeyer rounded up about thirty SOF troops and headed toward the city with American flags flying from the vehicle antennas. The goal, he said, "was to drive to city hall and plant an American flag." Waltemeyer had made himself clear but was in no position to control the city. Mosul was the third largest city in Iraq and multiethnic. To secure Mosul the SOF desperately needed to be reinforced.[14]

Jim Jones provided the initial help. With few forces in the north the NATO commander and four-star Marine general had come up with a stopgap: the 26th Marine Expeditionary Unit, which was afloat in the Mediterranean. Franks and the CENTCOM headquarters reluctantly accepted the offer. Commanded by Colonel A. P. Frick, the unit consisted of an infantry battalion, attack and transport helicopters, fixed wing AV-8 Harrier jets, tanks, LAVs, and artillery—some 2,200 Marines in all. An early plan had called for the MEU to block senior Iraqi officials from fleeing across the Iraqi-Syrian border. With the chaos in the north, Frick was ordered to deploy his Marines to Irbil "by the most expeditious means available." Given the considerable distance the MEU had to travel, that was easier said than done.

As a decision had been made to get as many boots on the ground as quickly as possible, the infantry debarked from their amphibious ships at Souda Bay, Crete, where they were to fly by C-130 and helicopter on a circuitous route to Irbil. Lieutenant Colonel David Hough, his command group, and 128 members of a rifle company were on the first flight. The next day twelve of their transport helicopters took off to begin a hopscotch journey to the landing strip at Bashur, the first step in a troop airlift that would take days. CENTCOM refused the Marines' request to bring along their Harrier jump jets and Cobra attack helicopters, saying they would not be needed. "We had no idea what our new mission was at that point. We were completely in the dark," said Major Paul Brickley, the battalion operations officer.

When Colonel Charlie Cleveland, the commander of the 10th Special Forces Group, told Frick he was going to Mosul, the Marine commander had one paramount question: "Where is that?" The Marines had no way to get there, so Cleveland said he would provide transport, which turned out to be Special Forces Pave Low helicopters and local buses. "What are we supposed to do?" Frick asked. "Link up with 5102 and work it out with them. There's civil unrest in the city," Cleveland said. "Who's 5102?" was the next question. "Special Forces," was the answer.[15]

At the Mosul airfield, Waltemeyer told Hough he wanted the Marines to establish a footprint at the airfield and set up a presence in the city to let the residents know the Americans were there. Early the following morning, SOF and Marines established checkpoints over the Tigris and, on April 14, a company of Marines and SOF drove to Mosul's city hall through an angry crowd protesting the lack of water and electricity. The situation turned deadly when Mishan al-Jabouri, a notorious local businessman, was seen entering city hall, which enraged the crowd. The Jabouri tribe had a Mafia-like reputation with ties to Saddam Hussein, and Mosul residents believed Jabouri's presence indicated that he was about to be installed as head of a regional government. Ignorant of local politics, the Marines made the mistake of letting Jabouri address the throng in the belief that this would somehow calm it down. Cars were overturned and set afire and the Marines reported taking small arms fire. They responded by firing over the crowd, but when a mob rushed city hall they lowered their sights and killed seven of the attackers. SOF put out a call for air support. In sequence, F-14s, F/A-18s, and F-16s arrived and made threatening low passes over the crowd, temporarily dispersing it. But soon the aircraft were gone.

By noon things had quieted down. When a relief convoy arrived, Waltemeyer and Hough decided to hold their position for the night. But things became worse the next day when firing at the beleaguered company and command group resumed with increased intensity. Frick, Hough, and Waltemeyer realized that a couple hundred Marines in the third largest city in Iraq were in an untenable position. Under cover of an SOF AC-130 gunship, the Americans withdrew to the Mosul airport when it became dark. Meanwhile in Ankara, U.S. officials were busy assuring the Turks that all was under control and that the Americans and not the Peshmerga were in charge of Mosul.

The Marine Expeditionary Unit commander sorely wished he had been allowed to bring his Cobra helicopter gunships, Harriers, and LAVs. He was further dismayed when on April 17 the Sixth Fleet commander ordered the Marines to halt further deployments to Iraq. The flow of his battalion was stopped in midstream. The 26th MEU had received little guidance about its mission and only a fraction of what it needed to do the job. Thereafter, the 750-man force had to content itself with providing security for the airfield. The deployment of the 26th MEU had been Jones's brainstorm, not CENTCOM's. Without strong backing from Franks or any real coordination with McKiernan's staff, the plan did not get very far.[16]

Osman, too, was convinced that the U.S. still needed more troops, and firepower, in the north. Already Turkish Special Forces operatives had been picked up in Kirkuk, disguised as humanitarian aid workers. Osman believed the Turks were meddling and that the threat of a Turkish intervention, if the Peshmerga took control of Mosul, was real. Osman called Abizaid and told him, "You've got to get a larger force in here and give them some tanks. They've got to see we're serious about this."

The deputy at CENTCOM responded that he would send Petraeus's 101st Airborne Division. McKiernan was thinking the same thing. With its heliborne forces and long reach, the 101st was ordered to conduct the longest airmobile operation in history, moving from well south of Baghdad to Mosul, with multiple refuelings en route.[17]

Overseeing Mosul was just about the last thing the 101st had had in mind when American forces invaded Iraq. Petraeus had been convinced his soldiers would be among the first to get to Baghdad. But after the American military was attacked by paramilitary forces in the rear, the 101st was ordered to clear the southern Iraqi cities of Najaf and Karbala before moving north. The 101st's new orders were to take charge of Mosul, the territory to the west that stretched to the Syrian border, as well as Kurdish areas to Mosul's north and east. Petraeus had a large area to cover—the entire Ninawa Province—but he had a full division of soldiers and firepower with which to do it.

Colonel Joe Anderson, the commander of the 2nd Brigade of the 101st, led his soldiers to the Mosul airfield on April 22. The situation did not appear encouraging. The Marines were hunkered down at the airport. The city was still in an uproar. Many of the Peshmerga had left, but not before looting the Iraqi V Corps's supply depot and retiring to the mountains with purloined artillery and every other piece of useful weaponry and equipment they could get their hands on. As a farewell salute they had also blown up the Iraqi ammunition dump, which exploded and burned for days.

Colonel Anderson quickly moved more than 1,600 soldiers into the city center. Within a few days, General Petraeus began negotiations with the various ethnic groups and tribes to form a local governing council and convene a caucus so the Iraqis could pick a new mayor. Petraeus had his troops assume a no-nonsense but nonaggressive posture. He himself took off his helmet and flak jacket while he walked through the streets and talked with neighborhood leaders. "He did it right and won over Mosul," said Osman. It was a far different approach from the one taken by Odierno in Tikrit.[18]

The campaign in northern Iraq relied more on finesse than

speed or firepower. More so than the campaigns in the south or west, it validated the strategy employed in the earlier war against the Taliban. As in Afghanistan, SOF relied on indigenous forces supported by American airpower to hold in place and ultimately defeat a 150,000-man Iraqi army along the Green Line. The political challenges had been more daunting than the military ones. Still, a handful of officers from different commands managed to tamp down ethnic tensions. The liberation of Iraqi Kurdistan owed much to their ingenuity and adaptability.

While Osman and his fellow officers were struggling to keep the lid on northern Iraq, the British were securing the southeast. Robin Brims, the British major general who commanded the 1 U.K. Armoured Division, had faced a different strategic situation than had most of his American counterparts. Unlike Buff Blount or Jim Mattis, Brims's goal was not to seize the enemy capital, defeat the Republican Guard, and throw Saddam out of power. The British mission was to stabilize and ultimately liberate the Shiite-dominated corner of Iraq.

In the opening days of the war, the British had quickly taken the Faw Peninsula and assumed control of the Rumaylah oilfields from Mattis's division. Taking advantage of the newly seized port of Umm Qasr, Albert Whitley, McKiernan's British deputy, scored an early public relations coup by organizing a very visible delivery of food and humanitarian assistance. Whitley had initially approached the Americans, who had tons of aid stockpiled but were slow to respond. The British government had little to offer. So Whitley convinced the Kuwaiti Red Crescent to donate aid and arranged for it to be loaded on the *Sir Galahad*, a British vessel. The arrival of the ship on March 28 was, as Whitley hoped, an international media event, though more show than substance.

After its initial operations, the British offensive had been methodical, even patient. Franks had pressed McKiernan during his visit to Camp Doha to seize Basra faster. But when McKiernan went to see Brims, he left the timing up to the British. As far as McKiernan was concerned, the British had already accomplished their main strategic purpose by fixing the Iraqi forces in Basra and in eastern Iraq. On Franks's computer screens in Qatar, the red icons looked like menacing formations but McKiernan saw them as hollow symbols of divisions that had little will to fight.

For Brims, the pace of the attack was less important than risking the destruction of Basra, Zubayr, and other southern cities. The population in the region was deemed to be largely anti-Saddam, presumed to be receptive, if not friendly, to the coalition but also under the thumb of hard-nosed Baathists who reported to Baghdad. Ali Hassan al-Majeed, Chemical Ali, who was in control of the network of Baath militia and Fedayeen in the south, was operating out of Basra.

Brims did not want to lay siege to Basra and cut off the city from food and other supplies. Nor was his goal to trap all the Baathists in the city. For Brims, it was enough to take the city more or less intact. The British commander was careful to leave an escape route for many of the regime forces—the road north of Highway 6 leading to Amara—unlike the Americans, who had hoped to set a cordon around Baghdad and trap as many senior officers as they could. Unlike Mattis, who gave orders to his commanders to destroy the enemy units they faced and not let them retreat to fight another day, Brims said, "I knew that they didn't want to fight, and I wanted to give those who didn't want to fight the opportunity to escape. So I exercised restraint there. I could mention any number of occasions when I restrained. But it was not because I was given 'limited freedom of action,' nor for 'legal reasons,' but because that is how we wanted to fight the war."

The strategy minimized the chances of a slugfest in Basra but allowed the Fedayeen to live to fight another day. In another contrast with the Americans, Brims also applied stricter rules of engagement. The V Corps and Marines routinely relied on counterbattery radar in their artillery duels with the Iraqis. Brims was reluctant to rely on unobserved fire, a procedure that was effective in quickly responding to enemy barrages but which increased the possibility of civilian casualties. The British general was also determined to draw on the lessons of Zubayr, which had been a hotbed of Fedayeen resistance. Instead of racing into the city, the

British 7 Armored Brigade had set up checkpoints on the outskirts, gathered intelligence about the resistance in the city, and
ambushed the Iraqi fighters who came out to contest their positions. Brims did much the same at Basra. The British conducted
raids in and out of the city and gradually moved into the outskirts.

During the Army's and Marines' approach to Baghdad, the
British had received intelligence pinpointing the location of
Chemical Ali. Within minutes, an air strike had been authorized.
An American F-16 dropped two JDAM satellite-guided bombs.
The first was a dud, but the second hit and blasted the suspected
hideout. On the morning of April 6, the Black Watch was conducting a raid in northern Basra, penetrating the city. After meeting no resistance in their Challenger tanks and Warrior armored
vehicles, the British drove farther until they encountered Iraqi
soldiers and Fedayeen at concrete pillboxes and in fortified
houses. After attacking the enemy positions it was clear that the
Iraqi defense was coming apart. Constant pressure from the
British and the attack on Chemical Ali had undermined enemy
morale. Brims could see that the Iraqi defense at Basra was hollow and it was time to strike. Officially, the decision to attack
into Basra was McKiernan's, so Brims called McKiernan's command and was given the green light.

At 11:00 a.m., Brims finally gave the order for British forces to
move deep into the city. The 7 Armoured Brigade, commanded by
Brigadier Graham Binns, drove over the western bridges while
Brigadier Jim Dutton's 3 Commando Brigade attacked from the
south. The 16 Air Assault Brigade under Brigadier "Jacko" Page
simultaneously moved into Diya, a town about ten miles north of
Basra that British intelligence indicated was the headquarters for
the Iraqi military's III Corps. Brims could have attacked the
headquarters but held back. By now it had been abandoned. The
mayor of the town came out waving a white flag. The Iraqi command had left several hours earlier.

The attack into Basra made for a long day of fighting, but only
three British soldiers were killed. The division commander was
duly proud of its accomplishment. "If you had said to me on
March 19 that you could attack into a defended city of one and a

quarter million people and only have three of your own soldiers killed I'd have taken it. I deeply regret the three but I think it was a pretty remarkable achievement by 7 Armoured Brigade."

At the Pentagon, officials released video of the strike on Chemical Ali's house. "We believe that the reign of terror of Chemical Ali has come to an end," Rumsfeld said. U.S. intelligence, however, later discovered that the Iraqi official had survived the attack and escaped the city. Like the failed F-117 strike at Dora Farms and the April 7 B-1 attack in Baghdad, the air strike had been precisely delivered but the target had eluded them.

Brims, who had also believed the early intelligence reports, was philosophical about the episode. The British general thought that the final collapse of the Iraqi defenses in Basra had been precipitated by reports among the residents of Basra that Chemical Ali had been killed. Here was an inadvertent case of psychological warfare. The Pentagon, CENTCOM, and the British Ministry of Defence were convinced that Ali was buried under the debris of his Basra headquarters, and for a while the Iraqis were as well. His body, however, was not found. Chemical Ali was still alive and well. Saddam and his top officials had scattered to the four winds, but they were not finished yet.[19]

CHAPTER 23

Hello, I Must Be Going

On April 15, President Bush convened a meeting of his top aides to consider the plan for withdrawing U.S. forces from Iraq. In his Citadel speech before assuming the presidency, Bush had vowed to avoid open-ended peacekeeping operations and massive nation-building operations. Rumsfeld had echoed the same themes in his address "Beyond Nation-Building" just a month before the war. With the Iraqi capital in American hands the administration was moving to put its precepts into action.[1]

Prepared by the Joint Staff, the plan was confidently titled "Iraq Phase IV: Gaining Coalition Commitment." There were to be three foreign divisions: a British-led division that would include other allied forces, a Polish-led division, and a Muslim force that would be led by the Saudis and Arabs from other Persian Gulf States. In addition, the administration would solicit foreign constabularies to help keep order and train the Iraqi police. The Italian Carabinieri were high on the wish list, as were constabularies from Denmark, Italy, Portugal, South Korea, and Singapore. Few of the potential contributors had been whole-hearted supporters of the war, but the administration assumed they would be willing to help keep the peace in a relatively benign Iraq, which controlled some of the world's largest oil reserves and which would be ruled by a new enlightened government.

The president applauded the plan to seek foreign troops, and the meeting yielded three additional decisions on post-Saddam Iraq. The United States would collect and publish information on Saddam's brutality. It would upgrade the Iraqis' health care system and accept an offer from Saudi Crown Prince Abdullah to establish a hospital in Baghdad.[2] In the early days after the fall of the capital, Baghdad had been racked by a spasm of looting, but the Bush administration was convinced its strategy was still on track. There would be no Balkans-like peacekeeping operation. The Iraq War would be like a thunderstorm: a short, violent episode that swept away the enemy but would not entail a burdensome, long-term troop commitment.

The next day, Tommy Franks flew to the Iraqi capital to discuss the path ahead. It was the CENTCOM commander's first flight to the sprawling Baghdad airport, which American forces had turned into a transportation hub for liberated Iraq. As Franks emerged from his C-130 he pumped a clenched fist into the air. Though the airport was in U.S. hands, Franks's security detail was not taking any chances. Apache attack helicopters prowled the skies as Franks made the ten-minute drive to Cobra Base, the new forward headquarters for McKiernan's land war command.

Cobra Base was situated at the Abu Ghraib North Palace, a massive white edifice set in the middle of an azure man-made lake. The war had robbed the palace of much of its splendor. Anticipating that the palace would be a target, the Iraqis had removed nearly all of its furnishings—paintings had even been taken from their frames—turning the once grand residence into a dusty hulk. One wing of the structure had been turned into a heap of rubble three weeks earlier thanks to a GBU-10 that Major Steven Ankerstar, the F-117 pilot, had dropped as "a show of force." When the palace was seized by Buff Blount's 3rd ID, its only residents were a small group of Syrian jihadists, one of whom was found hiding in a refrigerator, and some stray goats. The palace did not have electricity or even working plumbing. The U.S. soldiers who now occupied it had transformed its cavernous chambers and grand balconies into crowded dormitories and had taken to washing their clothes in the increasingly foul moat.

Franks took a quick tour of the grounds and then gathered his commanders in an enormous drawing room. Buzz Moseley had flown up from his command post in Saudi Arabia. Vice

Admiral Tim Keating, who oversaw the naval campaign from his headquarters in Bahrain, made the trip. So did Major General Dell Dailey, who commanded the most secret Special Operations Forces. McKiernan was the host. It was the first time the commanders had gathered in person since before the war. After embracing the officers, Franks issued his classified set of instructions.

The combat forces that had battled their way to Baghdad, Tikrit, Karbala, and Najaf should prepare to pull out within sixty days. New units would arrive to help stabilize the country but most would stay no longer than 120 days. Cutting back so quickly would leave much of Iraq uncovered, but Franks laid down the rule that was to guide the next phase of the operation: the generals should be prepared to take as much risk departing as they had in their push to Baghdad. The U.S. forces in Iraq should expect some form of functioning Iraqi government in thirty to sixty days.[3]

After their discussion Franks and the commanders sat down in front of a screen for a satellite video conference with President Bush. Turning his attention to Franks, the president asked about the effort to recruit a multinational force. Franks said he would give it a 6 on a scale of 1 to 10, noting that Colin Powell and Don Rumsfeld would be approaching allied nations while Franks himself would be lobbying the United Arab Emirates, which had expressed interest in sending a force of Arab peacekeeping soldiers to Iraq. As the Baghdad meeting drew to a close, the president congratulated the commanders. Afterward, Franks and his team posed for photos and puffed on victory cigars.

Rusty Blackman, the two-star Marine general who served as McKiernan's chief of staff, was dumbfounded by Franks's emphasis on a speedy U.S. troop withdrawal. The Army and Marines had taken the Iraqi capital just a week earlier. The U.S. had yet to send troops to cities like Fallujah and there were regions of the country—and even neighborhoods in Baghdad—that were still not secure. McKiernan had planned to oversee forces in Iraq for as long as six months before transitioning to a new command and nothing he or his staff had seen so far had suggested that it was time to think about leaving. If Franks's guidance was carried out, the more than 140,000 troops in Iraq could be down to little more than a "division-plus," about 30,000 troops, by September.

After the session, Blackman told Terry Moran about Franks's surprising guidance. Moran, in turn, called Mike Fitzgerald, the chief CENTCOM planner. "What the hell is going on?" asked Moran. McKiernan had just been told that U.S. forces would soon begin to leave Iraq. "Who said that?" Fitzgerald asked. "CENTCOM said that," Moran replied.[4]

After he retired, Franks explained that the guidance was part of the broader Bush administration effort to convince allied countries that Iraq was stable and encourage them in thinking that it was safe to send troops. "I wanted our troopers to work up their transportation plans, work up a process whereby they could begin redeployment in as little as sixty days," Franks said. To reinforce the point, Franks recommended that the White House proclaim that the major hostilities had come to an end. The idea, Franks said, was "to have the old man declare the end of major combat operations on the first of May because it opened the bank, so to speak, for us to go after additional international forces."[5]

Though Franks did not mention it, the CENTCOM commander had outlined his strategy in a private e-mail to Rumsfeld on the day of his Baghdad visit. Franks recommended that the United States declare a military victory in Iraq and announce that it was transitioning to postwar operations. To drive the point home, Franks's e-mail further recommended that Jay Garner move his team to Baghdad and that McKiernan be designated as the head of CJTF-Iraq—or Combined Joint Task Force Iraq.[6]

Several days later, McKiernan received another surprise. When McKiernan pitched Cobra II in December 2002 he had insisted that the initial invasion force be followed by the 1st Armored Division and the 1st Cavalry. Iraq was a big country with long, unsecured borders. The Fedayeen attacks in the south had only reinforced his assessment that the occupation could be more challenging than anticipated and that the follow-up troops were needed. Even with the reinforcements, McKiernan would have only half the 380,000 troops that Zinni had once determined would be necessary to secure the entire country. McKiernan hoped to strengthen his hold with the help of reconstituted Iraqi troops and foreign forces, but they were not available yet. For the foreseeable future, the only significant forces he had to control the country would be the Americans and British. Even if allied forces were to be drawn down soon, McKiernan still wanted all of the forces that were earmarked for the Cobra II plan.

Rumsfeld, however, had made it equally clear that he might off-ramp some Army units if Saddam's forces were quickly defeated. From the time he was briefed on Zinni's 1003 plan, Rumsfeld saw force requirements more in terms of what was needed to win the war than to secure the peace. Even before the war began Rumsfeld had discussed the possibility of off-ramping units if they were not needed to defeat Saddam. On February 20, the Joint Staff had developed a list of units whose deployment could be canceled or reversed: the 173rd Airborne, the 3rd Armored Cavalry Regiment, the 101st Airborne, the 1st Armored Division, and the 1st Cavalry Division. On March 8, Rumsfeld sent a note to Myers expressing his view that the flow of forces should be carefully metered so that an excessive number were not deployed. "I think I need a good deal more understanding of the units we may decide not to send over," Rumsfeld wrote, "so we make intelligent decisions and don't get stampeded into just sending them over." In response, the Joint Staff prepared weekly briefings on the subject. With victory seemingly at hand and the Republican Guard vanquished, the defense secretary had begun to press the issue again in video conferences with Franks, asking why the Pentagon needed to send both the 1st Armored and 1st Cavalry divisions. Rumsfeld had never accepted Shinseki's suggestion that more troops might be needed to stabilize postwar Iraq than to prosecute the war, and he was no more convinced now.[7]

Initially, Franks took the position that he needed both divisions: they would extend the military's reach into northern and western Iraq and enable CENTCOM to devote more resources to retraining the Iraqi army. But after discussing the matter for several days with Rumsfeld, Franks relented. The 1st Armored Division was sent, but the deployment of the sixteen-thousand-strong 1st Cavalry Division was officially canceled on April 21. Franks justified his change of heart on the grounds that allied forces would soon be on the way and that McKiernan and other commanders could manage with the divisions they had. While Franks insisted that he had not been browbeaten into going along, he acknowledged that Rumsfeld was the impetus behind the decision. "We had First Armored and First Cav in the flow," Franks said. "Don Rumsfeld did in fact make the decision to off-ramp the First Cavalry Division."[8]

Tom White, the civilian Army secretary, had a less charitable view. "Rumsfeld just ground Franks down," White said. "If you grind away at the military guys long enough, they will finally say, 'Screw it, I'll do the best I can with what I have.' The nature of Rumsfeld is that you just get tired of arguing with him." Since Rumsfeld and his aides were determined to keep the American troop presence in Iraq to a minimum, the decision was all but preordained. White explained, "Our working budgetary assumption was that ninety days after completion of the operation, we would withdraw the first fifty thousand and then every thirty days we'd take out another fifty thousand until everybody was back. The view was that whatever was left in Iraq would be de minimis."[9]

For his part, McKiernan was unhappy with the decision, which was made without his consultation, but he did not fight it. Making the best of the forces he had on hand, he decided how to distribute his troops. McKiernan told his Army and Marine commanders that the troops' main focus would be on keeping order in Iraq's cities. The rest of the country would be "economy of force" and there would be no more than an armored cavalry squadron in western Iraq. While military commanders would be making preparations to leave the country, McKiernan cautioned that the redeployment could be delayed or even halted if security in Iraq deteriorated or if the Bush administration failed to recruit the allied forces. The success of Jay Garner's postwar team, McKiernan noted, would facilitate the redeployment.[10]

One region with the smallest U.S. troop presence was the Anbar Province, which included Fallujah and Ramadi, where unbeknownst to the Americans Saddam and his sons had initially taken refuge. In mid-April, the United States had gotten by with a modicum of troops when an Iraqi general in the west indicated he was prepared to formally surrender his division. Colonel Curtis Potts, the commander of the 3rd Infantry Division's Aviation Brigade, flew on April 15 to an outpost in the Anbar region where he was joined by some of Terry Ferrell's troops. General Mohammed Jarawi officially submitted his surrender over a small folding table. The Iraqi troops in the division had already gone AWOL, but U.S. forces drove around the region afterward and destroyed the seventy-odd armored vehicles that were officially under Jarawi's command before dropping off the general at his home in Ramadi. It was the only time that an Iraqi unit had formally surrendered during the war. Though hailed as a confirmation of the U.S. victory, the Iraqi troops in the unit had blended into the population, and the U.S. did not have nearly enough troops to establish a presence in the province, let alone impose order. It was a grand photo op, but not much of a bellwether of what was to come.[11]

On April 24, troops from the 82nd Airborne took up positions in a schoolhouse in Fallujah, the first time that U.S. forces had installed themselves in the Sunni city. During an angry demonstration against the U.S. troops six days later, shots rang out. The 82nd fired back, killing seventeen Iraqis and wounding more than sixty. The 82nd insisted it had been fired at. The Iraqis claimed that the soldiers had overreacted. The next day, as angry protests continued in the city, seven soldiers from the 3rd Armored Cavalry Regiment were wounded by a grenade attack. "It's just a reaction to the shootings," said Emad Hassan, a well-dressed civil engineer. "If you kill my brother, then I will kill yours." On a wall outside the mayor's building next to the Army's makeshift compound protesters hung a sign in English that proclaimed, "U.S. killers, we'll kick you out." The region that the United States had hoped to control with just a smattering of forces was soon a tense battleground.[12]

On May 1, Bush flew to the deck of the *Abraham Lincoln* aircraft carrier. Standing before a banner announcing "Mission Accomplished," the president said that the major combat phase of the war had been completed and noted that U.S. forces were bringing order to the country and pursuing Saddam's henchmen. The White House was making an effort to suggest that Iraq was stable enough for allied nations to volunteer troops, but events on the ground were sending the opposite message.

At his hotel headquarters in Kuwait, Jay Garner was anxious to get to Baghdad. The day after Franks returned from the meeting with his commanders, Garner had contacted Franks and urged him to fly the postwar team to the fallen capital. Under CENTCOM's original plan, Garner and his team of postwar advisers and administrators were not to arrive until sixty days after the war. Franks and his staff figured that military civil affairs teams and combat engineers would do the heavy lifting in the early days. Garner and his civilian aides would come later.

With the rapid demise of Saddam's regime, however, Garner lobbied to get his Office for Reconstruction and Humanitarian Assistance to Iraq sooner rather than later, and Franks agreed. Garner's plan was to attach advisers to the Iraqi ministries and manage the country until an Iraqi government was put in place, a government that would be expected to include Ahmed Chalabi, Iyad Alawi, and the other exiles who had been meeting with Bush administration officials in Washington, London, Kurdistan, and Tallil.[13]

It was assumed that the dramatic ouster of Saddam would create a "*Wizard of Oz* moment" in Iraq, recalled Carl Strock, the two-star general from the Army Corps of Engineers and a Garner deputy. After the wicked dictator was deposed, throngs of cheering Iraqis would hail their liberators and go back to work under the tutelage of Garner's postwar organization and its teams of advisers attached to the Iraqi ministries—in some cases, no more than a single individual. It was, Strock acknowledged, a "simplistic approach." But simplistic or not, the strategy had been embraced by the White House. "The concept was that we would defeat the army, but the institutions would hold, everything from ministries to police forces," Condoleezza Rice had noted. "You would be able to bring new leadership but we were going to keep the body in place." Garner, for his part, was not anticipating that he would be taking on the political and physical reconstruction of Iraq, and he was hoping to find a partner among the Iraqis.[14]

Still, Garner thought Franks's admonition about risk-taking on the way out was plain crazy. Garner did not relish the prospect of watching U.S. forces leave just as he was setting up shop. Franks's embrace of audacity was fine for the invasion, since a U.S. victory had been all but preordained, but Garner thought it was reckless to take risks in postwar Iraq. Holding the country together and installing a democratic government in the heart of the Arab world would be hard enough without removing forces from the field. "There was no doubt we would win the war," Garner recalled telling McKiernan, "but there can be doubt we will win the peace."[15]

As unsettling as Franks's comments were, it was not the first time that Garner's team had heard that the U.S. might diminish the number of its troops in Iraq. In mid-April, Lawrence Di Rita, one of Rumsfeld's closest aides, had arrived in Kuwait to join Garner's team. Speaking to a group of Garner's aides, Di Rita had outlined Rumsfeld's vision. The Pentagon was determined to avoid open-ended military commitments like those in Bosnia and Kosovo, and to withdraw the vast majority of the American forces in three to four months. The State Department had mismanaged the postwar efforts in the Balkans, and Afghanistan was headed the same way. With the Defense Department now in charge of Iraq after the fall of Saddam things would run more smoothly. "The main theme was that DOD would be in charge, and this would be totally different than in the past," said Tom Gross, who was also at the session. "We would be out very quickly. We were very confused. We did not see it as a short-term process." In another meeting with Garner's team, Di Rita had also rejected the notion that the United States would supervise a lengthy and costly reconstruction of the country. Paul Wolfowitz had initially suggested that much of the long-neglected repair and upgrading of Iraq's infrastructure would be paid for by its oil proceeds; Di Rita stressed this with more passion. Garner's team had projected no more than $3 billion in reconstruction costs over three years at the February Rock Drill, but as the reconstruction plan was being laid out Di Rita slammed his hand on the table and erupted: "We don't owe these people a thing. We gave them their freedom." Rumsfeld's loyal lieutenant was passionately championing his boss's "Beyond Nation-Building" doctrine. Di Rita's views were much remarked on by Garner's aides, though he later insisted he had not made the statement, or he had been misinterpreted.[16]

There was a vicious circularity to the military and civilian planning. CENTCOM was hoping that the success of Garner's team would speed the withdrawal of U.S. troops; Garner was hoping that CENTCOM would provide the security he needed to begin to fashion a new Iraqi government, deliver humanitarian aid, and begin to rebuild the country.

When Garner's team flew to Baghdad on April 18, they stayed at the Abu Ghraib North Palace before moving into the Republican Palace, which Flip DeCamp's battalion had seized on the April 7 Thunder Run. Garner immediately took off on a nationwide tour, heading to Kurdistan, where he was greeted as a hero by throngs of pro-American Kurds who had been living in a virtual American protectorate for more than a decade and were grateful for Garner's role in managing the relief program after the Persian Gulf War. It was a veritable *Wizard of Oz* moment.

Baghdad, however, was nothing like Kurdistan. The Iraqi ministries Garner had hoped to use to run the country had been ransacked and looted. Communication systems were in shambles. When the Iraqi resistance had stiffened and Saddam had taken to the airwaves, Moseley had stepped up his efforts to cut Saddam off from his troops. The twelve telephone switching centers in Baghdad were hit hard and disabled. In its zeal to knock Saddam and his propaganda broadcasts off the air—and to sunder the regime's ability to command its forces—the U.S. had in effect disabled what Garner now needed. Moreover, the Iraqi electrical grid had become unstable, and the Iraqis had shut it down only to discover it could not be switched back on. It was all but impossible for Garner to communicate with officials across town, let alone get his message to the capital's residents. Two of the three sewage treatment plants in Baghdad had to be extensively rebuilt as a result of the looting. Security was tenuous.

Robert Gifford had been one of the first members of Garner's team to arrive in Baghdad. He was a longtime deputy in the State Department's Bureau for International Narcotics and Law Enforcement Affairs, and his job was to advise Iraq's Interior Ministry and get its police force up and running. Garner had given Gifford explicit instructions to arrange a "police event" as soon as he got to Baghdad: a public demonstration that the police were returning to work, a potential photo op for Garner shown meeting with Iraqi cops in charge of keeping the peace.

It did not take long for Gifford to discover that the Iraqi police force had abandoned their posts and that their police stations had been picked clean by looters—electrical wires, phones, light fixtures, even some of the door jambs had been stolen. If the police were not able to protect their own stations it did not look like they would be helping the Americans keep order in Iraq anytime soon. Without reliable information on Iraqi personnel, Gifford was also worried that Iraqi law enforcement officials might rustle up tainted loyalists of the old order for the new police force—hardly the kind of people Garner should publicly embrace.[17]

The dearth of qualified Iraqi police in the opening weeks and months of the occupation was precisely the kind of problem that Dick Mayer, the Justice Department expert, had anticipated in February when he pushed at the Rock Drill for a 5,000-person international civilian police force. Bob Perito had warned of it as well in his presentation at the Pentagon. The reluctance of the White House to plan for this scenario, in fact, had led David Kay to resign his position on Garner's team months before. Mayer's recommendation to deploy an international constabulary had been rebuffed by the White House, which was determined to rely on the Iraqis to get the job done and which took comfort from a CIA assessment that Iraq's police were true professionals.

Soon officers from U.S. military units across the country were trekking to Gifford's office asking him for help in organizing the

Iraqi police in their areas, but he had nothing to offer. Gifford was still operating with a mere $25 milion in seed money. Only the thirty-four-member assessment team that was to address Iraq's law enforcement needs and 150 private contractors still on standby in the United States had been authorized and funded.

When the assessment team showed up in May, Gifford immediately sent many of them into the field to try to encourage returning police station commanders, establish traffic control, help police leadership, and start training at the police academy. Appealing for more resources, Gifford and other experts prepared an internal report painting a bleak picture of the Iraqi police. The Iraqi police, the assessors noted, were corrupt, unprofessional, and untrustworthy. In fact, they were little more than traffic cops, were despised by the population, and were without any investigative competence. Molding them into a modern police force would be difficult work. The assessment recommended that 6,663 police advisers be sent. In effect, the report was making recommendations that had been rejected months before.[18]

Critics have complained that the Bush administration did not have a plan for postwar Iraq. But insofar as rebuilding the Iraqi police was concerned, the White House had not neglected the issue. It had considered and rejected the proposal by midlevel Justice and State Department officials for five thousand U.S. law enforcement personnel. It chose instead to rely on Iraqi forces, whatever gendarmes could be solicited from foreign countries, and several hundred U.S. contractors who would be sent only if the need arose. Looking back on the summer of 2003, Perito said, the Bush administration "did not have a training mission set to go." "Instead, they decided to do an assessment, offer recommendations, have them adopted, and then go for the money," he said. "What that does, it loses you the first six months of the operation. The doctrine on peace operations is that the initial month or so is critical."[19]

When Major General Carl Strock first joined Garner's team, he had been given an intelligence briefing on Iraq's electrical grid, but the intelligence focused on potential war damage to the system, not on the dilapidation of the power plants and generators—comprising a hodgepodge of parts from Europe and Asia—that had suffered as a result of more than a decade of economic sanctions and inadequate investment.

The infrastructure was not only antiquated but had collapsed. U.S. troops approaching Baghdad might have thought that Saddam had blacked out the city, but in fact the Iraqi shutdown of the electrical grid had been purely technical. The U.S. policy had been not to target Iraq's power plants or electrical system. But U.S. air strikes had undermined the system in two ways: fuel lines to power plants, as well as electrical transmission lines, had inadvertently been damaged in bombing raids. Under the strain, the already fragile system had begun to experience power surges. When the chief engineer of the south Baghdad plant shut it down as a precaution, the entire grid had collapsed. Adding to the difficulties, much of the system had been undergoing its annual spring maintenance when the war approached. Some of its machinery had been disassembled and was undergoing repair when the foreign contractors who were hired for the job evacuated the country. Compounding the problem, the main expertise of the Army Corps of Engineers in charge of rectifying matters was in hydropower.

The looting in Baghdad made the task of restarting the system all the more difficult. The computerized control center in the capital was stripped bare. "You have to have some kind of control to stop generators or raise it or throw a switch—it was gone," recalled Thomas Wheelock, a senior official with the U.S. Agency for International Development. Even the transmission lines, which contained copper and aluminum, were stolen. "They just started at one end of the transmission line and worked their way up, taking down the towers, taking away the valuable metals, smelting it down, selling it into Iran and Kuwait," Wheelock added. "The price of metal in the Middle East dropped dramatically during this period of time."[20]

In January 2003, the National Intelligence Council, a CIA-led panel of intelligence specialists, had cautioned that building democracy in Iraq would be difficult because of its authoritarian history and warned of the risk that the American forces would be seen as occupiers. "Attitudes toward a foreign military force would depend largely on the progress made in transferring power, as well as on the degree to which that force were perceived as providing necessary security and fostering reconstruction and a return to prosperity," it said. The report also noted that quick restoration of services would be important to maintain the support of the Iraqi public. It was a useful point, but had not spurred any extraordinary efforts on the part of the Pentagon and other agencies. Strock and his engineers had been prepared for a patch job, not an overhaul.[21]

The absence of electricity further undermined an already burgeoning security problem, encouraged crime, made it hard for Garner and McKiernan to communicate with the Iraqi public over television and radio, and rendered the oppressive summer heat more trying for the Iraqi citizenry. Saddam had been brutal, but at least he had kept the capital supplied with electricity, even if it meant diverting power from the Shiite-dominated south. Now the capital's residents were mystified that a nation that had sent a man to the moon could not supply electricity. Sensing the urgency of the situation, McKiernan ordered Steven Hawkins, the brigadier general who was picked by Casey to head JTF-4, to form a task force and get Iraq's electrical system working again. Hawkins plunged into the job, beginning with no funds or even radios for his team. Working with Iraqi engineers to the point of exhaustion, Hawkins gradually restored electricity on a part-time basis, but the system remained vulnerable to sabotage and blackouts.[22]

In allocating his forces, McKiernan continued to view Baghdad as the political center, symbolically and in practical terms. Even so, the U.S. military was hard put to keep order in the capital. Buff Blount's 3rd Infantry Division had plenty of tanks and Bradleys but relatively few infantry. While the division had about 18,000 troops, only 10,000 or so were in a position to patrol Baghdad after the collapse of the regime. Of these, just 1,200 would be dismounted infantry. With little guidance, the division took on the mission of guarding several hundred critical sites in the city, including hospitals, clinics, banks, government offices, palaces, refineries, shopping centers, and museums. There were also other sites that needed to be secured until the WMD investigation teams cleared them. Using tank crews to add to the foot patrols was easier said than done. There were only several hundred sets of body armor for the entire division. The Marines had lots of infantry, but they were needed to secure the Shiite-dominated area and moved south. The dearth of troops on the ground was only partially remedied by the arrival of the 2nd Armored Cavalry Regiment and other units in the capital.

The troops' considerable burden was aggravated by the need to protect Garner's teams. Each time one wanted to drive to an Iraqi ministry, two Humvees with soldiers had to be provided as escorts. "The moment I got there I put a demand on them for somewhere between fifty and sixty armed Humvees a day," Garner said. "That's a big demand. Plus, I put a demand on them for pretty much an infantry battalion to protect the palace that we had our people living in, had our office in. So there was instantly a huge security requirement."[23]

"We simply did not have enough forces for a city of six or seven million," Strock said. "The forces were stretched too thin and the troops on the ground often did not understand the significance of the stuff they were guarding." Wheelock noted that U.S. forces guarded the Oil Ministry and key power plants. "For the power lines we did not have enough assets," he said. "We didn't have enough troops in the country to provide security. They could not protect the power lines and they were not about to devote resources to them."[24]

As U.S. forces gradually extended their presence throughout Baghdad, the extent of weapons and munitions caches they discovered was enormous, and well beyond the intelligence estimates. Truckload after truckload of munitions were moved out of the city just to get them away from heavily populated areas. There was no way coalition forces could secure all the weapons and munitions storage sites across Iraq, a problem that grew over time. One of McKiernan's first major challenges was how to get weapons off the streets in a society where everyone seemingly had access to guns, there were barely contained ethnic tensions, and looting was still prevalent. He tried proclamations and meetings with political leaders, who were more concerned about arming their personal security teams than disarming the society. It was a seemingly impossible task.

While the Americans struggled with Iraq's infrastructure, their efforts to organize an interim government faltered. When U.S. forces had encountered the Fedayeen, Franks and Abizaid had implored Khalilzad to organize a series of meetings among the Kurds and exiles, and sessions were conducted at Tallil and later in Baghdad. The appeal to the resistance leaders was also a linchpin of the Pentagon's strategy for a quick turnover of the country to the Iraqis and for the rapid exit of most U.S. forces from Iraq. During his swing through Kurdistan, Garner had also urged Talabani and Barzani to come to Baghdad and work with members of the Iraqi resistance like Ahmed Chalabi and Iyad Alawi. Given their long-awaited opportunity to run the country, however, the eclectic collection of Iraqi leaders and opposition figures was hobbled by rivalries and ethnic politics. The hope to rapidly put an Iraqi face on the occupation was hampered by the Iraqi exile leaders themselves.

Qubad Talabani, the son of the Kurdish leader and a Kurdish representative to Washington, said that the American shortfalls were magnified by the failure of the Iraqi resistance to work together. "The first failure was an Iraqi failure," he said. "We were collectively unable to form this government because of what has plagued Iraq since then, quotas and who gets what share and what responsibility. This sent a message to Washington that the Iraqis were unable to administer themselves."[25]

While Garner and his team officially expressed confidence despite the challenges they faced, some began to fear that their reconstruction and political mission verged on the impossible. "It was supposed to be a Chalabi-centered effort with the five other parties," recalled Robin Raphel, a former U.S. ambassador to Tunisia and a senior member of Garner's team. "It was very obvious to me that we could not run a country we did not understand. We were not prepared. We went too soon. We should have waited until we built an international coalition." The White House had spurned the United Nations, but Raphel jested darkly to her colleagues that the United States would be on its knees in a week begging for help from the world body.[26]

The Bush administration's doctrine of preemption held that while the United States might act unilaterally, the success of its military operation would attract allies to share the postwar burden. Wolfowitz had even speculated before the war that France might be among those willing to send forces to post-Saddam Iraq. In foreign capitals, word soon spread that the United States was fumbling in Iraq. The country was disorderly, the interim Iraqi government had not congealed, and the invasion did not have the United Nations's imprimatur. There did not, as yet, seem to be an organized insurgency, but the proclamation that major combat operations had ended seemed hollow.

Talk of a Muslim peacekeeping division soon faded. The Saudis imposed all sorts of conditions on their participation, including the requirement that they not be under U.S. command. Even the hospital the Saudis volunteered was a worry after Washington became concerned that Wahhabis, Muslim zealots, had infiltrated it. Quiet discussions to deploy troops from the United Arab Emirates to protect the southern Iraqi oilfields also came to naught.

E. J. Sinclair, a brigadier general with the 101st Airborne, was ordered to New Delhi to try to secure India's agreement to deploy an entire division in northern Iraq. Dressed in his desert camouflage, the general flew from Mosul to Kuwait on a C-12 plane only to struggle with Kuwaiti officials who were reluctant to allow him to board a commercial flight to India without a passport. The U.S. embassy had to intervene to get Sinclair on the flight. The absence of a U.N. endorsement for the invasion was a major political obstacle for the Indians and nothing came of the trip. Turkey later offered peacekeeping troops, but the Iraqis saw their offer as an attempt by Ankara to meddle in Iraqi affairs and would not accept them. The Poles agreed to lead a division, but it was of uneven quality. At Washington's insistence, a contingent of Spanish troops was put under Polish command but they were limited by restrictive rules of engagement. A Ukrainian brigade was stationed in Kut, but they were barely able to defend themselves and retreated during their first serious challenge. Only the British-led division, fortified by Italian and other troops, became a reality.[27]

In early May, Tony Blair's government made John Sawers, the British ambassador to Egypt, its point man in Iraq. Four days after arriving, Sawers sent a confidential cable to top officials at 10 Downing Street, the British Foreign Office, the British Ministry of Defence, and the British International Aid Agency. His message was entitled "Iraq: What's Going Wrong?" It painted a bleak picture and noted that the U.S.-led coalition was gradually losing public support.

"A Baghdad First strategy is needed," Sawers wrote. "The problems are worst in the capital, and it is the one place we can't afford to get it wrong. But the troops here are tired, and are not providing the security framework needed. We need a clear policy on which Baathists can return, a more concerted effort on reconstruction, and an imaginative approach on the media. For all this, money needs to be released by Washington. The clock is ticking."

Sawers contended that Garner's team was ill-suited for the challenge ahead. "Garner's outfit, ORHA, is an unbelievable mess," he wrote. "No leadership, no strategy, no coordination, no structure, and inaccessible to ordinary Iraqis. . . . Garner and his team of 60-year-old retired generals are well-meaning, but out of their depth."

The effort to reconstruct the country needed to be stepped up to gain public support. Forty percent of Baghdad's sewage was pouring into the Tigris untreated. Garbage was piling up in the streets. A mobile phone system was desperately needed. Bechtel, the contractor the United States had turned to for its major reconstruction projects, was moving far too slowly. Water was running but not potable. Electrical power was intermittent. "We need visibly successful projects, however small: schools and hospitals reopening, new bakeries, food distribution points."

There was no television in the capital and no way for the coalition to get its message to the Iraqis. "Baghdad has no TV, and no newspapers apart from party political rags. I was given two fliers yesterday by an Iraqi, one calling for the assassination of all Baathists, the other for the killing of all U.S. forces. That, and rumour, are the only information flowing. An ORHA TV project is due to get going next week, but its content will be tightly controlled by ORHA, and it risks not being credible. I have pressed them, as a start, to broadcast a Premier League [British soccer] game each day, but the Americans don't yet get it."

Funding was scant. Unlike the British in Basra, the Bush administration was reluctant to use confiscated Iraqi funds to pay police and government workers. Security in the capital was a huge worry, as it did not seem that the United States had control of the city. The 3rd ID was exhausted by the fight to Baghdad and tied to their armored vehicles. "No progress is possible until security improves," Sawers warned. "Crime is widespread (not surprising as Saddam released all the criminals last autumn). Carjackings are endemic, with the cars driven to Iran for sale. Last week, the Ministry of Planning was re-kitted out ready to resume work; that night it was looted again. The evening air is full of gunfire. There is still a climate of fear on the streets, because of the level of crime, and that is casting a shadow over all else.

"Frankly, the 3rd Inf Div need to go home now, and be garlanded as victors," Sawers wrote, adding that the British should consider sending some troops of its own to Baghdad. "We, the Brits, do not have all the answers, but an operational UK presence in Baghdad is worth considering, despite the obvious political problem. Transferring one of our two brigades is presumably out of the question, but one battalion with a mandate to deploy into the streets could still make an impact."[28]

It was an uncharitable view of the army division that had been the first to get to Baghdad and which had struggled to keep order without sufficient assets and no guidance from on high.

There were also limits to how much the British government would help. That month Albert Whitley and a visiting British general advocated extending the tour of duty of the 16 British Air Assault Brigade and moving it to Baghdad so it could assist in training the Iraqi police and help the Americans safeguard the capital. The request was enthusiastically supported by McKiernan. But the war in Iraq was controversial in the United Kingdom and Baghdad was dicier than Basra. British officials in London overruled their British commanders in Iraq and decided against extending the brigade's tour of duty. For all of Sawers's warnings, the United States would continue to shoulder the burden in the Iraqi capital.

Four days after Sawers sent his cable, Franks met at his Tampa headquarters with Edmund Giambastiani, the head of the Joint Forces Command. Days before, Franks had briefed the Joint Chiefs. Relations between Franks and the JCS had been strained throughout the planning and execution of the military plan, and Jim Jones, the NATO commander, had sought to lighten the mood by buying purple T-shirts with "TTMF" emblazoned on the front and arranging for the chiefs to wear them when Franks arrived. "TTMF" alluded to Franks's denunciation of the chiefs as "Title Ten Motherfuckers." Franks recounted the episode to Giambastiani as the generals discussed lessons learned in the Iraq War. The private meeting also included Gene Renuart and Gary Luck, Franks's mentor, and an aide took notes.

Franks touted the virtues of joint military operations among the Army, Navy, Air Force, and Marines and dismissed his critics as behind the times. "The SECDEF has made his mark on the future, more joint, not less joint," Franks said, referring to Rumsfeld. "Where is the center of gravity of the U.S. military? It is jointness."

As the meeting proceeded, Franks discussed how operations in Afghanistan had influenced his strategy in Iraq. Afghanistan had taught him that relatively small groups of forces, coupled with precision weapons, could be effective against the enemy.

In the middle of the discussion, Franks was interrupted by a phone call. Franks's guidance to prepare for rapid deployment and his fascination with small formations—views supported at the highest levels of the Bush administration—no longer seemed so prescient. "That was the SECDEF," Franks confided to the group. "He said he's getting the hell beat out of him about the Baghdad security situation. He wanted to know if we needed more divisions in country. Tell John Abizaid to pick a brigade-size unit and get it to Baghdad now. I am not gratified by enough forces on the ground. Lawlessness is a problem and we need more people to accomplish the task."[29]

CHAPTER 24

Starting from Scratch

With Baghdad in disarray, the White House opted for a major course correction: Jerry Bremer would be brought in to oversee Iraq. L. Paul Bremer had worked as Henry Kissinger's chief of staff, served as ambassador to the Netherlands, and headed the State Department's office on counterterrorism. In Bremer, the administration saw a hands-on and assertive administrator: a veritable proconsul who would grab hold of the turmoil that was Iraq and get the Bush administration's program there back on track.

Bremer auditioned for the job by meeting with Rumsfeld, whom he knew from the Ford administration three decades earlier. Bremer was not an expert on the Middle East and in his years as a diplomat had never been posted in the region, but in Rumsfeld's Pentagon that was considered a plus. Rumsfeld had sought to block some of Jay Garner's picks because they were State Department Arabists who might be less than ardent supporters of Bush's bold plan to remake Iraq. With Bremer, he would not have that problem.

The day after Bremer's meeting with Rumsfeld, Bush offered him the post, stressing that it was important to take the time to build a broad-based government. Bremer fully intended to assert his authority. The initial version of the administration's plan called for Bremer to share responsibilities with Zalmay Khalilzad, who had been meeting with Iraqi leaders on the political arrangements for a new government. Bremer vetoed the collaboration. There would be a single chief in Iraq and he would be it. Khalilzad learned he had been excluded just minutes before Bremer's appointment was announced on May 6. At the State Department, Colin Powell was stunned by the decision to remove Khalilzad from the administration's team in Iraq. The matter had never been discussed in interagency meetings. Powell called Rice and asked for an explanation. Khalilzad, Powell said, was the only guy who knew the Iraqi players well and who was regarded by them as a trusted representative of the White House. Rice replied that she had nothing to do with the move. Here was yet another example of how the national security apparatus was sidestepped.[1]

Before he headed to Iraq, Bremer consulted with Rumsfeld's aides about the next moves in Iraq. Doug Feith's policy shop had been drafting an order that would bar senior Baathists from power. The concept of de-Baathification was not a new one and had in fact been approved by Bush when he was briefed on it in March. It had been understood all along that Saddam's power structure had to be eliminated. But how deeply did the U.S. need to dig? There was a balance between purging the old order and depriving the new Iraqis of the human capital they needed to run the country.[2]

Saddam's opponents themselves had been divided on the question. At the December meeting of the Iraqi opposition that Khalilzad had convened, Iyad Alawi had pushed for limited de-Baathification and an appeal for Iraqis affiliated with the old order to switch sides. There was a measure of self-interest in Alawi's position. Alawi had contacts among the Baathists and the Iraqi military and had calculated that they could be part of his power base. Ahmed Chalabi, for his part, had pushed for a strong de-Baathification policy and for disbanding the Iraqi military, figuring this would not only remove the vestiges of Saddam's regime but also undermine his rival. In London, Khalilzad had been more influenced by Alawi's position than Chalabi's.

During his first weeks in Iraq, Jay Garner had taken a pragmatic approach toward de-Baathification. Seeking to work through the ministries, Garner had planned to lop off the top organizational layer or two but keep most officials in place. Evicting the Baath Party loyalists would be more a matter of compiling a blacklist than a full-fledged purge. But Khalilzad and Garner were now out. Bremer was in. Not only was Bremer entirely comfortable with a strict de-Baathification policy but he wanted to be the one to issue the edict. As Bremer put it in a memo to his Pentagon colleagues, he wanted to ensure that "my arrival in Iraq be marked by clear, public and decisive steps to reassure Iraqis that we are determined to eradicate Saddamism." Bremer was not anticipating any *Wizard of Oz* moments. The edict on de-Baathification would be a way for Bremer to demonstrate his authority and take control. If Saddam's supporters thought they could take advantage of the confusion in Iraq to claw their way back to power, Bremer would demonstrate that the Baathists were through, once and for all.[3]

There was one important decision that gave Bremer pause: the number of U.S. military forces in Iraq. Bremer was friendly with James Dobbins, who had served as the Bush administration's special envoy for Afghanistan and had also done stints as a State Department troubleshooter for Kosovo, Bosnia, Somalia, and Haiti. Dobbins declined Bremer's invitation to join him in Baghdad as a senior deputy, but he provided Bremer with a forthcoming study he had overseen for the RAND Corporation on nation-building exercises from World War II through Afghanistan. Nation-building was an area Bremer had not been involved in during his earlier career as a diplomat.

The message of the RAND study was that large peacekeeping forces were better than smaller ones. Not only did small forces encourage adversaries to think they could challenge the peacekeepers but they also led the occupation force to rely more on firepower to make up for their limited numbers. That raised the risk of civilian casualties and increased disaffection among the population. "The highest levels of casualties have occurred in the operations with the lowest level of U.S. troops, suggesting an inverse ratio between force levels and the level of risk," the RAND study noted.

Beyond that, Dobbins thought the Bush administration was neglecting the lessons of the Balkans at its peril. Rumsfeld had portrayed the Balkans in his February speech "Beyond Nation-Building" as a textbook example of postwar policies gone wrong. But Dobbins thought there was much to learn from the NATO operations there. Like the former Yugoslavia, Iraq was a multiethnic state that had been held together by a dictator. Like Bosnia and Kosovo, it had a Muslim population. Unlike postwar Germany, which some in the Bush administration cited as an important historical baseline, Iraq did not have an ethnically homogeneous population or a First World economy. Nor had it been totally devastated by war. To safeguard the peace in the Balkans, NATO had deployed about twenty peacekeepers for every thousand civilians. In Iraq this rule of thumb would have yielded a peacekeeping force of more than 450,000, about three times the force commanded by McKiernan. The numbers were similar to those in the study that had been prepared in February for Rice and Hadley by the young Marine major on the NSC staff.

In its argumentation and analysis, the RAND study ran directly counter to the Bush administration's policy for securing postwar Iraq. If the study had been applied, Rumsfeld would not have off-ramped the 1st Cavalry Division but would have sent even more forces. Bremer sent an executive summary of the RAND study to Rumsfeld, but never received a response. When Bremer arrived in Baghdad on May 12 and was driven to his headquarters at the Republican Palace, he was struck by the paucity of U.S. forces in the streets: soldiers seemed glued to their tanks and were not patrolling. To Bremer, the situation appeared to confirm the cautionary lessons of the RAND report.

The next day, Bremer convened his staff and signaled that it was time for a no-nonsense policy on crime and looting in the capital. In Haiti, as the RAND report noted, the Marines had fired on a group of Haitian soldiers who made threatening gestures five days into the occupation. Seven of the Haitians were killed and the episode sent a signal that the United States was not to be trifled with. Bremer thought it might be time to send a similar message in Iraq by shooting some of the looters. His closed-door comments were leaked almost immediately and made headlines: Bremer had promulgated a new policy under which

Iraqi looters were now to be shot. Bremer's position came as a surprise to Buff Blount, who soon made clear that his soldiers had no intention of using deadly force to stop stealing by the impoverished Iraqis his soldiers had liberated. The military's general policy was not to talk about its rules of engagement, but Blount did not want any of his soldiers to confuse Bremer's tough talk with their actual instructions. "Unless the soldier's life is threatened, we are not going out and shooting looters," Blount said. Mattis expressed similar sentiments. It was not an auspicious start to the Bush administration's corrective policy and served only to indicate dissonance between Bremer and the generals. As impressed as Bremer was with Dobbins's work, the episode suggested that Bremer had not examined the RAND report carefully enough. Using firepower to compensate for an inadequate number of troops was not the best way to win over an occupied population.[4]

Wearing his trademark Brooks Brothers suits and hiking boots, Bremer established a new organization: the Coalition Provisional Authority. Garner stayed on for a while to smooth the transition, but he had been surprised that his role as the civilian administrator in Iraq had ended so soon and was unhappy when Bremer began to turn many of his policies on their head. On May 15, Bremer nullified a commitment by Garner and Khalilzad to convene a meeting in Baghdad by the end of May to set up an interim Iraqi government, opting instead for a methodical step-by-step approach in which a constitution would first be drafted and, ultimately, elections held. The delay in transferring control to the Iraqis was a change but not a new option for the Bush team. Just eleven days into the war, Rumsfeld sent a classified paper to Cheney, Powell, and George Tenet, the CIA director, stating that it could also be risky to hand over power too quickly to the Iraqis. Washington needed to first assure itself that the new government would be friendly to the United States.[5]

The next day, Bremer issued Order No. 1: "De-Baathification of Iraqi Society," promulgating the policy drawn up by Feith's staff. As Bremer interpreted the order, the top four levels of the Baath Party were to be barred from government jobs. Garner was with the CIA station chief when the de-Baathification order was issued. Bremer, the station chief opined, had just disenfranchised more than 30,000 people.[6]

The change in approach was fundamental and much more than a matter of differing personalities and administrative styles. When the Bush administration became anxious about the staunch resistance it encountered from the Fedayeen during the early days of the war, it was eager to put an Iraqi face on the problem. The United States decided to convene a meeting of Iraqi resistance leaders at the Tallil air base and pushed for the early establishment of an Iraqi interim government. But when Baghdad was quickly captured and Iraqi opposition leaders began to bicker, the administration became more confident that it could and should shape events in Iraq. The United States tugged on the reins of power and put off the day when the Iraqis would be entrusted to run their own affairs. With Bremer's appointment, the pendulum had swung back toward Washington. Despite the disorder and confusion, the Bush administration was convinced that it could dictate the terms of the peace.

Nowhere was the policy difference starker than on the plans to rebuild the Iraqi army. CENTCOM had hoped that there would be wholesale capitulations of Iraqi units. The forces would serve as the building blocks of a new Iraqi military, which would supplement the U.S. troops and help them to secure Iraq. Even though there had only been one such instance of capitulation—in Anbar Province when an Iraqi general had formally surrendered without his troops to Colonel Potts—Abizaid, McKiernan, and Garner calculated that they would still be able to recall AWOL soldiers and begin to put the Iraqi military back together again. They had a powerful incentive to do so.

Abizaid and McKiernan were looking for troops, as well as a means of avoiding the taint of occupation. From the start, they had counted on Iraqi troops and allied units to supplement the overstretched American forces. The use of Iraqi troops was vital for security and an eventual exit strategy. On April 17, little more than a week after American troops first entered Baghdad, Abizaid told a satellite video conference that a three-division interim Iraqi military should be formed using units that had "self-demobilized" as well as members of opposition groups, who would be invited to appear at processing centers. Abizaid was under no illusion that the new military would instantly be transformed into a crack fighting force and the idea was to initially arrange for the Iraqi soldiers to undertake minor tasks like guarding government buildings and monitoring border crossing points. But he believed that Arab armies were not just military organizations—they provided jobs, helping to hold Arab societies together. His goal was to field three divisions in three months.

McKiernan had sought to recruit a new Iraqi general staff after his arrival in Baghdad. On May 9, he and a select few senior U.S. officers met at the Abu Ghraib palace with Faris Naima, a former Iraqi officer, in a meeting coordinated by the CIA. Naima had the professional bearing of a soldier and spoke fluent English. He had been the commander of al-Bakr Military College, a training ground for Iraq's top officers. Suspect politically, but a Sunni who was still valued by Saddam's government, he was appointed as the Iraqi ambassador to the Philippines and then Austria. Naima later told Americans that working for Saddam's Stalinesque regime was a nerve-racking ordeal. When he was invited to one of Saddam's palaces for a meeting he was never sure whether he was going to be promoted or bundled off for execution. When Qusay ordered him and his wife to return to Baghdad after their tour in Vienna, Naima decided it would be safer to break with the regime and stay abroad.

Wearing a frayed business suit at the meeting with the American generals, Naima pulled out a folded piece of paper from his jacket that outlined his plan for how to proceed. Because looting had broken out in Baghdad and crime was rampant, a show of power was needed. The most important thing was security. Naima urged the Americans to establish three Iraqi military divisions to be deployed in northern, central, and southern Iraq. An army company would be stationed in each major town to back up the police. Naima said there were plenty of potential military leaders who were not committed Baathists. The idea, he said, would be to start at the top, create a new Iraqi Ministry of

Defense, and then work down. All officers would be required to denounce the Baath Party.

When the Americans wondered where they would find the officers, Naima had an answer: "I can bring them to you." He also offered some political advice. The United States, he stressed, needed to pay the military, the police, and the bureaucrats. Iraq was a nation of civil servants, he said, and they needed their salaries to survive. Beyond that, the Americans should announce a departure plan so Iraqis did not view them as occupiers. McKiernan was impressed. It looked like he could work from the top down as well as from the bottom up to summon Iraqi soldiers to duty, screen them, and quickly install a new force.[7]

While McKiernan and the CIA were working on reviving the army, Jay Garner's team had been making a parallel effort. Garner still wanted to use the former Iraqi army as a source of labor. To that end, he had arranged for contractors to retrain the Iraqi troops. RONCO, a Washington consulting company, had developed a proposal to screen Iraqi soldiers so they could join a new fighting force or be retrained for other duties. The company drew up a detailed plan for three screening centers in northern, central, and southern Iraq. MPRI, a consulting company that was run by Carl Vuono, the former Army chief of staff, had been awarded an initial contract for $625,000 to help prepare Saddam's former troops for reconstruction duties. As a preliminary step, it had sent a nine-member team to Kuwait.

Soon after arriving in Baghdad, one of Garner's top planners, Colonel Paul Hughes, heard that some former Iraqi officers had approached U.S. troops in Baghdad to ask how they might receive their salaries. After securing approval from senior officers, Hughes met with the group at one of the Republican Guard's officers clubs. Calling themselves the Independent Military Gathering, the Iraqi officers indicated that they wanted to cooperate with the Americans. Though many wanted to work outside the military, they were willing to supply names of potential recruits, including lower-ranking noncommissioned officers. Anticipating that the Defense Ministry would be bombed, they had wisely removed the computers containing military personnel records. Eventually, they gave the Americans a list of some 50,000 to 70,000 names, including the military police. The United States may not have had a ready-made military force but it seemed to have some of the pieces—if, that is, it wanted to use them.[8]

As with Bremer's edict on de-Baathification, the groundwork for the Coalition Provisional Authority's position on building a new Iraqi military had been laid in Washington. Before leaving for Iraq, Bremer had consulted with Walter Slocombe, who had held Feith's defense policy position in the Clinton administration. Though a Democrat, Slocombe had supported the Bush administration's decision to attack Iraq and had maintained cordial relations with the Rumsfeld team. One day as he was coming out of the Pentagon gym, Slocombe had run into Steve Cambone, one of Rumsfeld's closest aides, who asked him if he would be willing to join Bremer's team. Within a few days, Feith invited Slocombe to come in and talk about the possibility of running Iraq's new Ministry of Defense. Before leaving for Iraq, Slocombe and Bremer discussed the idea of formally disestablishing the Iraqi army and starting from scratch. In a sense, the proposal was part of Bremer's crusade against "Saddamism." With one blow he would purge the Baathists from their government posts and eliminate Saddam's army. Keeping a Sunni-dominated military, Bremer and Slocombe reasoned, would outrage the Kurds. The Shiites would refuse to join, creating more of an ethnic imbalance. Moreover, by dismantling the army, the United States would be relieved of the obligation to pay AWOL Iraqi officers and soldiers. There would be provisions for making termination payments, but no arrangements would be made to pay salaries to those ushered out of the force. What was the point of paying an army that had fled its post and did not exist? they thought. Nor was there a system on hand to retain former troops for other jobs, an important omission in a nation with a soaring unemployment rate.[9]

Bremer and Slocombe's position completely reversed the plan that Feith himself had briefed to Bush in March. The president, in fact, had been told that it would be reckless to throw 300,000 Iraqi soldiers out of work amid the confusion of postwar Iraq and far preferable to screen the force to identify Saddam loyalists. Feith, however, became a supporter of the new tack. Now that the Iraqi army had gone AWOL, Feith figured that the advantages of trying to recall it were not worth the potential liabilities of recruiting a military that might include officers loyal to Saddam. The Pentagon's closest Iraqi ally, Chalabi, had been pushing for months to do away with the old Iraqi army, as had the Kurds.

Once Slocombe arrived in Iraq, McKiernan made an effort to win him over by inviting him to a session with Naima and other former Iraqi officers. Slocombe heard the officers out, thanked them for their time, and made it clear that he did not view them as the nucleus of a new Iraqi command. Using ranking Iraqi officers to rebuild the Iraqi military, Slocombe reassured, would simply produce another Sunni-dominated force.

Sticking to his position, Slocombe drafted an edict—Order No. 2, "The Dissolution of Entities"—formally abolishing the army, the Defense Ministry, and Iraq's intelligence agencies. There would be a new force—the New Iraqi Corps, which would be "professional, non-political, militarily effective and representative of all Iraqis." Slocombe sent the text of the order to the Defense Department, where it was scrutinized by Rumsfeld's staff. Bremer secured Rumsfeld's consent. Plans for the new corps that were to follow were discussed with the Pentagon, too.

On May 19, Rumsfeld himself sent a classified set of planning instructions to Bremer on how to establish the New Iraqi Corps. "The NIC will contribute to setting the conditions necessary for a stable, self-sustaining Iraq, with a viable governing body," Rumsfeld's message noted. "Endstate is a viable force that is a source of Iraqi national pride, contributes to national unity and provides a model for ethnic cooperation." Rumsfeld added that the corps should initially consist of three motorized battalions that would be 800 strong. One battalion would be in the north, one in the central part of the country, and one in the southern region. Rumsfeld's message envisioned that it would take six months to field the initial force, which would be put under the control of a new Ministry of Defense. The corps would eventually grow to three divisions and 40,000 personnel. For all the talk of building Iraqi pride, the name of the new force betrayed a certain cultural insensitivity: NIC, when pronounced, sounded very much like "fuck" in Arabic. It was a graphic demonstration of just how little the liberators understood the nation they occupied.[10]

On May 23, Bremer formally issued Order No. 2. While Rumsfeld had been consulted in advance, other key players were blindsided by the edict. Peter Pace, the vice chairman of the Joint Chiefs of Staff, said later that the Joint Chiefs were not consulted about the decision. Powell did not know about it in advance. Condoleezza Rice was caught off guard but comforted herself with the thought that the White House needed to respect the judgment of their man in Baghdad. "I don't think that anybody thought it was wildly out of context with what we were trying to achieve, and the whole structure had been set up so that some of those decisions could be made in the field or through the Pentagon chain," she said later.[11]

In fact, Abizaid and McKiernan did consider the decision an abrupt and unwelcome departure from their previous planning. Just how great a departure became clearer when Slocombe outlined his plans for forming the New Iraqi Corps. To avoid the taint of Baathism, it was decided that no one from the rank of colonel and above could join without extensive vetting. Building the corps battalion by battalion meant that it would take a full year to field the first division of infantry—about 12,000 Iraqi troops—and two years to train and equip a three-division force. The generals wanted to use Iraqi forces as a means to generate the troop levels that would be needed to guard the borders and establish a military presence throughout the country. The decision to abolish the Iraqi army not only risked alienating some 300,000 Iraqi troops but upended CENTCOM's postwar plan. "We wanted to rapidly call the soldiers back, get them on our side, and then sort out who could and could not be trusted," said John Agoglia, the CENTCOM planner who became the command's liaison to Bremer's authority. "It would have been a lot faster than building one battalion at a time. And we wanted to send a psychological message that they were going to be part of the new Iraq, to prevent them from turning against us."[12]

Franks and his commanders were in an awkward position, trying to influence a decision that had already been made. In late May, Rear Admiral James Robb told Slocombe that Abizaid

believed that former senior Iraqi officers should not be disqualified and that the training should be accelerated. Franks followed
up in a video conference on June 2 with Bremer. "I think the
velocity of doing it can be characterized as a miscalculation,"
Franks said after the war.[13]

The reaction to Order No. 2 in Iraq was incendiary. The
decree prompted angry demonstrations in Baghdad. In Mosul,
Petraeus's 101st had been working tirelessly to win the support of
Iraqis. But the announcement led to violent protests that
wounded sixteen of its soldiers. On June 14, Petraeus spied Slocombe at a change-of-command ceremony for Scott Wallace at
the Abu Ghraib palace. He told him that the decision to leave the
Iraqi soldiers without a livelihood had put American lives at risk.
Trying to calm the roiling waters, Bremer later decided to pay the
Iraqi troops, which gave the United States the worst of both
options: it was paying money to a bitter, demobilized army but
was getting nothing in return, and had created a situation in
which the soldiers were unsupervised, had no stake in the new
order, and were free to create mischief, or worse.[14]

Soon after Bremer issued his order abolishing the army, the occupation authority made a discovery. Bremer's de-Baathification
program had disqualified Iraqis who held the top party ranks
from holding posts in the new Iraq—a policy that had mechani-
cally been applied to the military, barring the recruitment of all
senior Iraqi officers. After the Americans acquired and examined
the military's personnel records, they learned there were fewer
Baathists among the top ranks than they had thought. Only half
of the major generals were committed Baathists, and only a small
percentage of the brigadier generals. Only some 8,000 of the
140,000 officers and NCOs were committed enough Baathists to
be disqualified. That was one of the points Naima had made
with McKiernan, and in a sense it was not surprising. Saddam
had been so distrustful of the Regular Army that he made sure
the divisions were stationed far from Baghdad. Even the supposedly loyal Republican Guard had not been allowed to take up
positions inside the capital. Bremer had denied top-level officers
a role in the new Iraqi army based on a misunderstanding of the
Iraqis' civil-military relations.[15]

In his memoirs of his tour of Iraq, Bremer made much of the fact that Rumsfeld and his aides had signed off on the decision to abolish the Iraqi army, but he did not note the deep unhappiness of the U.S. military about the move.[16] Under pressure from Abizaid and Rumsfeld, Bremer sought to speed up the training of the new Iraqi forces. The Americans also created a new militia—the Iraqi Civil Defense Corps—but this militia was of widely inconsistent abilities, it was not a national force, and it was unable to fill the gap.

In fact, in their own way, Rumsfeld and Bremer each contributed to the security problem. Rumsfeld limited the number of American troops in Iraq, and Bremer limited the number of Iraqi forces that were immediately available. The two decisions combined to produce a much larger security vacuum.

Bremer's CPA, the Coalition Provisional Authority, was not the only organization that was starting from scratch. Before the war, the Joint Staff suggested that a new military organization be established and staffed in advance to control postwar Iraq. Abizaid had suggested that the task might be allocated to the III Corps. There were attempts to get a running head start. The idea, however, had gone nowhere. When Baghdad fell it was still unclear how long McKiernan's land war command would be in charge or what would follow.

In late April, Franks had gathered his officers to discuss the sort of organization that needed to be established and it was agreed that the military would establish a new Combined Joint Task Force, an organization that would be headed by a three-star general, would have a staff from throughout the services, and would oversee all the military units in Iraq.

When the time came to pick a name one aide suggested CJTF-13, a bit of black humor that pointed to difficulties ahead. Franks chimed in, "Let's make it CJTF-1369, unlucky cocksuckers." Gene Renuart, ever the dignified Air Force officer, quickly restored some civility to the conversation: the organization would be called CJTF-7. Renuart picked the number 7 because that was the number his son had worn on his soccer uniform.

Still, the episode was indicative of Franks's attitude about the postwar administration. For Franks, anything other than warfighting was an unglamorous and thankless burden. Franks was already considering retiring and negotiating a multimillion-dollar deal to write his memoirs, much as Schwarzkopf had done after the Gulf War. "I am going to get my mains," he told one of his senior officers. For Franks, postwar Iraq would soon be somebody else's problem.[17]

In Washington, Jack Keane thought that this was a time for continuity in command in the Iraqi region. A gruff but articulate New Yorker, Keane took over as the acting head of the Army after a period of considerable turmoil in the top ranks. Two weeks after Baghdad was taken, Tom White had been told to report to Rumsfeld's office for a five p.m. meeting. When the civilian Army secretary walked in, Rumsfeld came right to the point. "I want to make a change," he said. "Fine, that is your choice," White shot back. White's alliance with Shinseki had become an unpardonable offense for the defense secretary, who continued to believe that the service was too enamored of large forces and slow to change. White told Rumsfeld he would write a short resignation letter that day. The army secretary had planned to stay through the end of Shinseki's terms, but a week later Wolfowitz called to say that was no longer acceptable, and White left on May 9. When Shinseki retired the next month he lauded White for his principles. Rumsfeld, who was traveling, did not attend the event.[18]

Keane's big worry was not about the changes in Washington, but the ones that were being planned in the Persian Gulf region. Keane had contacted Myers and suggested extending Franks's tour at CENTCOM, which would enable Abizaid to focus more on Iraq. But Myers told Keane that that was not an option. Franks seemed exhausted by two wars and Myers was frustrated with trying to convince him to stay on and focus on the postwar situation.

Keane was also concerned about who was going to run CJTF-7. Keane's own choice—and that he presumed of the administration—was McKiernan. In mid-June, however, Keane was dumbfounded to learn that McKiernan was on his way out of Iraq and that the post was going to Ricardo "Rick" Sanchez. The two-star commander of the 1st Armored Division had replaced Scott Wallace as the head of the V Corps, a move that Wallace had only learned about two weeks earlier. Sanchez was now going to be elevated yet again to the head of CJTF-7. Almost overnight the commander of the last arriving division in Iraq would become the senior military commander for the most sensitive part of the operation. Compounding the problem, Sanchez would have to build a new team, drawing on the V Corps and senior officers from elsewhere in the army. McKiernan already had a team of general officers, one that had been focusing on Iraq. Keane called Abizaid and asked what the hell was going on. Keane respected McKiernan. Had Keane accepted Rumsfeld's offer to stay on as the Army Chief, he planned to make McKiernan the Vice Chief. Abizaid replied that the arrangements had been agreed upon between Franks and McKiernan.

In fact, it was something of a garble. McKiernan was prepared to stay on, but had asked that much of his staff, which had been deployed for almost two years, be rotated home. A larger factor seemed to be the attitude of civilians in Washington. McKiernan had decidedly less support from Rumsfeld and his staff than from his Army superiors. Larry Di Rita, a top Rumsfeld aide, had been overheard at Bremer's headquarters telling officials in Washington that McKiernan was not the right general to run the operations in postwar Iraq. It also did not help when Rumsfeld returned from an April 30 meeting with McKiernan and Wallace in Iraq and complained about the Army generals he had encountered there. Washington was prepared to rely on an untested general who was not the choice of the head of his own service.[19]

On the morning of June 15, McKiernan and Terry Moran said their goodbyes to Bremer. McKiernan gave Bremer an overview of the operation that the 4th ID was about to undertake near Taji and Baqubah to search for members of Saddam's regime. Bremer was comfortable with the plan. McKiernan then offered two pieces of advice. Bremer needed to increase the money provided to brigade and division commanders for projects in their area. They knew the country, had the security and the contacts. Bre-

mer's office, in contrast, was Baghdad-centric. It had no representative in most of Iraq's eighteen governorates.

McKiernan also raised again his concern over the Army. Bremer needed to go "bigger and faster." He could establish an Iraqi
general staff, recall the Iraqi soldiers and officers to their gar-
risons, and arrange for the Iraqi forces to conduct "low-risk"
missions like guarding gas stations, power plants, government
buildings, and bridges. It would not be pretty. The vetting would
have to be carried out quickly. The United States would need to
sort out those with "blood on their hands" over time. But Iraqi
brigades could quickly be deployed near Mosul, Baghdad, and
Basra. Bremer listened, but made no promises.[20]

Personalities aside, the summer of 2003 had been a time of
enormous turbulence in the American command. Franks was
preparing to leave his post to be replaced at CENTCOM by
Abizaid. Garner had been replaced by Bremer. McKiernan and
Wallace had left. The newest general on the block was in
charge, and his relations with Bremer were soon strained. The
changes and sheer transport of staff to and from Iraq was time-
consuming and distracting. At Bremer's headquarters, John
Agoglia was concerned that Americans were so preoccupied
with rearranging their headquarters that they were losing touch
with the deteriorating situation in Iraq.

Ten days after McKiernan left, John Sawers sent another confidential cable to London. The message was entitled "Iraq:
Progress Report," but there was not much progress to speak of.
Sawers noted that Bremer had become concerned that the U.S.
troop withdrawals had gone too far, prompting him to call the
president. Unemployment was running at 60 percent. "It has
been a difficult week in Iraq. Fire fights between Coalition forces
and Iraqi groups have been more frequent, with the Majar al-
Kabir incident the worst. That seems to have been due to local
causes and is in a known volatile area, but it shows how thin is
the veneer of security in many parts of Iraq," he wrote.

"The new threat is well-targeted sabotage of the infrastructure. An attack on the power grid last weekend had a series of
knock-on effects, which halved the power generation in Baghdad
and many other parts of the country. That, in turn, cut off the

water supply. Much of Baghdad has been without electricity and running water for the last three days. The oil and gas network is another target, with five successful attacks this week on pipelines. We do not yet have an answer to this threat. We are also seeing the first signs of intimidation of Iraqis working for the Coalition.

"Bremer's main concern is that we must keep in-country sufficient military capability to ensure a security blanket across the country. He has twice said to President Bush that he is concerned that the draw down of US/UK troops has gone too far, and we cannot afford further reductions. US forces are down to 60 percent of end-conflict levels, UK forces have reduced further to 40 percent. While other national contingencies are welcome, he questions whether they will be sufficiently robust when push comes to shove.

"In the medium term, my main concern is the Shia. The continued problem with security and essential services means that moderate Shia leaders are coming under pressure as their communities question whether supporting the Coalition is the right approach. Meanwhile, the Iranians are adding to their options in Iraq by cultivating the young Najaf radical, Muqtadr Al-Sadr, and that is worrying the moderate clerics. SCIRI, the pro-Iran party we are working with, are facing some tricky decisions. Iraqis remain resistant to Iranian attempts to exert influence. But the biggest threat in the next year is that, for a mix of reasons, we lose the Shia heartlands. The Iranians seem to be positioning themselves so they can make that threat more real."[21]

On July 16, John Abizaid used his debut press conference after taking over as CENTCOM commander to deliver a message of his own. U.S. forces in Iraq were now under attack from "a classical guerrilla-type campaign." The account was the first time that a senior officer had openly stated that the U.S. confronted an insurgency and made headlines. Rumsfeld, who had been stating for weeks that the U.S. was merely conducting mopping-up operations against "dead-enders," privately expressed his unhappiness to Abizaid about his blunt comments, military officials said.

Six days later, the Americans thought they might have struck a decisive blow. After escaping to Syria, Uday and Qusay Hussein had been turned away and found their way to Mosul. Tipped off by their anxious host, soldiers from Colonel Joe Anderson's brigade surrounded the house. In Baghdad, Dell Dailey's Task Force 20 began to head north. After a series of miscues the timing of the raid was delayed until daylight the next morning. Having surrounded the house, the Americans asked the Iraqis to come out peacefully. Then TF-20 went in after them. Four U.S. troops were wounded and the insertion force withdrew.

After a second failed attempt to attack the house, the TF-20 commandos told Anderson they wanted the building leveled by air strike and M1 tanks. "They come to me and say, 'We want tanks, we want CAS [close air support]. We want to level the building.' The reason is that they say they are in some fortified, interior bunker, bulletproof." Anderson was not about to launch an air strike in the middle of a crowded site. So he ordered his soldiers to launch ten TOW antitank missiles at the structure. When the soldiers finally took the building, they determined that there was no interior bunker, but Uday, Qusay, and Uday's fourteen-year-old son were dead. The damaged building was razed several days later. After months of growing insurgent activity, the Americans thought they might finally have reached a turning point. But the resistance continued to build.[22]

As the long, hot summer dragged on, Bremer sought to maintain tight control over the political life of Iraq. Since his Coalition Provisional Authority had little presence outside Baghdad he worked through the U.S. military.

To the south, Lieutenant Colonel Chris Conlin, whose battalion had taken the Crown Jewel on the opening day of the invasion, was given authority for Najaf. Conlin arrived to discover that the CIA had installed a Sufi as mayor who not only was unpopular with the city's residents, but was receiving bad notices in the Western media. Soon word came down from Bremer's office that Conlin was to fire the mayor.

Conlin suggested that an election be held and Mattis's and Bremer's staffs endorsed the idea. The Marines and an Army reserve unit from Green Bay, Wisconsin, devised a plan to register the Iraqis and build wooden ballot boxes. The upcoming balloting stimulated enormous interest and intensive campaigning.

The Shiites had been repressed for years by Saddam and now, having been liberated by the Americans, they would finally have an opportunity to govern themselves. Just a day before the registration process was formally to begin, however, Conlin received a call from Mattis. The election had to be canceled. Bremer was concerned that an unfriendly Islamic candidate would prevail.

With election fervor running high, Conlin urged Mattis to allow him to announce that the election had been postponed, not annulled. Appearing on local television, Conlin took the blame, saying that he had pushed the Iraqis to vote before they were ready. There would be an election, but not yet. Then Conlin went with Jim Conway, the top Marine commander, to Baghdad to plead the case for an election with Bremer. Bremer was not available, and the Marine officers had to settle for a deputy, who matter-of-factly explained that Bremer would not allow the wrong guy to win the election. The Marines were advised to select a group of Iraqis they thought were safe and have them pick a mayor. That way the United States would control the process. The Marines did not like the idea. That was not what the Marines had in mind after hearing the White House talk about bringing democracy to the Middle East. "A window of opportunity existed when the regime fell," Mattis recalled. "When the Marines went south I reminded my commanders that the kinetic phase was over, that we had come to Iraq to liberate and they should take off their helmets and help the people with what they need. It worked. Two things then created major problems: disbanding the Iraqi army and putting proud soldiers on the street unemployed. The other was shortstopping local elections."[23]

North in Tikrit, Ray Odierno was having his own problems. Unlike the Marines, Odierno was not operating in the Shiite heartland, but in the Sunni north. After a month of relative peace, insurgent activity had begun to heat up, and Bremer's de-Baathification edict was making things worse. In Saddam's old stomping grounds everybody who was anybody was Baathist. As the schools prepared to reopen, Odierno was instructed to fire a thousand schoolteachers in the province on the grounds that they were committed Baathists. Meanwhile, Bremer's authority cut off their pay. Odierno retained the teachers while he sought to argue the case with Bremer. The decision on the teachers had rippled through the community and fortified support for a growing resistance. It was jeopardizing the security of American soldiers. An exception was eventually made, but the episode had hardly improved the division's standing with the Iraqis.

Odierno fought a similar battle over the Iraqi police. Again, Bremer's authority said they were riddled with Baathists. Odierno went to Baghdad to plead his case with Bernie Kerik, the former New York City police chief who had taken over from Robert Gifford. Again, Odierno prevailed, but the wrangle had its cost. Relations with the Iraqis were soured and for weeks the police stopped coming to work. Odierno later concluded that it would have been better to let the U.S. military call the shots on such important policy issues. It was dispersed around the country and was working hard with the local communities. Bremer's CPA had been entrusted with important governance issues before it was ready to exercise the responsibility. "Decisions were taken out of our hands," Odierno recalled. "We lost the window of opportunity when it would have done the most good."[24]

In the west, Buff Blount had sent Perkins's 2nd BCT to Fallujah to restore order after the 82nd and 3rd Armored Cavalry Regiment had come under attack. Perkins had an entire brigade of troops. The brigade also reached out to the Iraqis. Blount authorized the payment of "blood money" for the Iraqis who had been shot by the 82nd, hoping to head off further revenge killings. The division's soldiers sought to cooperate with the local imams and to train the police. By July, however, it was time for the 3rd ID to return to the United States.

But Blount was worried that the inroads his soldiers had made with the Iraqi population would be erased if his soldiers were replaced by troops from the 82nd, whom the residents of Fallujah still hated with a passion. Blount went to see Sanchez and explained the sensitivity of the situation. As much as Blount wanted to take his soldiers home, he offered to extend the 3rd ID deployment in Fallujah. If the 82nd returned, there would be fewer forces in the area and fewer soldiers with a history of troubled relations with the Iraqis.

Sanchez was not sympathetic. It was time for the 3rd ID to leave and the 82nd was the only unit that was available to take over. Within weeks of the 3rd ID's departure, the 82nd shot and killed some of the policemen the 3rd ID had worked so hard to train after mistaking them for Iraqi insurgents. Hostility against the Americans continued to grow in Fallujah.[25]

After his marauding in the north, Pete Blaber made his way to Baghdad, where he and his Delta team were conducting operations. Stopping by the Green Zone with Saif Ataya, Blaber approached a CPA official and identified himself as the Delta commander to a State Department official on Bremer's staff. Blaber explained that Ataya had been useful to Delta and could guide the civilians in dealing with the welter of clashing cultures that is Iraq. Blaber was told that Ataya's services were not needed. The only job that the CPA could offer was working as an interpreter for $60 a day.

Ataya eventually found a role for himself funneling intelligence about terrorist cells and the situation to the U.S. military. No Iraqi had been more supportive of the invasion than Ataya, but what he found in Baghdad worried him greatly. There was no security on the streets, just the law of the gun. The people felt cut off from the Americans and their own interim government. There were few jobs. For $50 or $100, groups could hire local Iraqis to take a shot at the Americans. Corruption was rampant. Before he fled Iraq, Ataya recalled that Saddam had staged events, appeared on television, and masqueraded as a man of the people. It was all a charade but at least he had made the effort. But Ataya felt that the new Iraqi leaders who were setting up the interim government seemed as isolated as the Americans in the Green Zone and were not getting their message out.

When Ataya returned from Iraq in 2004 he was invited to the Pentagon to offer his impressions to Wolfowitz and Blaber. Ataya still held out hope that democracy would take root in Iraq and spread through the Middle East. But he warned that things were deteriorating. "I told them the situation would be worse because of the evidence of corruption." Returning to California, he got a job teaching Arabic to U.S. military personnel and rebuffed several lucrative offers to return to Iraq.[26]

In December 2005, McKiernan was awarded his fourth star and took command of U.S. troops in Europe. Looking back at the summer of 2003, McKiernan later saw the period as a lost chance to build support and to prevent the insurgency from gaining momentum. "With few exceptions we were not being shot at. I could walk the streets anywhere in Baghdad. Most Iraqis there still viewed us as liberators, even if they did not particularly like us culturally," said McKiernan. "From the beginning in planning for a post-Saddam Iraq, we failed to seize a window of opportunity to get military, political, economic, and informational effects harmonized to bring order to a chaotic situation. While the Baathist hard-liners would have opposed the coalition under any circumstances I believe the insurgency's mosaic of affiliations was not a preordained event."[27]

Some of McKiernan's aides were blunter still. With limited American troops, few allies, and no Iraqi army to draw on, the United States had lost the initiative at a critical moment. "My position is that we lost momentum and that the insurgency was not inevitable," said Spider Marks, who retired from the military after a stint running the Army's intelligence school. "We had momentum going in and had Saddam's forces on the run. But we did not have enough troops. First, we did not have enough troops to conduct combat patrols in sufficient numbers to gain solid intelligence and paint a good picture of the enemy on the ground. Secondly, we needed more troops to act on the intelligence we generated. They took advantage of our limited numbers."[28]

Jim Conway, who was later made the senior operations officer for the Joint Chiefs, agreed with McKiernan that while some level of resistance was inevitable, political, economic, and military steps could have been taken to mitigate the virulence of the insurgency. Preventing the Iraqis from holding local elections, he said, was a major blunder. "I think we underestimated the importance of Iraqi pride in our dealings with them," Conway said. "When we denied Iraqis the opportunities to elect local officials—vice appoint them by the area commander—we were increasingly seen as occupiers."

Like other senior military officers, Conway believed that the disestablishment of the army reinforced the impression that the U.S. was intent on acting like an occupying power while depriving the U.S. of security forces at a critical time. "We should have capitalized on—not dissolved—the Iraqi army," he said. "The most respected institution in the country was the army. It has been said that they 'melted away' during the initial fighting. That is only partially true. Nevertheless, I am certain that had we seriously attempted to reassemble them—and dismiss those with blood on their hands from the Saddam era—that could have been accomplished. We had no problem rounding them up to pay for no work done when that became the CPA policy."

Beyond that, the problems in winning the support of the Iraqi public, he said, were aggravated by the inability of Bremer's Coalition Provisional Authority to meet the Iraqis' expectations for rebuilding their country. Even the Marines were taken aback by the CPA's poor state of preparation and its inability to operate outside Baghdad. Conway's officers kept waiting for civilian "local governance teams" that never arrived, forcing Marine battalion commanders to become city managers, chiefs of policy, and agricultural experts.[29]

Brigadier General John Kelly, Mattis's assistant division commander, was made the Marines' chief liaison to Congress after his two tours in Iraq. Like Marks, he believed that the limited number of troops made it hard to contain the insurgency. "Numbers count. One of the truisms I found in my studies and experience is if you are forced to shift forces around in an insurgency to plug holes, you lose," Kelly observed. "No cooperation from the locals who need the presence and security." The multinational forces the United States recruited were often not very effective. Most of the newly arriving foreign troops were not authorized to conduct offensive operations by the governments that sent them and had to check with their respective capitals before they could carry out many of their orders. With little involvement with civil affairs and local Iraqis, they did not provide much of a stabilizing influence. The civilian effort in Baghdad never seemed to get organized. Frustrated with the insurgent attacks and unprepared to deal with the complexities of Iraq, there was a "default to meet violence with violence on the part of some U.S. forces," Kelly observed, which led to civilian casualties and hardened the attitudes of many Iraqis against the Americans.[30]

Buff Blount also thought the United States had missed an opportunity. "There was a time when the insurgency could have been headed off or greatly reduced and contained," he said. Blount cited several factors that allowed the insurgency to develop. One was the change in personnel. "There were several leadership changes that are questionable," Blount said. "The first is letting McKiernan and his headquarters go back to Kuwait and giving the responsibility for CJTF-7 to V Corps. McKiernan and his staff were the Army's experts on the Middle East. V Corps is European-based and had no experience in the region. You also had a brand-new corps commander who had not participated in the first phases of the war and had all the responsibility Bremer was soon to thrust on him. In the same time frame, Bremer replaced Garner and within a week or two all the people that the U.S. military and the Iraqis had been dealing with were replaced and everything started over."

Like the other generals, Blount said the decision to dismantle the Iraqi army and his de-Baathification decree made the military's job harder. "For a period of time we were perceived as and acted like liberators, but as more and more combat troops came, there was a shift to an occupation or fortress mentality."[31]

Jack Keane retired from the military after running the U.S. Army through the troubled summer of 2003. The United States mission in Iraq, he recalled later, was made all the more difficult by the administration's aversion to nation-building and its determination not to study the lessons of its predecessors. That attitude set the stage for many of the problems that were to come. "It was an ideology they came in with and an overreaction to the Clinton administration," Keane said. "The Bush administration looked at the Bosnia/Kosovo model and decided that it was fundamentally flawed. They concluded that it encouraged an artificial dependency on the part of the host country by committing a larger footprint of U.S. troops. They preferred a small presence to force the host country to do its own nation-building. I believe this is desirable but only if there is security. Without security, the model breaks down quickly, which was the case in Iraq."

Keane said military leaders, including the Joint Chiefs of Staff, the Vice Chiefs, and Franks, share responsibility for the problems in Iraq by not considering that guerrilla war was a serious possibility. "The fact is that the Baathist insurgency surprised us and we had not developed a comprehensive option for dealing with this possibility, one that would have included more military police, civil affairs units, interrogators, interpreters, and Special Operations Forces. If we had planned for an insurgency we probably would have deployed the First Cavalry Division and it would have assisted greatly with the initial occupation. This was not just an intelligence community failure, but also our failure as senior military leaders, including myself."[32]

Colin Powell left the administration soon after Bush's reelection. At the State Department, Rich Armitage, Powell's top deputy, stayed on for a month and made several fact-finding trips to Iraq before he also left government. Armitage had no love for Saddam and was happy to see him overthrown. He had questioned the timing of the invasion but not its purpose. Still, he was troubled by the way the transition was going. Reconstruction projects had slowed as a result of the violence. The insurgents seemed to know where the U.S. forces were and where they were headed. Time was not necessarily on the U.S. side. Meeting with Bush and his National Security Council in November 2004, Armitage provided his unvarnished assessment.

"We are not winning," Armitage stated. The president seemed taken aback.

"Are we losing?" Bush asked.

Armitage's reply was not reassuring: "Not yet."[33]

Epilogue

On December 5, 2005, Donald Rumsfeld visited the Johns Hopkins School of Advanced International Studies to give his appraisal of events in Iraq. Asked about the lessons of the still unfinished war, the defense secretary was quick to tout the virtues of military transformation. "I think if I had to pull out one lesson that we've learned over the past four or five years, it would be that in the twenty-first century we're going to have to stop thinking about things, numbers of things, and mass, and think also and maybe even first about speed and agility and precision."

It was the same message that George W. Bush had delivered in a Citadel speech in 1998 and the one lesson that Rumsfeld had sought to drum into the Pentagon. The secretary of defense, however, was only partially right. As a consequence, the United States has yet to achieve its victory and U.S. troops and the Iraqis themselves have paid an unnecessarily high price. The violent chaos that followed Saddam's defeat was not a matter of not having a plan but of adhering too rigidly to the wrong one.

From the start, American political objectives were bold and extraordinarily ambitious. The military operation was intended to strike a blow at terrorism by ousting a long-standing adversary, eliminating Iraq's weapons of mass destruction, and implanting a moderate and pro-American state in the heart of the Arab world. It was also to be a powerful demonstration of American power and an object lesson—for Iran, Syria, and other would-be foes—of the potential consequences of supporting terrorist groups and pursuing nuclear, biological, and chemical arms. The United States would not just defeat a dictator. It would transform a region and send the message that the American intervention in Afghanistan was not the end but just the beginning of Washington's "global war on terror."

But President Bush and his team committed five grievous errors. They underestimated their opponent and failed to understand the welter of ethnic groups and tribes that is Iraq. They did not bring the right tools to the fight and put too much confidence in technology. They failed to adapt to developments on the ground and remained wedded to their prewar analysis even after Iraqis showed their penchant for guerrilla tactics in the first days of the war. They presided over a system in which differing military and political perspectives were discouraged. Finally, they turned their back on the nation-building lessons from the Balkans and other crisis zones and fashioned a plan that unrealistically sought to shift much of the burden onto a defeated and ethnically diverse population and allied nations that were enormously ambivalent about the invasion. Instead of making plans to fight a counterinsurgency, the president and his team drew up plans to bring the troops home and all but declared the war won.

There is a direct link between the way the Iraq War was planned and the bitter insurgency the American-led coalition subsequently confronted. The ambitious plans that the president announced to transform American defense proved to be at odds with his bold plan to transform a region.

THE MISREADING OF THE FOE

Rumsfeld and his generals misread their foe by viewing the invasion of Iraq largely as a continuation of the Persian Gulf War. During the Desert Storm campaign Saddam Hussein's Republican Guard was the best equipped and most loyal force. Tommy Franks and his generals continued to regard the Republican Guard as their principal adversary. The allied ground forces, as few as they were, expected to run roughshod over the Guard units with a combination of maneuver and firepower and drive directly to Baghdad. Bypassed Iraqi units would be left to die on the vine. As it turned out, the generals were well prepared to fight the enemy that they had war-gamed against. But it would be the paramilitary Fedayeen that represented the principal challenge in Nasiriyah, Samawah, Najaf, Kifl, and Diwaniyah, and that fought tenaciously in Baghdad as well. The failure to understand the foe in part reflected a failure of intelligence. The CIA in particular was not only wrong on WMD, but failed to identify the importance of the Fedayeen or to uncover the tons of arms that had been cached in the cities and towns of southern Iraq. The CIA's assurances that the Iraqi military would capitulate and that the Army and Marines would be welcome in the southern cities were misleading and dangerous. Field commanders lost confidence in the agency and came to depend upon front-line reporting to gain knowledge of their enemy in the unexpected war they were fighting.

Just as Rumsfeld and Franks failed to understand the enemy, they also did not understand the actual structure of political power in Iraq. Rumsfeld and Franks believed that their victory would be sealed with the seizing of Baghdad, which was identified as Iraq's "center of gravity." But from the first day of the invasion the United States was not fighting a purely conventional war, one that would be suddenly brought to an end when the regime's ministries were seized and its leader toppled. The attacks by the Fedayeen on the road to Baghdad demonstrated that the American-led coalition was contending with a decentralized enemy that was fanatical, not dependent on rigid command and control, and whose base of operations was dispersed throughout the towns and cities of Iraq. The "center of gravity" was not a single geographic location—the Iraqi capital—but the entire Sunni Triangle and more broadly the Iraqi people themselves. The Fedayeen would not be defeated and the war not won until the Sunni region was under control, and the Iraqi population supportive or at least not actively antagonistic.

THE OVERRELIANCE ON TECHNOLOGICAL ADVANCEMENT

The administration put far too much confidence in American military technology, Special Operations Forces, and clandestine operations. Rumsfeld's principles of transformation were in large measure a codification of the long-promised "revolution in military affairs." With the aid of high-tech reconnaissance systems, precision weapons, and advanced communications, relatively small units could be even more lethal. For Rumsfeld his vision had been realized in Afghanistan and would be adapted for Iraq.

During the march to Baghdad, the approach was effective. Saddam's regime was caught off guard when the United States invaded with a force that was far smaller than the one it amassed for the 1991 Persian Gulf War and without waiting to carry out a long, preparatory air campaign. Speed was a vital element of the campaign. The rapid pace of the Army and Marine attack enabled the United States to secure the critical bridges and assure the Iraqis could not destroy them. It also made it possible for U.S. troops to move into the Iraqi capital before the enemy could stiffen its defenses. Improved reconnaissance and surveillance and precision munitions gave well-trained U.S. forces a decisive edge. The expanded cooperation among the military services added to the efficiency of the effort. The military campaign was more "joint" than ever before. The establishment of McKiernan's allied land war headquarters, an innovation compared with CENTCOM's arrangements for waging the Persian Gulf War, helped to harmonize the Army and Marine attacks.

But after the fall of Baghdad in April 2003, the requirements were reversed: mass, not speed, was requisite for sealing the victory. Military technology was less decisive against an opponent that faded away into Iraqi cities only to fight another day. Nor were SOF efforts and CIA operations generally effective against an elusive adversary. To gain control of the Sunni Triangle and pursue the Fedayeen, Baath Party militia, and enemy formations before they had a chance to catch their breath, rearm, and regroup, the United States needed more boots on the ground. As a result of a deficit of forces, Anbar Province in western Iraq, the heartland of Sunnism and Baathist support, was treated as an "economy of force" operation and only sparsely covered by American troops. There were not sufficient troops to seal the borders, guard the copious arms caches, and dominate the terrain, all of which allowed the province to become a sanctuary for insurgents. The Bush administration's assumptions that it could solicit substantial coalition troops for the postwar and quickly reorganize and use defeated Iraqi military manpower were either proved wrong or derailed by ill-informed decision-making like Bremer's edict to abolish the Iraqi army. Without sufficient forces, there was a constant turnover of U.S. troops in Fallujah, a key city just a short drive from Baghdad, which impaired the U.S. military's ability to develop a good working relationship with locals. The problem was not just one of numbers. The United States also lacked the right sort of troops for the postwar phase: it needed to have more civil affairs units, military police, and interpreters. The result was that Anbar Province became the seat of much of the resistance to the U.S. occupation and Fallujah became a metaphor for postcombat failure in Iraq.

THE FAILURE TO ADAPT TO DEVELOPMENTS ON THE BATTLEFIELD

There were numerous indications in the first days of the war that the United States was involved in a different war than it had anticipated. Instead of being welcomed at Nasiriyah, the Marines engaged in a bloody and casualty-inducing fight. After running into stiff resistance at Samawah, the V Corps dropped its plans for a feint up Highways 1 and 8. The clashes at Kifl and Objective Floyd were fierce. The first Marine to be killed in action died at the hands of an Iraqi dressed in civilian clothes who fired from a pickup truck, not a tank. Moreover, the Americans encountered primitive roadside bombs, suicide car bombs, foreign jihadists, and guerrilla-style ambushes, hallmarks of the insurgency to come.

American troops themselves were quick to identify the nature of their enemy. Shocked by the early battles at Nasiriyah and near Najaf, they adapted and successfully developed tactics to deal with the real as opposed to expected enemy—tactics used effectively in the assault on Baghdad. The troops' training and the leadership in the field and at the allied land command paid off.

But the American war plan was never adjusted on high. Tommy Franks never acknowledged the enemy he faced nor did he comprehend the nature of the war he was directing. He denigrated the Fedayeen as little more than a speed bump on the way to Baghdad and never appreciated their resilience and determination. Franks threatened to fire Scott Wallace, the V Corps commander, when he noted publicly that his soldiers were battling a different enemy than the one that had been featured in the military's war games. Once Baghdad was taken, Franks turned his attention elsewhere in the belief that victory was his, never realizing the irregulars he maligned constituted the real military center of gravity, one that had not surrendered. In his book, *American Soldier,* Franks claims credit for a winning strategy. At best he had won the first round of the war thanks largely to his subordinate commanders, but neither he nor they had won the war.

More important, Rumsfeld failed to heed his own counsel on defense planning. From the day he returned to the Pentagon as George W. Bush's defense secretary, Rumsfeld underscored the need to be prepared for the unexpected. There were, Rumsfeld cautioned, unknown dangers so unanticipated that experts could not even imagine them. Success depended on agility: the ability to adjust the battle plan in the face of threats that could be neither predicted nor foreseen. Yet Rumsfeld was so confident of the validity of the prewar plan that he questioned the need to deploy the 1st Cavalry before Baghdad fell. Just a week after Baghdad was seized, the White House, Defense Department, and CENTCOM were focused on withdrawing troops and replacing them with less capable foreign troops instead of deploying the assets that would be needed to hedge against new threats.

The failure to read the early signs of the insurgency and to adapt accordingly was all the more surprising given the Bush administration's repeated assertions that Saddam's regime was allied with Osama bin Laden and terrorist organizations like Abu Musab al-Zarqawi's and given confirmed intelligence reports that jihadists had infiltrated from Syria. Had the administration taken its own counsel to heart, it would have been planning to wage a counterinsurgency and conduct antiterrorist operations as soon as Baghdad fell.

THE DYSFUNCTION OF AMERICAN MILITARY STRUCTURES

During the Persian Gulf War, Defense Secretary Dick Cheney had a strong and independent-minded counterpart in Colin Powell, the chairman of the Joint Chiefs. The two differed over strategy and even the imperative of going to war. The dynamic provided for a more informed debate over strategy and force requirements. In the Iraq War, Rumsfeld and Franks dominated the planning; the Joint Chiefs of Staff were pushed to the margins and largely accepted their role. Richard Myers was picked to be the JCS chairman because of his track record as a team player and largely fulfilled Rumsfeld's expectations. Even Shinseki, who stirred up a debate over the number of troops needed for the postwar period in his remarks to Congress, did not press the issue inside the JCS, according to former chiefs.

With his experience as defense secretary, his ties to the Iraqi opposition, and his role as advocate of the war, Cheney had the authority to serve as a counterweight to the Pentagon's optimism on postwar planning. But the vice president never once challenged the realism of Rumsfeld's expectations. Rather, he ratified the hopeful and unrealistic plan. Colin Powell raised both the issue of insufficient troops and the difficulties the U.S. would encounter in postwar Iraq, but he was the odd man out in an administration that was dominated by Bush, Cheney, and Rumsfeld and later told the president that he considered the policy-making machinery to be broken. Given the many indications that Rumsfeld and his aides viewed the building of a new Iraq as a relatively undemanding pursuit, the nation would have been better served if Powell had objected when the secretary of defense moved to seize control of postwar planning.

The problem was compounded at lower levels by the improvised military and political structures that were established in Iraq by the Americans. No military headquarters or staff was selected in advance to secure postwar Iraq. The summer of 2003 was one of turmoil in which McKiernan's command, which was focused on the Middle East region, was supplanted by a command led by Ricardo Sanchez, a junior three-star general whose last assignment was in Europe. The changeover occurred as Franks was nearing retirement and preparing to hand CENTCOM over to John Abizaid, and as Jay Garner and his team were replaced by L. Paul Bremer and his Coalition Provisional Authority. Determined to solidify his authority, Bremer squeezed out Zalmay

Khalilzad, the one official who knew the Iraqi politicians well. Exacerbating the situation, relations between Sanchez and Bremer were not strong. The personnel changes and infighting were distracting and diverted attention and energy from Iraq at the precise moment when the insurgency was beginning to gain traction.

THE BUSH ADMINISTRATION'S DISDAIN
FOR NATION-BUILDING

When he first visited Kosovo, President Bush confided to the U.S. commander that his imperative was to extract American forces from the region while Rumsfeld publicly cast the Balkans as an object lesson of a policy gone wrong. Many critics have assailed the administration for lapses in its planning. But it is striking how much of the United States postwar strategy was the product of careful deliberation. The failure to organize a civilian constabulary for immediate duty in Iraq was not an oversight. Rejecting recommendations from officials of the Justice and State departments, senior administration officials decided they would not be needed and decided to rely on the Iraqi law enforcement apparatus. The cost of reconstructing postwar Iraq was assessed at no more than $3 billion, which assumed that Iraq would soon be on its feet and able to pay its own way. Bush received a comprehensive briefing on the postwar plans for Iraq on March 10 and 12, 2003, barely a week before the war.

Without a focused and realistically derived commitment to Iraq's future, the administration's political plan veered wildly from quickly transferring power and employing the Iraqi military to putting off Iraqi rule and formally disbanding the Iraqi armed forces. The disregard for the nation-building efforts of Bush's predecessor was largely an exercise in wishful thinking. The administration convinced itself it could dislodge the regime without doing the hard work of rebuilding a new Iraq or without committing itself to the troop levels that were needed in most other postwar conflicts, as documented in a study prepared for Condoleezza Rice and Steve Hadley by a young Marine on their staff, and by a RAND Corporation report provided to L. Paul Bremer.

The war planning took about eighteen months. The postwar planning began in earnest only a couple of months before the invasion. Bush, Cheney, Rumsfeld, and Tommy Franks spent most of their time and energy on the least demanding task— defeating Saddam's weakened conventional forces—and the least amount on the most demanding—rehabilitation of and security for the new Iraq. The result was a surprising contradiction. The United States did not have nearly enough troops to secure the hundreds of suspected WMD sites that had supposedly been identified in Iraq or to secure the nation's long, porous borders. Had the Iraqis possessed WMD and terrorist groups been prevalent in Iraq as the Bush administration so loudly asserted, U.S. forces might well have failed to prevent the WMD from being spirited out of the country and falling into the hands of the dark forces the administration had declared war against.

In making the case for its preemptive war, the Bush administration made it clear that it was prepared, if need be, to act unilaterally. But the consolidation of the United States's gains assumed that Washington would eventually elicit the cooperation of others: the Iraqis and allied nations that in the main were all too happy to keep their distance from postwar Iraq. There was a disparity of ends and means: the unilateral foreign policy required that others move in later to fill the security and nation-building void. Apart from the British, the "coalition of the willing" much touted by the United States was few in number, hobbled by restrictive rules of engagement that precluded them from launching effective offensive actions, or ill-prepared for the civil affairs requirements needed to stabilize Iraq after the war.

As for the Iraqis, Saddam Hussein's strategy was no more prescient than that of the Americans. Classified interrogations conducted after the war reveal that Saddam and his aides repeatedly dismissed the threat that the American-led forces in Kuwait posed to Baghdad. Saddam viewed Iran as his principal external enemy. The Iraqi leader had initially calculated that he could maintain the ambiguity over his WMD program to deter Iran, his opponents at home, and other adversaries even as he complied with the letter of the U.N. inspection demands. It was a fine line to walk and a misreading of his American adversary. The "deterrence by doubt" strategy encouraged suspicions within the Bush administration that the Iraqi leader really did have something to hide. Having publicly promulgated a doctrine of preemption, the Bush team was not about to be restrained by lack of support at the United Nations.

Saddam's military calculations were similarly deficient. Saddam's formative military crisis was not his lopsided defeat in the 1991 Persian Gulf War, but the sudden Shiite uprising in the south that followed. With preservation of his regime his top priority, Saddam oversaw the development of the Baath Emergency Plan, which called for squelching the sort of uprisings that the Shiites had mounted after the Gulf War. The idea was for the Fedayeen and other militia to contain any uprising long enough for Republican Guard units to arrive and crush the opposition. Saddam assumed that local Baathists would be cut off for a period of time and would have to survive on their own until the army or Republican Guard arrived to rescue them. Each village, town, and city would become a small semi-independent citadel. Fedayeen units would put down local revolts, drawing on caches of light weapons like AK-47s, machine guns, mortars, and RPGs, which would be kept under close guard by the Baathists. Ultimately, the very force designed to counter an insurgency became the regime's stoutest defender and ultimately the core of the insurgency against the Americans.

Saddam's preoccupation with internal security precluded him from taking measures that would have slowed the American advance. The Ring Plan he approved was a stolid positional defense that ceded much of Iraq, and was held in poor regard by his more capable generals; it stood a poor chance of thwarting the Americans. The Iraqi leader refrained from ordering the destruction of bridges early in the war, calculating that he would need them to rush his own forces south to quell a possible uprising. Fearful of the potential for a coup, he prohibited Republican Guard troops from taking up positions inside the capital. Distrustful of his own officer corps, he did not allow contacts among neighboring units. The scenarios that most worried the

Bush administration—the willful destruction of the Iraqi oil-fields and the blowing up of dams—were in fact never planned. Saddam's miscalculations were so great that he never expected to lose the war.

While there are indications that Iraq's intelligence service and other diehards prepared to battle after the regime was toppled, there is no convincing evidence that Saddam anticipated and planned a guerrilla campaign. As the CIA debriefings of captured regime officials made clear, Uday and Qusay were on the run with a meager support network after Baghdad fell while Saddam was apprehended in a spider hole. Saddam was no more far-sighted than the Americans in preparing for the aftermath. But while the Fedayeen were not part of a deliberate plan to carry on a guerrilla war in the event the regime was toppled, it provided much of the wherewithal for an insurgency: thousands of committed fighters, decentralized command and control systems, and massive caches of arms.

The combination of miscalculations on both sides led to an outcome that neither expected. Saddam failed to prevent the fall of the capital, his own capture, and the ascendancy of Shiite and Kurdish groups that he had long suppressed. His supporters were forced to wage a bloody guerrilla war that threatened to tear the country apart and offered no promise of restoring the Iraqi leader to power. The United States's hopes for a lightning victory were quickly dashed and it suffered mounting casualties.

None of this was inevitable. The U.S military commanders who battled their way to Baghdad and endured the long, hot summer of 2003 believe that there was a window of opportunity in the early weeks and months of the invasion, which was allowed to close. Though some degree of opposition was unavoidable, the virulent insurgency that emerged was not inevitable but was aided by military and political blunders in Washington. Having failed to prepare for postcombat burdens, undertaken the war with the minimal acceptable forces, and canceled the deployment of badly needed reinforcements, the Bush administration compounded the problem by disbanding the Iraqi army, putting more than 300,000 armed men on the streets, and denying local elections that would have allowed the Iraqis a measure of control over their own affairs. When it looked like a candidate not to Washington's liking might win in Najaf, Bremer canceled the vote. The difficulties were compounded when Washington installed a new military headquarters and civilian authority that did not work well together and were ill-prepared for their tasks.

As poorly positioned to keep order as the Americans were, many Iraqis at first were thankful for the removal of Saddam's regime or simply too numbed by the rapid turn of events and display of American power to complain. But when order and essential services were not immediately restored, American prestige eroded quickly. There was a chink in the victor's armor. As local Iraqis were quick to note, the Americans could put a man on the moon but could not provide electricity.

The cost to the administration's foreign policy was considerable: instead of sending a cautioning message of American strength to Iran and North Korea, the United States was bogged down in a conflict that absorbed its military efforts. Instead of demonstrating the liberating power of democratic rule, the United States had inadvertently sent a message that the transition to a representative government was fraught with peril. Instead of demonstrating the sort of success that would have attracted allies to send forces to share the burden of occupation, American and British forces found themselves virtually alone.

For all this, the future of Iraq still hangs in the balance. The determination of American forces to fill the void left by the civilian policymakers and to engage the Iraqis, as well as fight the insurgents, has kept alive the hope of an outcome that would justify their sacrifice. The valor and resilience of the Iraqis who have flocked to the polls have also preserved the possibility that a representative government may emerge from the ruins of Saddam's totalitarian Iraq. The price for the American and allied troops, and for the Iraqis themselves, though, was higher than it need have been: chaos, suffering, and a future that is still vexed.

Afterword to the
Vintage Books Edition

Even for a nation accustomed to violence the summer of 2006 marked a disturbing milestone in Iraq. No fewer than 2,625 roadside bombs and other explosive devices were planted in July. It was the highest monthly total since the American-led invasion, double the figure recorded at the start of the year, and a telling indication that the insurgency was stronger than ever.

Three years after the fall of Saddam Hussein, Iraq was an independent nation. It had a new prime minister, a new parliament, and an ambassador to the United Nations. The Iraqi government had the trappings of a sovereign government, including national elections and a ten-division army. But while Iraq's government was officially recognized abroad it faced enormous challenges at home. The Sunni Triangle was still infested with insurgents. Baghdad was rife with militias and death squads. Basra was home to organized crime and squalid fights over the proceeds from the export of Iraqi oil. Crime and corruption simply added to the impression that Iraq had a government that was all but powerless to keep the peace.

Pentagon analysts dubbed the phenomenon the "cycle of violence and insecurity." The debate was no longer whether the United States was winning in Iraq. It was whether the cycle could be broken and a modicum of order established in a country that was likely to be plagued by violence for years to come.

In essence, there were two wars in Iraq: a bitter test of wills with an array of ruthless Sunni-based insurgents and an escalating sectarian struggle in which Shiites and Sunnis fought for control. The parallel conflicts fueled each other, producing a vicious circle of violence. Terrorist attacks against the Shiite majority encouraged the rise of Shiite militias, which in turn carried out their own raids, thus aggravating the fears of Sunnis, who responded by expanding their support, tacit or otherwise, for an insurgency that was as resilient as ever.

The United States, in part, was still paying the price for the shortage of American forces in 2003. The limited number of American troops and the ill-advised decision to dismantle the Iraqi army gave insurgents a chance to catch their breath. The insurgents turned this lapse to their advantage, building support among disillusioned Sunnis and using the reprieve to organize their forces.

Saddam's regime, in fact, had all the tools to mount an insurgency. Iraq was a heavily militarized society that was awash in arms. American intelligence also determined after the fall of Baghdad that the Iraqi Intelligence Service or Mukhabarat, the Special Security Office, and Baath Party militia had established safe houses throughout Iraq prior to the war and filled them with weapons and bomb-making materials. The Mukhabarat had sixteen safe houses in Kirkuk alone, each of which contained bomb-making materials and official documents to enable agents to move around the country. The intent in establishing the safe houses was to wage a counterinsurgency against the Kurds, Shiites, or other groups that might seek to wrest control from the regime in parts of Iraq. While not aimed at the United States, this network provided an infrastructure that the insurgency could use to challenge American occupiers.

Saddam himself was involved in some of the early planning meetings in the summer of 2003. There was a large base of potential supporters to draw on. Including the Special Republican Guard, the only conventional military force to be entrusted with security of the capital, the key security organizations that were intended to protect the regime from internal as well as external threats included no fewer than 110,000 personnel. The security organizations derived much of their personnel from six tribes and eighteen clans; they also provided the initial core of the resistance in a multifaceted insurgency. The nascent insurgency developed a fourfold plan in 2003 to drive out the American occupiers, weaken the Iraqi institutions that had supplanted Saddam's regime locally as well as nationally, and create dissatisfaction with the new order on the part of the Iraqi population while maintaining influence over its Sunni base.

By 2006, there were 20,000 insurgents actively fighting the American and Iraqi forces. A cohort of eighteen- to twenty-five-year-olds provided the foot soldiers while tribal leaders, businessmen, and clerics who had close ties to the old government—what American intelligence calls "regime beneficiaries"—provided much of the leadership, financing, and other backing. The active insurgency was supported by a much larger network of part-time intelligence gatherers, lookouts, couriers, and hosts. Including the broader base of part-time support, some American officials estimated that the insurgency might be as large as 75,000 to 80,000. The head of the Iraqi Intelligence Service, Muhammad Abd Allah al-Shahwani, put the figure higher still, estimating that the number of part-time supporters could exceed 200,000, a fraction of the estimated 26 million Iraqis but still a formidable base for sustaining an insurgency.[1]

About 95 percent of the resistance was made up of Iraqi Sunnis. Long-standing links to foreign terrorist and Islamic groups, however, were also reenergized. Before the American invasion, Saddam had not established an operational alliance with Al Qaeda, according to American intelligence. But Saddam's regime had trained an array of Islamic militants from North Africa and the Middle East, including terrorists from Algeria, Morocco, Sudan, as well as the Palestinians and the Egyptian Islamic Jihad. The aim was to harass some of the Arab regimes that had supported the Americans in the 1991 Persian Gulf War and to keep an eye on extremist groups that might otherwise cause problems in Iraq. It was an example of the old adage that the best way to survive is to keep your friends close, but keep your enemies closer. The secular Baathist regime had also maintained ties with several Muslim religious organizations, such as the Society of Islamic Scholars and the Iraqi Islamic Party, for the same reasons.

As the war approached, Saddam's regime exploited these relationships to bring in Syrian, Palestinian, and other foreign fighters to add to the ranks of the Saddam Fedayeen. After the fall of

Baghdad, these relationships were expanded to strengthen the insurgency. The members of the old regime decided that Islam was a better banner for mobilizing support against the Americans than the restoration of Baath Party power, and a marriage of convenience developed between members of the old order and radical jihadists. Mosques became centers for mobilizing support for the insurgency. Foreign jihadists were also recruited.

American intelligence obtained a window into this network in the fall of 2003 when five suicide bomb attacks were directed at Iraqi police posts. One of the would-be suicide bombers failed to carry out his mission and was captured. He was a Sudanese who had passed through a safe house in Ramadi. When Americans searched the site they found Salafist as well as Baathist literature. The house next door belonged to a former Iraqi major general who was a leader in the Ramadi area in the nationalist insurgency. It was what American intelligence called a "transactional relationship" in which former regime figures enlisted the cooperation of future "martyrs."

For all the debate over force levels in Iraq, the American military never deployed sufficient combat power to establish control throughout the Sunni-dominated areas of Iraq. The Americans had sufficient combat power to operate where they pleased but not enough to stop the insurgents from striking elsewhere or intimidating the population.

The Anbar province, which includes the towns of Ramadi, Fallujah, and Haditha and remains a base for many insurgents, for example, remained an "economy of force" operation. Every time the Americans massed force to put out one fire they created a vacuum elsewhere that the insurgents rushed to fill. When the Marines gathered forces to clear Fallujah in 2004 they drew troops from the Haditha area, where the insurgents promptly moved in and executed the defenseless local police near the town's soccer field, setting back the effort to establish order there. "In our perfect world we could use some more infantrymen to be able to patrol the streets and partner with the Iraqi army," said Lieutenant Colonel Ronald Gridley, executive officer with the Marines' 7th Regimental Combat Team, which had responsibility for a major swath of Anbar Province, including Haditha. Colonel Gridley said that his regiment has told its superiors that it could use a battalion or two of additional troops, but acknowledged that "What we recommend and what we get is going to be two different things."[2]

Nor could the Iraqi army fill the gap. The effort to field the army had been set back by the dismantling of the force. Just finding the troops to man what was intended to be a national institution was a problem. The two Iraqi divisions in Anbar were more than 5,000 troops short of their authorized levels. The Iraqi army's practice of granting generous leaves reduced the day-to-day strength of the division further. As with the old army, each month Iraqi soldiers were granted a week or so leave to deliver their pay to the families, who often live hundreds of miles away, a tradition that reflects the fact that there is not an effective banking system in Iraq. Unlike the old army, the new army was made up entirely of volunteers. After an Iraqi enlisted there was no penalty for going AWOL or dropping out to find another line of work. It was the most volunteer army in the world. With all the dangers, hardships, and problems in receiving pay the soldiers did not always come back.

Factoring in the leaves, the day-to-day strength of the 7th Iraqi Division was about 35 percent of its authorized level during the summer of 2006. The 1st Iraqi Division, which had the responsibility for parts of Fallujah, was at about 50 percent strength. The Shiite-dominated Baghdad government was inclined to ignore the Sunni Anbar Province, and the two divisions were in more difficult shape than other divisions, as they were deployed in remote and dangerous areas. But the two Anbar divisions were not the only ones that were short of personnel. The Iraqi division in the difficult Diyala region was also "challenged" in terms of troop strength, according to senior American officials. Most Iraqi divisions did better and had 85 to 90 percent of the troops they were authorized. Still, when leaves were taken into accounts, even these had 65 to 70 percent strength.[3]

The Iraqi army thus was at best a useful supplement for the United States's military and still far from a force that could sup-

plant the need for American troops. Nor could it effectively protect those Iraqis who cooperated with the United States and the
new Iraqi government from intimidation and assassination, a
prerequisite for any successful counterinsurgency campaign.

The counterinsurgency efforts did not rely entirely on military
factors. A major part of the strategy called for making inroads
with the Sunnis, a group that made up only 20 percent of the
population in Iraq but which had been supporting an insurgency
to thwart the rise of a new order in Iraq. Enlisting the support of
the Sunnis, who had become accustomed to ruling over the Shiites and Kurds, would have been a tall order under the best of circumstances. But security problems and poor planning for the
war's aftermath made the task much harder.

The violence in Iraq seriously hampered the American-
supported effort to rebuild Iraq, an important element in the
effort to create support among the population. According to estimates by the World Bank and L. Paul Bremer's Coalition Provisional Authority in 2003, the four-year cost of rebuilding Iraq
was $55 billion. But these estimates did not take into account the
growing violence in Iraq, which led funds to be reallocated for
security purposes and interfered with the execution of projects to
help Iraqi civilians. By 2006, $34 billion in American funds had
been appropriated for Iraq, 40 percent of which was for training
and equipping the Iraqi security forces. Much of the funding for
civilian purposes had not been spent. Infighting among Iraqi
politicians and the repeated efforts to organize a new government also diverted energies that would have been better spent
trying to meet the needs of the population. Almost 200 state-
owned enterprises remained to be privatized and no legislation
had been prepared to get them up and running.[4]

The failure to quickly establish a true unity government in
Baghdad also played into the insurgents' hands as well by feeding
Sunni resentments. Sunnis voted heavily in the parliamentary
elections in December. The nationwide turnout was more than
70 percent of eligible voters, and more than 50 percent of the
Sunnis voted. During the months it took to form a new Iraqi gov-

ernment, however, Sunnis concluded that it would be dominated by Shiites, and Sunni attitudes began to harden. Forty-three percent of Iraqis who live in the Anbar and Diyala provinces—two Sunni-dominated areas—disapproved of the way Prime Minister Nouri Kamel al-Maliki was handling his job, while only 25 percent approved, according to a June 2006 survey by the International Republican Institute, a nonpartisan group that seeks to support elections and the rule of law abroad. In Ninawa, Salahaddin, and Kirkuk provinces, which also have a high concentration of Sunnis and include Saddam Hussein's base of support in Tikrit, opposition to the Maliki government was even higher. In those areas, 75 percent disapproved of the prime minister's government and only 5 percent approved.[5]

As Sunni skepticism of the new political process grew so did the violence. The number of roadside bombs—or "improvised explosive devices" as they are known by the military—is an especially important indicator of enemy activity. Bomb attacks are the largest killer of American troops. They also require a well-organized network of operatives: a bomb-maker, financiers to pay for the effort, operatives to dig holes in the road, plant the explosives, watch for approaching American and Iraqi forces, and trigger the blast when American and Iraqi forces approach.

According to the count by the American military, 1,454 bombs were planted in January 2006. Of these, 834 exploded, while 620 were found before they went off. As politics in Iraq became more polarized bomb attacks grew. The number of IEDs rose in February, increased again in March, grew some more in April, and expanded in May. According to American military statistics, 2,615 bombs were planted in May, while 2,384 were laid in June. (American officials point out that one reason there was a slight dip in June is that the month has only thirty days.)

The killing of Abu Musab al-Zarqawi in June 2006 deprived the insurgents of one of their most visible leaders. But like the capture of Saddam in December 2003 or the killing of his sons Uday and Qusay in July of that year, Zarqawi's death did not prove to be a turning point. By July, bombings reached another new high with 1,666 explosions and 959 more cases in which bombs were discovered and cleared. This was the largest monthly total and roughly twice as many as were recorded a year earlier. According to military officials in Baghdad, 10 percent of the bombs that exploded targeted civilians, twice the rate from 2005. The percentage of bomb attacks that struck Iraqi security forces increased from 15 percent in January to 20 percent in July 2006. But the vast majority of these bombs struck American or other coalition troops.

"The insurgency has gotten worse by almost all measures with insurgent attacks at historically high levels," a senior Defense Department official said during the difficult summer of 2006. "The insurgency has more public support and is demonstrably more capable in numbers of people active and in its ability to direct violence than at any point in time." According to insurgent messages monitored by American intelligence, their strategy was to bleed the Americans on the assumption that the United States was not prepared to endure repeated attacks in Iraq for more than five to seven years. One year after Vice President Dick Cheney proclaimed that the insurgency was in "its last throes" it was stronger than ever.[6]

In addition to a resilient insurgency, the United States was confronted by the parallel problem of escalating ethnic strife. The February 22, 2006, attack on the Al Askari Mosque in Samarra, which is believed to have been organized by Zarqawi's Al Qaeda of Iraq, stirred up already smoldering sectarian tensions. Shiite militias retaliated against Sunni groups and the internecine fighting escalated. Some of the violence was perpetrated by Iraqi security forces that had been co-opted by Shiite groups. One of the Iraqi organizations that was infiltrated by militias was the Facilities Protection Service, which had some 150,000 members and was established to protect twenty-seven of Iraq's ministries.

The results were felt in Baghdad, which has a mixed Shiite and Sunni population. To improve security, Prime Minister Maliki, who was sworn in on May 20, 2006, announced a plan dubbed "Together Forward" in which the Iraqis would take the lead in securing the capital. It entailed the deployment of some 51,000 troops and police—including 7,200 American soldiers. Even before the plan the Americans were in the process of handing over much of the responsibility for securing the capital to the Iraqis. In mid-June 2005, for example, American troops conducted an average of 360 patrols a day. By the middle of February 2006, the patrols were down to ninety-two a day—a drop of more than 70 percent. By the summer, Iraqi soldiers or police had the lead role in protecting 70 percent of the city, including its most violent neighborhoods, and controlled all of Baghdad's 6,000 checkpoints.[7]

But the spiraling violence illustrated the limitations of the new Iraq security forces, particularly the Iraqi police. No sooner did Maliki outline his plan than the violence reached dangerous proportions. According to Zalmay Khalilzad, the American ambassador to Iraq, there were 558 violent incidents in Baghdad in July 2006, which represented a 10 percent increase over an already large monthly toll. These attacks resulted in 2,100 deaths, and 77 percent of these casualties were the result of sectarian attacks.[8]

Many Iraqis were relocating, spurring fears that much of Iraq might, in effect, become ethnically cleansed with separate Sunni and Shiite enclaves. Sunnis, for example, lined up to get through the checkpoints surrounding Fallujah, a largely Sunni city. The sectarian violence also poised the separate but very real danger that a full-fledged civil war might engulf areas where many Shiites and Sunnis continued to live together: specifically, the Iraqi capital, the "center of gravity" for the broader effort to stabilize the country. Avoiding civil war became an even greater worry to the United States than was the stubborn Sunni-based insurgence, and the surge in the violence forced the United States military to rethink its plans on troop withdrawals.

While the passions in Iraq had a dynamic of their own, the Americans charged that Iran was fueling tensions by supporting Shiite factions in Iraq. Tehran had already intervened in Iraq by providing advanced bomb-making technology—"shaped charges" capable of penetrating the armor on American vehicles—to militant groups in Iraq. Iran's broader goal was to prevent the emergence of a strong and unified Iraq, especially one in which the Sunnis, who once led a bloody eight-year war with Iran, had a major role. Iran also wanted to raise the cost of regime change in

Iraq for the Americans in case the Bush administration had any thoughts about a similar enterprise in Tehran.

The developments prompted the Americans to reverse course and take a more active military role in the capital. The plan was for American and Iraqi troops to cordon off sectors of the city, sweep the area for militia leaders or insurgents, and establish control of Baghdad a neighborhood at a time. After securing an area, Iraqi police (with American advisers) would be sent in to maintain control, and American and Iraqi funds would be spent to improve basic services such as medical care and trash removal and to create jobs, especially among young Iraqis, who have frequently been recruited by the insurgency and sectarian militias. All told, $500 million in Iraqi funds and at least $130 million in American funds was budgeted for this effort. In effect, the scheme was a version of the "inkblot" counterinsurgency strategy of grabbing a piece of terrain, stabilizing it, and gradually expanding it. Only this time the objective was not a far-flung Iraqi city or town, but the capital, the seat of the fledgling government and home to some seven million Iraqis. "Baghdad is truly a must-win," said Major General William B. Caldwell IV, the senior spokesman for the American-led military command in Iraq. "We have to win in Baghdad. We don't have an option."

To carry out the plan, the United States committed the remainder of its military reserve in Kuwait. (Much of that reserve force was already involved in the fight to reclaim control of Ramadi.) It also diverted military police companies to Baghdad that had been earmarked for duty in Anbar. And it dispatched Army units equipped with Stryker vehicles from northern and western Iraq to the capital. The end result was an operation that by October 2006 involved about 25,200 troops, some 15,600 of whom were American, as well as more than 30,000 Iraqi police. It was a conscious strategy to assume greater risk in regions already overflowing with violence in order to improve security in the Iraqi capital.

While the violence in Anbar and Baghdad received much attention, even some relatively quiet areas gave reason for concern. Three years after the fall of Saddam Hussein's Baathist regime in Baghdad, Iraqi Kurdistan had emerged as the most stable sector of the country. Already semiautonomous as the result of the

American no-fly-zone protection after the 1991 war, the oil-rich region enjoyed a large measure of self-rule, even flying a Kurdish rather than an Iraqi flag at some locations, as the national flag was considered "Saddamist."

The two traditional rival parties, the Patriotic Union of Kurdistan (PUK) and the Kurdistan Democratic Party (KDP) were formally at peace. Massoud Barzani, head of the KDP and president of the Kurdish Regional Government (KRG) in Irbil, and Jalal Talabani, founder of the PUK and president of Iraq in Baghdad, were both officially committed to a unified pluralistic Iraq, a pledge they reaffirmed to the White House. A Kurdish Regional Assembly was elected in 2005, but the Kurds also held seats in the national unity government parliament. While the Kurds maintained a 100,000-man militia that had been effective against the Iraqi army during the war, they sanctioned the participation of Peshmerga in the national security forces.

Yet despite this stability, ethnic tensions were simmering here as well. The Kurdish enclave in northern Iraq had become a sanctuary for some 40,000 refugees of all persuasions from the sectarian violence elsewhere in Iraq. Meanwhile, the "Arabization" of Kirkuk—begun in the 1980s by Saddam Hussein, who forcibly replaced Kurds with Sunni Arabs to ensure his control of the region's oil reserves—had reversed after the war as thousands of Kurds returned to the area to reclaim their homes. This led to armed clashes between Sunnis and Kurds. Although the scale of violence did not match that of central Iraq, Kirkuk, Mosul, and Sulaymaniyah were frequent targets of terrorist bombings.

The most serious threat to stability in the Kurdish region, however, was not internal. It came from its neighbors, Turkey and Iran. Both nations had significant Kurdish minorities with aspirations of Kurdish independence, and Ankara and Tehran remained fearful that Kurdish autonomy in Iraq would ignite a pan-independence movement throughout the region. After the fall of Saddam's regime, tensions increased and local clashes occurred along the shared borders. The 5,000-man military wing of the terrorist Kurdistan Workers Party (PKK) and its Iranian counterpart, PJAK, sequestered in the rugged Qandil Mountains of northeastern Iraq, conducted cross border raids into Turkey.

This prompted little-publicized Turkish and Iranian retaliatory artillery and air strikes on the guerrilla hideouts in Iraq. The Bush administration cautioned Turkey against any overt action against Iraqi Kurdistan and appointed former NATO commander General Joseph Ralston special coordinator to Ankara to deal with the PKK problem. The fragile equilibrium in the north was endangered by the possible colllapse of the national unity government in Baghdad and an ensuing civil war.

The difficult realities on the ground raised questions about the United States's strategy. In March 2006, President Bush reaffirmed his "strategy for victory" in Iraq. The president cited the 2005 attack to retake Tal Afar, the largest city in Ninawa Province. Instead of clearing the city and then moving out only to let the insurgents and terrorists return, as they had done in the past, Bush said that the United States had left well-trained Iraqi soldiers behind to secure the city and allow reconstruction, an approach he called "clear, hold, and build."

If that indeed was the approach it was being applied selectively. With limited American forces to do any clearing, an uncertain Iraqi force to do the holding, and an Iraqi government that was having difficulty delivering needed programs and services to its citizens, the strategy looked more like "hang on and hand over." Hang on against an insurgency that seems to be laying roadside bombs as quickly as they are discovered, and hand over to an Iraqi military that is still a work in progress.

Indeed, as the violence was growing in Iraq in 2006, General George Casey, the top American commander, developed a plan that called for a steady reduction in American forces, presenting it at the White House and the Pentagon in June 2006. Casey divided the future American role in Iraq into three phases. The first twelve months were described as a period of stabilization. The period from the summer of 2007 through the summer of 2008 would focus on the restoration of the Iraqi government's authority. During the period from the summer of 2008 though the summer of 2009 the Iraqi government would supposedly become increasingly self-reliant.

In line with this vision, Casey envisioned that troop cuts might begin soon. The United States had fourteen combat brigades in Iraq, each of which numbers about 3,500 soldiers, plus many other support troops. Under the plan, the United States would shrink this force to twelve combat brigades in September. A combat brigade would be kept on alert in Kuwait or elsewhere in case American commanders needed to augment their forces to deal with a crisis. Another brigade would be kept on a lesser state of alert elsewhere in the world, but still prepared to deploy quickly. As a result, the plan was called 12-1-1.

By December the number of American combat brigades in Iraq would be in the range of ten to twelve. They could be further reduced to seven to eight combat brigades by June 2007 and finally to five to six by December 2007. At the same time, the number of bases in Iraq would decline as American forces consolidated. By the end of the year the number of bases would shrink to fifty-seven from the current sixty-nine. By June 2007, there would be thirty bases, and by December 2007 there would be only eleven. By the end of 2007, the United States would have three principal regional military commands: in Baghdad and the surrounding area, in Anbar Province and the west, and in northern Iraq.

The plan depended on the development of competent Iraqi security forces, a reduction in Sunni Arab hostility toward the new Iraqi government, and the assumption that the insurgency would not expand beyond Iraq's six central provinces. Within a month it had been overtaken by events, and the plan to reduce the combat brigades was temporarily suspended. By October 2006, the total number of American forces in Iraq had grown to 142,000 from a level of 125,000 in June.[9]

By the summer of 2006 the United States was caught in the middle of an internecine struggle for power over which it had limited influence. A case could be made for sending substantially more troops to work alongside the Iraqi forces, but there was little political support in Washington for upping the ante. With midterm elections in the fall of 2006 and a presidential contest approaching in 2008, neither the Republicans nor the Democrats were talking seriously about adding forces in Iraq. Rather, the politics centered on the pace and timing of force reductions.

Dividing Iraq into disparate Sunni, Shiite, and Kurdish enclaves under a highly decentralized Iraqi government was another option. The United States policy was to maintain a unified Iraq but some Americans argued that a divided nation needed to be on the policy horizon. Indeed, many Iraqis already were—in effect—creating ethnically separate zones as they fled the sectarian strife. Still, public opinion surveys showed that most Iraqis preferred a unitary state, though they had very different ideas of who should be in control of that state. Some prominent areas—Baghdad in particular—were home to Sunnis and Shiites alike and would be very difficult to divide. A big problem was that many Sunnis did not trust the Shia-dominated government to share oil revenues fairly under a decentralized power-sharing arrangement.

Withdrawing in the face of civil strife was another possibility, but one that seemed likely to remove the remaining constraints against a full-fledged internecine conflict. Having taking the lid off Pandora's box in Iraq it seemed cynical to leave the Iraqis to their fate.

Substantially increasing American forces in Iraq was another possibility. Yet, having failed to significantly expand American ground forces soon after the fall of Baghdad—only a 30,000 increase in Army troops strength was authorized—this option was problematic. In theory, the United States could build up its military presence in Iraq by extending the combat tours of forces already deployed and reallocating the Pentagon budget to increase the military's end strength. That would enable the United States to work in concert with an expanding Iraqi security force to beat back the insurgents and militia and protect the populace, a key objective in any successful counterinsurgency strategy. But the Bush administration seemed to have little interest in assuming the political and financial burden of such an approach.

That left Washington's basic approach: progressively build up Iraq's security forces, encourage the Iraqi government's efforts to improve the capacity of its ministries to take care of the needs of its own citizens, and gradually reduce the number of American troops in Iraq. This was a prescription for a long struggle, albeit at somewhat reduced cost, and a far cry from the in-and-out victory the Bush administration had once hoped to achieve. It was a sign of the difficulties that by 2006 the fulfillment of this pared-back series of goals would appear to be a major victory.

The American plan for reducing its forces in Iraq was premised on the establishment of effective Iraqi security forces, the minimization and containment of the insurgency, a well-managed campaign to win over the public by reconstruction and restoring services, and the securing of borders to limit the influence of external players. To the degree these goals were met, U.S. forces could be proportionately reduced. However, the conditions were not being met midway through 2006. Notwithstanding some relatively quiet sectors, the overall situation had deteriorated.

The hoped-for unity government was fracturing along ethnic and sectarian lines with Sunnis, Shiites, and Kurds advancing their own agendas. Sectarian militias and criminal groups were running wild. Efforts to put the country's economy back in working order were crippled by insurgent attacks, looting, and corruption. The Iraqi army had made only marginal gains against the insurgency and the police were not only ineffective, but often untrustworthy.

As of November 2006, the toll has been higher than the Bush administration ever imagined. It has involved the loss of more than 2,800 American lives and the wounding of more than 21,000 American troops. More than 200 British and other coalition personnel have been killed, as well as hundreds injured. There have been tens of thousands of Iraqi casualties. And yet, despite these costs, more than ever, the future of Iraq hangs in the balance.

Acknowledgments

This book is heavily indebted to the soldiers, Marines, airmen, and sailors, of all ranks and stripes, who fought in the conflict and met with us over the past three years. They spent hours telling their story, gave us access to their personal diaries and after-action reports. They were generous with their time and never asked anything in return other than our best effort to get the story right.

We owe a special thanks to David McKiernan's Coalition Forces Land Component Command, where Michael Gordon was embedded as a reporter for the *New York Times* during the war. McKiernan's staff there gave him extraordinary access and spent many months afterward answering questions about the complex events. Terry Moran, William Webster, James "Spider" Marks, J. D. Thurman, Robert "Rusty" Blackman, Kevin Benson, Albert Whitley, and Daniel Leaf were among the many who provided valuable insights during the war. Rick Thomas, Gregory Julian, and Dave Connolly provided public affairs support.

We are also grateful to Scott Wallace's V Corps, which granted interviews with key participants before, during, and after the invasion. Buford Blount's 3rd Infantry Division was particularly helpful. When the division sought to document its fights, it allowed Gordon to participate in the effort and visit the battlefields with the very soldiers who fought in the engagements. It was a unique opportunity to meet the participants and understand the clashes when memories were fresh right after the war.

All of the division's brigades and their commanders were extremely helpful, but a special appreciation must be extended to David Perkins's 2nd BCT, which allowed Gordon to live with its battalions in Baghdad and Fallujah. Rock Marcone's 3-69 Armored Battalion also allowed Gordon to visit briefly in Baghdad, and Terry Ferrell's 3-7 Cavalry Squadron facilitated interviews there. David Petraeus's 101st Airborne Division hosted Gordon after it moved to Mosul and other points north, and James Mattis's 1st Marine Division hosted him in Hillah. Timothy Keating was most helpful during visits to his naval headquarters in Bahrain and later at the Pentagon. Robin Brims and his able deputy Chris Vernon met with Gordon at the British headquarters in Kuwait before the war and Gordon was also able to speak with senior British officers during and after the capture of Basra.

In the United States, we traveled extensively to meet with a large variety of military units to fill in the story. The trips took us to Camp Lejeune to interview Richard Natonski's Task Force Tarawa Marines and Camp Pendleton and Twenty-nine Palms to interview Marines of Mattis's division. We visited Miramar Air Station to meet with Marine aviators from James "Tamer" Amos's 3rd Air Wing and Fort Hood to talk to some of the officers of the 4th Infantry Division, which Raymond Odierno had handed off to J. D. Thurman. At Fort Hood, we also interviewed the aircrews with Dan Ball's 1-227 Apache squadron. Special Operations Forces explained their war to us.

Our research also took us to CENTCOM's headquarters in Tampa, the Joint Forces Command near Norfolk, and Nellis Air Force Base, where T. Michael "Buzz" Moseley allowed Gordon to sit in on an internal briefing on the air war. We are also grateful to the assistance provided by officers from Moseley's Combined Forces Air Operations Center, which oversaw the air war, and to some of the F-117 pilots and aircrews who helped with our account.

The military's war colleges also allowed us to interview students and staff who fought in the war and, on occasion, consult their archives. Thanks to the Army War College at Carlisle Barracks, Pennsylvania; the Army Command and General Staff College at Fort Leavenworth, Kansas; the Naval War College in Newport, Rhode Island, and the Air War College at Maxwell Air Force Base in Alabama; and the Marine Corps Command and Staff College at Quantico, Virginia.

The services' historical centers were most helpful and allowed us to consult the work done by their industrious field attachments. Thanks to Frank R. Shirer of the U.S. Army Center of Military History and Vicki Hester, Fort Stewart Museum Historian. We would also like to extend our appreciation to Chuck Melson of the U.S. Marine Corps Historical Center. Gregory Fontenot and E. J. Degen, co-authors of the Army's official history of the conflict, *On Point,* were most helpful.

At the Pentagon, we were granted interviews with virtually all of the Joint Chiefs of Staff, as well as key members of the Joint Staff. Current and former Army, Navy, Marine, and Air Force officers patiently explained important decisions. Senior Defense Department officials made themselves available, including Paul Wolfowitz and Douglas Feith and his staff.

Thanks must also be extended to Condoleezza Rice and other White House officials who agreed to interviews on the war planning as part of a *New York Times* series that served as a foundation for some of our chapters, and to Richard Armitage and other senior State Department officials. Paul Pillar, formerly of the CIA, and other intelligence officials also provided their perspective.

Jay Garner, Paul Hughes, and other key members of the Office for Reconstruction and Humanitarian Assistance team were readily accessible. L. Paul Bremer and members of the Coalition Provisional Authority were helpful during their tour of duty in Baghdad. Rick Sanchez gave a *New York Times* interview to Gordon during his Baghdad tour, which was useful for this book.

Many of our important contacts cannot be openly thanked because of the documents and sensitive information they provided, information they believed should be made public to fill in the record of the war and enlighten the public on how the campaign in Iraq was actually planned and fought.

Some government and military officials chose not to cooperate. Secretary of Defense Donald Rumsfeld turned down a long-standing interview request. General Tommy Franks gave an hourlong interview in the fall of 2004 for a *New York Times* article on the postwar planning, much of which is drawn on in the book. But he did not agree to a follow-up session to go over issues in depth despite repeated requests. Vice President Dick

Cheney also declined to be interviewed, a decision we were told was made after consultation with his then chief of staff, Scooter Libby.

This book would not have been possible without the support of the Center for Strategic and International Studies, where Gordon was a writer-in-residence from the fall of 2003 to the spring of 2005. John Hamre, the president of CSIS, and Kurt Campbell, a CSIS senior vice president and director of its international security program, were most supportive. Bruce Blair, the president of the World Security Institute, was also instrumental to the completion of the book. The institute named Gordon as its distinguished media fellow through the balance of 2005.

Jeremiah Cushman and Christopher Mann, our dedicated and talented research assistants, were indispensable. They scoured military archives, reviewed many hours of transcribed interviews, sifted through hundreds of documents, carried out vital research, and reviewed the book text. We were also aided by a variety of interns, including Mike Alpern, Tom Hommel, Sam King, Milady Ortiz, and Michael Petillo. Eric Schmitt, John Burns, and other members of the *New York Times* staff offered their insights. David Rampe, assistant foreign editor at the *Times*, read through the early drafts and provided helpful recommendations. Elisabeth Bumiller was an able guide to the White House.

Andrew Wylie, our erudite agent, guided us through the publishing world. Erroll McDonald, our patient publishing executive, had numerous perceptive and important suggestions as to how to improve the telling of a very complicated tale. Fred Chase, our keen-eyed copy editor, worked assiduously on the text. Joyce Pendola, our talented cartographer, prepared the maps. Thanks also to Pantheon's diligent production team: Peter Andersen, Lydia Buechler, Archie Ferguson, Avery Flück, Wesley Gott, Andy Hughes, Altie Karper, Maria Massey, and Robin Reardon.

Our heartfelt appreciation to many others, too numerous to name, who also helped us tell the inside story of the Iraq War.

Notes

CHAPTER 1: *Snowflakes from the Secretary*

1. Central Command, or CENTCOM, is the U.S. combat command assigned responsibility and authority for U.S. military operations in the Middle East.
2. Interview, Lieutenant General Gregory S. Newbold (Ret).
3. George W. Bush, "A Period of Consequences," 23 September 1999, the Citadel, available from http://citadel.edu/r3/pao/addresses/pres_bush.html, accessed 1 November 2005. Richard Armitage, who later served as deputy secretary of state under Colin Powell, drafted much of the text.
4. Interview, former Pentagon official. Also see James Mann, *Rise of the Vulcans* (New York: Viking, 2004), pp. x–xiii, and Midge Decter, *Rumsfeld: A Personal Portrait* (New York: Regan Books/Harper-Collins, 2003), for accounts of Rumsfeld's career.
5. Interview, former senior military officer.
6. Interview, former senior official.
7. Quadrennial Defense Review Report, 30 September 2001.

   > For the United States, the revolution in military affairs holds the potential to confer enormous advantages and to extend the current period of U.S. military superiority. . . . Moving to a capabilities-based force also requires the United States to focus on emerging opportunities that certain capabilities, including advanced remote sensing, long-range precision strike, transformed maneuver and expeditionary forces and systems, to overcome anti-access and area denial threats, can confer on the U.S. military over time.

8. Interview, Douglas Macgregor.
9. Dick Cheney, "Defense Strategy for the 1990s: The Regional Defense Strategy," DOD publication, January 1993.
10. Quadrennial Defense Review Report, 30 September 2001.
11. Interview, Tom White.
12. Donald Rumsfeld, "Bureaucracy to Battlefield," speech, 10 September 2001, available from http://www.defenselink.mil/speeches/2001/s20010910-secdef.html, accessed 1 November 2005.
13. Interview, Douglas Feith.

14. Thomas Kean et al., *The 9/11 Commission Report* (New York: Norton, 2004), pp. 559–60; Interview, Douglas Feith.

15. Letter to the authors from former President George H. W. Bush, as published in Michael R. Gordon and Lieutenant General (Ret.) Bernard E. Trainor, *The Generals' War* (New York: Little, Brown, 1995), p. 517.

16. The cease-fire arrangements agreed on at the March 1991 talks at Safwan also inadvertently gave the regime a badly needed boost. When the Iraqi generals complained that their bridges had been bombed and asked H. Norman Schwarzkopf, the chief allied commander, for the right to fly helicopters throughout southern Iraq, Schwarzkopf agreed. The Iraqi commanders quickly exploited the concession to mount ferocious helicopter attacks on the Shiites—including, American intelligence learned more than a decade later, with chemical weapons—prompting Schwarzkopf to complain that he had been duped. At the forward headquarters of the Third Army, Brigadier General Steve Arnold, the command's chief operations officer, drew up a top secret contingency plan to march on the Iraqi capital and dislodge Saddam, which he dubbed fittingly enough "The Road to Baghdad." Concerned that Saddam had survived the Desert Storm campaign and anxious to create problems for him at home, the Saudis proposed a covert program to arm the Shiite rebels during a visit to Riyadh by Secretary of State James Baker and a team of Bush officials. "The Road to Baghdad" plan, in possession of the authors.

17. Gordon and Trainor, *The Generals' War,* pp. 455–56.

18. Interview, Brent Scowcroft.

19. Wayne Downing, "An Alternative Strategy for Iraq" plan, in possession of the authors. It called for assembling a core of 300 to 500 Iraqi expatriates with military experience, which would be trained in the U.S. In addition, a 2,000- to 10,000-man force would be recruited and transported to a base in the Middle East. Two special units would be formed, including a 200-man Commando Company trained for raids and ambushes and strike operations, and a 150-man vehicle Anti-Tank Company armed with medium- and long-range antitank missiles.

20. William J. Clinton, "The Iraq Liberation Act," statement by the president, 31 October 1998, available from http://www.library.cornell.edu/colldev/mideast/libera.htm, accessed 28 October 2005.

21. Alfred B. Prados, "Iraqi Challenges and U.S. Military Responses: March 1991 Through October 31, 1998," *CRS Report for Congress,* 20 November 2002.

22. Interview, former Pentagon official.

23. Interview, former Clinton aide.

24. Interview, former Pentagon official; George W. Bush, "Remarks by the President to the American Troops in Kosovo," 24 July 2001, available

from http://www.whitehouse.gov/news/releases/2001/07/20010724-1 .html; David E. Sanger, "Bush, in Kosovo, Tells U.S. Troops Role Is Essential," *New York Times*, 25 July 2001, Section A, p. 1.

25. Interview, former member of the Joint Staff.

Wolfowitz was influenced by the views of Laurie Mylroie, who argued that the 1993 attack was an Iraqi plot. As dean of the Johns Hopkins School of Advanced International Studies, a post he held after leaving the administration of George H. W. Bush, Wolfowitz informally looked into the matter. See Laurie Mylroie, *The War Against America: Saddam Hussein and the World Trade Center Attacks: A Study of Revenge* (New York: Regan Books/HarperCollins, 2001).

26. Interviews, former Joint Staff officials.

27. Interview, Lieutenant General Gregory S. Newbold.

28. Saddam Hussein, "Open letter from Saddam Hussein to the American peoples and the western peoples and their governments," 15 September 2001, available from http://www.everything2.com/index .pl?node_id=1172306, accessed 20 October 2005. The second letter is available from http://web.archive.org/web/20010922151907/www .uruklink.net/iraqnews/enews12.htm.

> We say to the American peoples, what happened on September 11, 2001, should be compared to what their government and their armies are doing in the world, for example, the international agencies have stated that more than one million and a half Iraqis have died because of the blockade imposed by America and some Western countries, in addition to the tens of thousands who died or are injured in the military action perpetrated by America along with those who allied with it against Iraq. Hundreds of bridges, churches, mosques, colleges, schools, factories, palaces, hotels, and thousands of private houses were destroyed or damaged by the American and Western bombardment, which is ongoing even today against Iraq. . . . There is, however, one difference, namely that those who direct their missiles and bombs to the targets, whether Americans or from another Western country, are mostly targeting by remote controls, that is why they do so as if they were playing an amusing game. As for those who acted on September 11, 2001, they did it from a close range, and with, I imagine, giving their lives willingly, with an irrevocable determination. . . . Americans should feel the pain they have inflicted on other peoples of the world, so as when they suffer, they will find the right solution and the right path. . . . America needs wisdom, not power. It has used power, along with the West, to its extreme extent, only to find out later that it doesn't achieve what they wanted. Will the rulers of America try wisdom just for once so that their people can live in security and stability?

29. Interview, senior official.
30. Interview, former senior official.
31. Kean et al., *The 9/11 Commission Report,* 2004, p. 335.
32. Interview, Francis Brooke.
33. Interview, Lieutenant Colonel Charles Danna.
34. Interview, Lieutenant Colonel Chuck Eassa.
35. Review of Rumsfeld's talking points by the authors.

CHAPTER 2: *The Generated Start*

1. Tommy Franks, *American Soldier* (New York: Regan Books/Harper-Collins, 2004).
2. Interview, former aide.
3. Interview, Newt Gingrich.
4. Interview, General Anthony Zinni (Ret.).
5. Even after Clinton signed legislation giving him the authority to train and equip the INC, Zinni declared that the idea was a prescription for disaster. Invoking memories of the failed, CIA-sponsored Bay of Pigs invasion of Cuba, Zinni predicted it would lead to a "Bay of Goats" incited by Ahmed Chalabi's "Gucci Guerrillas." The comments sparked angry complaints from the Republican supporters of the plan, most notably John McCain, who, in a sharp exchange with Zinni, complained that the CENTCOM commander was not following the law. Zinni did little to defuse the confrontation by telling the senator that the Iraq Liberation Act had not revoked his constitutional right of free speech and that his responsibility as a commander was to call the shots as he saw them. The exchange upset the White House, which thought it had managed to finesse a potent political issue. JCS Chairman General Hugh Shelton, who agreed wholeheartedly with Zinni, later called him to say he had been asked by the White House to reprimand the CENTCOM commander. Shelton dryly told Zinni that he should consider himself chewed out.
6. Interview, General Anthony Zinni (Ret.).
7. Ibid. "Desert Crossing Seminar, After Action Report, June 28–30, 1999." A declassified version of the still secret report was obtained by the authors through the Freedom of Information Act. In keeping with the prevailing intelligence at the time there was also a discussion on how to respond if weapons of mass destruction were used against American personnel or by one faction against another within Iraq.

   There was discussion prior to the war game on what to call the exercise. Under the original plan the code name was "Desert Resolve." After a discussion among military intelligence officers, the name was changed to "Desert Crossing." They noted that the Arabic term "Aboor" ("crossing" in English) was used by Saddam Hussein and his aides to suggest that Iraq was in the process of crossing from a troubled period to better times. The thinking, as one internal 1998 memo from an intelligence officer noted, was that if the title of the exercise leaked it would add to the psychological pressure on the regime. "By co-opting the term, we would deliver a frightening and ominous message to regime supporters and a heartening sign to regime opponents," the memo noted. The memo also noted that the name might be interpreted by the Iraqis as implying that the United States was planning "another left hook through the desert areas west of Kuwait and the Tigris-Euphrates river valleys" when CENTCOM's invasion plan, in fact, called for moving primarily "up the fertile valley plain around Highway 8." Thus, the name would add to the American deception plan if force was used.

8. Plan details provided by former CENTCOM officials.
9. Interview, Lieutenant Colonel John Agoglia.
10. Interview, former CENTCOM official.
11. Franks, *American Soldier,* p. 198.
12. Ibid., pp. 346–56; Interview, former CENTCOM official.
13. Interviews, former CENTCOM officials.
14. Interview, Douglas Macgregor. The briefing provided to Rumsfeld was entitled "Transforming the Way America Fights," and contained the following slide:

What the Enemy Does Not Expect
   - The enemy does not expect a swift, sudden ground attack without warning that begins without air or missile strikes.
   - The enemy does not expect the United States to attack with a ground combat force of fewer than 100,000 troops.
   - The enemy does not expect a ground attack aimed directly at Baghdad and its oil fields.
   - The enemy does not expect US forces to rapidly "lean into" potential WMD fires making their use very unlikely.
   - The enemy does not expect the United States to act without prior international sanction.

   Therefore, that is exactly what the United States must do to swiftly remove the Iraqi regime.

15. Interview, Douglas Macgregor.
16. Franks was sent a summary of James P. Wade's "Rapid Dominance Concept," a strategy "based on four core characteristics—'total' knowledge, rapidity, brilliance in execution, and control of the environment." Also included was an article by retired Air Force General Charles Horner, who oversaw the air campaign during the 1991 Persian Gulf War. It was entitled "How and Where to Apply Shock and Awe." This six-page paper cited historical examples as far back as Genghis Khan and concluded with the passage, "In the end, if we are

going to lead then we must be considered the madmen of the world, capable of any action, willing to risk anything to achieve our national interests. It is only our ends that must be admired, if we seek to be loved then our capacity to act will be weak, as our threat will not be credible. If we are to achieve noble purposes we must be prepared to act in the most ignoble manner."

17. President George W. Bush, "State of the Union" speech, 29 January 2002, available from http://www.whitehouse.gov/news/releases/2002/01/20020129-11.html, accessed 1 November 2005.
18. Interview, CENTCOM official.

CHAPTER 3: *Smaller Is Beautiful*

1. Franks, *American Soldier,* pp. 372–73; Interview, former CENTCOM official.
2. Interviews, former State Department officials.
3. Interview, Dick Cheney, 1991.
4. Interviews, officials on trip and U.S. diplomats. Also see Michael R. Gordon, "Cheney, in London, Receives Strong Support from Blair on Tough Stance Against Iraq," *New York Times,* 12 March 2002, Section A, p. 14; Michael R. Gordon, "Saudis Warn Against Attack on Iraq by the United States," *New York Times,* 17 March 2002, Section A, p. 16; Michael R. Gordon, "Cheney, in Jordan, Meets Opposition to Military Move in Iraq," *New York Times,* 13 March 2002, Section A, p. 12; Michael R. Gordon, "U.S. Offers Aid to Turkey to Lead Kabul Force," *New York Times,* 20 March 2002, Section A, p. 14; Michael R. Gordon, "Cheney Asks Yemen to Join the Pursuit of Al Qaeda's Remnants," *New York Times,* 15 March 2002, Section A, p. 10; Michael R. Gordon, "Cheney Says Next Goal in U.S. War on Terror Is to Block Access to Arms," *New York Times,* 16 March 2002, Section A, p. 8.
5. Interview, former CENTCOM official.
6. Interview, meeting participant.
7. Notes of a participant. A war game presentation at the Component Commanders' Conference, 23 March 2002, Ramstein, Germany, recommended a "near simultaneous" air and ground campaign. That is, one in which the air and ground action would be separated by twenty-four to sixty hours. But it noted that Moseley did not concur. It also noted that the summer months would reduce the ability to wage war. It supported the idea of attacking from Turkey if the air- and sea-lift could be worked out. It reported "no major holes in current plan."
8. Notes of a participant of the CENTCOM meeting.
9. John McCain, Senate Armed Services Committee hearing, 23 September 2004. After listening to Rumsfeld, McCain said: "I don't need

General Myers' response. I know it will be exactly the same as yours. I would like the personal opinions—I would—and I don't mean that as in any way a criticism, General Myers. I would like the personal opinions of the other CINCs, if I could, since my time has expired."

10. Franks, *American Soldier,* p. 277; Interviews, former members of the Joint Chiefs of Staff.

11. Interview, General John Jumper.

12. Interviews, former CENTCOM officials.

13. Notes of a participant.

14. Interview, former CENTCOM planner.

15. Interview, former CENTCOM official.

16. White House transcripts: "President Bush Meets with German Chancellor Schroeder," 23 May 2002, available from http://www.whitehouse .gov/news/releases/2002/05/20020523-1.html, and "President Bush Meets with French President Chirac," 26 May 2002, available from http:// www.whitehouse.gov/news/releases/2002/05/20020526-2.html. Bush made a similar comment to a reporter from ITN, the British television channel, on April 4. See "Interview of the President by Sir Trevor McDonald of Britain's ITV Television Network," available from http://www.usembassy.it/file2002_04/alia/a2040709.htm.

17. DOD news briefing transcript, CENTCOM CINC General Tommy Franks, Tuesday, 21 May 2002, available from http://www.globalsecurity .org/military/library/news/2002/05/mil-020521-dod01b.htm.

18. Notes of a participant.

19. Interview, former member of the Joint Staff.

20. No reliable census had been carried out for years. The Iraqi population was estimated variously at 24 to 25 million.

21. "Iraq: Prime Minister's Meeting, 23 July," memorandum prepared by Matthew Rycroft, a Downing Street policy aide, 1 May 2005, available from http://www.timesonline.co.uk/article/0,,2087-1593607,00.html.

CHAPTER 4: *The Other Side of the Hill*

1. "Comprehensive Report of the Special Advisor to the Central Intelligence on Iraq's WMD, with Addendums (Duelfer Report)," vol. 1, Regime Strategic Intent, 30 September 2004, p. 25.

2. "U.S. Joint Forces Command Combat Study: Iraqi Perspectives on Operation Iraqi Freedom Major Combat Operations," classified "secret." Reviewed by the authors. Much of the research was done for JFCOM by the Institute for Defense Analyses, a Pentagon-funded research center. The study also had the support of the CIA, the Defense Intelligence Agency, and the Iraq Survey Group, a panel that studied Iraq's WMD programs and efforts, and CJTF-7, the U.S.-led military command in Iraq.

3. Visit to Babylon by Michael Gordon.
4. "Comprehensive Report," vol. 1, pp. 11–12, 19, 72; Interview, intelligence official.

    Reports that Saddam made extensive use of doubles, so prevalent in the West, however, were a myth, U.S. officials determined from their interrogations with the Iraqi hierarchy after the war. Saddam did not use doubles, perhaps because it introduced the potential for mischief by would-be coup plotters.
5. JFCOM briefing.
6. "Iraqi Perspectives," pp. 10, 26, 34.

    While Saddam seems to have understood that those around him actively distorted their views to please him, after 1998 he became increasingly reclusive and less inclined to personally verify claims made by subordinates. Grossly exaggerated assessments were left unchecked, and few among Saddam's closest confidants risked bringing the dictator bad news.
7. Ibid., p. 36.
8. Ibid., p. 26.
9. JFCOM briefing; "Iraqi Perspectives," p. 10.
10. JFCOM briefing.
11. JFCOM briefing.
12. George W. Bush, graduation speech at West Point, 1 June 2002, available from http://www.whitehouse.gov/news/releases/2002/06/20020601-3.html, accessed 1 November 2005.
13. "Excerpts from Pentagon's Plan: 'Prevent the Re-emergence of a New Rival,'" *New York Times,* 8 March 1992, Section A, p. 14.
14. The National Security Strategy of the United States, September 2002, available from http://www.whitehouse.gov/nsc/nss.html, accessed 1 November 2005; Michael R. Gordon, "In Bush's 'Axis of Evil,' Why Iraq Stands Out," *New York Times,* 9 September 2002, Section A, p. 8; Interview, senior administration official.
15. George W. Bush, "President Salutes Troops of the 10th Mountain Division," 19 July 2002, available from http://www.whitehouse.gov/news/releases/2002/07/20020719.html, accessed 1 November 2005.
16. "Iraqi Perspectives," p. 29; Interview, intelligence official.
17. Comprehensive Report," vol. 1, p. 25.

    With sixteen of Iraq's eighteen provinces in open revolt, the Iraqi regime felt the urgent need to rapidly overpower the growing resistance movement. Husayn Kamil, head of a key military ministry and personal confidant to Saddam Hussein, first ordered a strike on rebel positions at Najaf using VX liquid. When the oily nerve agent could not be found, Kamil instructed subordinates to use mustard gas instead. This option was also ruled out, however, after Iraqi commanders considered the high risk of detection by coalition forces. Another substitute would have to be found.

In early March 1991, roughly a dozen Iraqi Mi-8 helicopters loaded with Sarin nerve gas launched from Tamuz air base and began a series of chemical strikes against rebel Shiite positions in the Karbala region. The attacks were judged to be ineffective—probably due to improper delivery—but the regime did not abandon its efforts to dislodge insurgents with chemical weapons. Several hundred more aerial bombs filled with CS (tear gas) fell on Karbala and Najaf over the following weeks. Anecdotal reports gathered from Iraqis fleeing the country after the Gulf War also described a variety of chemical strikes executed against Basra and Nasiriyah.

18. "Comprehensive Report," vol. 1, p. 58. Evidence suggests these resolutions were never implemented, and it remains a mystery what Saddam's real motivation in passing them had been.

19. JFCOM briefing.

20. USCINCCENT Commanders' Conference, Operation Iraqi Freedom (CENTCOM slides with backups), 1–2 August 2002, slides 19–21. The CENTCOM slides put it this way: "eliminate Saddam's regime through the destruction of his security apparatus, exposing Saddam to threat of a population uprising, coup, assassination, or direct attack by U.S. forces, while eliminating Iraq's WMD threat to neighbors."

21. USCINCCENT Commanders' Conference, 1–2 August. Slide 103 describes thirty-two to forty-five months of total Phase IV work and an additional American security commitment of two years.

22. Interview, James Moschgat, 26 May 2004. Aircrews grew increasingly frustrated as they were ordered to leave hostile (SAM) antiaircraft sites untouched in favor of alternative targets. Other operational constraints included a marked Saudi reluctance to allow offensive strikes from their territory. Also see Michael R. Gordon, "U.S. Air Raids in '02 Prepared for War in Iraq," *New York Times,* 20 July 2003, Section A, p. 1.

23. Elizabeth Bone and Christopher Bolkcom, "Unmanned Aerial Vehicles: Background and Issues for Congress," *CRS Report for Congress,* 25 April 2003, p. 16.

24. Component Commanders' Conference, 1–2 August 2002, component commanders' meetings; notes of a participant.

25. Interview, senior British officer.

26. Interview, Richard Armitage. Other State Department officials say there was a general perception that the White House had concluded that military action had to occur no later than the spring of 2003 so the war would be won before the 2004 election. Robin Raphel, a senior State Department official who later served as an aide to Paul Bremer, said, "There were two pressures [on the administration to move forward]. One was the clear political pressure, election-driven and calendar-driven. And the other was, the troops were deployed forward

for Afghanistan and to let that kind of fall back and then reenergize everybody is very difficult. That's a real issue." U.S. Institute for Peace oral history interview by Charles Stuart Kennedy, 13 July 2004. The USIP is a government-funded research center.

27. Interview, Lieutenant General Gregory S. Newbold.
28. A draft of the classified statement was read to the authors by a senior administration official.
29. George W. Bush, "President Discusses Security and Defense Issues," 21 August 2002, available from http://www.whitehouse.gov/news/releases/2002/08/20020821-1.html, accessed 1 November 2005.
30. Bush meeting with NSC on September 6, account from notes of a participant.

CHAPTER 5: *Back to the Future*

1. Notes of a participant.
2. Interviews, CENTCOM and CFLCC officials.
3. "Fortress Baghdad" slide, viewed by the authors.
4. "Report of the Select Committee on Intelligence on the U.S. Intelligence Community's Pre-War Intelligence Assessments on Iraq, Together with Additional Views," 7 July 2004.
5. Interview, Major General James "Spider" Marks.
6. Interview, Colonel Kevin Benson.
7. Interview, Lieutenant General David D. McKiernan, Army oral history interview by Major John Aarsen, 30 November 2002.
8. Notes of a participant.
9. Some of McKiernan's staff, notably Benson and Marks, favored moving G-day ahead of A-day to gain surprise, as did Lieutenant General James Conway, but McKiernan did not go that far.
10. The CENTCOM commander was intrigued by early regime collapse. Gary Harrell, the commander of CENTCOM's Special Operations Forces, noted that Task Force 20 would need two days' heads-up to carry out the seizing of the Baghdad airport. He noted that he had plans to stop the flight of top Iraqi officials to Syria and Iran. Franks wanted the Navy to provide sufficient security to ensure that cargo ships could transit unmolested through the Suez Canal and the Bab al-Mandab Strait near the Horn of Africa. "Keep the ditch open," he said.
11. Notes of participants.
12. "Rumsfeld, Franks Address Press," CNN International transcript, 12 December 2002.

> FRANKS: You know, for more than two years now we have talked a lot about transformation, and we have thought a lot about what transformation means, and we have thought about the way we field our assets, the way we train our people, the sorts of technologies we

use, and a great many other things. The power of this Exercise Internal Look, in my view, has been—or is that it is giving us an opportunity to get at all those points. You know, the doctrines that existed for our armed forces several years ago really don't apply to the first war of the 21st Century.

Franks also suggested that there was not a link between the Internal Look exercise and tensions with Iraq. "Well, actually I wasn't aware that any threat had been issued. The purpose of the Internal Look exercise is as I described it: move the command post a long ways and gain the effect of this training and increased readiness."

13. Notes of a participant.
14. Franks and other CENTCOM officials provided a similar account to Bob Woodward, who wrote in *Plan of Attack* that the U.S. forces had executed the Hybrid 5-11-16-125 Plan. Gregory Hooker, CENTCOM chief intelligence analyst, noted in his monograph *Shaping the Plan for Operation Iraqi Freedom* that a close examination of the record "runs counter to the frequently repeated suggestions by senior participants in OIF [Operation Iraqi Freedom] that the Hybrid plan was the version ultimately executed. Hybrid, with its thirty-two-day buildup to G-day and its sixteen-day separation between A-day and G-day, does not accurately describe OIF's execution." Hooker cites Franks's book, *American Soldier,* and Woodward's *Plan of Attack*. Bob Woodward, *Plan of Attack* (New York: Simon & Schuster, 2004), pp. 287, 401. Gregory Hooker, *Shaping the Plan for Operation Iraqi Freedom* (Washington, D.C.: Washington Institute for Near East Policy, 2005), pp. 32–33.

CHAPTER 6: *'Round and 'Round We Go*

1. Among other units, the MODEP sought theater missile defense systems that were to be deployed in Kuwait and other Arab nations offering bases, and Odierno's 4th Infantry Division.
2. Interview, Colonel Kevin Benson.
3. CFLCC briefing slide.
4. Interview, Major General James D. "J. D." Thurman, Army oral history interview by Lieutenant Colonel Steven Holcomb, 27 May 2003.
5. Interview, Lieutenant Colonel Thomas Reilly, Army oral history interview by Major Gregory A. Weisler, 15 May 2003.
6. "Final Report of the Independent Panel to Review DOD Detention Operations," August 2004, p. 54. The report wrongly blames the Army's Forces Command for failing to use the TPFDL system.
7. Interviews, CFLCC staff; Interview, Newt Gingrich.
8. Interview, senior civilian official.
9. Interview, Brigadier General Steve Hawkins.

10. "U.S. Senate Armed Services Committee Hearing on FY 2004 Defense Authorization," transcript, 25 February 2003. The exchange between Senator Carl Levin and General Eric Shinseki follows:

    SENATOR LEVIN: General Shinseki, could you give us some idea as to the magnitude of the Army's force requirement for an occupation of Iraq following a successful completion of the war?

    GENERAL SHINSEKI: In specific numbers, I would have to rely on combatant commanders' exact requirements. But I think . . .

    LEVIN: How about a range?

    SHINSEKI: I would say that what's been mobilized to this point, something on the order of several hundred thousand soldiers, are probably, you know, a figure that would be required. We're talking about post-hostilities control over a piece of geography that's fairly significant with the kinds of ethnic tensions that could lead to other problems. And so, it takes significant ground force presence to maintain [a] safe and secure environment to ensure that the people are fed, that water is distributed, all the normal responsibilities that go along with administering a situation like this.

    LEVIN: And what effect would that type of an occupation to that extent have on two things, one is our OPTEMPO [operations tempo], which you've talked about, already stressed, and also on the ability of the Army to fulfill the other missions that we have?

    SHINSEKI: Well, if it were an extended requirement for presence of U.S.-only Army forces, it would have a significant long-term effect. And therefore, I think the kind of assistance from friends and allies would be helpful.

11. Interview, Tom White.

12. Briefing reviewed by authors; Interview, senior administration official.

13. Unlike a "surrender," which makes the defeated combatants prisoners under the Geneva Convention and prohibits them from switching sides, when an enemy unit "capitulates," it can be enlisted to serve the victor.

14. Interview, General Anthony Zinni.

15. SCIRI, the Iranian-backed Supreme Council for the Islamic Revolution in Iran, had a militia dubbed the Badr Corps, but did attend the London meeting.

16. Interviews, Department of Defense and White House officials.

17. Interview, Kanan Makiya. Also Kanan Makiya, "Our Hopes Betrayed," *The Observer,* 16 February 2003, available from http://observer.guardian.co.uk/iraq/story/0,12239,896611,00.html, accessed 8 November 2005.

18. Interview, Colonel Kevin Benson.

19. Interview, senior official.

20. "Iraqi Perspectives," p. 13; Interview, General Michael Hagee, commandant, United States Marine Corps.
21. Notes of a participant at the CENTCOM meeting.
22. Notes of a participant.
23. Michael R. Gordon, "NATO, the Inside Story," *New York Times,* 25 February 2003; interviews with senior U.S. and NATO officials.
24. Notes of a participant.
25. Dexter Filkins, "Turkish Deputies Refuse to Accept American Troops," *New York Times,* 2 March 2003, Section A, p. 1.
26. In the end, cooler heads prevailed and the United States offered the Turks $1 billion in credits despite their refusal to open a northern front. The credits were never used.
27. Interview, General J. D. Thurman, 27 May 2003.
28. Joseph Collins's memo, "Rear Area Forces Gap."

CHAPTER 7: *The Red Line*

1. "Comprehensive Report," vol. 1, p. 65.
2. Ibid.
3. Ibid., p. 63.
4. Ibid., p. 34.
   Saddam never discussed using deception as a policy, but he used to say privately that the "better part of war was deceiving," according to Ali Hassan al-Majeed. He stated that Saddam wanted to avoid appearing weak and did not reveal he was deceiving the world about the presence of WMD. The U.N.'s inconclusive assessment of Iraq's possession of WMD, in Saddam's view, gave pause to Iran. Saddam was concerned that the U.N. inspection process would expose Iraq's vulnerability, thereby magnifying the effect of Iran's own capability.
5. "Iraqi Perspectives," pp. 39–42.
   According to senior Iraqi officers, the plan was not drawn up through the customary deliberate staff process. A later study to support the new plan was in fact formalized by an al-Bakr University team on 23 February 2003, only weeks before the war. The February enemy courses of action study postulated multiple attacks on multiple fronts, south, west, and north.
6. Ibid., pp. 32–33. "Saddam: there is no way the air force would win a battle or a war as long as there is an infantry soldier," said the director general of the Republican Guard general staff.
7. Visit to the facility by Michael Gordon.
8. Philip H. Gordon and Jeremy Shapiro, *Allies at War* (New York: McGraw-Hill, 2004), p. 100.
9. Michael R. Gordon, "German and Spanish Navies Take on Major

Role Near Horn of Africa," *New York Times,* 15 December 2002, Section A, p. 36.

10. "Iraqi Perspectives," p. 11.

11. "Comprehensive Report," vol. 3, pp. 107–10.

12. Interview, General Anthony Zinni.

13. "Report of the Select Committee on Intelligence on the U.S. Intelligence Community's Pre-War Intelligence Assessments on Iraq, Together with Additional Views," 7 July 2004.

14. "Prior to the Gulf War, America's top intelligence analysts would come to my office in the Defense Department and tell me that Saddam Hussein was at least five or perhaps even 10 years away from having a nuclear weapon. After the war we learned that he had been much closer than that, perhaps within a year of acquiring such a weapon," Vice President Dick Cheney, 26 August 2002 speech to the Veterans of Foreign Wars, available from http://www.whitehouse.gov/news/releases/2002/08/20020826.html, accessed 3 November 2005.

15. "Report of the Select Committee on Intelligence," p. 276. The Bush administration was not alone in pointing to the risk. The Carnegie Endowment for International Peace, which was critical of many administration policies, issued a report in June 2002 entitled *Deadly Arsenals,* which asserted that Saddam was determined to develop nuclear weapons, may have hidden up to 600 metric tons [600 short tons] of CW agents, had the capability to conduct clandestine BW research, and quite possibly possessed an arsenal of two dozen Scud missiles. Joseph Cirincione et al., *Deadly Arsenals,* 1st ed. (Washington, D.C.: Carnegie Endowment for International Peace, 2002), pp. 271–80.

16. "Report of the Select Committee on Intelligence," pp. 307–12.

17. Interview, Paul Pillar.

18. Declassified version of October 2002 National Intelligence Estimate, "Iraq's Continuing Programs for Weapons of Mass Destruction." The estimate read: "Baghdad, for now, appears to be drawing a line short of conducting terrorist attacks with conventional or CBW against the United States, fearing that exposure of Iraqi involvement would provide Washington a stronger cause for making war. Iraq probably would attempt clandestine attacks against the U.S. homeland if Baghdad feared an attack that threatened the survival of the regime were imminent or unavoidable or possibly for revenge," the NIE noted. "Saddam, if sufficiently desperate, might decide that only an organization such as al-Qa'ida—with worldwide reach and extensive terrorist infrastructure—and already engaged in a life-or-death struggle against the United States—could perpetuate the kind of terrorist attack that he would hope to conduct. . . . In such circumstances, he might decide that the extreme step of assisting the Islamist terrorists in conducting a CBW attack against the United States would be his

last chance to exact vengeance by taking a larger number of victims with him."

19. Declassified National Intelligence Estimate, October 2002, and Senate testimony; George Tenet interview with Alison Mitchell, *New York Times* congressional reporter; "C.I.A. Letter to Senate on Baghdad's Intentions," *New York Times,* 9 October 2002, Section A, p. 12; Alison Mitchell and Carl Hulse, "C.I.A. Sees Terror After Iraq Action," *New York Times,* 9 October 2002, Section A, p. 1; Michael R. Gordon, "U.S. Aides Split on Assessment of Iraq's Plans," *New York Times,* 10 October 2002, Section A, p. 1. Tenet declined an interview request by the authors.

20. Senator Bob Graham voted against and was among the first to drop out of the campaign for the presidential nomination.

21. As Washington has no embassy in Pyongyang, the U.S. team was taken to the British consulate in two British Land Rovers, went to a secure room, and reviewed the statement again with three linguists. After studying the translation, James Kelly and other members of his delegation concluded that there was only one way to interpret it: North Korea had defiantly declared that it was pursuing nuclear weapons. The conclusion was transmitted via encrypted British communications to Washington.

22. Interview, Charles "Jack" Pritchard, former U.S. ambassador to the talks with North Korea. Also see articles: Barbara Slavin, "N. Korea Admits Nuclear Program," *USA Today,* 17 October 2002, Section A, p. 1; Ryan Lizza, "Nuclear Test," *New Republic,* vol. 227, no. 19, 4 November 2002, pp. 10–11. After being contacted for comment by Slavin and by Chris Nelson, who writes a daily e-mail newsletter on Asian policy, the Bush administration organized a 7:00 p.m. conference call with the *New York Times* and other major publications and disclosed the story. Senator Richard Lugar and Representatives Jim Kolbe and Jim Leach, all Republicans, were briefed in closed session by Kelly on the meetings, and they did not publicly discuss the events. No Democratic lawmakers were briefed prior to the news disclosures.

23. Cheney made the argument in a 26 August 2002 address to the Veterans of Foreign Wars. "Some concede that Saddam is evil, power-hungry, and a menace—but that, until he crosses the threshold of actually possessing nuclear weapons, we should rule out preemptive action. That logic seems to me to be deeply flawed. The argument comes down to this: yes, Saddam is as dangerous as we say he is, we just need to let him get stronger before we do anything about it. Yet if we did wait until that moment, Saddam would simply be emboldened, and it would become even harder for us to gather friends and allies to oppose him."

24. Interview, Larry Wilkerson.

25. On January 27, Hans Blix told the Security Council, "Iraq appears

not to have come to a genuine acceptance even today of the disarma-
ment which was demanded of it and which it needs to carry out to win
the confidence of the world and to live in peace." Text of speech available from http://www.globalpolicy.org/security/issues/iraq/unmovic/
2003/0127entblixrep.htm, accessed 11 November 2005.

26. Interview, Larry Wilkerson. Also, see transcript of Wilkerson's 19 October 2005 talk, "Weighing the Uniqueness of the Bush Administration's National Security Decision-Making Process: Boon or Danger to
American Democracy?," hosted by the New America Foundation,
available from http://www.newamerica.net/Download_Docs/pdfs/Doc_
File_2644_1.pdf, accessed 3 November 2005.

> The consensus of the intelligence community was overwhelming.
> I can still hear George Tenet telling me, and telling my boss in the
> bowels of the CIA, that the information we were delivering—
> which we had called considerably—we had called it very much—
> we had thrown whole reams of paper out that the White House
> had created. But George was convinced, John McLaughlin was
> convinced that what we were presented was accurate. And con-
> trary to what you were hearing in the papers and other places,
> one of the best relationships we had in fighting terrorists and in
> intelligence in general was with guess who? The French. In fact,
> it was probably the best. And they were right there with us.
>
> In fact, I'll just cite one more thing. The French came in in the
> middle of my deliberations at the CIA and said, we have just
> spun aluminum tubes, and by god, we did it to this RPM, et
> cetera, et cetera, and it was all, you know, proof positive that
> the aluminum tubes were not for mortar casings or artillery
> casings, they were for centrifuges. Otherwise, why would you
> have such exquisite instruments? We were wrong. We were
> wrong. . . . He was going to wait until the international tension
> was off of him, until the sanctions were down, and then he was
> going to go back—certainly go back to all of his programs. I
> mean, I was convinced of that.

27. "Report of the Select Committee on Intelligence," p. 249.
28. Douglas Jehl, "Report Warned Bush Team About Intelligence
Doubts," *New York Times,* 5 November 2005, Section A, p. 14.
29. Interview, Paul Pillar.
30. "Comprehensive Report," vol. 1, p. 67.
31. Ibid., p. 62.
32. V Corps classified operations order in possession of the authors.
33. I Marine Expeditionary Force classified operations order in possession of authors.
34. Interview, Major General Robert "Rusty" Blackman, Marine Corps
oral history interview by Colonel Nicholas Reynolds, 31 May 2003.

CHAPTER 8: *A Little Postwar Planning*

1. Interview, General Anthony Zinni.
2. Interview, Major Ray Eiriz, Operation Iraqi Freedom Study Group interview by Major Craig Borchelt, 28 May 2003.
3. Interview, Colonel John F. Agoglia, Office for Reconstruction and Humanitarian Assistance (ORHA) history interview by Gordon Rudd, 28 June 2003.
4. Interview, Pentagon officials.
5. Interview, senior military official.
6. General Richard Myers's notes on the October 16 meeting were described by a Pentagon official.
7. Interview, Condoleezza Rice.
8. Doug Feith's office also produced a seven-page PowerPoint brief dealing with their view of Phase IV, but it was not coordinated with the Joint Staff, and key planners, including Jewett, were not allowed to keep a copy of it. Military officials recall that it listed a number of long-term-objective bullets, including building a new Iraq that had no WMD, installing a government that was friendly to the U.S. and Israel, and the use of oil to pay for the reconstruction.
9. Interview, Brigadier General Steve Hawkins.
10. Interviews, CFLCC officials.
11. Briefing to CINC (28 February), "CFLCC Stability Operations," slide prepared 16 February 2003.

   The CFLCC briefing on stability operations contained a number of slides. "Commanders' Intent" said the goal was to "Control as we go," "Rolling transition to stability operations," "Balance effects of control and destruction." The idea was also to use existing Iraqi organizations and administration. Before regime collapse, V Corps, I MEF, and 4ID would work with Iraqi provincial administrations. Following regime collapse, an interim national military authority would work with "Iraqi ministries." A proclamation would be issued to establish the authority of the interim military administration. The briefing proposed the establishment of a seven-member Iraqi council. Three members would come from the exile community. Four would come from Iraqis who had lived under Saddam. All main ethnic groups would be represented.

   The priorities for the first thirty to sixty days included the following: Defeat pockets of resistance; Secure key infrastructure; Provide emergency HA (humanitarian assistance); Control DCs (displaced civilians)/secure EPWs (enemy prisoners of war); Locate/Secure WMD/Conduct SSE (sensitive site exploitation); maintain public order and safety; Empower selected Iraqi officials at local/state/national level (Provisional Commissions); Repair mission essential LOCs (lines of communication); Restore critical utilities/basic services; Support sustainment HA (humanitarian assistance); Exercise military authority at local levels; Begin reintegration of Iraqi military.

12. Interview, Colonel (Ret.) Jim Rabon.

13. Lieutenant Colonel Steven W. Peterson, "Central but Inadequate: The Application of Theory in Operation Iraqi Freedom," National War College, available from http://www.ndu.edu/library/n4/n045602I.pdf.

14. Interviews, Colonel Tom Greenwood, NSC officials.

15. Interview, Jay Garner.

16. Interview, Major General Carl Strock.

17. Donald Rumsfeld, "Beyond Nation-Building," speech given at the 11th Annual Salute to Freedom, Intrepid Sea-Air-Space Museum, New York City, 14 February 2003, available from http://www.defenselink.mil/speeches/2003/sp20030214-secdef0023.html.

18. Interview, former official.

19. Interview, Colonel Paul Hughes.

20. According to Brookings's 14 November 2005 update of the "Iraq Index," the U.S. has thus far appropriated $20.9 billion, obligated $17.3 billion, and actually disbursed $11.5 billion under the Iraq Relief and Reconstruction Funds (IRRF I and II). Available from www.brookings.edu/fp/saban/iraq/index.pdf.

According to the Center for Strategic and International Studies' Post-Conflict Reconstruction Project's December 2004 publication on reconstruction spending, $24.1 billion has been appropriated for the reconstruction of Iraq. ("Progress or Peril? Measuring Iraq's Reconstruction," available from www.csis.org/media/pubs/iraq_funds.pdf).

21. Briefing slides from the meeting obtained by the authors, as well as the review of an informal transcript of the meeting.

22. ORHA briefing prepared by Colonel Tom Gross and Colonel Paul Hughes, in the possession of the authors.

ORHA Rock Drill briefing:

Law Enforcement

BACKGROUND: The early establishment of public order through the rule of law is critical to ORHA's effective execution of its civil administration tasks.

DISCUSSION: Several issues require decisions:
1. Need to determine the legal code that will be employed by the coalition.
2. Law enforcement personnel requirements must be resourced by the U.S.
3. Funding must be secured ($30M for 1st 3 months; $93M for next 9 months)
4. Premature to determine U.S. law enforcement footprint.

RECOMMENDATION: Develop these issues and present to the PC for decision.

Use & Reorganization of the Iraqi Army

BACKGROUND: The Iraqi military, principally the Army, must be reorganized and retrained. Selected portions of the military will be demobilized and abolished.

DISCUSSION:

1. Necessary to keep Iraqi Army intact for a specified period of time.
2. Serves as a ready resource pool for labor intensive civil works projects.
3. Provides a command & control structure and available mobility assets that can be used in Phase IV (under U.S. supervision).

RECOMMENDATION: Contract out this functional mission area as soon as possible.

Vetting Process & Coordination

- BACKGROUND:
  - Every functional area will require the use of indigenous Iraqis.
  - Coalition must weed out "bad" Iraqis.
- DISCUSSION:
  - Vetting process is lengthy and bureaucratic.
  - Refugee/IDP camps will register all Iraqi personnel.
  - Use of NGO/IO-built rosters for vetting purposes is not a certainty.
- RECOMMENDATION:
  - ORHA be granted control of vetting process and be resourced to do so.
  - State coordinate with NGOs/IOs to use their rosters.

Achieving the Use of Service from Neighboring States
(TURKEY, IRAN, SYRIA, JORDAN, KUWAIT, SAUDI ARABIA)

- BACKGROUND: The reconstruction of Iraq is costly and time consuming. Estimates to be over 3 billion dollars and 3 years to complete.
- DISCUSSION: There is significant potential that gaps will exist in requirements (use) of services (water, power, medical, and economic) and our ability to provide. It is important there not be a gap as it will be interpreted by the international community as a failure by the USG. Iraq's neighbors are capable of providing a level of interim service to bridge this gap and mitigate costs and time by the USG.
- RECOMMENDATION: Engage Turkey, Jordan, Syria, Iran, Saudi Arabia, and Kuwait to develop policy and plans for use of available water, power, medical and other goods and services.

23. Interviews, participants of the meeting.

24. Interview, Qubad Talabani, Washington representative of the Patriotic Union of Kurdistan and Jalal Talabani's son.
25. Interview, David Kay.
26. Interview, Robert Perito. Perito's memo is excerpted below:

> The US-military administration will be responsible for security, public order, and law enforcement. In meeting this responsibility, the US will not be able to rely on the local authorities. Saddam's security services must be disbanded. Prior experience indicates the regular Iraqi police will be unavailable, intimidated or unprepared to act in the chaotic postwar environment. . . . Given the political and practical realities, it's doubtful the US will be able to turn to the EU, NATO and OSCE, which provided police and legal experts in Bosnia and Kosovo. . . . Relying on Coalition military forces is not the answer. Experience in the Balkans demonstrated that regular soldiers are neither trained nor equipped to deal with mob violence or engage in law enforcement. . . . To ensure a stable post-conflict environment in Iraq, the US should create a civilian US "Stability Force." Such force should include civilian constabulary, police and teams of judicial and corrections experts to establish the rule of law. This force could work with Coalition military forces that will remain to ensure a safe and secure environment. . . .

> For Iraq, a US civilian Stability Force would have the following components:
> - CONSTABULARY: A force of 20 companies with appropriate headquarters and administrative staff for a total of 2,500 personnel. Primary deployment would be in Baghdad, with contingents in four regional centers (Mosul and Kirkuk in the North and Basra and Kut in the South). These forces would have access to a helicopter airlift to ensure maximum mobility.
> - CIVIL POLICE: A force of 4,000 US civil police with its headquarters in Baghdad and contingents co-located in the regional and provincial headquarters of the Iraqi National Police. These officers would require wheeled transport, light weapons and effective communications to ensure coordination with constabulary and military backups.
> - JUDICIAL TEAMS: There should be ten teams of twenty lawyers, judges, court administrators and corrections officers supported by a headquarters staff, paralegals, translators and a training unit for a total of 300 personnel. They would be deployed to major population centers where they would work directly with local judicial authorities.

> . . . The fact that we may be within weeks of a decision by the President to intervene in Iraq should not deter us. Experience in

the Balkans, East Timor and Afghanistan shows that Coalition forces will have to deal with high levels of violence for the first two years of the mission.

27. Interview, David Kay; "Future of Iraq Study," in possession of the authors.
28. Interview, Colonel Paul Hughes.
29. Presentation to the NSC on March 10 and March 12, reviewed by the authors; Interviews, senior NSC and DOD officials.
30. Joseph Collins memo, 7 March 2003.

CHAPTER 9: *Dora Farms*

1. Interviews, senior allied officials who participated in the meeting.
2. "Comprehensive Report," vol. 1, p. 66.
3. Interview, Chief Warrant Officer Henry Crowder.
4. Interview, Pentagon official.
5. Interviews, CFLCC officials.
6. Interviews, CENTCOM and military officials.
7. Interview, U.S. Air Force officer.
8. Informal transcript of Richard Perle's briefing by a participant.
9. Interview, Colonel Mace Carpenter.
10. Interviews, Air Force officials.
11. Interviews, Colonel Matthew McKeon, Major Steven Ankerstar.
12. Eric Schmitt, "Back from Iraq, High-Tech Fighter Pilots Recount Exploits," *New York Times*, 25 April 2003, Section A, p. 12.
13. Interviews, Navy officials.
14. Interviews, Colonel Matthew McKeon, Major Steven Ankerstar.
15. President George W. Bush, "President Bush Addresses the Nation," 19 March 2003, available from http://www.whitehouse.gov/news/releases/2003/03/20030319-17.html.
16. "Iraqi Perspectives," p. 55.
17. Interview, Pentagon official.
18. Interview, Brigadier General Howard Bromberg. Also 32nd AAMDC Operation Iraqi Freedom briefing, available from http://www.globalsecurity.org/military/library/report/2003/32aamdc_oif-patriot_sep03.ppt.

CHAPTER 10: *The Opening Gambit*

1. Major General James Mattis, e-mail to the authors. Also see 1st Marine Division draft history for other details.
2. Internal report acquired by the authors.
3. Interview, Lieutenant General James Conway.

4. Interview, Major General James Mattis.
5. Interview, Captain David Banning. Also see Captain David Banning, Marine Corps interview by Major Carol Harris, 1 June 2003.
6. Interview, Lieutenant Colonel Jerome Driscoll, Marine Corps oral history interview, date unknown.
7. Interview, Lieutenant Colonel Fred Padilla.
8. Ibid.; Hampton Sides, "The First to Die," *Men's Journal,* vol. 12, no. 11, December 2003.
9. Interview, Lieutenant Colonel Chris Conlin.
10. Interviews, CFLCC officials.
11. Interview, Lieutenant Colonel Jerome Driscoll. Also see Lieutenant Colonel James R. Braden, Marine Corps oral history interview by Lieutenant Colonel Michael D. Visconage, 24 April 2003.
12. Tapes of meetings of Marine commanders made available to the authors. See video conference meeting of USMC commanders, 21 March 2003.
13. Major Craig Wonson, e-mail to the author.

CHAPTER 11: *Objective Liberty*

1. Interviews, aides to Major General Buford Blount.
2. Remarks by Captain Douglas Phillipone and 3rd Infantry Division staff ride attended by Michael Gordon.
3. During a normal year a tank battalion puts 800 miles on its M1s. During the first six months in Kuwait, 2-69 Armor, part of Allyn's brigade, put 1,660 miles on its tanks. It also used three times its normal expenditure of ammunition.
4. Interview, Colonel Daniel Allyn.
5. Interview, Lieutenant Colonel Jeffery R. "J. R." Sanderson.
6. Interview, Colonel Daniel Allyn. Also Special Forces after-action report in possession of the authors.
7. 6-6 Battalion after-action report.
8. Interview, Colonel Thomas Torrance.
9. Interview, Lieutenant Colonel John D. Harding conducted by Michael Gordon during 3rd ID staff ride to Tallil.
10. Interviews, Colonel Curtis Potts, Major James Desjardin, and Sergeant First Class Juan Rodriguez; 1st Lieutenant William Adams, Army oral history interview by Sergeant Daniel Goerke, 24 April 2003; Staff Sergeant John Thompson, Army oral history interview by Sergeant Daniel Goerke, 25 April 2003.
11. Interview, Major James Desjardin.
12. Interview, James Roche.
13. Interview, Captain Michael Downs.
14. Notes of a military aide.
15. Interviews, Colonel Matthew McKeon, Major Steven Ankerstar.

CHAPTER 12: *Everyone Loves a Parade*

1. Interview, Lieutenant Colonel Terry Ferrell.
2. Interviews, soldiers of the 3-7 Cavalry Squadron. See also Colonel (Ret.) Gregory Fontenot, Lieutenant Colonel E. J. Degen, and Lieutenant Colonel David Tohn, *On Point: The United States Army in Operation Iraqi Freedom* (Fort Leavenworth: Combat Studies Institute Press, 2004), pp. 126–27.
3. Interviews, Staff Sergeant Dillard J. Johnson and Sergeant First Class Anthony Broadhead.
4. Ibid.
5. Fontenot, Degen, and Tohn, *On Point*, pp. 130–31.
6. Interview, Lieutenant Colonel Terry Ferrell.
7. Interviews, Lieutenant Colonel Terry Ferrell, Staff Sergeant Dillard J. Johnson, Sergeant First Class Anthony Broadhead, and Captain Jeff McCoy.
8. First Lieutenant Stephen C. Gleason, Army oral history interview by Major Norman Childs, 28 May 2003; Lieutenant Colonel Scott Rutter, Army oral history interview by Major Norman Childs, 28 May 2003; Captain James Lee, Army oral history interview by Staff Sergeant Aaron McLeod, 28 May 2003.
9. Interview, Lieutenant Colonel Terry Ferrell.
10. Interview, Colonel Daniel Allyn.
11. Interviews, Captain Clay Lyle, Lieutenant Colonel Terry Ferrell, and Sergeant First Class Paul Wheatley.
12. Interview, Colonel Terry Ferrell.
13. Ibid.
14. Ibid.

CHAPTER 13: *Task Force Tarawa*

1. Task Force Tarawa intelligence summary, S//MCFI 24–72 Hour Assessment:

> The 11th ID will remain in survivability positions to garrison locations and is expected to fracture once U.S. forces draw closer to An Nasiriyah. The 45th and 47th will most likely remain in their current locations in the marshes east of An Nasiriyah, which will enhance their survivability. The 45th and 47th will most likely capitulate once U.S. forces prosecute ground operations into Iraq. Iraqi intelligence, security, and paramilitary units attempt to set up defenses in An Nasiriyah in order to delay U.S. movement and to discourage civil uprisings. However, this is expected to be short lived due to HUMINT reporting and FIF debriefs, which strongly suggest that paramilitary groups closely allied with the regime will

ultimately break and run for fear of retribution from the local populace.

2. Interview, Lieutenant Colonel Joseph Apodaca.

3. Interview, Colonel Ronald Bailey; Colonel Ronald Bailey, Marine Corps oral history interview by Colonel Reed Bonnadonna, 8 May 2003.

4. Interview, Major Andrew Kennedy, Marine Corps oral history interview by Colonel Reed Bonnadonna, 7 May 2003.

5. Interview, Lieutenant Colonel James Reilly.

6. Interview, Colonel Ronald Bailey; also Colonel Ronald Bailey, Marine Corps oral history interview, 8 May 2003.

7. Copy of I MEF Frago 017-03 in possession of the authors.

8. Interview, Colonel Ronald Bailey; Major Andrew Kennedy, Marine Corps oral history interview, 7 May 2003.

9. Interview, Lieutenant Colonel Rick Grabowski.

10. Interviews, Major William Peeples; Major William Peeples, Marine Corps oral history interview by Colonel Reed Bonnadonna, 1 May 2003.

11. "Attack on the 507th Maintenance Company, 23 March 2003, An Nasiriyah, Iraq," after-action report of the 507th, U.S. Army.

12. Major William Peeples, Marine Corps oral history interview, 1 May 2003.

13. E-mail from Lieutenant Colonel Andrew Kennedy, in possession of the authors.

14. Major William Peeples, Marine Corps oral history interview, 1 May 2003.

15. Interviews, Colonel Ronald Bailey, Lieutenant Colonel Eddie Ray, and Lieutenant Colonel Rick Grabowski.

16. Lieutenant Colonel Rick Grabowski, Marine Corps oral history interview by Colonel Reed Bonnadonna, 6 April 2003. Of eight vehicles mired in the sludge three had to be stripped of sensitive materials, their radios zeroed, and abandoned. The following day the Marines returned to retrieve them and found that during the night the Iraqis had looted them. In the words of one Marine, "You couldn't have a cleaner strip job in New York. These people definitely knew how to take stuff apart. They took every wire, radio, every instrumentation out of the panels . . . the Humvees . . . we couldn't get them out of the mud. Somehow they were able to jack those vehicles up, get the tires off them, and put them back down in the mud. These people just stripped *everything*. Engines, everything."

17. Interview, Captain Michael Brooks.

18. Later, trail marks of the Iraqi artillery indicated that the guns were oriented westward in the direction of the bridge connecting Highway 7 to the center of Nasiriyah. They were apparently hastily redirected

toward C Company, further indication that the Iraqis expected the American attack to come through the middle of the city.

19. Interview, Captain Daniel Wittnam, Marine Corps oral history interview by Colonel Reed Bonnadonna, 1 May 2003.

20. Ibid.

21. Interview, Captain Eric Garcia; Lieutenant Colonel Rick Grabowski, Marine Corps oral history interview, 6 April 2003; Captain Michael Brooks, Marine Corps oral history interview by Colonel Reed Bonnadonna.

22. Under the Marine Corps Table of Organization only two of the three rifle companies had forward air controllers (FACs). C Company did not have one.

23. FACs employ three different types of close air support (CAS) control. Type 1 requires the controller to visually acquire the attacking aircraft and the target under attack. Type 2 control occurs when either visual acquisition of the attacking aircraft or the target at weapons release is not possible or when attacking aircraft are not in a position to acquire the target prior to weapons release. FACs were authorized to employ the first two types of CAS with approval of the Fire Support Coordination Center (FSCC). Type 3 is used when the attack imposes a low risk of fratricide. Authorization rests only with a commander, who, if he sees fit, can grant a blanket weapons release clearance. Prior to crossing into Iraq, Lieutenant Colonel Grabowski specifically reminded his FACs that only he could authorize Type 3 CAS.

24. USCENTAF Friendly Fire Investigation Board, "A-10 Marine Friendly Fire Incident," 6 March 2004.

25. Ibid.

26. Interview, Major William Peeples.

27. Captain Timothy Dremann, Marine Corps oral history interview by Colonel Reed Bonnadonna, 22 April 2003.

28. Interview, Lieutenant Colonel Rick Grabowski.

29. Interviews, Major General James Mattis, Brigadier General John Kelly, and Lieutenant Colonel Lewis Craparotta.

30. Interview, Task Force Tarawa officer.

31. Interview, Task Force Tarawa official.

CHAPTER 14: *Vampire 12*

1. Interview, Major General James "Spider" Marks.

2. Video conference transcript, notes of a participant.

3. The regiment had two different types of Apaches: 1-227 and 6-6 had AH-64Ds, which could fire the Longbow, while 2-6 had the older AH-64A, which was not capable of firing the Longbow.

4. Notes taken from Major Michael Gabel's diary.

5. Interview, Lieutenant Colonel Daniel Ball. Also see Sig Christenson, "Flight into Ambush," a three-part series in the *San Antonio Express News*, 21–23 March 2004, for a detailed and informative account, available from http://www.mysanantonio.com/news/military/stories/MYSA21.01A.Longbow_1_0321.7d24b3c.html. Also Fontenot, Degen, and Tohn, *On Point*, pp. 179–92; and "Battle Summary, 6th Squadron, 6th Cavalry Operation Iraqi Freedom" and "Battle Summary of Attack Conducted Against the Iraqi Republican Guard, 2d Ar Bde, Medina Divisions," 1-227 Attack Helicopter Battalion.

6. Captain Karen Hobart, Operation Iraqi Freedom Study Group interview by Major David Tohn, 8 May 2003.

7. Wallace knew nothing of the timing of the ATACMS firing.

8. Interview, Chief Warrant Officer 5 Lance McElhiney.

9. The regiment was assigned to go to Tactical Assembly Area Vicksburg, which was inside Objective Rams.

10. Interview, Captain Andy Hilmes; 3rd ID staff ride attended by Michael R. Gordon (MRG), Najaf.

11. Interview, Lieutenant Colonel Eric Schwartz; 3rd ID staff ride attended by MRG, Objective Rams.

12. Interview, Colonel David Perkins; notes from 3rd ID staff ride attended by MRG, Objective Rams.

13. Captain Andrew Caine, "Task Force 3-5: The Odyssey to Fuel the Deep Fight."

14. Lieutenant Colonel Michael J. Barbee, Operation Iraqi Freedom Study Group interview by Major Jonathan Gass; Colonel William Wolf, Operation Iraqi Freedom Study Group interview by Colonel Gregory Fontenot (Ret.), 13 November 2003.

15. Interview, 1st Lieutenant Jason King; Chief Warrant Officer 2 John Tomblin, Operation Iraqi Freedom Study Group interview by Major Jonathan Gass, 16 May 2003.

16. Interview, Chief Warrant Officer 5 Lance McElhiney.

17. Interviews, Chief Warrant Officer 2 Joe Goode and Chief Warrant Officer 2 Cynthia Rosel.

18. Interview, Lieutenant Colonel Daniel Ball.

19. Interview, Chief Warrant Officer 2 Dave Williams.

20. Ibid.

21. Diary entry of Major John Lindsay reviewed by the authors; Interview, Captain Karen Hobart.

22. Interview, Colonel William Wolf, Operation Iraqi Freedom Study Group interview, 13 November 2003.

23. "Power Grid and ADA Ground Fire," follow-up report to 6-6 Cavalry Medina Mission. Also "Iraqi Perspectives," p. 51.

24. "AAR Comments from TF 11 AVN FSO/FSE," document in possession of the authors.

CHAPTER 15: *A Sanctuary for the Fedayeen*

1. Interview, Colonel Will Grimsley.
2. Interview, Lieutenant Colonel Ernest "Rock" Marcone.
3. Interview, 2nd Lieutenant John Rowold.
4. Interviews, Major Mike Oliver and 2nd Lieutenant John Rowold.
5. The bridging assets were for crossing at Objective Peach and were arrayed accordingly in the division's linear formation.
6. Interviews, Captain Dan Hibner and Lieutenant Colonel Ernest "Rock" Marcone; Captain Dan Hibner, Operation Iraqi Freedom Study Group interview by Lieutenant Colonel James Knowlton, 15 May 2003.

    Captain Hibner noted that the Iraqis crossed their detonation wires, which meant when one cord exploded, it rendered the second harmless, thus defeating the mechanism that would have destroyed the other side of the bridge.
7. Interview, Captain Dave Benton; 3rd ID staff ride attended by MRG.
8. Interview, soldier who participated in the action.
9. Interview, 1st Lieutenant Brad Castro; 3rd ID staff ride attended by MRG.
10. Interviews, Colonel Terry Ferrell and Lieutenant Colonel J. R. Sanderson.
11. Interview, Lieutenant Colonel Terry Ferrell.
12. Interview, Captain Jeff McCoy; 3rd ID staff ride attended by MRG.
13. Interview, First Sergeant Roy Griggs; 3rd ID staff ride attended by MRG.
14. Interviews, Lieutenant Colonel Terry Ferrell and Captain Jeff McCoy.
15. Interviews, Lieutenant Colonel J. R. Sanderson and Colonel Will Grimsley.
16. Interview, Lieutenant Colonel Herman "Stacy" Clardy.
17. Interview, Major General James Mattis.
18. Interview, Lieutenant Colonel Herman "Stacy" Clardy. Two weeks passed before Clardy's men admitted a call for Slingshot had been issued and subsequently aborted.
19. 1st Marine Division draft history.
20. Interview, Lieutenant Colonel Duffy White.
21. First Lieutenant Brian Chontosh, Marine Corps oral history interview by Lieutenant Colonel Nicholas Reynolds, 4 May 2003.
22. Interview, Lieutenant Colonel Sam Mundy.
23. Interview, Lieutenant Colonel Duffy White.
24. Ibid.; Lieutenant Colonel Sam Mundy e-mail to the authors. Also 1st Marine Division draft history.

CHAPTER 16: *Back to the Drawing Board*

1. Notes of a participant; Major General James D. "J. D." Thurman, Army oral history interview by Lieutenant Colonel Steven Holcomb, 27 May 2003; Interview, Lieutenant General William Scott Wallace; Major General Buford Blount, Army oral history interview by Major Norman Childs, 24 May 2003; Interview, Major General James Mattis. The commanders, Major General Blount and Major General Mattis, were of like mind. Slowing down or pausing would mean loss of momentum and make their divisions vulnerable to chemical attack.

2. Informal transcript of conversation between General Tommy Franks and Admiral Edmund Giambastiani on lessons learned from OIF, 14 May 2003; Interview, senior administration official.

3. Major General J. D. Thurman, Army oral history interview, 27 May 2003.

4. The following morning, General Conway relayed to his commanders the results of the meeting and estimated it would take another thirty days of air strikes before Iraqi forces could be reduced to 50 percent. Video conference transcripts.

5. Interview, Major General Charles Swannack; Lieutenant General William S. Wallace, Operation Iraqi Freedom Study Group interview by Lieutenant Colonel (Ret.) Gregory Fontenot, Lieutenant Colonel E. J. Degen, and Major David Tohn, 7 August 2003. Also Fontenot, Degen, and Tohn, *On Point*, p. 211.

6. Notes of a participant; Fontenot, Degen, and Tohn, *On Point*, p. 245.

7. Notes of a participant. Also see Jim Dwyer, "A Gulf Commander Sees a Longer Road," *New York Times,* 28 March 2003, Section A, p. 1; Rick Atkinson, "General: A War Likely; Logistics, Enemy Force Reevaluation," *Washington Post,* 27 March 2003, Section A, p. 1.

8. Notes of a participant.

9. Interviews, senior military officials.

10. Notes of a participant.
    "Phone call with Dave Halversen—CC still unhappy with our temp; feel like we have lost contact with the enemy. 101 Deep Attack last night with moderate BDA [bomb damage assessment] confirms CINC suspicion that we do not know where enemy is."

11. Notebooks, Major General James A. "Spider" Marks.

12. Interview, Colonel Ted Seel.

13. Interviews, senior officials.

14. Ibid.

15. Interview, Major General James D. "J. D." Thurman.

16. Donald Rumsfeld, DOD news briefing, 1 April 2003; available from http://www.defenselink.mil/transcripts/2003/t04012003_t0401sd.html.

17. Donald Rumsfeld, remarks on ABC's *This Week with George*

Stephanopoulos, 30 March 2003, available from http://www
.defenselink.mil/transcripts/2003/t03302003_t0330sdabcsteph.html.
18. In his March 25 memo, Macgregor wrote:

> The advance must continue without pause. There is no reason
> to stop. The force in place is massive, and so far has taken
> almost no casualties. True, there may be some supply problems,
> but hardening the supply convoys and implementing a C-130
> airlift will solve that problem. Holding one's nerve is funda-
> mental. Tikrit should be flattened. The RG [Republican Guard]
> should be destroyed. Urban resistance should be eradicated
> with armor and precision bombing. . . . Saddam, who is already
> winning the media battle, would win a huge psychological vic-
> tory even if he hangs from a lamppost in a few weeks time. He
> will be seen as the Arab leader who is able to fight the United
> States to a stand-still. . . . Stopping will damage the morale of
> the average American soldier out there more than just about
> anything else. The soldiers are out there to win, and they will
> win if allowed to but they need momentum on their side. Stop-
> ping will be a betrayal. Stopping will send entirely the wrong
> message to the Kurds and the Shiites and the many Iraqis who
> hate Saddam. Stopping will be a signal that the United States
> absolutely cannot be trusted. Stopping will encourage the
> Turks to play games. Stopping will give more time for the Rus-
> sians and the Iranians to interfere. Stopping will allow the
> French, the Germans, and world public opinion to have a field
> day at this country's expense to the point where a combination
> of world opinion and the United Nations may be able to pre-
> vent us from re-taking the offensive. Stopping will open the
> door to destructive partisan politics. Public support could well
> evaporate.

19. Interview, Major General Buford Blount. Also see Lieutenant General
    William S. Wallace, Operation Iraqi Freedom Study Group interview
    by Lieutenant Colonel (Ret.) Gregory Fontenot, Lieutenant Colonel
    E. J. Degen, and Major David Tohn, 7 August 2003; Colonel David
    Perkins, Army oral history interview by Major Norman Childs,
    25 May 2003. Also, interview, Lieutenant Colonel Philip "Flip"
    DeCamp: "Our job was initially to seize the bridge, attack across the
    bridge and put almost two tank companies on the other side of the
    bridge."
20. Fontenot, Degen, and Tohn, *On Point,* pp. 245, 258.
21. Interviews, Colonel David Perkins, Captain Christopher Carter, and
    Lieutenant Colonel Philip "Flip" DeCamp.
22. Chris Tomlinson, "Battling for a Bridge and a Town, U.S. Troops Risk
    Their Lives to Rescue an Elderly Woman," Associated Press

newswires, 31 March 2003; Interviews, Captain Christopher Carter and Sergeant Luis Javier Sanchez.

23. As American forces withdrew, Iraqi civilians poured into the streets, onto the Hindiyah bridge, and toward an arms cache collection point that had been wired for demolition. If one inattentive U.S. soldier had not prematurely detonated the captured Iraqi weapons, the subsequent explosion may have severely injured hundreds of civilian spectators.

24. Major General James Mattis, Marine Corps oral history interview by Dr. Gary Solis, 24 January 2004. On the final day of the pause, Iraqi tanks and school buses filled with infantry soldiers rushed to prevent the Marine advance, having apparently deduced the American path to Baghdad.

25. Notes of March 26–27 VTCs.

26. Interview with Moseley aides.

27. Air war briefing attended by authors.

28. Colonel Mace Carpenter, "Deliberate, Disciplined, Proportional and Precise: The Operation Iraqi Freedom Air and Space Strategy; Initial Assessment," draft copy, pp. 19–20; Interview, Major General James Amos.

29. E-mail to the authors from Brigadier General Kurt Chicowski and interviews with Colonel Mace Carpenter and Major General T. Michael "Buzz" Moseley.

30. Interview, Colonel Matt McKeon.

31. Notes of a Moseley aide and interview with Colonel Mace Carpenter.

32. Notes of March 27 VTC.

33. Interview, Major General James D. "J. D." Thurman; notes of a participant, 27 March video conference.

34. Interview, military official.

CHAPTER 17: *Team Tank*

1. Interview, military officer.

2. Ibid.

3. Ibid.

4. Ibid.; Robert W. Jones, "Team Tank: Armor in Support of Special Operations," *Veritas: Journal of Army Special Forces History,* Winter 2005, pp. 69–73.

5. James Schroder, "The Rangers Take Hadithah Dam," *Veritas: Journal of Army Special Forces History,* Winter 2005, pp. 55–60. Also Michael R. Mullins and Cherilyn A. Walley, "Holding Back the Flood at Hadithah Dam," *Veritas: Journal of Army Special Forces History,* Winter 2005, pp. 65–68.

6. Interview, military officer.

7. While the Turkish parliament debated U.S. entry, prominent Kurdish leaders told Khalilzad they planned on attacking Turkish troops who entered northern Iraq.

8. Interview, Major General Henry "Pete" Osman.

9. Ibid.

10. Lieutenant Colonel Robert Waltemeyer, Operation Iraqi Freedom Study Group interview by Lieutenant Colonel Rob Walsh, date unknown.

11. Interview, Major General Henry "Pete" Osman.

12. Interview, General James Jones.

13. Fontenot, Degen, and Tohn, *On Point*, pp. 222–29.

14. Interview, Major General Henry "Pete" Osman.

    General Abizaid had suggested to Osman that inflating the importance of the 173rd would help to mislead and fix Saddam's defenses in the north. Osman's terse presentation from Salahuddin did receive significant press coverage. However, it could not have allayed Kurdish fears of a Turkish intervention. The meeting opened with a statement by Colonel Keith Lawless indicating the MCLC (Military Coordination and Liaison Command) would coordinate among "all the various factions in the north, including the Turks, if in fact Turkish forces cross."

15. Interviews, Major General Henry "Pete" Osman, administration official; Fontenot, Degen, and Tohn, *On Point*, p. 230; Kenn Finlayson, "Operation Viking Hammer: 3/10 SFG Against the Ansar Al-Islam," *Veritas: Journal of Army Special Forces History,* Winter 2005, pp. 15–18.

16. Interview, Major General Henry "Pete" Osman. Also see Kenn Finlayson, "This Is What You Signed Up For: The Attack on Ayn Sifni," *Veritas: Journal of Army Special Forces History,* Winter 2005, pp. 75–78.

17. Nathan S. Lowrey, "The Battle for Debecka Crossroads," *Veritas: Journal of Army Special Forces History,* Winter 2005, pp. 79–85. Also Harvey Morris, "Eighteen Kurdish Soldiers Killed, Many Injured in US 'Friendly Fire,' " *Financial Times,* 7 April 2003, p. 3.

18. Interview, U.S. State Department official.

19. Interview, Rear Admiral John Stufflebeam.

20. Interview, General James Jones.

CHAPTER 18: *The Red Zone*

1. "Iraqi Perspectives," pp. 25, 52.

2. Lieutenant Colonel Ernest "Rock" Marcone, Army oral history interview by Major Norman Childs, 30 May 2003. Also Lieutenant Colonel Rock Marcone, Army oral history interview by Colonel

(Ret.) Gregory Fontenot and Lieutenant Colonel E. J. Degen, 22 October 2003.

3. Interviews, Colonel William Grimsley, Lieutenant Colonel Ernest "Rock" Marcone, Captain Dan Hibner, Sergeant Jay Bliss, First Lieutenant Ramon Brigantti, First Lieutenant Kevin Caesar, and Sergeant Robert Stevens.

4. Ibid.; Lieutenant Colonel Ernest "Rock" Marcone, Army oral history interviews, 30 May 2003, and 22 October 2003.

5. CENTCOM Patriot investigation report.

6. Interviews, Colonel Dave Perkins, Major General Buford Blount. Also Colonel William Grimsley, Army oral history interview by Lieutenant David R. Manning, May 2003.

7. Interview, Lieutenant Colonel Ernest "Rock" Marcone, 30 May 2003.

8. "Iraqi Perspectives," p. 44.

9. Captain Matthew Paul, Army oral history interview by Lieutenant Colonel (Ret.) Arthur A. Durante, 15 May 2003; Captain Matthew Paul, Army oral history interview by Sergeant Troy Hester, 28 May 2003.

10. First Lieutenant Mark Schenck, "2-7 Infantry Unit History."

11. Sergeant First Class Paul R. Smith citation.

12. Interview, Colonel Dave Perkins.

13. Lieutenant General Raad al-Hamdani, *Frontline* interview, available from http://www.pbs.org/wgbh/pages/frontline/shows/invasion/interviews/raad.html

14. Interview, Lieutenant Colonel Duffy White.

15. Major General James Amos, Marine Corps oral history interview by Colonel Charles J. Quilter and Lieutenant Colonel Michael Visconage, 16 May 2003.

16. Interviews, Major General James Amos and Major Craig R. Wonson. Also see Lieutenant Colonel Michael Oehl, "2nd Tank Battalion Unit Chronology."

17. "Comprehensive Report," vol. 3, p. 110. Many Iraqi generals and high-level defense officials also believed that Saddam had some sort of plan to use chemical weapons despite his statements that he had no WMD. In a compartmentalized military, many officers accepted that there were secret plans of which they would have no knowledge and of which some other unit would have the task.

18. Interviews, Lieutenant Colonel Steven Ferrando and Lieutenant Colonel Lew Craparotta.

19. An Air Force A-10 mistakenly attacked the Marines' command group at the intersection due to erroneous coordinates. The attack was called off before it inflicted casualties.

20. Interview, Lieutenant Colonel Lew Craparotta.

21. Interview, Colonel Joseph Dowdy.

22. Interview, Major General James Mattis.

23. Interviews, Colonel Joseph Dowdy, General James Mattis, and Brigadier General John Kelly.

24. "Iraqi Perspectives," p. 52.

25. Interviews, senior CFLCC and Marine officials.

26. Lieutenant Colonel Carl E. "Sam" Mundy, Marine Corps oral history interview by Lieutenant Colonel Michael Visconage, 4 May 2003; First Lieutenant Brian Chontosh, Marine Corps oral history interview, 4 May 2003; Interview, Lieutenant Colonel Duffy White.

27. Lieutenant Colonel Carl E. "Sam" Mundy, Marine Corps oral history interview, 4 May 2003; First Lieutenant Brian Chontosh, Marine Corps oral history interview, 4 May 2003; Colonel Joseph F. Dunford, Marine Corps oral history interview by Lieutenant Colonel Nicholas Reynolds, 2 May 2003. Also see Oehl, "2nd Tank Battalion Unit Chronology."

CHAPTER 19: *The Thunder Run*

1. Interviews, Colonel J. D. Johnson, Lieutenant General William S. Wallace, and Major General Buford Blount.

2. Michael R. Gordon, "Baghdad Targets Picked if Hussein Holes Up There," *New York Times,* 7 March 2003, Section A, p. 11.

3. Major General Buford Blount, Army oral history interview by Major Norman Childs, 24 May 2003.

4. Interview, Lieutenant Colonel Eric Schwartz.

5. Sergeant First Class Eric R. Olson, "Operation Iraqi Freedom Journal."

6. Interview, Sergeant Jason Diaz; 3rd ID staff ride attended by Michael Gordon.

7. Interview, Colonel Dave Perkins.

8. Olson, "Operation Iraqi Freedom Journal," p. 42. Also see Steven Lee Myers, "U.S. Tanks Make Quick Strike into Baghdad," *New York Times,* 6 April 2003, Section A, p. 1.

9. Interview, First Lieutenant Roger Gruneisen; 3rd ID staff ride attended by Michael Gordon.

10. Interview, Staff Sergeant Jeffery Empson, Operation Iraqi Freedom Study Group by Lieutenant Colonel David Manning, 19 May 2003.

11. Interviews, Captain Jason Conroy and Captain Michael Dyches; 3rd ID staff ride attended by Michael Gordon.

12. Interview, Colonel Dave Perkins.

13. 3rd ID staff ride attended by Michael Gordon.

14. 1-64 Armor officers, Operation Iraqi Freedom Study Group interviews by Lieutenant Colonel David Manning, 18 May 2003. Also see Ron Martz, "I Owe These Heroes My Life," *Atlanta Journal-Constitution,* 6 April 2003, p. A1.

15. Interview, Captain Erik Berdy.
16. Olson, "Operation Iraqi Freedom Journal," p. 47. Also 3rd ID staff ride attended by Michael Gordon.

　　For additional information on the Thunder Run, see David Zucchino, *Thunder Run* (New York: Atlantic Monthly Press, 2004).

CHAPTER 20: *The Accidental Victory*

1. "Iraqi Perspectives," p. 83. This site (33 17'29"N, 44 21'16"E) also served as an alternate Republican Guard command post for Qusay Hussein. During Saddam's visit, he commanded those present to begin coordinating Fedayeen and Republican Guard forces in urban operations against Americans.
2. Interview, Colonel Dave Perkins.
3. 3rd ID staff ride attended by Michael Gordon.
4. Interview, Colonel Dave Perkins. Also Perkins, Army oral history interview by Major Norman Childs, 25 May 2003; 3rd ID staff ride attended by Michael Gordon.
5. Interview, Colonel Dave Perkins.
6. Interview, Lieutenant General William S. Wallace. Also see Lieutenant General William S. Wallace, Operation Iraqi Freedom Study Group interview by Colonel (Ret.) Gregory Fontenot, Lieutenant Colonel E. J. Degen, and Major David Tohn, 7 August 2003.
7. Interview, Major General Buford Blount.
8. Interview, Colonel Dave Perkins.
9. 3rd ID staff ride attended by Michael Gordon.
10. Captain Felix Almaguer, Operation Iraqi Freedom Study Group interview by Major Daniel Corey, 19 May 2003. Some captured foreign fighters had both Saddam Fedayeen and Hezbollah tattoos.
11. Fontenot, Degen, Tohn, *On Point*, p. 352.
12. Lieutenant Colonel Peter Bayer, Army oral history interview by Major Norman Childs, 25 May 2003.
13. Interview, Colonel Dave Perkins; Perkins, Army oral history interview, 25 May 2003; Interview, Lieutenant General William S. Wallace.
14. Interviews, General J. D. Thurman, Major General Buford Blount, and Lieutenant General William S. Wallace.
15. Interview, Lieutenant Colonel Stephan Twitty; Command Sergeant Major Robert Gallagher, Operation Iraqi Freedom Study Group interview by Arthur Durante, 19 May 2003.

　　"The Objectives were originally called Golf 231, Golf 232, and Golf 233. We changed the names . . . to add some humor into it," remarked Twitty.
16. Intelligence provided by Special Forces and extrapolated from the April 5 Thunder Run led Captain Felix Almaguer, the task force intel-

ligence officer, to predict that each of the three objectives would be defended by 150 to 200 dismounted infantry. Interviews, Colonel Stephan Twitty and Captain Zan Hornbuckle.

17. Interview, Sergeant Major Robert Gallagher; Gallagher, Army oral history interview, 19 May 2003; Interview, Captain Zan Hornbuckle.

18. "Regime Isolation," 2 BCT history, pp. 23–25; Interviews, Captain Zan Hornbuckle and Sergeant Major Robert Gallagher; Gallagher, Army oral history interview, 19 May 2003.

19. Captain William Glaser, Operation Iraqi Freedom Study Group interview by Major Peter Kilner, 18 May 2003.

20. Interviews, Colonel Dave Perkins and Captain William Glaser; Glaser, Operation Iraqi Freedom Study Group interview, 18 May 2003.

21. Interview, Lieutenant General William S. Wallace.

22. Captain J. O. Bailey, Army oral history interview by Sergeant Troy Hester, 20 May 2003; First Lieutenant Aaron Polsgrove, Infantry School manuscript, pp. 7–8.

23. Polsgrove, Infantry School manuscript, pp. 8–10; Interviews, Major Everett Denton Knapp and Captain Steve Hommel.

24. Interview, Captain Steve Hommel.

25. 3rd ID staff ride attended by Michael Gordon.

26. Interview, Captain Erik Berdy.

27. Some of the foreign fighters had been paid to fight Americans. "They had the money on them," said Task Force 3-15's executive officer Major Everett Denton Knapp. "Syrians captured at Objective Curley indicated they had been paid thirty days before U.S. troops arrived in Baghdad."

28. Captain Felix Almaguer, Army oral history interview, 19 May 2003.

29. "Iraqi Perspectives," p. 17.

CHAPTER 21: *The Second Battle for Baghdad*

1. Draft 1st Marine Division official history, Chapter 6, p. 30.

2. Interview, Lieutenant Colonel Niel E. "Rick" Nelson.

3. Interview, Lieutenant Colonel Duffy White.

4. Interview, Lieutenant Colonel Niel E. "Rick" Nelson.

5. Draft 1st Marine Division official history.

6. Corporal Jeremiah J. Day, Marine Corps oral history interview by Lieutenant Colonel Michael Visconage, 12 June 2003.

7. The Army Canal, which ran northeast from the Diyala to Highway 2, became the boundary between RCT-1 and RCT-7.

8. Draft 1st Marine Division official history, Chapter 6, p. 44.

9. Captain Phillip Wolford, Army oral history interview by Major Norman Childs, 19 May 2003.

10. Interviews, Captain Phillip Wolford and Sergeant Shawn Gibson.

11. Interview, Chris Tomlinson.

12. Colonel Daniel Allyn, Operation Iraqi Freedom Study Group interview by Colonel Timothy Cherry, 13 May 2003.

13. Interviews, Lieutenant Colonel Terry Ferrell, Captain Clay Lyle, Sergeant First Class Matthew Chase, and Sergeant First Class Paul Wheatley. Also commanders and staff of 3-7 Cavalry, Operation Iraqi Freedom Study Group interviews by Major Peter Kilner, 25 May 2003.

14. Interview, Lieutenant Colonel Jeffrey "J. R." Sanderson.

15. Interview, Colonel Daniel Allyn.

16. Interview, Staff Sergeant James E. Harrison. Also see Staff Sergeant James E. Harrison, Army oral history interview by Sergeant Daniel Goerke, 14 May 2003.

17. Interviews, Lieutenant Colonel J. R. Sanderson, Colonel Daniel Allyn, and Captain Stu James.

18. 3rd ID staff ride attended by Michael Gordon.

19. Draft 1st Marine Division official history.

20. Interview, Lieutenant Colonel Frederick Padilla.

21. Ibid.

22. Captain Larry Brown, Marine Corps oral history interview by Lieutenant Colonel Michael Visconage, 18 May 2003; Hospitalman 2 Michael O'Leary, Marine Corps oral history interview by Lieutenant Colonel Michael Visconage, 12 May 2003.

23. Interview, General John Jumper; accounts by Air War Command officials.

CHAPTER 22: *Saddam's Great Escape*

1. Interview, Rashid Abudullah Ibrahim al-Huraymis; "Iraqi Perspectives," p. 80.

2. "Iraqi Perspectives," p. 80.

3. Interview, Brigadier General John Kelly.

4. Draft 1st Marine Division official history, Chapter 7, p. 9.

5. Interview, Lieutenant Colonel Herman "Stacy" Clardy.

6. Interview, Chief Warrant Officer 2 David Williams.

7. Interviews, Brigadier General John Kelly and Lieutenant Colonel Herman "Stacy" Clardy.

8. Interview, military official; Jones, "Team Tank," *Veritas*, pp. 71–72.

9. Interview, Lieutenant Colonel Duffy White.

10. Ibid.; Interview, Brigadier General John Kelly; Draft 1st Marine Division official history, Chapter 7, p. 32.

11. Interviews, Brigadier General John Kelly and Major General Ray Odierno; draft 1st Marine Division official history, Chapter 7, pp. 35–36. Also see Gian P. Gentile, "The Risk of Velvet Gloves," *Washington Post*, 19 January 2004, Section A, p. 21.

12. Interviews, Lieutenant Colonel Kenneth Tovo and Lieutenant General Henry "Pete" Osman.

13. Interview, Lieutenant General Henry "Pete" Osman. Also see Philip P. Pan, "Kurds' Seizure of City Alarms Turkey; Officials Threaten Force but Say U.S. Will Be Given Time to Urge Withdrawal," *Washington Post*, 11 April 2003, Section A, p. 35.

14. Lieutenant Colonel Robert Waltemeyer, Army interview.

15. Major Paul Brickley. "The original MEU mission required ACE helicopters to pick up BLT Marines and equipment at Irbil, fly them to positions along designated 'rat lines,' and establish checkpoints to intercept HVTs attempting to flee Iraq. Having planned for the intended mission of establishing security checkpoints to stop HVTs from escaping Iraq, the MEU was surprised by the sudden change in mission. The environment was unknown to MEU Marines as they climbed on board civilian buses for insertion into Mosul." Captain Arnaldo L. Colon, "Marines in North Iraq: A Certain Force," 26 MEU(SOC) official report, p. 15.

16. Colon, "Marines in North Iraq," pp. 21–29.

17. Interview, Lieutenant General Henry "Pete" Osman. To help pacify the Turks, liaison officers were allowed to join U.S. forces in Kirkuk. Turkey also wanted to send humanitarian aid with a large military escort. They were told that was unacceptable, but they could send the aid trucks without the troops. That Turkish SOF were part of the contingent became known when a fifteen-year-old Turkish youth turned in an AK-47 to the Americans, explaining that he didn't know how to use it.

18. Interviews, Colonel Joseph Anderson and Lieutenant General Henry "Pete" Osman.

19. Interview, Major General Robin Brims.

CHAPTER 23: *Hello, I Must Be Going*

1. Donald Rumsfeld, "Beyond Nation-Building," speech, 14 February 2003, available from http://www.defenselink.mil/speeches/2003/sp20030214-secdef0023.html; George W. Bush, "A Period of Consequences," 23 September 1999, available from http://citadel.edu/pao/addresses/pres_bush.html.

2. Interview, Pentagon official.

3. Interviews, senior military officials. Lieutenant General Earl Hailston, the senior Marine in the Persian Gulf region, who operated out of Bahrain, and Major General Gene Renuart also attended the meeting.

4. Interview, CFLCC official.

5. Interview, General Tommy Franks, 5 October 2004.

6. Interview, Pentagon official.

7. Ibid.

8. Interview, General Tommy Franks.

9. Interview, Tom White.

10. Interviews, CFLCC officials.

11. Interview, Colonel Curtis Potts.

12. Ian Fisher, "U.S. Force Said to Kill 15 Iraqis During an Anti-American Rally," *New York Times*, 30 April 2003, Section A, p. 1.

13. Interview, Jay Garner, PBS *Frontline*, "Truth, War and Consequences," available from http://www.pbs.org/wgbh/pages/frontline/shows/truth/interviews/garner.html, accessed 9 January 2006.

14. Interviews, Major General Carl Strock and Condoleezza Rice. Also see Michael R. Gordon, "Poor Intelligence Misled Troops About Risk of Drawn-Out War," *New York Times*, 20 October 2004, Section A, p. 1, available from http://www.nytimes.com/pages/world/worldspecial3/, accessed 9 January 2006.

15. Interview, Jay Garner.

16. Interview, Colonel Paul Hughes.

17. Interview, ORHA official. Also see Michael R. Gordon, "For Training Iraq's Police: The Main Problem Was Time," *New York Times*, 21 October 2004, Section A, p. 13, available from: http://www.nytimes.com/pages/world/worldspecial3/, accessed 9 January 2006.

18. Also see "Iraq Police: An Assessment of the Present and Recommendations for the Future," draft report, 30 May 2003, for the Coalition Provisional Authority Interior Ministry. Also "Iraq Police: An Assessment of the Present and Recommendations for the Future," draft, 2 June 2003.

19. Interview, Robert Perito.

20. Interview, Tom Wheelock, United States Institute of Peace Association for Diplomatic Studies and Training, Iraq Experience Project, by W. Haven North, 8 September 2004.

21. For an excerpt from the report, see "A Long, Difficult and Probably Turbulent Process," *New York Times*, 20 October 2004, Section A, p. 12, available from http://www.nytimes.com/pages/world/worldspecial3/, accessed 11 January 2006. The thirty-eight-page report, entitled "Principal Challenges in Post-Saddam Iraq," chronicled a long list of potential problems. It noted, but did not emphasize, the issues. The discussion of this threat was left to the last paragraph of the report. The key judgments of the report are the following:

> The building of an Iraqi democracy would be a long, difficult and probably turbulent process with potential for backsliding into Iraq's tradition of authoritarianism. Iraqi political culture does not foster liberalism or democracy. . . . The principal positive elements in any effort at democratization would be the current relative weakness of political Islam in Iraq and the con-

tributions that could be made by 4 million Iraqi exiles. Iraq would be unlikely to split apart, but a post-Saddam authority would face a deeply divided society with a significant chance that domestic groups would engage in violent conflict with each other unless an occupying force prevented them from doing so.

Sunni Arabs would face possible loss of their longstanding privileged position, while Shia would seek power commensurate with their majority status. Kurds could try to take advantage of Saddam's departure by seizing some of the large northern oil fields, a move that would elicit forceful responses from Sunni Arabs and from Turkey. Score-settling would occur throughout Iraq.

Iraq's large petroleum resources, its greatest asset, would make economic reconstruction less difficult than political transformation. Iraq's economic options would remain few and narrow without forgiveness of debt, a reduction in reparations from the previous Persian Gulf war or something akin to a Marshall plan. If they remained relatively unscathed and any administrative issues involving organization of Iraq's oil industry were resolved, it would be possible to increase oil production in three months from 2.4 million barrels per day to 3.1 million barrels.

The foreign and security policies of a new Iraqi government necessarily would defer heavily in the near term to the interests of the United States, United Nations or an international coalition. But it would also reflect many continuing Iraqi perceptions. Unless guaranteed a security umbrella against its strategic rivals, Iraq's interest in acquiring weapons of mass destruction would eventually revive.

A new Iraqi government would have little interest in supporting terrorism, although strong Iraqi support for the Palestinians would continue. If Baghdad were unable to exert control over the Iraqi countryside, Al Qaeda or other terrorist groups could operate from remote areas.

22. Interview, Brigadier General Steven Hawkins.
23. Interview, Jay Garner, PBS *Frontline,* "Truth, War and Consequences."
24. Interview, Major General Carl Strock; Interview, Tom Wheelock, Iraq Experience Project, 8 September 2004.
25. Interview, Qubad Talabani.
26. Interview, Ambassador Robin Raphel, United States Institute of Peace Association for Diplomatic Studies and Training, Iraq Experience Project, by Charles Kennedy, 13 July 2004.
27. Interview, Brigadier General E. J. Sinclair.

28. "Iraq: What's Going Wrong," cable from John Sawers to British officials, in possession of the authors.

29. Informal transcript of conversation between General Tommy Franks, Admiral Edmund Giambastiani, Major General Gene Renuart, Major General Gary Luck, Lieutenant General Michael "Rifle" DeLong, 14 May 2003, obtained by the authors.

CHAPTER 24: *Starting from Scratch*

1. Interviews, Coalition Provisional Authority, White House, and State Department officials.

2. Jeremiah Cushman, "The Ba'ath Party and U.S. De-Ba'athification Policy," unpublished paper, August 2004.

3. Interview, former CPA official.

4. Interview, James Dobbins. Also see James Dobbins et al., *America's Role in Nation-building: From Germany to Iraq,* RAND Corporation, 2003.

5. Interview, Pentagon official.

6. Interview, Jay Garner. Also Coalition Provisional Authority Order No. 1, "De-Baathification of Iraqi Society," issued May 16, 2003.

7. Michael R. Gordon, "Debate Lingering on Decision to Dissolve the Iraqi Military," *New York Times,* 21 October 2004, Section A, p. 1, available from http://www.nytimes.com/pages/world/worldspecial3/, accessed 11 January 2006. See also Coalition Provisional Authority Order No. 2, "Dissolution of Entities," May 23, 2003.

8. Interview, Colonel Paul Hughes.

9. Interview, CPA official.

10. "19 May 2003 SecDef Planning Instruction—Establishment and Training of the NIC," reviewed by the authors.

11. Condoleezza Rice, quoted in Gordon, "Debate Lingering on Decision to Dissolve Iraqi Military," 21 October 2004. Also see "A Conversation with Peter Pace," 17 February 2004, Council on Foreign Relations, available from http://www.cfr.org/publication/6785/conversation_with_peter_pace.html.

12. Interview, Colonel John Agoglia.

13. Interview, General Tommy Franks.

14. Gordon, "Debate Lingering on Decision to Dissolve the Iraqi Military," 21 October 2004.

15. Interviews, CPA staff.

16. L. Paul Bremer, *My Year in Iraq* (New York: Simon & Schuster, 2006).

17. Interviews, military and Pentagon officials.

18. Interview, Tom White.

19. Interviews, military officials.

20. Interviews, CFLCC and CPA officials.

21. "Iraq: Progress Report," 25 June 2003, John Sawers, confidential British diplomatic report obtained by the authors.
22. Interviews, Colonel Joe Anderson and officers of the 101st Airborne Division.
23. Interviews, Lieutenant Colonel Christopher Conlin and Major General James Mattis.
24. Interview, Major General Ray Odierno.
25. Interview, military official.
26. Interview, Saif Atiyah.
27. Interview, Lieutenant General David McKiernan.
28. Interview, Major General James "Spider" Marks.
29. Interview, Lieutenant General James Conway.
30. Interview, Brigadier General John Kelly.
31. Interview, Major General Buford Blount.
32. Interview, John Keane.
33. Interview, meeting participant.

AFTERWORD TO THE VINTAGE BOOKS EDITION

1. Interview, Defense Department officials.
2. Michael R. Gordon, "An Army of Some," *New York Times Magazine*, 20 August 2006.
3. Ibid.
4. See "Iraq: Recent Developments in Reconstruction Assistance," Congressional Research Service, June 2006.
5. "Survey of Iraqi Public Opinion, June 14–24, 2006," International Republican Institute.
6. Michael R. Gordon, Mark Mazzetti, and Thom Shanker, "Insurgent Bombs Directed at G.I.'s Increase in Iraq," *New York Times,* 17 August 2006.
7. Dexter Filkins, "Baghdad's Chaos Undercuts Tack Pursued by U.S.," *New York Times,* 6 August 2006.
8. Zalmay Khalilzad, "The Battle of Baghdad," *Wall Street Journal,* 23 August 2006.
9. Michael R. Gordon, "Top U.S. General in Iraq Outlines Sharp Troop Cut," *New York Times,* 25 June 2006. Also see Will Dunham, "Pentagon Moves to Buttress U.S. Troop Levels in Iraq," Reuters, 12 October 2006.

Appendix

What follows are internal documents concerning the planning and execution of the war and the situation in Iraq following the fall of Baghdad. They have not previously been released. Also included is L. Paul Bremer's public order dissolving the Iraqi military.

Chronology of the war prepared for President Bush, May 6, 2003

6MAY CINC to POTUS Briefing
Author: CCF6-D USCENTCOM

CHRONOLOGY

28 Nov: OSW aircraft dropped 360,000 leaflets IVO Al Kut,Al Basrah.
01 Dec: OSW Coalition Aircraft targeted air defense near Tallil, Iraq.
02 Dec :   OSW aircraft dropped 240,000 leaflets IVO Al Kut Iraq.
6-16 Dec: Exercise INTERNAL LOOK at Camp As Sayliyah, Qatar.
16 Dec: The Iraqi opposition conference concluded in London, reps from
           over 50 opposition parties met.
19 Jan: 350 personnel depart MacDill AFB to Al Saliyah, Qatar, CENTCOM's
           Forward HQ.
5 Feb: Colin Powell delivers remarks to UN.
25 Feb: Red Cross workers built warehouses in three
           countries next to Iraq in the event of war.
27 Feb: Blix on Iraq "Still hasn't committed to disarming".
1 Mar: Turkish Parliament voted no to U.S. troops being based along Iraq border.
17 Mar: UN orders all UN personnel out of Iraq.
           Pres. Bush addresses nation setting an ultimatum for Saddam Hussein.
19 Mar: **(D-DAY)**   - OIF War Begins.
           - SOF / OGA recon Iraqi units along Green Line.
           - SOF / OGA infils and link ups continue in the South.
           - CFACC initiates counter-TBM operations.
           - 2100L: 1) Special forces destroy VISOBS and assault into western Iraq
(S-DAY), 2) TF-20 destroys western VISOBS and moves into Iraq, 3) Ground forces
recon into southern oil fields with SOF / OGA; I MEF conducts RIP with Kuwait forces.
20 Mar (D+1): - Robust counter-TBM operations.
           - 0001L: TF-20 raid on Ar Rutbah
           - 0530L: TST 2 X F-117 and 24 TLAMs attack leadership target.
           - 2000L: Aerial and ground recon into southern oil fields.
           - 2100L: Air operations conducted to shape the battlespace; 537 air strike sorties;
34 TLAMs; 143 PGMs.
           - 2200L: SOF forces attack to; seize Tallil AB and Euphrates river crossings, and
secure MABOT/KABOT and Al Faw Manifold.
21 Mar (D+2):- Coalition forces seize Iraqi tugboat with 50 naval mines in Khor Abd
Allah waterway; 20 enemy detained; first evidence of mine warfare.
           - 0600L: I MEF seizes western Rumaylah oil fields. Accepts surrender of the
senior ledership of the 51st Iraqi Mech Inf DIV (**G-DAY**).
           - 2100L: Initiate strategic air operations (**A-DAY**); 832 air strike sorties, 381
TLAM's, 124 CALCM's, 231 PGM's.
           - 2200L: Strike on Khurmal terrorist facility.
22 Mar (D+3):- 0700L: V CORPS seizes Tallil AB; controls Euphrates river
           crossings; establishes a FARP south of An Nasiriyah.

- TF TARAWA conducts RIP with 3rd ID to secure Euphrates crossing sites.
- CA Teams begin food and water deliveries and restoring local
- Continue air operations; 878 air sorties, 45 TLAMs, 3 CALCMs, 644 PGMs, 15 ATACMS.
- General Franks met with journalists for the first time since war began.

23 Mar (D+4): - Ground forces attack toward Baghdad
- Military Coordination and Liaison Command infiltrates into Northern Iraq.
-UK SOF and OGA with Iraqi assets expand the interdiction of HVTs.
- CA teams facilitate humanitarian support in southern and northern Iraq.
- Twelve soldiers assigned to the 507th Maint Comp, 3rd ID missing near An Nasiriyah. Iraqi's take PFC Lynch and five other soldiers prisoner.
- Conducted strategic air operations; 827 air strike sorties, 72 TLAMs, 690 PGMs.
- Weather and dust storms impact operations.

24 Mar (D+5) : - Damage Assessment Response Team made final preparations to support the Iraqi people.
- US SOF and OGA insert assets into An Najaf; TF-7 (UK) emergency exfil from western Iraq.
- TF-20 conducts raid on Thar Thar Palace; H2 AB surrenders.
- Conducted strategic air operations: 944 air strike sorties, 11 TLAMs, 2 CALCMs, 559 PGMs.
- CFLCC continues attack toward Baghdad; holds Euphrates crossing sites and attacks north toward Al Kut with I MEF.
- 11th AHR attacks RG Medina DIV south of Baghdad; 1 AH-64 shot down; 2 POWs.
- CA teams restore local government and identify seaport workers in Umm Qasr; facilitate humanitarian assistance in southern Iraq.
- "Boots and Coots" begin oil field fire fighting.
- Engineers from International Red Cross repaired water facilities in Basrah to 40% capacity.

25 Mar (D+6) :- TF-20 attacks H1 airfield.
- Mamals begin Mine Counter-measure operations at Umm Qasr.
- 1st UK Armored DIV secures Al Faw southern oil fields.
- Blacklist issued to components.
- V (US) CORPS seizes An Najaf, continues ops to secure city.

26 Mar (D+7) : - 4th Inf DIV decision made to move to Kuwait.
- Began lethal aid to PUK in norther Iraq IVO Bashur airfield.
- 1st UK Armored DIV isolates Basrah.
- 173rd Airborne BDE executes airborne assault into Bashur airfield via 15 X C-17.
- Dr. Khalilzad and LTG Broadwater infiltrate northern Iraq IVO As Sulaymaniyah.
- Umm Qasr port open and ready for HA delivery.
- V (US) CORPS defeats enemy forces vic An Najaf and As Samawah.

27 Mar (D+8) : - 24th MEU commences offload.

28 Mar (D+9) : - Mine clearing operations in KAA complete; channel open to Umm Qasr.

- Khurma assault/sensitive site exploitation commences.

29 Mar (D+10) : - A-10 refueling opds begin at Tallil AB.

- 101st Air Assault DIV conducts deep attack vicinity Karbala.

- 4th Infantry DIV ADVON commences RSOI in Kuwait.

- TLAM shooters move from Eastern Med and Red Sea to NAG.

- H1 airfield seized.

30 Mar (D+11) : - Thar-Thar Palace direct action by TF-20.

- V (US) CORPS and I MEF occupy attack positions vicinity Karbala and Al Kut.

31 Mar (D+12) :

- First HA ship (UK) at Umm Qasr offloads.

1 Apr (D+13) - TF-20 seizes Hadithah Dam.

- PFC Lynch rescued and remains of 11 soldiers recovered.

- 3 ID attacks north through Karbala Gap to secure Baghdad

- I MEF attacks north towards Al Kut to secure Baghdad.

2 Apr (D+14): - 3 ID secures Euphrates crossing site 17 miles south of Baghdad.

3 Apr (D+15): - 1st UK DIV begins Phase IV transition VIC Umm Qasr.

- I MEF cuts Hwy 6 to isolate Baghdad from southeast.

4 Apr (D+16): - Operation MOUNTAIR THUNDER--air strikes against Iraqi V Corps in the north.

- Khurma samples and 11 human remains enroute to CONUS.

- 3 ID attacks to seize Al Hillah (Medina DIV) and BIAP.

- I MEF attacks to seize Al Kut (Baghdad DIV).

- 82 ABN attacks north of As Samawah.

- UK raid Said traffic circle in Basrah.

5 Apr (D+17): - FIFF move from northern Iraq to southern Iraq.

- 1st "Thunder Run" into central Baghdad by 3 ID.

- I MEF isolates Baghdad from the southeast.

6 Apr (D+18): - 1st UK DIV executes attack into Basrah.

7 Apr (D+19): - EUCOM heavy and medium immediate reaction company begins flow into Bashur airfield.

7 Apr (Cont):   **- CDR USCENTCOM visits Coalition troops in Iraq.**

8 Apr (D+20):   - I MEF raids Rasheed district.

- TF-20 armed recce along Syria/Iraq border.

- 3 ID completes outer cordon of Baghdad from Tigris north to Tigris south.

- 2nd "Thunder Run" into central Baghdad by 3 ID.

- TF-20 commences Hwy 1 interdiction ops north of Baghdad.

9 Apr (D+21):- I MEF secures Al Rasheed complex southeast Baghdad.

- 2 MOABs arrive Al Udeid.

- Spanish ship delivers HA to Umm Qasar.

- Regime fractured; Saddam statue toppled by people of Baghdad. 10 Apr (D+22) - All roads leading into Baghdad interdicted.

- 3 ID holds BIAP, completes outer cordon from Tigris to Tigris.
- BIAP open for Intra-theater lift.
- Kirkuk and northern oil fields secured by JSOTF-N.

11 Apr (D+23): - 1 UK DIV secures the west Qurna and Majnoon oil infrastructure.
- JSOTF-N accepts surrender from Iraqi V CORPS Cdr.
- MV Manar (UAE) delivers HA to Umm Qasr.
- CFLCC early entry command post flows to Baghdad.
- CFSOCC jump command post flows to Baghdad.
- CENTCOM releases "playing cards" displaying the55 most wanted members of Iraqi regime.

12 Apr (D+24): - I MEF attacks north toward to Baqubah and Tikrit.
- 26 MEU commences air movement from Cyprus to Bashur.
- Civilian authorities turn Mosul over to Coalition.
- USS Abraham Lincoln CVBG outchops.

13 Apr (D+25): - Ar Ramadi surrenders to OGA and Tribals.
- Oil flow to Syria stopped.
- 18 of 27 population centers under Coalition influence.
- Naval mine clearing begins north of Umm Qasr.
- 4th ID starts movement into Iraq.
- 7 POWs recovered VIC Tikrit.

15 Apr (D+27): - MEK signs "Cease Fire" agreement.
- Interim Iraqi Authority conference held at Tallil.
- CFLCC begins repositioning of forces to Phase IV stance.
- CDR USCENTCOM announces counter-TBM mission in west is complete.

16 Apr (D+28): - 3/7 CAV secures Ar Ramadi.
- **CDR USCENTCOM visits Baghdad.**

19 Apr (D+31): - USS Kitty Hawk CVBG outchops.

20 Apr (D+32): - USS Constellation CVBG outchops.
- 1.0 CVBG presence USS Nimitz CVBG in NAG.

21 Apr (D+33): - 101st RIP with TF-20 at H1 airfield and Hadithah Dam.
- ORHA begins insertion into Baghdad.
- 1st UK AR DIV secures Umm Qasr.

22 Apr (D+34): - JOR and KSA field hospitals arrive Baghdad.
- 1st Shia pilgrimage in 25 Yrs commences between karbala and An Najaf; 82nd ABN provided security.
- 101st air assaults into Mosul.

24 Apr (D+36): - 26 MEU commences reconstitution.

26 Apr (D+38): - 3 ID secures 125 sites in support of SSE and ORHA.

27 Apr (D+39): - TF-Tarawa hires 100 police officers; curfew in Al Kut to stabilize civil unrest.
- Central Iraq meeting in Baghdad (IIA).

1 May (D+43): - CJTF-7 established.
- POTUS announces end of major combat operations while aboard USS Abraham Lincoln.
- **CDR USCENTCOM visits Basrah.**

3 May (D+45): - I MEF and V (US) CORPS conduct SASO throughout the battlespace.
4 May (D+46): - CJTF-7 assumes West Iraq battlespace.
- 3 ID seizes Republican Presidential Palace in Baghdad.
- 3 ID isolates Baghdad from the northwest
- USS Nimitz CVBG inchop.

PERSONNEL (as of 5 MAY)

– Total military supporting OIF in AOR: 359,029
– US - 316,260
– Coalition - 42,769
– Military in Iraq: 173,218
– US - 150,816
– Coalition - 22,402
– Total Nations in Tampa: 52
– Total Nations in Iraq Theater: 23
– 12 in Iraq – US, AL, AU, CZE, IT, JO, LI, PO, SA, SP, UAE, GB

OIF CASUALITIES   (as of 5 MAY)

- Total Deaths: 171
  - US - 138
  - UK - 33
- Total KIA: 138
  - US - 110
  - UK - 28

BOMBS DROPPED/SORTIES FLOWN
(as of 2 MAY)

Bombs Dropped: 30,501
PGMs: 20,142 (67%)
TLAMs: 802

Sorties Flown: 47,694
  - Strike: 16,969
  - Refueling: 9,656
  - Cargo: 9,974
  - Reconnaissance: 1,795

TONNAGE MOVED (as of 2 MAY)
559,622 short tons (includes OEF; sea, air, rail and ground transport)

SENSITIVE SITE EXPLOITATION
(as of 2 MAY)

Major actions in CENTCOM's campaign. Prepared by the Coalition Forces Land Component Command.

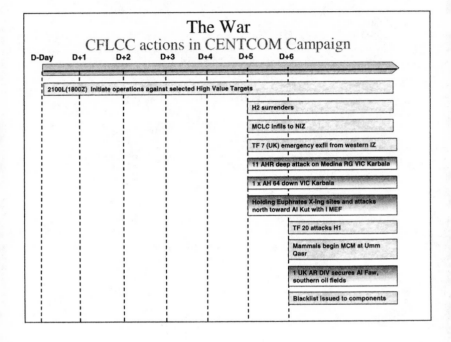

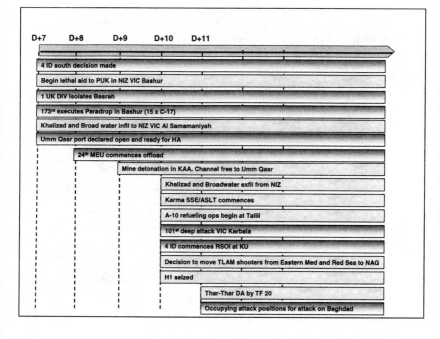

D+7   D+8   D+9   D+10   D+11

4 ID south decision made

Begin lethal aid to PUK in NIZ VIC Bashur

1 UK DIV isolates Basrah

173rd executes Paradrop in Bashur (15 x C-17)

Khalizad and Broad water infil to NIZ VIC Al Samamaniyah

Umm Qasr port declared open and ready for HA

24th MEU commences offload

Mine detonation in KAA. Channel free to Umm Qasr

Khalizad and Broadwater exfil from NIZ

Karma SSE/ASLT commences

A-10 refueling ops begin at Tallil

101st deep attack VIC Karbala

4 ID commences RSOI at KU

Decision to move TLAM shooters from Eastern Med and Red Sea to NAG

H1 seized

Thar-Thar DA by TF 20

Occupying attack positions for attack on Baghdad

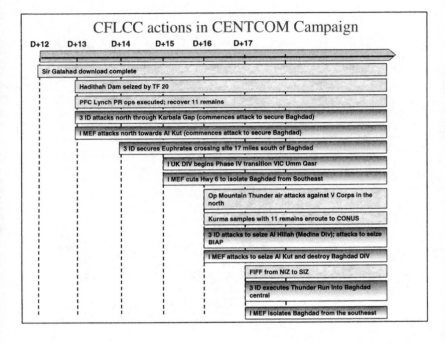

CFLCC actions in CENTCOM Campaign

D+12 D+13 D+14 D+15 D+16 D+17

Sir Galahad download complete

Hadithah Dam seized by TF 20

PFC Lynch PR ops executed; recover 11 remains

3 ID attacks north through Karbala Gap (commences attack to secure Baghdad)

I MEF attacks north towards Al Kut (commences attack to secure Baghdad)

3 ID secures Euphrates crossing site 17 miles south of Baghdad

I UK DIV begins Phase IV transition VIC Umm Qasr

I MEF cuts Hwy 6 to isolate Baghdad from Southeast

Op Mountain Thunder air attacks against V Corps in the north

Kurma samples with 11 remains enroute to CONUS

3 ID attacks to seize Al Hillah (Medina Div); attacks to seize BIAP

I MEF attacks to seize Al Kut and destroy Baghdad DIV

FIFF from NIZ to SIZ

3 ID executes Thunder Run into Baghdad central

I MEF isolates Baghdad from the southeast

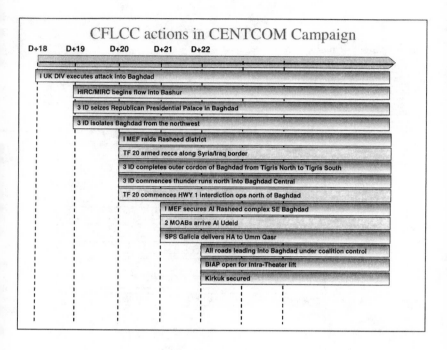

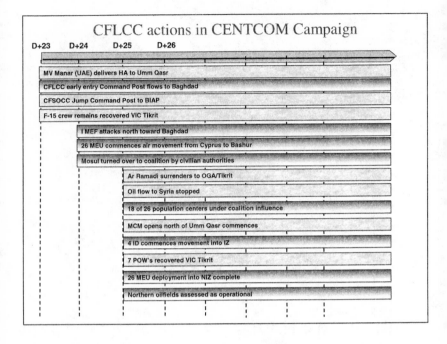

CFLCC actions in CENTCOM Campaign

D+23　　D+24　　D+25　　D+26

- MV Manar (UAE) delivers HA to Umm Qasr
- CFLCC early entry Command Post flows to Baghdad
- CFSOCC Jump Command Post to BIAP
- F-15 crew remains recovered VIC Tikrit
- I MEF attacks north toward Baghdad
- 26 MEU commences air movement from Cyprus to Bashur
- Mosul turned over to coalition by civilian authorities
- Ar Ramadi surrenders to OGA/Tikrit
- Oil flow to Syria stopped
- 18 of 26 population centers under coalition influence
- MCM opens north of Umm Qasr commences
- 4 ID commences movement into IZ
- 7 POW's recovered VIC Tikrit
- 26 MEU deployment into NIZ complete
- Northern oilfields assessed as operational

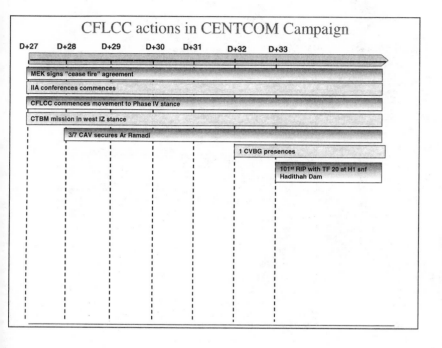

CFLCC actions in CENTCOM Campaign

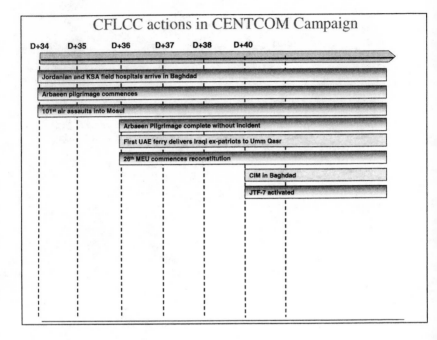

Evolution of the land war plan. Prepared by the Coalition Forces Land Component Command.

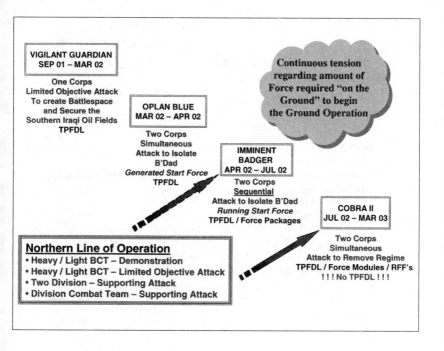

Plan to use the Iraqi army after the war. Prepared by Jay Garner's postwar team and presented at the February 2003 Rock Drill.

Iraqi Security Forces: Post-War Use of Regular Army

Office of Reconstruction and Humanitarian Assistance

- Cannot immediately demobilize... 300K-400K unemployed
- Take advantage of ready labor force w/C2 structure & organic mobility
- Use for reconstruction of Iraq:
  - Reconstruction is labor-intensive
  - Skill set matches tasks: Selected security, construction, demining, engineering, etc.
    - Reestablishes prestige of Regular Army
    - Over time identifies leaders, units to retain
    - Uses Army to rebuild Nation, assist Iraqi population
- Long process (2-3 years), establish lead contractor

Recommendation: Contract now, begin planning and initiate immediately in Phase IV

Briefing on the need for civilian constabulary to keep order in postwar Iraq

DEFENSE POLICY BOARD
BRIEFING
FEBRUARY 28, 2003

EASTABLISHING POST-CONFLICT SECURITY IN IRAQ

Robert M. Perito
United Institute of Peace

- If the President decides to take military action, the US will quickly face the challenge of creating post-conflict security in Iraq. This task will be difficult, confusing and dangerous for everyone involved.

- The US-military administration will be responsible for security, public order, and law enforcement.

- In meeting this responsibility, the US will not be able to rely on the local authorities. Saddam's security services must be disbanded. Prior experience indicates the regular Iraqi police will be unavailable, intimidated or unprepared to act in the chaotic postwar environment.

- Given the political and practical realities, its doubtful the US will be able to turn to the EU, NATO and OSCE, which provided police and legal experts in Bosnia and Kosovo.

- Relying on Coalition military forces is not the answer. Experience in the Balkans demonstrated that regular soldiers are neither trained nor equipped to deal with mob violence or engage in law enforcement.

- There is also a distinct difference between military and police forces. Military forces are trained to concentrate mass and firepower and to destroy the enemy.

- Police are trained to deal with civilians, to preserve and protect and to use only the amount of force required to control the situation.

- LA Rodney King Riot or Montgomery County sniper.

- The US has the world's finest military, but the US military has no civilian security partner. There is no federal department or agency that has responsibility for post-conflict stability.

- The US does not have civilian constabulary forces. It lacks a national police force.

- The US is the only country that uses commercial contractors to staff its police contingents in UN peace operations.

- There is no Federal agency authorized to provide prosecutors, judges and corrections officers for stability operations. However, experience in Kosovo has shown that such personnel are needed to perform judicial functions and to reform local judicial and penal systems.

US STABILITY FORCE

- To ensure a stable post-conflict environment in Iraq, the US should create a civilian US "Stability Force." Such force should include civilian constabulary, police and teams of judicial and corrections experts to establish the rule of law. This force could work with Coalition military forces that will remain to ensure a safe and secure environment.

- A civilian Stability Force would provide the US military with an effective civilian partner. Establishing the rule of law from the outset will free the military to perform its duties and speed its withdrawal.

- Creating the rule of law will provide a foundation for political, economic and social reconstruction.

- The civilian Stability Force would consist of three elements:

Constabulary Units

- Constabularies are police forces with military characteristics.

- They are formed units that fill the place in the force continuum between the military and the civil police.

- In Kosovo, the UN and NATO deployed highly mobile, company-size constabulary units that operated independently or in combination with other forces.

- These constabulary forces were equipped with armored vehicles and heavy weapons and could fight as light infantry, if required.

- Their primary function was civil disorder management and they were highly trained and properly equipped with non-lethal weapons for crowd control.

- They were also trained and equipped to perform police functions and could engage in law enforcement.

- In Kosovo, these "UN Special Police Units" handled crowd control, but they were also able to perform a long list of other functions.

- They protected the airport, guarded prisons, escorted convoys, protected refugees, provided close protection for officials and patrolled the border. Of particular importance was their ability to conduct high-risk arrests of organized crime figures and terrorists.

Civil Police

- The US Stability Force should include civil police (street cops). Like the UN Police in Haiti, Kosovo and East Timor, these police officers should be armed and have 'executive authority' to make arrests, conduct investigations and use deadly force.

- This would enable them to engage in police operations and to operate independently, if required. The civil police contingent would include a liaison and training unit to train and monitor the local police.

- The US has several thousand police officers that have served in UN police missions. These veterans could form the core of the police component of the US Stability Force.

Judicial Teams

- Constabulary and police are important, but they cannot function without the other parts of the judicial system, courts and prisons. The US Stability Force would include teams of prosecutors, defense attorneys, judges, court administrators and corrections officers.

- As in Kosovo, these teams could act independently and could decide to handle sensitive cases on their own authority. Their primary mission, however, would be to ensure that local courts function fairly and effectively.

- Judicial teams would deal with war criminals, ensure respect for human rights and assist with judicial reform. They would also train local attorneys, jurists and court administrators.

- Corrections officers would ensure the proper handling of war criminals, release of political prisoners and the rehabilitation of prison facilities.

- A cadre of American legal veterans with experience in Haiti, Bosnia, and Kosovo is available and could be recruited to perform these functions.

Iraq

- For Iraq, a US civilian Stability Force would have the following components:

- Constabulary: A force of 20 companies with appropriate headquarters and administrative staff for a total of 2,500 personnel. Primary deployment would be in Baghdad, with contingents in four regional centers (Mosul and Kirkuk in the North and Basra and Kut in the South.) These forces would have access to a helicopter airlift to ensure maximum mobility.

- Civil Police: A force of 4,000 US civil police with its headquarters in Baghdad and contingents co-located in the regional and provincial headquarters of the Iraqi National Police. These officers would require wheeled transport, light weapons and effective communications to ensure coordination with constabulary and military backups.

- Judicial Teams: There should be ten teams of twenty lawyers, judges, court administrators and corrections officers supported by a headquarters staff, para-legals, translators and a training unit for a total of 300 personnel. They would be deployed to major population centers where they would work directly with local judicial authorities.

BENEFITS

- Creating a US Stability Force will be challenging. Its contribution to creating post-conflict stability would more than justify the effort.

- Such a force would:

  (1) Join together all of the elements required to effectively achieve sustainable security under a single, unified authority;

  (2) Close the security gap that has plagued previous peace operations by providing for a smooth transition from war fighting to institution building;

  (3) Establish police and judicial authority from the outset, thus freeing the military to perform its functions and speeding its withdrawal;

  (4) Establish the rule of law as a platform from which the other aspects of political, economic and social reconstruction could go forward in an environment conducive to achieving success; and,

  (5) Provide the US with a force that could partner with similar forces from other countries or international organizations.

CONCLUSIONS

- Given the operational realities, the US must take responsibility for establishing the rule of law in Iraq. Other countries may play a role and contribute as conditions stabilize.

- If previous experience is a guide, countries will be more willing to contribute personnel, if the US participates and Americans provide leadership.

- This would mean assuming additional burdens, but it would prevent mistakes and shorten the period before the US can hand off to international or local authorities.

- The challenge is getting started. The people, skill sets and equipment exist in civilian law enforcement, but they need to be brought together by a federal government agency. This will require new funding and, possibly, new legislation. The key ingredients will be leadership and political will.

- The fact that we may be within weeks of a decision by the President to intervene in Iraq should not deter us. Experience in the Balkans, East Timor and Afghanistan shows that Coalition forces will have to deal with high levels of violence for the first two years of the mission.

- The faster we begin, the faster the US will be able to deploy effective civilian security forces and rule of law teams. The faster these units begin their work, the faster Coalition military forces will be able to withdraw and responsibility can be passed to a new Iraqi government.

PRINCIPAL CHALLENGES IN POST–SADDAM IRAQ

In January 2003, the National Intelligence Council issued a thirty-eight-page classified report entitled "Principal Challenges in Post-Saddam Iraq." The report noted that the failure to provide security, restore basic services, and make progress in transferring power to the Iraqi people would lead to the perception that the United States was an occupying power. But the report did not emphasize the possibility of an insurgency. Key sections of the report follow.

—"The building of an Iraqi democracy would be a long, difficult, and probably turbulent process, with potential for backsliding into Iraq's tradition of authoritarianism. Iraqi political culture does not foster liberalism or democracy. Iraq lacks the experience of a loyal opposition and effective institutions for mass political participation. Saddam's brutal methods have made a generation of Iraqis distrustful of surrendering or sharing power. The principal positive elements in any effort at democratization would be the current relative weakness of political Islam in Iraq and the contributions that could be made by four million Iraqi exiles, many of whom are Westernized and well educated, and by the now impoverished and underemployed Iraqi middle class. Iraq would be unlikely to split apart, but a post-Saddam authority would face a deeply divided society with a significant chance that domestic groups would engage in violent conflict with each other unless an occupying force prevented them from doing so.

—"Sunni Arabs would face possible loss of their long-standing privileged position while Shia would seek power commensurate with their majority status. Kurds could try to take advantage of Saddam's departure by seizing some of the large northern oil fields, a move that would elicit forceful responses from Sunni Arabs and from Turkey. Score settling would occur throughout Iraq between those associated with Saddam's regime and those who had suffered most under it.

—"Iraq's large petroleum resources, its greatest asset, would make economic reconstruction less difficult than political transformation. Iraq's economic options would remain few and narrow without forgiveness of debt, a reduction in reparations from the previous Persian Gulf War or something akin to a Marshall plan. Iraq's economic and financial prospects would vary significantly depending on how much damage its oil facilities sustained in war. If they remained relatively unscathed and any administrative issues involving organization of Iraq's oil industry were resolved it would be possible to increase oil production in three months from 2.4 million barrels per day to 3.1 million barrels per day. A less oil-dependent economy with a strong private sector would be required to generate the more than 240,000 new jobs needed each year to accommodate the rapidly growing labor force.

—"Major outside assistance would be required to meet humanitarian needs. Increasing numbers of refugees and internally displaced persons combined with civil strife would strain Iraq's already inadequate health care services, food distribution networks and supplies of potable water. Most Iraqis depend on government food rations and are not equipped to deal with hoarding, looting or price gauging. Rapid reconstitution of the distribution system would be critical to avoiding widespread health problems. Iraqis have restored their physical infrastructure quickly after previous wars. The difficulty of restoring such services as water and electricity after a new war would depend chiefly on how much destruction was caused by urban combat.

—"The foreign and security policies of a new Iraqi government necessary would defer heavily in the near term to the interests of the United States, United Nations or an international coalition. But it would also reflect many continuing Iraqi perceptions and interests. Those perceptions, particularly of threats from regional states, such as Iran, Turkey and Israel, would increasingly shape the Iraqis' policies as they reasserted their independence. These threat perceptions along with a prideful sense of Iraqi's place as a regional power probably would sustain Iraq's interest in rebuilding its military. Unless guaranteed a security umbrella against its strategic rivals Iraq's interest in acquiring weapons of mass destruction would eventually revive. A new Iraqi government would have little interest in supporting terrorism, although strong Iraqi support for the Palestinians would continue. If Baghdad were unable to exert control over the Iraqi countryside Al Qaeda or other terrorist groups could operate from remote areas.

—"Once the most pressing needs became less of a worry for most Iraqis, however, politics and the nature of the ruling authority would become increasingly important to them. Iraqis would expect progress in transferring power from foreign occupiers, however much they had been welcomed as liberators, to indigenous leaders. Attitudes toward a foreign military force would depend largely on the progress made in transferring power as well as on the degree to which that force were perceived as providing necessary security and fostering reconstruction and a return to prosperity."

Results of "Desert Crossing" war game organized by General Anthony Zinni in June 1999 to study how to manage a post-Saddam Iraq (declassified).

EXECUTIVE SUMMARY (U)

(U) On June 28–30, 1999, the United States Central Command (USCENT-COM) sponsored the Desert Crossing Seminar to identify interagency issues and insights on how to manage change in a post-Saddam Iraq. The Seminar structure focused the participants on crucial interagency issues that would bear on the situation, as well as interagency interests and responsibilities. USCENTCOM briefed a draft plan, known as "Desert Crossing," to participants for discussion of the proposed phases and concepts, as well as the risks, threats, opportunities, and challenges that are likely to be present under those conditions. Over 70 participants, including the Department of State, Department of Defense, National Security Council, and the Central Intelligence Agency took part in the seminar.

(U) Participants were organized into various teams to facilitate the development of insights, but were not asked to "solve" the problems. In fact, there was a consensus that this seminar should be the beginning of much more robust discussions. The observations below summarize participant views and suggest matters for further deliberation. These views do not represent consensus of the individual participants, the various Departments, agencies, or entities, or the U.S. Government.

Deliberate planning needs to become interagency (S)

- **(U) Political/Military planning should begin immediately.**
  (U) The dimensions of preparing a post-Saddam policy for Iraq and the region are vast and complex. Early preparation of a political-military plan as called for in Presidential Decision Directive 56 should be a priority. The accompanying policy debate will expose a variety of contentious positions that must be reconciled and managed. Key discussion points include: benefits and risks associated with various strategic options; information requirements; and the likelihood that intervention will be costly in terms of casualties and resources.

- (U) **Regime crisis may require rapid U.S. action on short notice.**

  (U) When the crisis occurs, policy makers will have to deal with a large number of critical issues nearly simultaneously, including demonstrating U.S. leadership and resolve, managing Iraq's neighbors, and rapid policy formulation. Successfully doing so depends on identifying "Red Lines," the crossing of which is likely to lead to U.S. reaction, in order to facilitate crisis planning. Such Red Lines may include large-scale humanitarian crisis, use (or imminent use) of Weapons of Mass Destruction (WMD), or imminent Iraqi attack on a neighboring state.

- (U) **Regime change may not enhance regional stability.**

  (U) A change in regimes does not guarantee stability. A number of factors including aggressive neighbors, fragmentation along religious and/or ethnic lines, and chaos created by rival forces bidding for power could adversely affect regional stability. Even when civil order is restored and borders are secured, the replacement regime could be problematic—especially if perceived as weak, a puppet, or out-of-step with prevailing regional governments. These consequences must not be ignored during political-military planning.

- (U) **WMD issues warrant additional attention.**

  (U) Participants concluded that U.S. policy in reaction to the use of WMD against U.S. personnel or allies was clear. However, U.S. policy on the possibility of Iraqi use of WMD under other circumstances is ill defined and probably does not address the full range of situations. For example, how should the United States respond to an Iraqi faction that employs WMD against a competing faction or a non-coalition or non-ally neighbor? Although the likelihood of WMD use by Iraq was hotly debated, planners and policy makers should review potential WMD situations now to determine the scale, scope, and nature of such use and the likely U.S. response.

Management of Iran is critical to mission success (U)

- (U) **Iran's anti-Americanism could be enflamed by a U.S.-led intervention in Iraq.**

  (U) Iran has substantial interests in developments in Iraq, perhaps its most bitter rival in the region, nor have relations with the United States been any better. The influx of U.S. and other western forces into Iraq would exacerbate worries in Tehran, as would the installation of a pro-western government in Baghdad. More than any other country in the region, the principals were most concerned by how Iran would respond to a U.S.-led intervention in Iraq.

- **(U) Iran possesses the ability to raise the costs and consequences of intervention.**
  (U) Many participants felt that Washington should attempt to leverage the crisis to improve the present U.S.-Iran relationship. They believe the worst-case scenario is one in which Iran feels pressured and lashes out asymmetrically in moves that range from harassment of U.S. forces to terrorist attacks. Such attacks will likely shake U.S. determination and perhaps undermine public and political will. To preclude this, the United States and its partners should ensure that Iran does not support counterproductive activities in Iraq and should engage Tehran in a productive fashion wherever possible.

- **(U) Lifting sanctions on Iran may be part of a full Iraq policy.**
  (U) Whether the lifting of U.S. sanctions on Iran will be required to gain Tehran's cooperation is unclear. Some participants expressed the view that the United States should use the possibility of lifting them as an incentive for Iranian cooperation. Other participants expressed concern as to how to control Iran in the long term if it continues its support for terrorism, continues WMD programs, and/or exports its revolutionary principles to other countries in the region once sanctions are lifted.

Ambiguous role of Iraqi opposition clouds U.S. policy development

- **(U) Lack of information on internal Iraqi opposition conditions severely hampers contingency planning.**
  (U) The United States lacks sufficient information on individuals and groups within Iraq to plan for, or respond to, Saddam's departure. Information for planning and to facilitate dialog with key internal groups or individuals is currently lacking; the United States does not have a clear understanding of their policies and agendas. The intelligence community should initiate actions to determine potential Iraqi leadership groupings that might "naturally" evolve when Saddam departs and to establish the basic criteria and conditions under which such individuals or groups should be approached.

- (U) **Iraqi exile opposition weaknesses are significant.**
  (U) The debate on post-Saddam Iraq also reveals the paucity of information about the potential and capabilities of the external Iraqi opposition groups. The lack of intelligence concerning their roles hampers U.S. policy development. Although participants disagreed as to whether exiled opposition leaders could be useful during the regime transition period, there was no dispute that if the United States were to support them, much must be done in order for these groups to be politically credible within Iraq.

- (U) **The United States should be prepared to initiate, on short notice, a dialog with leaders of key ethnic groups within Iraq.**
  (U) A variety of power struggles might occur during the early stages of a post-Saddam crisis. Because events are likely to occur rapidly, consideration should be given now to individuals and groups and their policies and agendas in order to develop a range of options. To this end, the United States should initiate, or at least prepare to initiate, dialogs with key leaders in the PUK, KDP, and Shia tribes as early possible.

Coalition dialogue should begin immediately

- (U) **Active support from coalition partners is critical to mission success.**
  (U) There are many unknowns as to how potential partners think about coalition participation. To facilitate rapid reaction, the United States must begin the process of planning for coalition operations and developing the basis for a coalition now. The risks to U.S. regional interests are too high and events are likely to unfold too rapidly to wait until the crisis begins.

- (U) **Differing visions of a unified Iraq complicate end-state articulation.**
  (U) The seminar demonstrated that there are differing visions of what a post-Saddam Iraq should look like to various coalition partners. These differences will complicate developing a common coalition end state, much less reaching consensus on such a state. This will delay coalition formation during the critical early stages of the crisis and may complicate exit strategies.

- (U) **Arab coalition may undermine accomplishment of U.S. policy objectives.**
  (U) A paradox exposed during the Seminar is that while an Arab coalition will be required for legitimacy in the region, such a coalition may make it more difficult for the United States to attain its objectives. Solutions envisioned by U.S. coalition partners (especially our Arab partners) may be

significantly different than those envisioned by U.S. planners. For example, the Iraq Liberation Act specifies a democratic outcome that contrasts starkly with the predilections of some Arab governments. Also, some participants believe that no Arab government will welcome the kind of lengthy U.S. presence that would be required to install and sustain a democratic government.

- (U) **A long-term, large-scale military intervention may be at odds with many coalition partners.**
  (U) The nature of the region's relationships with the United States and other western nations in the post-intervention era are likely to be vastly different. What participants referred to as the "Japanese Option," (long-term presence and directed change) is not likely to be well received by coalition partners. Changes that could result from intervention at various levels will involve political and military relationships; religious and ethnic conflicts; economic relations; and differing views of social justice. While differences with Arab allies concerning the U.S. presence in the region were managed reasonably well in the past (owing in part to common threats), intervention in Iraq may alter the way these relationships are handled dramatically enough to produce new frictions and conflicts.

Iraq's economic viability is key to long term regional stability

- (U) **Iraqi stabilization requires debt/claims forgiveness.**
  (U) Mounting a large intervention will be costly, as regional partners may not be willing to reimburse the United States to the extent that they have in the past. One possibility, using Iraqi oil revenues to pay for the intervention, would come at the expense of long-term reconstitution and may affect regional and global economic stability if oil prices fluctuate too rapidly. Also, Iraq still faces claims estimated at $300 billion as a result of its 1990 invasion of Kuwait. If these claims are relentlessly pursued, economic recovery, and thus stability, may be delayed. Policymakers in the United States and abroad should investigate debt and claims forgiveness, as a stable Iraq can evolve only if it is economically viable.

- (U) **The relaxation of economic sanctions early in the crisis may be a key determinant in the ability of the United States to influence events in Iraq.**
  (U) Some seminar participants believed that one of the most important things the United States could do to improve its image in the eyes of the Iraqi people would be the announcement of immediate lifting of eco-

nomic sanctions early in the transition crisis. The United States should expect immediate pressure from others, including coalition members, to lift sanctions, even while the outcome of the internal Iraqi situation is unclear. Seizing the "high ground" and immediately lifting the sanctions upon a change in the Iraqi regime—even if its policies and orientation are unknown—might be advantageous for U.S. interests.

Personal message from David McKiernan, Commanding General, Coalition Forces Land Component Command, to all personnel assigned, attached, or supporting Operation Iraqi Freedom. It was issued on March 19, 2003, on the eve of the war.

RMKS/1. YOU ARE ABOUT TO REMOVE THE REGIME OF SADDAM HUSSEIN AND ELIMINATE THE THREAT OF HIS WEAPONS OF MASS DESTRUCTION.

2. HE IS A BRUTAL DICTATOR WHOSE REGIME HAS A HISTORY OF RECKLESS AGGRESSION, TIES TO TERRORISM, ATTEMPTS TO DOMINATE A VITAL REGION OF THE WORLD AND A HISTORY OF DEVELOPING AND USING WEAPONS OF MASS DESTRUCTION. THERE ARE NO FURTHER OPTIONS OTHER THAN MILITARY OPERATIONS. TO DATE, NOTHING HAS RESTRAINED SADDAM HUSSEIN FROM PURSUING HIS GOALS OF INTIMIDATING NEIGHBORING STATES AND ATTACKING AND TYRANNIZING HIS OWN PEOPLE. HIS CONTINUING REFUSAL TO DESTROY WEAPONS OF MASS DESTRUCTION, TO FULLY COOPERATE IN INSPECTIONS TO VERIFY COMPLIANCE WITH UNITED NATIONS' MANDATES OR DESIST FROM ACQUIRING NEW WEAPONS PROVIDES NO REAL ALTERNATIVE TO THE ATTACK THAT WE WILL EXECUTE.

3. YOUR TASK WILL NOT BE AN EASY ONE, BUT IT IS JUST AND YOU WILL TRIUMPH. YOUR ARE A MEMBER OF THE BEST TRAINED AND EQUIPPED MILITARY FORCE IN HISTORY. THIS CAMPAIGN WILL PLACE EXTRAORDINARY DEMANDS ON INDIVIDUAL SOLDIERS, SAILORS, MARINES, AIRMEN AND SMALL UNIT LEADERS WHO MUST BE PREPARED TO FIGHT AS THEY HAVE BEEN TRAINED, WHILE, AT THE SAME TIME, PROVIDING A HELPING HAND TO THOSE IRAQIS THAT WELCOME THE COALITION AS LIBERATORS. YOUR COURAGE, TRAINING AND DETERMINATION, BACKED BY THE WILL OF ALL FREEDOM LOVING PEOPLES, ENSURES YOUR VICTORY.

4. WITHIN THIS FORCE, EACH OF US HAS A JOB TO DO, AND EACH OF US SERVES THE WHOLE. EVERY SINGLE CFLCC UNIT IS IMPORTANT IN THE CAMPAIGN TO REMOVE THIS DICTATOR AND RESTORE IRAQ TO THE PEOPLE OF IRAQ. LIKEWISE WE ARE PART OF A LARGER JOINT AND COALITION TEAM UNDER COMCENT. EACH OF US HAS A DUTY TO OUR UNIT, OUR SERVICE, AND OUR COUNTRY, BUT WE HAVE AN EQUALLY IMPORTANT DUTY TO EACH OTHER. YOUR COURAGE WILL BE TESTED BUT YOU WILL DRAW STRENGTH FROM THOSE ON YOUR LEFT AND RIGHT. YOU WILL NOT FALTER. I KNOW THAT ALL OF YOU WILL REPRESENT YOURSELVES, YOUR UNITS AND YOUR RESPECTIVE COUNTRIES WITH HONOR AND VALOR IN THE DAYS AHEAD. WE WILL FIGHT AS A TEAM AND WILL BE VICTORIOUS AS A TEAM THAT IS FIGHTING FOR A COMMON AND JUST GOAL.

5. I HAVE TOTAL CONFIDENCE IN YOU. THERE IS NO FINER TEAM GATHERED ANYWHERE IN THE WORLD; NO TEAM MORE CAPABLE OF ADDRESSING THE TASK AT HAND. WE ARE COMRADES IN ARMS AND I HAVE UNBOUNDED PRIDE IN LEADING YOU. TRUST YOUR INSTINCTS, TRAINING AND LEADERSHIP IN THE DAYS AHEAD. YOU ARE WARRIORS IN A HISTORIC CAMPAIGN THAT WILL BENEFIT OUR FAMILIES, LOVED ONES AND OUR COUNTRIES, AS WELL AS THE PEOPLE OF IRAQ.

6. STRIKE FAST AND HARD! MCKIERNAN

Marine e-mail from Lieutenant Colonel Andy Kennedy, the operations officer for RCT-2, on confusion during the battle at Nasiriyah

```
                                    RE concern.txt
From: RCT-2 S3
Sent: Wednesday, June 04, 2003 02:50
To: Starnes LtCol Glenn T; 2 MEB 1/2 BN CMDR
Subject: RE: concern

Gentlemen,
why did we not pass the timeline for siezing the bridges?
I'm not sure.  I thought I passed we would attack them after we gathered
ourselves at the 20 northing. I may not have done so. I wanted to see what
the situation was in the area before we went to attack the bridges (all
concerned about level of violence and urban suck etc.). The MEB had told me
verbally to plan to attack them "sometime around 04-0700 if possible".  I
did not produce any written orders and did not recieve any from the MEB so I
have nothing to fall back on but my memory of the events. It is possible
that I never mentioned attacking the eastern bridges, I can't remember.  My
intentions were to not go in half cocked but to assess the situation.  The
orders we'd recieved (verbally) were sufficiently annoying that I did not
want to execute them as briefed and so I asked Col J about why and when.  He
got me to shut up by telling me we need not attack until we were ready.  In
the rush of events that night I have no idea why I did not mention the fact
that MEB wanted us to attack the bridges.  I thought I passed this.  I have
no excuse except the press of events.  I am not trying to "soft pedal" this
in any way.  I obviously did not convey everything properly to our
subordinate units. I know it does no good to say so, but I am sorry.
Semper Fi
the newest LtCol on the block
```

British assessment by John Sawers on waning Iraqi suppport for the coalition and the need to improve Baghdad security, May 11, 2003

```
CONFIDENTIAL
PERSONAL
FM IRAQREP
TO IMMEDIATE FCO
TELNO 2
OF 111430Z MAY 03
INFO IMMEDIATE BAGHDAD, UKMIS NEW YORK, WASHINGTON
INFO IMMEDIATE ACTOR, DFID, MODUK, WHIRL, NO 10


PERSONAL FROM SPECIAL REP FOR IRAQ FOR:

NO 10: POWELL, MANNING, CAMPBELL, RYCROFT
FCO: PS/SOS, PS/O'BRIEN, PUS, RICKETTS, EHRMAN, CHAPLIN, CHILCOTT
MOD: PS/SOS, CDS, CGS, PUS, WEBB, PIGOTT
DFID: PS/SOS, PUS, BREWER, MILLER, AUSTIN

SUBJECT: PERSONAL: IRAQ: WHAT'S GOING WRONG?

SUMMARY

1. A Baghdad First strategy is needed.  The problems are worst
in the capital, and it is the one place we can't afford to get
it wrong.  But the troops here are tired, and are not providing
the security framework needed.  We need a clear policy on which
Ba'athists can return, a more concerted effort on reconstruction,
and an imaginative approach on the media.  For all this, money
needs to be released by Washington.  The clock is ticking.

DETAIL

2. Four days in Iraq has been enough to identify the main reasons
why the reconstruction of Iraq is so slow.  The Coalition are
widely welcomed, but are gradually losing public support.

3. Garner's outfit, ORHA, is an unbelievable mess.  No
leadership, no strategy, no co-ordination, no structure, and
inaccessible to ordinary Iraqis.  Bremer's arrival is not a day
too soon, and he needs to be radical.  Garner and his top team
of 60-year old retired generals are well-meaning but out of their
depth.  Tim Cross is widely seen as the only senior figure
offering direction to the many able individuals here from the US,
Britain and Australia.  Garner points to a glass half-full, but
much of this is despite, not because of ORHA.  The political
point is that progress is lagging behind the reasonable
expectations of ordinary Iraqis.

4. I have not yet been out of the capital, but it is clear that
Baghdad is the biggest problem.  Other parts of Iraq are getting
organised: there are minimal Shia/Sunni tensions; town councils
have been agreed in the sensitive cities of Mosul and Kirkuk;
and so on. But Baghdad has the worst security, a poor level
of essential services, and no information flow.  I will
recommend to Bremer a Baghdad First strategy.  We can afford
some of the regions to languish.  But failure in Baghdad would
be fatally undermine our success in the conflict.  What
would such an approach require?

SECURITY
```

5. No progress is possible until security improves. Crime is widespread (not surprising as Saddam released all the criminals last autumn). Car-jackings are endemic, with the cars driven to Iran for sale. Last week the Ministry of Planning was re-kitted out ready to resume work; that night it was looted again. The evening air is full of gunfire. There is still a climate of fear on the streets, because of the level of crime, and that is casting a shadow over all else.

6. A big part of the problem is the US Third Infantry Division. They fought a magnificent war, exhausted themselves and now just want to go home. Unlike more mobile US units like the marines (now gone) and the 101st Airborne Division (in Mosul), 3rd Inf Div are sticking to their heavy vehicles and combat gear, and are not inclined to learn new techniques. Our Paras company at the Embassy witnessed a US tank respond to (harmless) Kalashnikov fire into the air from a block of residential flats by firing three tank rounds into the building. Stories are numerous of US troops sitting on their tanks parked in front of public buildings while looters go about their business behind them. Every civilian who approaches a US checkpoint is treated as a potential suicide bomber. Those trying to set up Baghdad's police find the military here a hindrance, not a help. Frankly, the 3rd Inf Div need to go home now, and be garlanded as victors, but sadly that isn't due for several weeks. Can it be brought forward?

7. The military culture in the capital needs to change before their replacements (another heavy armour division) arrives. We, the Brits, do not have all the answers, but an operational UK presence in Baghdad is worth considering, despite the obvious political problem. Transferring one of our two brigades is presumably out of the question, but one battalion with a mandate to deploy into the streets could still make an impact. CGS saw the problem last Friday and can offer more professional advice. There are US units who could also contribute if there is any gap in coverage to be filled.

8. Re-forming the Baghdad police has begun, but needs to be accelerated. I visited them today and the work is being pushed forward by an excellent team of US military police and two civilian advisers (one a Brit). It is beginning to happen but is not getting the priority it needs. The police need to start patrolling with sympathetic soldiers, rather than with one police car sandwiched between four Humvees. Weapons, uniforms, funds, vehicles, access to fuel and a functioning judicial process are all problems. Bringing Kurdish Peshmerga down to the capital, as Barzani and Talebani are suggesting as a stopgap, would be at best only one small part of the solution. There is already a risk of Iraqi Arabs reacting against the prominent Kurdish role in the apres-guerre.

DE-BA'ATHIFICATION

9. The other fear among ordinary people in Baghdad is that the Ba'athists could still come back. ORHA have made mistakes here, appointing quite senior party figures as their main partners in the trade and health ministries, at Baghdad University and so on. Several political leaders I have seen say a line should be drawn at the "firqa" level of the Ba'ath Party and all those at that level and the three above should be excluded, about 30,000 in all.

This would represent between five and ten per cent of total party membership. But it is still a lot of people and may be one level too many, at least for now. Whatever, we need to set out a clear policy, plus a process for dealing with contested cases, even though it means starting again in some institutions.

RECONSTRUCTION

10. With security and credible de-Ba'athification will come the chance for durable reconstruction. Power is back, though the network is not robust. Water is running but is not potable. 40% of Baghdad's sewage is said to be pouring into the Tigris untreated, contributing to disease downstream. Garbage is piling up on the streets, and will be a health hazard here. A GSM mobile phone system is desperately needed in the capital as communications are dire. And so on. Bechtel, who have the main contract for re-connecting essential services, are moving far too slowly. They need to swamp Baghdad with engineers and skilled labour. They will have no difficulty in finding local workers.

11. Quick results projects are also needed to show there is progress on the way. We need visibly successful projects, however small: schools and hospitals re-opening, new bakeries, food distribution points. That is not a substitute for long term development, but it would meet genuine needs and also the political requirement. DfID and USAID could play a role here, as well as NGOs and the UN.

INFORMATION

12. Baghdad has no TV, and no newspapers apart from party political rags. I was given two fliers yesterday by an Iraqi, one calling for the assassination of all Ba'athists, the other for the killing of all US forces. That, and rumour, are the only information flowing. An ORHA TV project is due to get going next week but its content will be tightly controlled by ORHA, and it risks not being credible. I have pressed them, as a start, to broadcast a Premier League game each day, but the Americans don't yet get it.

13. More progress is being made with radio: the BBC (English and Arabic) should be up on FM this week. But, as all political leaders have stressed, Baghdad needs independent newspapers, radio stations and terrestial TV stations. One idea is to give satellite dishes and screens to cafes so that people can have access to pan-Arab channels - but it needs funding.

14. ORHA also needs a public face. Bremer's people already have this in mind, as ORHA's bunker image is painfully apparent. Security and the threat of swamping are real problems. But they are better than isolation and ignorance.

FUNDS AND PUBLIC SECTOR SALARIES

15. Finally, money needs to be available, not least to pay police and public service workers. This is held up in Washington (as ORHA gleefully point out). First, the US Administration are refusing to release Iraqi money to pay salaries - even the $740m in cash found here is being blocked (unlike the cash our troops found in Basra). That on its own should be enough to pay salaries into 2004. Second, early decisions are needed on salary levels and which

currency (dollars, Saddam dinars, or new Swiss dinars) should be used. The actual decisions are less important than getting them taken, so that a big information campaign can begin to distribute back pay in mid-June.

15.   There are hundreds of small problems needing attention - petrol and cooking fuel distribution, paying farmers for this season's harvest and so on. But the big five are as set out above, and security is both the most important and the most sensitive.   There will be an instinct in Washington to allow Bremer time to find his feet and reach his own conclusions. But that will take another week or more - and the clock is ticking. I will talk to him once he gets here, but will have to feel my way at first. No harm if the ground in Washington can be prepared.

16.   I am reporting separately about politics.

Contact: iraqrep@gtnet.gov.uk.; +88 216 521 00272

SAWERS

YYYY

SVLNAN 7523

NNNN

British assessment by John Sawers on declining security and Bremer's argument for more troops, June 25, 2003

SIC
FROM SPECIAL REPRESENTATIVE FOR IRAQ

SUBJECT: IRAQ: PROGRESS REPORT

SUMMARY

1. Security has worsened in Baghdad, especially at night. Continued attacks against the Coalition in the Sunni triangle. Majar al-Kabir was the first major incident in the Shia south. Sabotage of the infrastructure is a new threat. Law and order capability is slowly improving, but Bremer is concerned that the troop draw down may have gone too far.

2. Unemployment remains very high. Salaries and pensions help keep people going but aren't substitute for economic activity. CPA economic policy is becoming more coherent. We have to resolve whether our net obligations are to help reform the economy or preside over the Saddam era structures with minimum change. De Mello is inclined to the former.

3. The political process is edging forward. The UN are on board and would like to move more quickly. A big effort will be needed to line up all the party leaders in an agreed Political Council by mid-July. Moderate Shia leaders are coming under pressure as problems persist with essential services. With Muqtadr al-Sadr's return from Iran, the Shia radicals are becoming more active. Retaining Shia support is a sine qua non.

DETAIL

4. It has been a difficult week in Iraq. Fire fights between Coalition forces and Iraqi groups have been more frequent, with the Majar al-Kabir incident the worst. That seems to have been due to local causes and is in a known volatile area, but it shows how thin is the veneer of security in many parts of Iraq. Our law and order capability in Iraq is slowly improving, with police numbers rising and retraining beginning. The Courts and prison sys-

tems are also edging back up bit by bit. The need to transform Saddams brutal structures makes it a slow process.

5. US operations against hostile targets in the Sunni areas seem to have had some effect. Only two US soldiers were killed in action in the last week, but the number of incidents remains high—over 20 a day. Fortunately, ethnically-mixed cities like Kirkuk and Mosul remain calm and there are no significant Arab/Kurd or Shia/Sunni flashpoints.

6. The new threat is well-targeted sabotage of the infrastructure. An attack on the power grid last weekend had a series of knock-on effects which halved the power generation in Baghdad and many other parts of the country. That in turn cut off the water supply. Much of Baghdad has been without electricity and running water for the last three days. The oil and gas network is another target, with five successful attacks this week on pipelines. We do not yet have an answer to this threat. We are also seeing the first signs for intimidation of Iraqis working for the Coalition.

7. Bremer's main concern is that we must keep in-country sufficient military capability to ensure a security blanket across the country. He has twice said to President Bush that he is concerned that the draw down of US/UK troops has gone too far, and we cannot afford further reductions. US forces are down to 80 percent of end-conflict levels, UK forces have reduced further to 40 percent. While other national contingents are welcome, he questions whether they will be sufficiently robust when push turns to shove. General Reith assured Bremer today that we have the necessary forces in the south, and can reinforce if necessary.

THE ECONOMY

8. The attacks on the infrastructure are making it more difficult to build up electricity supply and to restart Iraq's economy. Food distribution is running smoothly, and the CPA are catching up with the backlog of salary payments to the public sector. The decision on military pensions has gone down well and protests on that front have gone quiet. But unemployment remains at an estimated 60 percent, and handouts arent a substitute for economic activity.

9. Economic policy making in the CPA is beginning to come together. As usual with the Americans, they start with the most radical ideas but usually end up with a more modest decision. An emergency budget for the rest of the year should be finalised in two weeks. A limited IMF-backed currency reform is in hand. Bremer is working up plans for a social safety net.

10. But there are big issues ahead: how do we get Iraq's state-owned industries running again? Can we attract foreign investment? How can the controls on the Iraqi economy and society be lifted to encourage enterprise? The World Bank and the IMF are pressing for reform of Iraqs state-controlled economy. Some say this would be contrary to our legal obligations. Others point to the requirements of SCR 1483 where the Coalition must promote the welfare of the Iraqi people, must effectively administer the country, and must restore conditions of security and stability (which covers the economy as much as civil society). De Mello told me today he favours more change, not less, and he regrets not doing more in East Timor when he had the power. We need to engage in this debate and do so in the knowledge that failing to get the economy moving will make it more difficult to achieve a successful transition.

POLITICAL PROCESS

11. Standing up a roughly 25 member Political Council by mid-July remains the goal. The main party leaders are playing hard to get. The Americans will need to twist Chalabi's arm to get him to take part personally. If he distances himself, then it will be harder to get other party leaders to join up. The UN Representative, de Mello, is supportive of our approach and asked me today why we couldn't move more quickly. I explained that we had to allow internal figures to come forward, and work for broad consensus among the parties, but we were stepping up the pace.

12. In the medium term, my main concern is the Shia. The continued problem with security and essential services means that moderate Shia leaders are coming under pressure as their communities question whether supporting the Coalition is the right approach. Meanwhile, the Iranians are adding to their options in Iraq by cultivating the young Najaf radical, Muqtadr Al-Sadr, and that is worrying the moderate clerics. SCIRI, the pro-Iran party we are working with, are facing some tricky decisions. Iraqis remain resist-

ant to Iranian attempts to exert influence. But the biggest threat in the next year is that, for a mix of reasons, we lose the Shia heartlands. The Iranians seem to be positioning themselves so they can make that threat more real.

CPA

13. The CPA is gradually strengthening itself. Bremer has found his feet, and he is open to our concerns when we articulate them. The arrival of key figures like Slocombe, Bearpark and Belka have improved the top team. Bearpark's first task is to build up the regional structure, especially CPA South which remains in a sorry state. The South is going to remain a UK responsibility, and we should not shed tears if the Dane, Olsen, opts to leave. Rather, we should seize the chance to put in a top quality Brit.

14. The other big gap is Communications Director. John Buck has done an excellent job over the last month, but the White House have let Bremer down and failed to find a good quality candidate prepared to spend the next 8 months in Baghdad. This is a crucial problem: we cannot communicate easily with the Iraqi people and that remains a fundamental weakness of the Coalition. We need someone to tackle that problem.

CONCLUSION

15. It's three steps forward and two steps back. We have to carry on steadily building up the Coalitions and Iraqs capabilities, and putting out fires where they occur. We cannot allow those responsible for killing Coalition soldiers and destroying Iraq's infrastructure to think they can get away with it. Nor should we despair: it was always on the cards that security would get worse before it improved. We just have to make sure we have the right resources, people and level of effort to keep driving this forward, including through August when the West might be on holiday but the terrorists and saboteurs won't be.

SAWERS

YYYY

WSLNAN 9565

SUBJECT: IRAQ: POLITICAL CONSULTATIONS, 19 JUNE

SUMMARY

1. Iraqi and Coalition agreement on the need to establish a Political Council rapidly. Coalition more concerned than Iraqis to see a Constitutional Conference convened soon. Bremer concludes that he hopes both will be established by the end of July.

DETAIL

2. Ambassador Bremer and I held a second expanded political consultation with Iraqi representatives on 19 June. 24 Iraqis were present, including the seven political parties, Pachachl and Sherif Ali. Over half were Shia, and there was even balance (for the first time) of externals and internals. Four women were invited, though one failed to show.

3. Bremer opened the meeting with the Coalition objective: a free Iraq at peace with its neighbours and governed by a democratically elected government representative of all strands of society. Getting there would be a challenge, since Iraq was a complex country. The Coalition wanted to move quickly to establish the interim administration provided for by UNSCR 1483, with a Political Council (PC) and a Constitutional Conference (CC).

4. The PC, with 20–30 members, would have substantial executive authority and responsibility from the time it was created. It would have two immediate tasks: to propose men and women who could run the Ministries, and to advise the Coalition on long-term strategic issues which would determine the kind of society we had in Iraq, for example on regulation of political parties and educational and judicial reforms. Bremer said that he imagined that the PC would establish a series of commissions or councils of experts. The PC would consider the experts recommendations, and forward proposals to the Coalition for action or decision. The PCs actions would have an impact in Iraq long after the Coalition left.

5. Bremer continued that the 1970 interim constitution did not provide a basis for democratic elections. A new constitution would be needed. He

envisaged a Constitutional Conference of 100–200 representatives of all strands of Iraqi society. It would meet and select a drafting committee. The drafting of a new constitution would be by Iraqis for Iraqis. There should be a very intense dialogue between the drafters and the people: Bremer envisaged a series of meetings with town councils, governorate representatives and others. Once the constitution was agreed by the CC, there would be a referendum and an election. He could not say how long this would take: that was for Iraqis to decide. As soon as there were elections, a fully sovereign Iraqi government would be formed.

6. Bremer asked for input on the process, and for ideas for people to be on the PC and CC. He stressed that President Bush and the Prime Minister were in complete agreement on these issues.

POLITICAL COUNCIL

7. There appeared to be consensus on the need to establish the PC rapidly, many arguing that establishing the PC was essential to achieving security. None argued for more time. Dr Othman (Al-Khair Financial Investment Company) said that an interim administration should have been established by now, but Iraqis as well as the Coalition were to blame for the delay. Mehdi (SCIRI) said that the PC should be established within a few weeks, and urged Bremer to set a date, which Bremer said he would do.

8. Sheikh Qizwini (Hilla Religious University) raised the powers of the PC, arguing that the PC should have to approve all Interim Administration decisions. He also put forward ideas for the PCs own organisation and chairmanship; and urged the need for clear laws. Bremer replied that the 1969 Criminal Code was, by his order, in effect and being implemented. On 17 July he had ordered that the 1971 Criminal Procedure should apply, with three amendments (defendant to have the right to legal representation from the moment of appointment of an investigative judge; right to silence; torture outlawed). Iraqi laws were being applied in Iraqi courts. He said that the internal organisation of the PC would be for its members: he could envisage an elected Chair and Vice-Chair, or a rotating Chair, or a Standing Committee of 3–5 members to act as Chair. He undertook that, once the interim administration was established, the CPA would not take any major decisions without prior consultation of the PC.

CONSTITUTIONAL CONFERENCE

9. There was much less sense of urgency over the Constitution. Sheikh Qizwini said that the political process should focus on the PC for the time being: the CC came later. Drafting a constitution would take 2–3 years. Ibrahim Shaboot (Islamic Democratic Trend) Talabani (PUK) and Jaafari (Da-wa) also counselled patience. Nabil Musawi (INC) and Mukliss argued that a referendum on the kind of state (republic/monarchy) was necessary before calling a CC (there is a surprising degree of support for the constitutional monarchy among the politicians). Ibrahim Bahr al-Ulum, speaking on behalf of his father, argued for a directly elected CC, however long direct elections would take, a point echoed by SCIRI and Dawa.

10. I endorsed Bremers opening statement about the strength of President Bushs and the Prime Ministers agreement and desire for progress, and expressed concern at the implications of having a directly elected CC. Ideally, we would want elected representatives too. But an election would require a census, a register of electors and agreement on electoral boundaries. Did we really want to wait for 6–9 months before starting on the constitution. That could mean that elections were two years away. The alternative would be to bring together a CC representing all the main strands of opinion and traditions in Iraq, and ensure that it consulted widely and that the resulting constitution was put to a referendum for adoption.

SERVICES

11. A few of those attending a political consultation for the first time argued that politics was not the key issue. Dr Othman said that Baghdad remained a paralysed city. Traffic, electricity, water, telephones, unemployment and salaries were most important. Iraqis should be addressing these; the US should stay in camps outside the cities. Bremer said that services and security were first priority. Baghdad was far better than when he arrived, 5 weeks ago. More than USD 500 million had been paid to the Iraqi people in the past 3 weeks alone. Petrol supplies were no longer a problem. 85,000 canisters of LPG for cooking were being distributed every day. He did not accept that the Coalition was not doing everything it could to improve services.

CONCLUSION

12. Bremer concluded that it was urgent to establish the PC, and important to establish the CC. He hoped both would be established by the end of July. He added that he was anxious to demonstrate that Iraqis were taking responsibility for Iraq. Recognising concerns expressed earlier by Dr Pachachi (IID), Bremer said he would be going to the World Economic Forum meeting in Amman this weekend with a party of Iraqis. He also said that there would be an Iraqi voting member on the Programme Review Board he had established to determine how to spend the Development Fund for Iraq (into which oil revenues would be paid), and that the International Advisory and Monitoring Board for the Fund would include Iraqis.

COMMENT

13. A polished performance from Bremer, and a constructive meeting, revealing a large measure of agreement on the Political Council. The discussions (reported separately) on the currency and payment to the ex-military, were also constructive.

14. I shall offer further comment on the direction of the political process over the weekend.

SAWERS

Decree that officially dissolved the Iraqi army

COALITION PROVISIONAL AUTHORITY ORDER NUMBER 2

DISSOLUTION OF ENTITIES

Pursuant to my authority as Administrator of the Coalition Provisional Authority (CPA), relevant U.N. Security Council resolutions, including Resolution 1483 (2003), and the laws and usages of war,

Reconfirming all of the provisions of General Franks' Freedom Message to the Iraqi People of April 16, 2003,

Recognizing that the prior Iraqi regime used certain government entities to oppress the Iraqi people and as instruments of torture, repression and corruption,

Reaffirming the Instructions to the Citizens of Iraq regarding Ministry of Youth and Sport of May 8, 2003,

I hereby promulgate the following:

Section 1
Dissolved Entities

The entities (the "Dissolved Entities") listed in the attached Annex are hereby dissolved. Additional entities may be added to this list in the future.

Section 2
Assets and Financial Obligations

1) All assets, including records and data, in whatever form maintained and wherever located, of the Dissolved Entities shall be held by the Administrator of the CPA ("the Administrator") on behalf of and for the benefit of the Iraqi people and shall be used to assist the Iraqi people and to support the recovery of Iraq.

2) All financial obligations of the Dissolved Entities are suspended. The Administrator of the CPA will establish procedures whereby persons claiming to be the beneficiaries of such obligations may apply for payment.

3) Persons in possession of assets of the Dissolved Entities shall preserve those assets, promptly inform local Coalition authorities, and immediately turn them over, as directed by those authorities. Continued possession, transfer, sale, use, conversion, or concealment of such assets following the date of this Order is prohibited and may be punished.

CPA/ORD/23 May 2003/02

Section 3
Employees and Service Members

1) Any military or other rank, title, or status granted to a former employee or functionary of a Dissolved Entity by the former Regime is hereby cancelled.

2) All conscripts are released from their service obligations. Conscription is suspended indefinitely, subject to decisions by future Iraq governments concerning whether a free Iraq should have conscription.

3) Any person employed by a Dissolved Entity in any form or capacity, is dismissed effective as of April 16, 2003. Any person employed by a Dissolved Entity, in any form or capacity, remains accountable for acts committed during such employment.

4) A termination payment in an amount to be determined by the Administrator will be paid to employees so dismissed, except those who are Senior Party Members as defined in the Administrator's May 16, 2003 Order of the Coalition Provisional Authority De-Baathification of Iraqi Society, CPA/ORD/2003/01 ("Senior Party Members") (See Section 3.6).

5) Pensions being paid by, or on account of service to, a Dissolved Entity before April 16, 2003 will continue to be paid, including to war widows and disabled veterans, provided that no pension payments will be made to any person who is a Senior Party Member (see Section 3.6) and that the power is reserved to the Administrator and to future Iraqi governments to revoke or reduce pensions as a penalty for past or future illegal conduct or to modify pension arrangements to eliminate improper privileges granted by the Baathist regime or for similar reasons.

6) Notwithstanding any provision of this Order, or any other Order, law, or regulation, and consistent with the Administrator's May 16, 2003 Order of the Coalition Provisional Authority De-Baathification of Iraqi Society, CPA/ORD/2003/01, no payment, including a termination or pension payment, will be made to any person who is or was a Senior Party Member. Any person holding the rank under the former regime of Colonel or above, or its equivalent, will be deemed a Senior Party Member, provided that such persons may seek, under procedures to be prescribed, to establish to the satisfaction of the Administrator, that they were not a Senior Party Member.

Section 4
Information

The Administrator shall prescribe procedures for offering rewards to person who provide information leading to the recovery of assets of Dissolved Entities.

Section 5
New Iraqi Corps

The CPA plans to create in the near future a New Iraqi Corps, as the first step in forming a national self-defense capability for a free Iraq. Under civilian control, that Corps will be professional, non-political, militarily effective, and representative of all Iraqis. The CPA will promulgate procedures for participation in the New Iraqi Corps.

Section 6
Other Matters

1) The Administrator may delegate his powers and responsibilities with respect to this Order as he determines appropriate. References to the Administrator herein include such delegates.

2) The Administrator may grant exceptions any limitations in this Order at his discretion.

Section 7
Entry into Force

This Order shall enter into force on the date of signature.

L. Paul Bremer, Administrator
Coalition Provisional Authority

CPA/ORD/23 May 2003/02

3

ANNEX

COALITION PROVISIONAL AUTHORITY ORDER NUMBER 2

DISSOLUTION OF ENTITIES

Institutions dissolved by the Order referenced (the "Dissolved Entities") are:

The Ministry of Defence
The Ministry of Information
The Ministry of State for Military Affairs
The Iraqi Intelligence Service
The National Security Bureau
The Directorate of National Security (Amn al-'Am)
The Special Security Organization

All entities affiliated with or comprising Saddam Hussein's bodyguards to include:
-Murafaqin (Companions)
-Himaya al Khasa (Special Guard)

The following military organizations:
-The Army, Air Force, Navy, the Air Defence Force, and other regular
military services
-The Republican Guard
-The Special Republican Guard
-The Directorate of Military Intelligence
-The Al Quds Force
-Emergency Forces (Quwat al Tawari)

The following paramilitaries:
-Saddam Fedayeen
-Ba'ath Party Militia
-Friends of Saddam
-Saddam's Lion Cubs (Ashbal Saddam)

Other Organizations:
-The Presidential Diwan
-The Presidential Secretariat
-The Revolutionary Command Council
-The National Assembly
-The Youth Organization (al-Futuwah)
-National Olympic Committee
-Revolutionary, Special and National Security Courts

CPA/ORD/23 May 2003/02 4

All organizations subordinate to the Dissolved Entities are also dissolved.

Additional organizations may be added to this list in the future.

GLOSSARY

Air Weapons Systems

Bombers

B-1—A multi-role long-range bomber designed to penetrate sophisticated air defenses (large bomb/missile load) (Lancer).

B-2—Low-observable "stealthy" multi-role bomber (large bomb/missile load) (Spirit).

B-52—High-altitude subsonic long-range bomber (large bomb/missile load).

Fighter/Attack

F-117 (USAF)—Low-observable "stealthy" attack aircraft (small load) (Nighthawk).

F-15 (USAF)—All-weather tactical fighter (Eagle).

F-16 (USAF)—Fighter attack aircraft (Falcon).

F/A-18 (USN/USMC)—Multipurpose fighter/attack aircraft (Hornet).

F-14 (USN)—Primarily an all-weather fighter aircraft (Tomcat).

AV-8 (USMC)—V/STOL light attack aircraft (Harrier).

A-10 (USAF)—Close-air-support, anti-armor aircraft (Thunderbolt/Warthog).

AC-130U (USAF)—Propeller-driven night close-air-support aircraft (Spooky).

EA6B—(USN/USMC)—Electronic warfare and jamming aircraft.

Lift/Support

C-141—Long-distance troop carrier.

C-5—Long-distance heavy-cargo carrier.

C-130—Intratheater troop and cargo carrier.

KC-10, 130, 135—Aerial refuelers.

UAV (Unmanned Aerial Vehicle)—A remotely piloted aircraft that can carry cameras, sensors, communications equipment, or other payloads (e.g., Predator).

AWACS (Airborne Warning and Control System)—A Boeing E-767 air-space surveillance aircraft.

JSTARS (Joint Surveillance Target Attack Radar System)—A Boeing 707 long-range air-to-ground surveillance system.

Helicopters

UH-1—Utility helicopter (transport, Medevac, command) (Huey).

UH-60 (USA)—Medium troop/cargo/Medevac carrier (Black Hawk).

CH-46 (USMC)—Medium troop/cargo/Medevac carrier (Sea Knight).

H-47 (USA)—Medium troop/cargo carrier (Chinook).

CH-53 (USMC)—Heavy-lift troop and cargo carrier (Sea Stallion).

MH-53 (USAF)—Special Operations (Pave Low).

AH-64 (USA)—Attack helicopter (Apache).

OH-58 (USA)—Armed reconnaissance (Kiowa).

Ground Weapons Systems

Infantry

M203 40mm grenade launcher—A rifled launcher attached to a rifle.

MK19 40mm machine gun (USMC)—A belt-fed grenade-launching machine gun.

M240G 7.6 machine gun—A belt-fed general-purpose machine gun.

M249 5.6 Squad Automatic Weapon (SAW)—A belt- or magazine-fed light machine gun.

AT-4—An expendable shoulder-fired assault rocket launcher.

Shoulder-Launched Multi-Purpose Assault Weapon (SMAW)—An 83mm man-portable rocket launcher.

Javelin—A man-portable, medium-range, fire-and-forget anti-tank missile.

M220 Tube-Launched Optically Tracked, Wire-Guided Missile Weapons System (TOW)—A vehicle- or ground-mounted heavy antitank assault weapon.

Rocket-Propelled Grenade (RPG)—Iraqi shoulder-fired medium-range antitank missile system.

Fire Support

M198 155mm towed howitzer—An indirect artillery fire support system.

M270 Multiple-Launch Rocket System (MLRS) (USA)—A tracked, self-propelled multiple-rocket system. **ATACMS** long-range missiles are fired from MLRS.

M252 81mm mortar—A man-transportable, crew-served smooth-bore mortar.

ZSU—Russian-designed family of antiaircraft guns and machine guns.

Vehicles

M1A1/2 Main Battle Tank—A crew-served tracked heavy tank mounting a smooth-bore 120mm main gun and machine guns (Abrams).

T-54/55, T-72 Main Battle Tanks (Iraq)—Russian-designed crew-served heavy tanks mounting 100/125mm main guns and machine guns.

M2/M3 Bradley Fighting Vehicle (BFV) (USA)—Fully mechanized, crew-served, and weaponized armored troop carrier.

Assault Amphibious Vehicle (AAV) (USMC)—A medium armored tracked amphibious troop carrier capable of operating at sea and on land.

Light Armored Vehicle (LAV) (USMC)—A crew-served lightly armored wheeled multipurpose vehicle (weapons platform, command, etc.).

High Mobility Multi-Purpose Wheeled Vehicle (HMMWV) "Humvee"—An unarmored light tactical vehicle.

M60A1 Assault Vehicle Landing Bridge (AVLB)—A crew-served self-contained armored vehicle carrying an internally operated sixty-foot scissor bridge.

M113—(USA)—Tracked, lightly armored personnel carrier and command and control vehicle.

BMP—Soviet-designed lightly armored fighting vehicle.

Miscellaneous

Blue Force Tracker—A satellite/sensor system that acquires, tracks, and displays designated entities with Global Positioning System (GPS) accuracy.

MOPP (Mission-Oriented Protective Posture)—the wearing of chemical and biological resistant clothing.

PGM (Precision-guided munitions—"smart bombs")—Bombs that can be aimed and directed against a single target, relying on external guidance or their own guidance system.

JDAM (Joint Direct Attack Munition)—Conventional bombs with attached tail kit to improve accuracy in all weather conditions.

IED (Improvised Explosive Device)—A homemade ambush antipersonnel/antivehicle weapon constructed from a variety of explosives.

HARM—Antiradiation high-speed air-launched missile.

INDEX

Page numbers in *italics* refer to maps.